A Field Guide
to the Butterflies

THE PETERSON FIELD GUIDE SERIES

EDITED BY ROGER TORY PETERSON

THE PETERSON FIELD GUIDE SERIES

A Field Guide
to the Butterflies

of North America, East of the Great Plains

BY ALEXANDER B. KLOTS

*The City College of New York and
The American Museum of Natural History*

*Illustrated with color paintings of 247 species
by Marjorie Statham
and 232 photographs by Florence Longworth*

HOUGHTON MIFFLIN COMPANY BOSTON

PRINTED IN THE U.S.A.

The Field Guide Series

WHEN the *Field Guide to the Birds* appeared in 1934, it met with instant approval. Intended as a short cut to recognition, its system, based on comparative patterns, field marks and distinctions between species, has proved to be very practical. It was inevitable that nature students everywhere should urge the author and the publisher to extend this plan to other fields of natural history. Inasmuch as it would take a lifetime for one man to complete such a series, it was thought best to assign each subject to a specialist, while I acted as advisor and editor.

A Field Guide to the Butterflies is one of the first of the new books to reach completion. Much more than a guide to recognizing the butterflies, it also makes a solid contribution to entomology. In addition to applying the Field Guide system to these attractive insects it brings butterfly taxonomy up to date and contains more new life-history data than any other popular work in a generation.

Today, a bird watcher does not confine himself just to birds. He becomes curious about the birds' environment — what the plants are where birds live — what insects they eat. Likewise, botanists no longer limit their activities to pressing plants, but study also the environmental factors that have affected the plants' evolution and survival. This living approach to natural history — ecology — is the modern one.

Every student of the outdoors will want this book, whether he is primarily interested in butterflies or not. It is really "a guide to field natural history as illustrated by the butterflies." The special sections on life zones and their indicator plants, on ecology, on the hows and whys of nomenclature, and the discussions of subspecies and geographic variation will be as enlightening to the serious bird student or mammalogist as to the insect collector, for they will throw light on their specialties. This guide, then, is a key book in the *Field Guide* series, for many of the general discussions will not be repeated elsewhere in the series.

When the author and I were based in Florida during World War II, we often went collecting together. It was there I learned how broad his interests were. Few men have his understanding of the interlocking partnerships of the outdoor world. He is not only one of the country's foremost lepidopterists, but his knowledge of birds, other animals, and plants is extensive. His book will have a prominent place on every natural history bookshelf.

ROGER TORY PETERSON

Acknowledgments

IN PREPARING this book all of the standard books on North American butterflies (the chief ones of these will be found listed in Appendix 2), and probably at least a thousand articles were consulted. Even with this survey of the literature, however, the work would have been inadequate without the help very generously given by a great number of people. It is impossible to list all of them, for many have contributed information about only a single point or two. To the following, however, I am heavily indebted for assistance and information of a major sort. Many of them have looked over parts of the manuscript or check list for errors or omissions, and have even, in some cases, contributed unpublished data of their own. In all fairness, however, I must state that I have not in all cases followed their advice; and so I accept full responsibility for all errors of omission or commission.

E. L. Bell, American Museum of Natural History (*Hesperioidea*); Dean Berry, Orlando, Fla. (Florida records); F. M. Brown, Fountain Valley School, Colorado Springs (*Phœbis* and *Aphrissa*); Otto Buchholz, Roselle Park, N.J. (field notes and records); R. L. Chermock, University of Alabama (*Satyridæ*); Austin Clark, United States National Museum (field notes and records); H. K. Clench, University of Michigan (*Incisalia*); W. P. Comstock, American Museum (*Anæa* and *Lycænidæ*); Cyril dos Passos, American Museum (*Œneis* and *Erebia*); W. T. M. Forbes, Cornell University (general taxonomy, *Danaidæ* and *Phyciodes*); Marguerite S. Forsyth, Florida City, Fla. (Florida records and localities); H. A. Freeman, Southern Methodist University (Texas records and *Hesperioidea*); T. N. Freeman, Department of Agriculture, Ottawa (Arctic and Canadian records and taxonomy); Florence Grimshawe, Miami, Fla. (Florida records); E. Irving Huntington, American Museum (*Lycænidæ*); A. W. Lindsey, Denison University (*Hesperia*); J. McDunnough, American Museum (general taxonomy); Don B. Stallings and J. R. Turner, Caldwell, Kansas (distribution records).

I am very deeply indebted to the Department of Insects and Spiders of the American Museum of Natural History, and to Dr. Mont Cazier, its chairman. Without the facilities of the department and of the Museum Library I would not have even attempted this work. The majority of the illustrations were made from museum specimens. Others were made from specimens loaned by Mr. dos Passos; and by Mr. T. N. Freeman. Mr. dos Passos has

vii

also helped with many special problems of bibliography, especially by means of his unique catalog of original references and photographs of type material.

Professor Joseph J. Copeland of the City College has very kindly checked over the botanical and ecological portions of the text. It has been especially pleasant to have had his help in this, for he and I have been field companions for many years on collecting trips in both the east and the west.

Roger Tory Peterson, who needs no introduction to students of natural history, has most generously given of his time, placing his wide knowledge of illustrations and books at my disposal. The arrangement of much of this book follows the concise identification methods developed largely by him in his *Field Guides* to the eastern and western birds.

The paintings for the color illustrations were made by Miss Marjorie Statham, who somehow found time to do them while preparing many others for American Museum research publications. My only regret is that no system of reproduction can do full justice to the unequaled accuracy and delicacy of her work, which is as fine as anything ever done of butterflies. The photographs of specimens were all taken and prepared by Mrs. Florence Longworth, already distinguished as a photographer of technical medical subjects. To both of these illustrators I am indebted more than I can say for their interest and their unfailing care, patience, and accuracy. I am also very deeply indebted to Mrs. Annabel Ryan for the skill with which she has interpreted my at times rather chaotic and cryptic manuscript, and the perseverance with which she prepared and proofread its final copy.

Foreword

I SUPPOSE that I have been preparing this book for some thirty-odd years, for it was in 1917 that I first became interested in butterflies. Since then my interest has never flagged; and I shall never regret that what was once only my hobby has become a part of my profession as well.

I was more fortunate than most boys in having, nearly at my doorstep, the collections of a great museum and the guidance of its staff. So I was spared most of the tribulations of beginning collectors. When I caught an unknown butterfly or found a strange larva I had only to look through the collection or ask a curator.

Since then, however, I have come to realize what inadequate information about our butterflies has been available to most people. To be sure, several books about butterflies have been published during the twentieth century, but only one of these has even attempted to include all of the species in eastern North America. And that one, although an excellent compilation for its time, has long been outdated by our increased knowledge, changed names, and new approaches to natural history. Moreover it told very little about the life histories, habits, environments and similar interesting things.

Accordingly, I have tried in writing this book to include the essential facts about our butterflies in the light of modern knowledge and approach. I trust that no important details about any of the species of our area have been omitted. And I have tried especially hard to give at least a skeleton outline of the many interesting approaches to butterfly study other than mere identification and naming.

Probably the chief attraction of butterfly study is the ease and practicability of making a collection. In these days, when birds are quite rightly protected, butterflies are the most popular group of animals with collectors. And not only can one collect specimens which he, himself caught, but also he can exchange specimens with some of the thousands of collectors in all parts of the world.

But collecting will be, it is hoped, only the first step. Those who pass beyond it, and become more interested in studying the life histories, habits, behavior and environments of the butterflies, will reap far greater rewards. And it must be noted that we are as yet comparatively ignorant about such details in the lives of a great many species, so that such studies may very easily bring the satisfaction of discovering important facts new to human knowledge.

As I look back on my many years of butterfly work I find that I have come to care less and less for individual specimens themselves. Instead I cherish them as reminders of a climb above timberline in the Rockies, or of my first visit to the teeming Everglades, or of the sight of a world of nothing but grasses billowing in the wind on the Great Plains. The Morphos and Heliconians that I caught in Brazil are now only specimens in a museum cabinet. But they take me back to the days when I caught them in the lush Amazon jungle and knew that they were the lineal descendents of the butterflies studied in the same spot by Bates and Wallace a hundred years ago. The best thing that I can wish for you is that you, too, will come to have such memories and that this book may help you to do so.

Contents

PART 1

PART 2

PART 3

Illustrations

Plates

Introduction

Why a New Butterfly Book? Recent years have seen the development of the Houghton Mifflin *Field Guides*, led by Roger Tory Peterson's famous *Field Guides* to eastern and western birds. These books, concise and compact, superbly illustrated and packed with essential information organized for the greatest ease and accuracy of use, have proved a boon to both amateur and professional naturalists. It was therefore a welcome opportunity to add to this series a guide to butterflies, so as to make our modern knowledge of these insects readily available to all.

During the last generation we have found out a great many new facts about our butterflies. Hundreds of articles have been published, but these, scattered throughout the scientific journals of the world, are not available to the majority of collectors. Rather few new species have been named from the east, but there are dozens of new subspecies and records of tropical immigrants, and much additional life-history and distribution information. There obviously is great need for a new book merely to assemble our recent increments of knowledge.

Again, a new book is needed because of the recent re-orientation of our attitude toward natural science. We are getting away from the old "descriptive" natural history that was concerned only with naming things and describing them. The new natural history is dynamic by comparison in every way. It regards different *kinds* of plants and animals (different *species*) not as separate and fixed things, but as fluid and plastic products of evolutionary change. It probes for the relationships between species not as a convenience in classification, but as a clue to their origins and past histories. In doing this it attaches almost greater importance to "subspecies" than to species which is why so much space has been given to these in this book. And it also recognizes the great importance, as well as interest, of studying the living thing in the field; for it realizes that habits and behavior, and the relations of an organism to the other organisms around it, are all major factors in its dynamic changes through the ages.

The Scope of the Book. The area covered includes all of North America east of the 100th meridian, from the northernmost limit of land to the Mexican boundary. Biologically this means that our area extends westward as far as the arid Great Plains, of which the 100th meridian forms an approximate eastern border. Of course, plants and animals pay no attention to straight meridians or international boundaries, so that we find in our area many species which are really western or tropical, our representatives being merely individuals on the edges of their natural ranges. All such species have been included, although they have not been treated in as great detail as those which are truly natives of our area.

Every butterfly recorded from within this area has been included, even though it has been recorded only once or twice. If any have been omitted I hope that they may be brought to my attention.

The Material Included. Every species of importance has been illustrated. Color has been used where it is most important for identification. Usually only the upper- or underside has been shown, whichever shows the better identification characters. In general, species which merely stray into our area have not been illustrated, unless they occur widely enough to cause confusion in identifying native forms.

In addition to illustrations, I have tried to give the following for every "native" species, no matter how rare: a description of the chief characteristics; notes on habits and habitats; a condensed description of the mature larva; the number of annual broods or generations; the method of hibernation; the average dates of appearance of spring adults; the geographic range in our area; and the type locality, range, and a brief characterization of each of the valid subspecies in our area. Naturally, everything has had to be greatly condensed, and much of interest has had to be omitted. Again, it is possible that I have omitted important facts. When such are noticed, I hope that they will be brought to my attention.

Part 1

CHAPTER ONE

How to Use This Book

BEFORE YOU CAN do any butterfly work some equipment is necessary. Perhaps you can make much or all of this for yourself. If not, it can be bought. In Chapter 2 you will find information about equipment and, in Part III, lists of leaflets and books which tell much more.

When you are ready to do so, go out and collect. Start right by taking along your notebook. Keep a record of just where you collect, and in what kinds of environment. Read the section on "Environments and Habitats" in Chapter 3, and that on "How to Collect" in Chapter 2. Try to visit as many different environments as possible, and whenever you are driving in a car keep your eyes open for new possibilities.

Having obtained some specimens you will wish to identify them. I hope that you will have taken this *Field Guide* along on the collecting trip, too. Leaf through it and look at the pictures, and find the one that seems to correspond to your specimen. Check the short list of characters on the legend page. Then, if all still seems well, turn to the text.

With most species a short description, or a list of the chief characters, is given in the text. Close and confusing species are mentioned under the heading "**Similar Species.**" If any such are mentioned turn to them, too, and check the differences on your specimen. It would be wise first, however, to look at the "**Range**" of the species, so as to make sure that it can occur in your part of the country. We do not expect to find Greenland butterflies in Ohio.

If your specimen belongs to one of the larger genera, do not fail to turn to the *genus* discussion. Much general information is given there which applies to all the species of the genus, and perhaps a "key."

If you encounter new words or terms, look in the Index to Technical Terms at the back of the book. All technical terms used in the book are listed there with either a definition or a page reference to an explanation.

You will do well to check on the information about the habits and environment of each species. Here, if you are identifying a specimen caught some time ago, is where your notebook can be of real value. Do not trust your memory.

The above procedure is well enough for a start. As time goes on, however, try to learn the *main groups* of butterflies, so as to save time leafing through the illustrations. Some of the families and other groups are very distinctive. It should take no more than a glance to identify a butterfly as a Swallowtail, a Pierid, a Skipper, a Blue, a Copper, or a Hairstreak. Looking over the illustrations of these just a few times should fix the groups in your mind. The Satyrs all have a certain general look, with their soft, brown colors and eyespots; and their characteristic flights are almost instantly recognizable in the field. Then there are a few easily "spotted" groups of the Nymphalids, such as the Fritillaries, the Anglewings, and the Crescents and Checkerspots. If you then will learn the Monarch and the Viceroy, the Snout Butterfly and a few other odds and ends, you will find yourself prepared to identify a large percentage of the more common butterflies without wasting any preliminary time.

One of your greatest aids can be the Check List (Part III). Use it primarily to check off the species of which you have specimens. In addition to this you can make it an index of the species which may occur in your region, or in any region in which you are particularly interested. Going through the text, note if each species may occur in the region. If so, a particular mark can be placed opposite the species name in the check list. This, too, can save much time in the long run. This system can be expanded in a number of ways, depending on your taste for systems, to mark down all kinds of possibilities.

To Teachers and Nature Leaders. I have given considerable thought to your needs. I am, myself, a biology teacher. I progressed in Scouting from Tenderfoot to Scoutmaster, and have worked much with summer camps. So I have encountered many of your problems. Throughout this *Field Guide* ideas of broad interest are brought out as much as space permits. Not only will the book serve its primary purpose, that of identifying butterflies; but it can also be used as a source book for building a broader program of natural history. The Nature Study taught in our schools and camps needs such broadening. Too often it leads to no appreciation of the essential kinship and the interdependence of all living things. The ecology that is here stressed is the surest and, in many ways, the easiest way of showing this.

We cannot, of course, develop a detailed formula for teaching butterfly work that will be suitable for all groups. We can list the chief points that should be covered, starting with those applicable to less advanced work, and then leave it to the teacher or leader to use what seems appropriate or is available. Only suggestive details are given below, since all subjects are covered more fully in the following chapters. A certain amount of equipment must be procured (Chapter 2). All of this except insect pins and a pair of forceps can well be homemade. If possible, enlist the cooperation of a manual training, shop, or crafts instructor and have the work done by the students. Do not forget exhibit mounts, such as "Riker Mounts," for display.

The first approach will probably be through collecting, or perhaps through having a collection already made. In either case the use of this book for identification has been covered in the first part of this chapter; and the specimens, once identified, can be used to illustrate such points of interest as the text may give for each species. Actually, collecting your own specimens is enormously preferable; and it is surprising how many species can be taken even within the limits of cities like Chicago and New York. Except in the most formal city parks, there are seldom any restrictions against collecting insects.

The outlines and suggestions given below are, practically without exception, applicable to either students or campers. The potentialities for field work at organized camps are, of course, far greater.

Group Organization. If a large enough group is available, some organization of tasks may be possible. Thus members of the group may volunteer for or be assigned to:

(a) Making net frames and handles, spreading boards, specimen boxes, etc.
(b) Sewing net bags
(c) Field work — collecting specimens
(d) Rearing larvæ brought home from the field or obtained from eggs
(e) Collecting and identifying the plants involved
(f) Keeping records
(g) Curatorial work — mounting and caring for the specimens collected.

Advance Preparation. The teacher or counsellor is advised to study the following list of organized suggestions carefully in advance, checking each point to which a reference is given. The task of identifying butterflies is relatively simple; but the "ecological" and "biological" details need careful study.

Group Trips. As many group trips as possible should be held. If these are not feasible, the following ideas should be suggested to the individuals. If possible, plan the route of a trip in advance, so as to have it run as follows:

(a) First collect around homes and gardens, on cultivated flowers. Wide ranging species will be secured here. Keep and label these separately.
(b) Next follow a roadside or railroad track away from cultivation for species in more natural conditions. In the route try to include dry meadow, wet meadow, and woodland environments. Label and keep separately the specimens secured in these or other distinctive environments.
(c) Collect also where some intensive agriculture is being practiced. If possible include a clover or alfalfa field where concentrations of Sulphurs (*Colias*) may be expected; or a cabbage, mustard, cauliflower, etc. field where European Cabbage Butterflies (*Pieris rapæ*) usually swarm. The lesson teaches itself. Look for damage to the crops. Ask a farmer what he does to protect the crops.
(d) Locate a good flowering bush or patch of a single species of flower and collect and list all butterflies visiting it. Decide which is the major butterfly species in its pollination. You might also count and calculate the relative numbers of butterflies and bees.

- (e) Concentrate on one common butterfly and list all the different flowers which it visits. Do this with several species if possible. Do the different species seem to have different choices?
- (f) In all the work watch sharply for female butterflies laying eggs (Chapter 3). When one is found watch her and get the eggs as they are laid as well as the plant on which the eggs are deposited. Finally collect her too. She will probably lay more in captivity. Collect some other females and bring them back alive for the same purpose. You may also note and call attention to mated pairs, flying in amplexus. Note also "chasing" reactions of males and, if possible, courtships.
- (g) Collect plenty of extra specimens of good-sized species for practice in spreading. Collect also a good supply of fresh larval food plants if needed. Take along *Field Guides* to trees and flowers on the trip.
- (h) Collect at least a few specimens of a few other orders of insects, such as Beetles (*Coleoptera*) both on plants and under stones, logs, and bark; Flies (*Diptera*); Bees, Wasps, and Ants (*Hymenoptera*); and Dragonflies and Damselflies (*Odonata*); also Spiders and Crayfish if possible.
- (i) Study Chapter 2 (pp. 13–20) for details of care of specimens.

Study of the Material. Below are the chief subjects and ideas that can be brought out in later study of the material from even one such trip. Only a few suggestive details are given here; there are more details in the other chapters to which references are given. All of these basic subjects can be covered, at least in simple form, with even the least advanced groups. They can be expanded almost indefinitely for older or more advanced students.

- (a) *Classification.* At least some related species, possibly congeneric ones, will be caught. Even the existence of different degrees of relationship is worth pointing out. The idea of the *species* as the "particular kind of butterfly" and that of the *genus* as a group of species that are "first cousins" is easily assimilated. From that the idea of the *family* goes across surprisingly easily (easiest: *Papilionidæ*, *Pieridæ*), and leads very obviously to that of the *order*. A couple of Spiders and a Crayfish complete an elementary lesson on "taxonomy" very simply. Practical reasons for using scientific names may well be pointed out.
- (b) *Food.* "All flesh is grass." The butterfly, like the cow and the rabbit, is only one stage removed from the plant food it eats. The Dragonfly, the Phœbe, and Man are another step removed. The Cooper's Hawk that catches the Phœbe that ate the butterfly is another step.

  Food habits are very specialized. Clover butterflies do not lay their eggs on cabbage or thistles, nor will their larvæ eat anything but clover or very closely related plants.

  Most butterflies are *herbivores*, but one, the Harvester (*Feniseca* — try to find larvæ of this widespread species) is a *predator*. So are Dragonflies — often called "Mosquito Hawks." The mosquitoes and horseflies which bite you are *parasites*. So are the parasitic Tachina Flies and Ichneumon Wasps (Chapter 3). Ants, Houseflies, etc. are *scavengers*; so is the Clothes Moth. What is Man?

(c) *Protection*. Adult butterflies escape from predators by swift flight (Hairstreaks, Skippers), dodging into cover (Satyrs), or concealment (Angle Wings, Goatweed Butterfly, Purple-wings). The Monarch "advertises" its bad taste; the Viceroy "mimics" this. Go as deeply as you wish into the protective aspects of butterfly colors and patterns (Chapter 3).

Larvæ and pupæ cannot flee. They survive by escaping notice, looking like leaves, twigs, dead debris, or bird droppings; by living concealed in nests; or by spending the day hiding (see *Speyeria*), feeding only at night. How many larvæ did you see on the trip; how many adults? You probably were within ten feet of more larvæ than of adults.

In the temperate zone hibernation is essential for survival. Butterflies hibernate in various specialized ways. Compare the Viceroy, the Swallowtails and Sulphurs, the Angle Wing and Mourning Cloak; and the Monarch which flies south for the winter.

Where and how do butterflies, for example *Papilio*, sleep at night? How do they take shelter from storms?

(d) *Life Histories*. Details for the study of life histories are given in Chapter 4. Butterflies can be reared easily even from the egg, in small containers on a schoolroom shelf or window ledge. Cleanliness and constant supplies of fresh food are the chief requisites. Such work is extremely valuable for the interest aroused, as well as for the training in care and reliability. For older students the details of insect metamorphosis may be taken up, and the value to the insect of this specialization of stages in its life cycle (Chapter 4).

(e) *Relations with Plants*. As larvæ, butterflies do some (but seldom extensive) damage to plants. As adults, however, they carry on an enormous amount of the cross-pollination essential for the survival of many plants. The habit of concentrating on only one or a few species of flowers makes this more efficient. The butterfly and the plant are mutually dependent; the relationship is *symbiotic* or *mutualistic*.

(f) *Relations with Other Animals*. (See Chapter 3.) Butterflies are preyed upon by a vast assortment of other animals; but even more important than these attacks are those of the parasitic wasps and flies that are the chief factors in limiting their numbers. But if these enemies were eliminated, the butterflies would increase so rapidly in numbers that their destruction of their larval food plants would itself diminish them again, very likely below the original level. I think that this idea, which implies that the "normal" enemies of a species are an integral part of its life and are not wholly harmful, is decidedly worth bringing out. Consider also the part played by competition between members of the same species. In an extreme form this is manifested by the occasional cannibalism practiced by various butterfly larvæ, especially those of the *Lycænidæ*. See also *Pieris rapæ, napi,* and *protodice* for competition between butterfly species.

The somewhat symbiotic relations of the larvæ of some butterflies (*Pieridæ, Lycænidæ*) with Ants should also be mentioned here.

(g) *Relations with Man*. Butterflies affect man directly in only a minor way. Very few species attack valuable plants in significant numbers. But the indirect benefits which we receive from the cross-pollination activities of the adults are incalculable, not only because of our direct use of many insect-pollinated plants, but also because of the great indirect importance of all such plants as soil conservers and builders.

(*h*) *Conservation*. Ideas (see Chapter 3) may well be gained from knowing even the simplest facts of butterfly "ecology" above. Where, for example, would our programs of conservation be if we had no insect-pollinated plants to form humus and to hold soil from erosion?

Exhibits. Exhibits are most valuable. A crude homemade exhibit may teach far more than an elaborate "boughten" one. Use exhibits as concise summaries of principles. A conventional exhibit would be merely a set of the butterflies collected; it would teach little besides names. Far better, split up such an exhibit into smaller ones each illustrating some principle. Such an exhibit might well be displayed in the local public library, together with an assortment of books on butterflies and related phases of natural history work.

(*a*) *Size*. Largest and smallest butterflies (Swallowtail and Blue)

(*b*) *Life History*. All stages possible, pressed larval food plant and adults' favorite flower

(*c*) *Environment*. Woodland, meadow, marsh species, etc.

(*d*) *Protection from Enemies*. Species illustrating flight, hiding, protective form and color, mimicry

(*e*) *Protection from Weather*. Species illustrating hibernation in various stages (i.e., a piece of hollow log or a tin can with a "Mourning Cloak" in it), a butterfly sleeping under a wide leaf; the migratory Monarch (with map), etc.

(*f*) *Food*. Examples of larval eating (pressed leaves), adult feeding (pressed flowers) with preserved larvæ in vial and adult (proboscis uncoiled) on flowers

(*g*) *Friends and Foes*. Cut-out pictures of birds; predatory insects; ants; flowers

(*h*) *Habits*. A set of the "mud puddle club" species; a set of the pugnacious species

(*i*) *Colors*. Different types of butterfly colors, both pigment and "structural"

CHAPTER TWO

Collecting and Preserving Specimens

EQUIPMENT

A CERTAIN amount of special equipment is necessary. Nearly all of this can be homemade, or it may be purchased. The following are basic equipment: net, killing bottles, forceps, "glassine" envelopes or paper triangles, insect pins, spreading boards, glass strips, relaxer, specimen boxes, notebook, black India ink, bond paper (for labels) and scissors. To these may be added many other items, depending on the size of your pocketbook, the extent of your work, and your fondness for gadgets.

Net. The ring must be of a strong, *spring* wire. Personally, I do not like rings of flat metal — the folding fishnet type; they are too wobbly. Ring diameter should be 12 or 15 inches; although still larger nets are used by some collectors. The handle must be strong, of hickory, ash, birch, etc., a 3½ foot length of ¾ inch diameter will do. I have seen excellent nets with steel golf club shafts. Have the ring and handle easily detachable for changing bags. Length of the bag should be at least two and a quarter, not over three times the diameter of the ring; it should taper to a broadly rounded point not less than 3 inches in diameter. These specifications make for ease in flipping the bag over the rim to prevent a captured butterfly getting out, and for avoiding crushing the wings of large specimens by too narrow a point. The tougher, yet more transparent and lighter the material, the better. In a pinch, ordinary cheesecloth or mosquito netting can be used; they are cheap, their only advantage. Bobbinet is much better, having a locked mesh, but tears easily. Silk or nylon bobbinets if *tough* are very good but expensive. Probably the best material is the silk or nylon "bolting cloth" used as a screen in flour mills. It is very expensive; but will in the long run repay the extra cost. I have such a bag which I used for eight years in the Arizona desert, the Florida scrub, and the Amazon and West African jungles. The top edge of the bag should be sewed to a two or three inch strip of heavy cloth which fastens around the ring; never pass the net bag itself around the ring. Some collectors prefer dark nets (I do), others light, just as some prefer longer handles. Take at least one spare bag along on your trips.

Killing bottles are a "must," even if you "pinch" most of your specimens (see "Collecting Techniques" below). The standard for generations has contained potassium cyanide. This is a deadly poison. If you do not wish to use it, liquid carbon tetrachloride is advised; this is not very poisonous unless inhaled deeply. It is very toxic to insects but often sets their muscles so rigidly as to make relaxing and spreading difficult. It *must not* be allowed to wet the specimen. Ether, chloroform, gasoline, etc. can be used in an emergency.

Use a wide-mouth tube or jar of strong glass, not too deep. To make a tetrachloride bottle, chop up rubber bands, old rubber scraps, etc. into small pieces and pack these in to a depth of $\frac{1}{2}$ to $1\frac{1}{2}$ inches. Fit some circles of heavy blotting paper over this. With a medicine dropper add the tetrachloride through a small hole in the blotter. The rubber will absorb and hold carbon tetrachloride. Do not put in too much or you will wet the specimens. Keep a pad of absorbent cotton over the blotting paper. Add more tetrachloride as necessary. Carry a spare supply in your collecting bag.

For a cyanide bottle put a $\frac{1}{4}$ to $\frac{3}{4}$ inch layer of granular cyanide on the bottom of the jar, and cover this with an inch of fine, *thoroughly dry* sawdust. On this pour $\frac{1}{4}$ to $\frac{1}{2}$ inch of plaster of paris mixed thick. Leave the jar open until the plaster is *completely* dry. Such a bottle will last from one to three or more seasons if kept perfectly dry inside. Wrap the whole bottom part with adhesive tape in case of breakage. Label the jar very plainly "Poison." Remember that potassium cyanide is altogether deadly — and this includes the gas it gives off, with its characteristic bitter almond smell. Make bottles outdoors or with all windows open. Take no chances with cyanide.

Forceps. Probably the handiest for butterfly work are those tapering to sharp, curved points. Fix up a forceps case so that you will not stab yourself, and *always* carry forceps on collecting trips. *Pinning forceps* of a number of types can be purchased. They are excellent for handling specimens on slender insect pins.

Envelopes. "Glassine" envelopes of sizes ranging from $1\frac{1}{2}$ to $3\frac{1}{2}$ inches square are excellent for "papering" specimens. Insist on envelopes made without mucilage, glue, or other water soluble adhesives. If you wish to fold your own triangles prepare and press a good supply in advance. Ordinary newsprint and pulp pages are good. Porous paper is better in very damp, hot regions; the specimens dry out more quickly and do not mold.

Insect Pins of standard lengths are practically a necessity. The following are important: (1) a head that will stay on; (2) a good, stiff steel; (3) a thorough coating with lacquer to prevent rusting; or a good stainless steel; and (4) a sharp, yet not too tapering point that will not "fishhook." Sizes run as follows: 1 to $1\frac{1}{2}$ for smallest butterflies, 2 for small ones, 3 for nearly everything else, 4 for a few very large species. Get mostly 3's, then 2's, then the extremes. Use the largest size practical for each specimen.

Spreading Boards are necessary for proper preparation of specimens. The essential design is simple. Adjustable spreading boards are available, but expensive. It is probably best to have at least three sizes, perhaps four. Size is determined by the width of the center groove. In this, $\frac{1}{8}$ inch will do for very small butterflies; $\frac{3}{16}$ inch for most small and small-medium sized ones; $\frac{1}{4}$ inch for the majority of specimens; $\frac{3}{8}$ inch for large-medium ones; and $\frac{1}{2}$ or even $\frac{5}{8}$ inch for very large butterflies and moths. A good starting set would be one $\frac{3}{16}$ inch, two $\frac{1}{4}$ inch, and one $\frac{3}{8}$ inch. The side pieces must, of course, be proportionately wide. Boards 19 to 20 inches long are more economical than short ones; start at the middle and work to the ends. Side pieces should slant upward slightly. Here are some very important features: (1) The side pieces must be of a soft wood, with no hard grain, that will not pick up in tiny splinters. "Whitewood" or soft pine is best. (2) The inner, upper edges of the side pieces must both be at absolutely the same level above the center strip. (3) The center strip must be of a very soft material; thin, natural cork and *soft* balsa wood are best. The strip must be locked in place so as not to loosen. (4) The board must not be allowed to become loose jointed. (5) The bottom must be absolutely flat and extend the whole width and length. Sandpaper or steel-wool your boards satin smooth frequently.

Strips of Glass, or pinned-down cardboard or paper strips, must be placed over the wings of specimens on the spreading boards to prevent curling. Standard microscope slides 1×3 and 2×3 inches are very handy and cheap, and have nicely rounded edges.

A *Relaxer* may be almost any small metal box or wide-mouthed glass jar. Elaborate (and expensive) ones are available at dealers. The top must be reasonably close fitting. An inch or so of clean sand in the bottom is thoroughly wetted. A perforated false bottom or screen holds papered specimens above this; a piece of cork or balsa will be needed if pinned specimens are to be relaxed. Specimens *must not be wetted*, but merely kept in saturated, humid air. *Keep plenty of flake naphthalene in the bottom to discourage mold.* Avoid sudden cooling of the box which will produce a miniature rainstorm and wet specimens. Do not leave specimens in the box too long or they will rot.

Specimen Boxes may be bought quite cheap, or may be made if you are a good carpenter. Cardboard boxes are cheap but leaky. Glass-topped boxes are fine for exhibits but are heavy. The all-wood box, properly made, is probably best for the private collector unless he can afford a cabinet of glass-topped drawers.

Primary necessity is tightness to keep out "museum pests." These are chiefly the larvæ of several small beetles (*Anthrenus* and *Dermestes*), Clothes Moths, Meal Moths, and Ants. Some are very tiny—but potent. All are very destructive and must be kept out at all costs. So the cover should fit down outside of an inner collar, and fit *tight*. The outer edge of this collar should have a rounded bevel to admit air gently when the box is opened. There should be two inches clear depth inside. The inner "pinning bottom" should be of a soft enough material for the pins to penetrate readily, at least $\frac{3}{8}$ inch thick. The best material is patent cork, obtainable in sheets from dealers. This should be papered *on both sides*, not just the top, or it will curl. It is expensive. Cheap corks with glue binders are anathema. Selected, soft balsa wood is very fine; composition construction boards like celotex and masonite are very good if soft enough. The pinning bottoms *must not* come loose; and there should be a solid bottom below for tightness. Tops and bottoms are best made of a light 3-plywood. Shellac or lacquer the box *thoroughly*; it must be thoroughly waterproofed externally. Light weight is a virtue. A standard "Schmitt Box" size is 9 × 13 × 2½ inches. Larger sizes are more practicable for larger butterflies.

Of course any shallow, reasonably tight box will suffice in a pinch. Every museum in the world is full of cigar boxes. Two layers of corrugated cardboard with the grains at right angles make a good emergency pinning bottom.

Notebook. This is an essential for every good collector. I use a "Lefax" myself, and keep past years in a file. A waterproof cover that will hold both the notebook and this *Field Guide* would be very handy. Keep notes of all collecting trips, rearing, etc. They will be invaluable later on. I have at my elbow now my original notes of twenty-nine years ago, and I wouldn't trade them for twenty-nine times the specimens I caught that day (which was a good day, too, in the Tetons).

Paper, Ink, and Scissors. Use the best grade of heavy bond paper for pin labels and mounting strips. Use an eternal India ink. A really sharp, stiff pair of scissors is advised. Scissors that flip labels all over the place are an abomination.

Other Items. I consider the above items essential; but you will probably accumulate many others in time. Entomologists are the most gadget-minded people I know, more so even than fishermen. Each one swears by some particular pet; and spends much time devising new ones.

A *Collecting Bag* is almost essential. It should be roomy, of stout canvas, and hang from one shoulder only, so you can drop it in a hurry. The army musette bags are good, though a trifle small. A metal *botanical vasculum* in addition is very good for food plants.

Cans for larvæ and other live specimens are a necessity. Take along plenty! Don't worry about insects needing air. You can shut larvæ up all day as tight as you want, providing they are clean and cool.

A *Magnifying Glass* is practically a necessity. You will seldom need one more than 10 ×. If you intend real work on insects a prism binocular dissecting microscope of a good make is almost a necessity; these are very expensive.

Mounting Needles or Pins are a great help. I make mine of very fine sewing needles, putting on heads by dipping them into sealing wax. Their slender, stiff, sharp points may break but will not fishhook and tear specimens' wings or the spreading board.

A *Labeling Block*, used to push small labels up on the specimen pins, is strongly advised. You can get along very well using small holes in a piece of wood or the edge of a table. A cross-section two inches thick from the flower stalk of a Century Plant or large Yucca is excellent.

Printed Pin Labels (available through dealers) for recording locality and collector on each specimen are great time savers. They should be printed with smallest type. Leave a space for the date.

A *Pin Block* with a number of holes for supplies of different sized insect pins is useful. *Vials* for preserving larvæ are almost a necessity. *Blowing Outfits* can be purchased from dealers. They are used for preparing mounts of caterpillars' skins. Wide-mouthed jars can be used for rearing larvæ; but better are "lamp chimney cages" or wooden frame cages covered with wire netting.

COLLECTING TECHNIQUES

AND HINTS

Netting. Only experience will tell you whether to clap your net down over a butterfly or to sweep at it. If the former, hold the end of the bag up immediately; most specimens will fly up into it. If the latter, flip the bag across the ring immediately to prevent escape. Get the butterfly up into the end, grasp the bag just below this and hold it up. Then slip the bottle in (I hold the net stick between my thighs) with the other hand, push it vertically up through the hand holding the bag, get the specimen into it, and push and hold it hard against the net. With the free hand slip on the cork or cap. Many specimens are lost in bottling. Do this all as fast as possible. Holding the end of the bag against the sky helps you to see what you are doing.

The experienced collector wastes very little motion and misses few shots. He tries "wing shots" only as a last resort. When you see someone cavorting madly across the landscape making round-house swings with a net, the odds are that he is a rank beginner. Of course there will be times when a chase is necessary. But a little observation of the butterfly, of the flowers it is visiting, or of whatever else it is doing, and a bit of careful stalking and a "sitting shot," will get more and better specimens.

Be careful to avoid hitting plants with the net whenever possible. You may tear the bag; and you will probably also get leaves and flowers in the net that will damage the specimens and make bottling difficult. Moreover you will be very unpopular if you knock the flowers off someone's prize-winning delphinium. And swing no harder than necessary; most specimens suffer damage from contact with the bag anyway. Keep the bag clean of weed seeds, which damage many specimens.

Pinching is a time honored technique favored by many collectors of various fauna. With the specimen in the end of the bag, pinch the sides *of its thorax only* with fingertips or forceps. Do this *only*

WHEN ITS WINGS ARE TOGETHER OVER ITS BACK: *do not pinch the wings, head, or abdomen.* You had better not pinch small species, skippers, or very active, strong butterflies, at least until you are an expert. Properly done, pinching produces more perfect specimens; but it is not an easy technique.

"Folding Back" specimens is an essential. Many butterflies will die with the wings folded *below* the body. *With the forceps* maneuver the wings together above the body and do this *within thirty seconds* or the wings will lock in position and then you will only do damage. Promptly done, positioning is easy; there is a simple but indescribable knack.

Papering should be done as soon as possible. Thoroughly pinched specimens may be papered at once, others after 10 to 30 minutes in the killing jar. Or you may use the jar merely to stun them, then pinch and paper at once. If you are using killing bottles, do not let specimens accumulate in one. Have a large "stock" jar for the accumulations. If possible don't carry this; set it down in a central spot. You can paper any specimens immediately if your stock jar is large enough to hold the envelopes. Don't kill strong species in a jar containing any fragile specimens. If a killing bottle "sweats" inside, don't use it until it has been dried — and remember that cyanide "sweat" is very poisonous.

Where to collect is always a puzzle for the beginner. Of course, the best collecting is on flowers. Only experience will teach you which are the best at any given time and place. The *Field Guide to the Flowers* will prove invaluable. The Milkweeds and orange Butterfly Weed (*Asclepias*), Dogbane (*Apocynum*), Clovers (*Trifolium*), Blueberries (*Vaccinium*), Huckleberries (*Gaylussacia*), Honeysuckle (*Lonicera*), Thistles (*Cirsium*), Burdock (*Arctium*), Buttonbush (*Cephalanthus* — in swampy places), and New Jersey Tea (*Ceanothus*) are all prime favorites. Especially in the South the white flowers of that pestiferous weed, Spanish Needles (*Bidens*) are extremely fine collecting — but the little forked, stick-tight seeds are an invention of Satan. Cultivated flowers are often good collecting, but may not attract a great many species.

Probably best at the start is to collect along a country roadside or a railroad track. This gives you a cross section of the country and a chance to collect in different environments. At first do not tarry too long in one spot. Read the list of environments given in Chapter 3 and see how many of these you can find. Without doing this you will miss many species, especially the rare ones, which are usually strongly limited in their environment. The best butterfly collectors I know are men with a keen eye for environment who know and watch for *typical plants* as keenly as for butterflies. I know such collectors who have time and again gone into perfectly strange country and found rarities that the local collectors scarcely ever saw. There is, I suppose, a trick to it — but the trick is based on preparation. Plan your trip, know what you are doing and why, and you will find good collecting. Check off in the text the species you may find in your region. See if a note as to habitat is given. See what the favorite flower is, if any, and the larval food plant. Look up these plants so that you may recognize them. You will then have a ten times better chance to find the butterfly than if you went out blindly. This is good "rainy day" and winter work.

Some miscellaneous hints. Don't trespass and don't leave farmers' gates open. In thirty years I have never yet been refused permission to collect on anyone's property. Learn to read and use topographic maps. Learn to avoid Poison Ivy, and other such plants. Use the automobile in reason; I know people who spend half their collecting time in a car, with proportionately poor results. Don't think you have to go to the wilderness to get good collecting. Over a hundred species of butterflies have been taken within twenty miles of New York City. Don't fail to keep plenty of notes on what you see and do, as well as catch. Above all, know your plants; get and carry the *Field Guides* to trees and flowers, and study them as hard as you do this one.

Baits and Lures. Many butterflies are strongly attracted to manure, carrion, excrement, rotting fruit, fermenting fruit juices, etc. Many species visit mud puddles in large numbers. Some will come down to a colored paper imitation of one of their kind, or to a specimen thus used as a lure. By keeping such possibilities in mind you may be able to lure in specimens that otherwise could hardly be caught. This is a standard technique for tropical collectors.

Care of Specimens. Adult butterflies need no preservatives; when thoroughly dried and kept dry they last almost indefinitely. I once dissected a specimen that was caught in 1819; it was as sound as you would wish. Field-papered specimens need merely to have the data recorded on each envelope and to be stacked loosely for fast drying. In very humid climates gentle artificial heat is advisable. Dust plenty of flake naphthalene in the box to deter mold and "museum pests." Take special care that ants do not get into the boxes, especially in the field or in camp.

Full directions for further care of specimens are contained in the various leaflets, obtainable either free or at little cost, listed in Part III.

Spreading. Everybody develops his own pet techniques. I give here merely fundamentals. The illustrations tell the story, but here are the steps (for a right-handed person).

Pin on the board two strips of good, tough paper. With forceps grasp the sides of the thorax of the specimen just below the wing bases; pinch gently, and the wings will spread apart (Fig. 3). Push pin *straight down* through the center of the thorax, pushing it down to within about $\frac{3}{8}$ in. of its head. Then pin the specimen in the center of the center groove of the board, again pushing the pin *straight down.* Pass the paper strips over the antennæ and wings so as to hold these out flat to the sides on the smooth boards. Pin strips down (Fig. 1). Insert a stiff pin straight down to left of body just behind the hindwing base, to prevent specimen turning

ARCTIC ALPINE AND
CANADIAN LIFE ZONES

Arctic Alpine Zone (*upper picture*). The Tableland Plateau of Katahdin, Me. at Governors Spring, alt. 4636 ft. In the background Baxter Peak, alt. 5267 ft. This is the sole locality of the Katahdin Arctic (*Œneis polixenes katahdin*) a subspecies of a truly Arctic butterfly. Many other Arctic insects occur here. The plant life is limited to low, stunted or mat-forming species, many of them characteristically Arctic, too. The dark patches are Spruce and Fir trees, forming low mats ("krumholz" or "elfin wood") only a foot or so high. Some typical plants are the Alpine Willow (*Salix Uva-ursi*), Labrador Tea (*Ledum grœndlandicum*), Lappland Rhododendron (*Rhododendron lapponicum*), Bearberry (*Arctostaphylos Uva-ursi*), Dwarf Bilberry (*Vaccinium cœspitosum*), Bog Bilberry (*V. uliginosum*), Pale Laurel (*Kalmia polifolia*), Diapensia (*Diapensia lapponica*), Mountain Sandwort (*Arenaria grœnlandica*), Alpine Holy Grass (*Hierochloë alpina*), Cotton Sedge Grass (*Eriophorum* sp.), Alpine Rush (*Juncus trifidus*), Club Mosses (*Lycopodium selago* and *annotinum* var. *pungens*) and a great variety of Lichens. The foot of the Hunt Trail, which leads up to this famous collecting ground, can be reached by driving from Millinocket, Me. to the Nesowadnehunk Tote Road. Use the Katahdin Quadrangle of the U.S. Geological Survey "topo" map.

Other accessible areas of Arctic-alpine Zone in the east are found on Mt. Washington, N.H. and on the summits of Mt. Albert and other peaks of the Gaspé Peninsula, Que. Each area has its special butterflies of the genera *Œneis* and *Boloria*, as well as Arctic moths, other insects and plants.

Canadian Zone Forest (*lower picture*) near West Bridgewater, Vt. Much of the Canadian Zone forest is of almost unmixed evergreen trees such as the White and Red Spruce (*Picea alba* and *rubra*), Balsam Fir (*Abies balsamea*), and Red and Jack Pines (*Pinus resinosa* and *banksiana*). Other great areas are composed of broad-leaved, deciduous trees such as the Sugar and Mountain maples (*Acer saccharum* and *spicatum*), Beech (*Fagus*), Yellow and White Birches (*Betula lutea*, *pendula* and *alba* var. *papyrifera*), Quaking Aspen, Large Toothed Aspen, and Balsam Poplar or Tacamahac (*Populus tremuloides*, *grandidentata*, and *balsamifera*). You will not find good butterfly collecting in the extensive areas of unbroken forest. But in spots such as that shown here, where the character of the forest is mixed and where there are meadows, trails or roads, butterflies may abound. Some characteristic ones are: Northern Wood Nymph (*Cercyonis pegala nephele*), Atlantis Fritillary (*Speyeria atlantis*), Satyr Angle Wing (*Polygonia satyrus*), Green Comma and Hoary Comma (*Polygonia faunus* and *gracilis*), Compton and Milbert's Tortoise Shells (*Nymphalis j-album* and *milberti*), White Admiral (*Limenitis a. arthemis*), Acadian Hairstreak (*Strymon acadica*), Early Hairstreak (*Erora lœta*), Sæpiolus Blue (*Plebeius sœpiolus*), Mustard White (*Pieris napi*), and Arctic Skipper (*Carterocephalus palœmon*). There are large areas of Canadian Zone in our northern states; and the Zone can be traced southward even to Georgia along the ridge of the Alleghany Mountains, although in very dilute form.

Plate 2   17

ACID BOG AND FRESH WATER MARSH

Acid Bog in Canadian Life Zone (*upper picture*). Such bogs are also known as "Sphagnum Bogs" or "Muskegs." This one is the "Klondike," near Mt. Katahdin, Me. Extreme acidity of soil and water characterizes such true bogs, permitting only certain plants to flourish. These are chiefly plants of the great Hudsonian and Arctic areas of the far north; many of them also characterize Arctic-alpine Zone above timberline. Some special butterflies, really far northern species, occur well to the southward in these bogs. Such are the Jutta Arctic (*Œneis jutta*), the Bog and the Purple Lesser Fritillaries (*Boloria eunomia* and *titania*), the Bog Elfin (*Incisalia lanoraieensis*), and the Bog Copper (*Lycæna epixanthe*). Acid bogs occur in typical form in Canadian Zone in Me., N. H., Vt., and N. Y., along the mountains south to Va. and in the coastal plain south to the Carolinas. They are quite common in Canada. Characteristic plants are: Tamarack (*Larix laricina*) and Black Spruce (*Picea mariana*) in the North and White Cedar (*Chamæcyparis thyoides*) in the South; Leatherleaf (*Chamædaphne calyculata*), Pitcher Plants (*Sarracenia*), Sundews (*Drosera*), Labrador Tea (*Ledum grœnlandicum*), Pale Laurel (*Kalmia polifolia*), Andromeda (*Andromeda polifolia*), the Cranberries (*Vaccinium oxycoccus* and *macrocarpon*), Mayflower (*Maianthemum canadense*), Bog Solomons Seal (*Smilacina trifolia*), and many Lichens ("Reindeer Mosses"). Deep spongy mats of Sphagnum Moss cover the ground, into which one sinks to the knees. In the northern bogs you may find nests of the Lincoln Sparrow, a characteristic breeding bird in such areas. No special environment will better repay the efforts of the butterfly collector. Famous bogs are those at Orono and Passadumkeag, Me. In southern Canada there are many; those at Mer Bleue, Ont. Lanoraie, Que. and in the Laurentides Park are noteworthy. Bogs occur in the northern middle west states, especially in northern Mich., Minn. and Wis. In the N.J. "pine barrens" are famous bog collecting areas, such as at Lakehurst and Forked River.

Fresh Water Marsh near Putnam, Conn. (*lower picture*). There are thousands of marshes in the eastern area that are far more extensive and typical than this one, and are such a familiar sight as hardly to warrant illustration. But I have collected in this little marsh since 1917, and cherish it particularly. Actually it is not a truly normal marsh area, for along one side is a tiny bit of acid soil in which Cranberry grows. Here, many miles from any other population of its species, is a little colony of the Bog Copper (*Lycæna epixanthe*). Typical and normal marsh butterflies are the Silver Bordered and Meadow Fritillaries (*Boloria selene* and *toddi*), Harris' Checkerspot (*Melitæa harrisii*), the Baltimore (*Euphydryas phæton*), the Two Spotted Skipper (*Atrytone bimacula*) and the Broad Winged Skipper (*Poanes viator*). Many other butterflies of other areas visit the flowering plants in the marshes (Blue Flag and Buttonbush are very good for collecting). The marsh butterflies are also found along the inland edges of salt and brackish marshes.

on pin. If you are left-handed, insert this pin to the right of the specimen and then spread the right side first.

Insert needle point behind strong radial vein of FW, slide wing part way forward. When doing this you may leave the paper strip pinned down (not too tight) or may unpin it and hold it down with the fingers. Do not move the FW so far forward that the HW will slip out from under it. Note: the needle point must move in the arc of a circle, since a straight forward movement will rip the wing. Push needle lightly into board to hold FW (No. 2). Move HW forward, then FW some more, then HW, etc., alternating. In proper position the inner margins of the FW should stand at right angles to the body and therefore form a straight line with each other (No. 3). The HW should not be so far forward as to hide any marks on it. If necessary hold wings in final position with needles through paper strip behind strong veins. Repeat the process on the right side.

After positioning antennæ and wings, cover them with a glass strip to prevent the wing edges curling up. A paper strip may be

Fig. 1

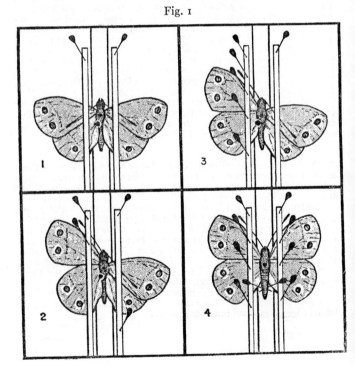

placed over them first if desired. Standard (3×1 in.) microscope slides are excellent for this. Pin glass strips securely in position to prevent any motion whatsoever. Adjust position of abdomen with pins crossed above or below it (No. 4). Make out pin label with full data and pin it alongside specimen. Place spreading board in a dry place, secure from ants or other pests. Allow at least several days for specimens to dry.

Special Note on Skippers. The muscles set so strongly that most specimens cannot be spread without tearing the wings, unless special precautions are taken. Two cuts should be made on each side of the thorax just below the base of each wing (see Fig. 2). Use a very thin, slender-pointed knife, or a razor blade broken diagonally. Do not cut too deeply, and be careful not to cut too high and remove the wings. Practise on some common specimens before trying valuable ones.

Data. Full, and above all *accurate*, data should be kept with every specimen. I cannot emphasize this enough. A specimen without data is, perhaps, of some interest; but it has little value. The minimum data consist of locality, date of capture, and name of collector. Beyond this any pertinent information of possible interest should be added, such as the environment (acid bog, deep woods, open field, etc.), the flowers visited ("visiting Lilac"), or other such. If a male and female are taken in copula this should be indicated on each. If a specimen is reared from the larval or pupal stage this should always be noted (ex larva, Hickory, emerged 7 Apr. '49). It is best to abbreviate the month *with letters*; do not use numerals, for some people put the month first, others in the middle (so, 7–9–52 would mean the seventh of September to one man and the ninth of July to another). For the locality use a name found on standard maps, and always include the name of an unmistakable town or county. There are probably hundreds of "Deer Creeks" and "Maple Hills" in the country and perhaps several in each state. Use a standard abbreviation for the state or

Fig. 2   Fig. 3

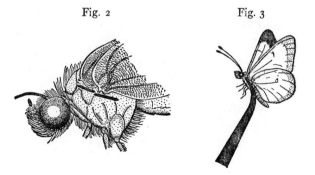

province. Remember that someone may be studying your material many years after you are dead and gone. Keep your pin labels as small as possible. Big "barn door" labels cause many accidents in the boxes.

Preserving Larvæ and Pupæ. Specimens of larvæ and pupæ should be kept in a liquid preservative. Simplest is to kill by dropping into very hot or gently boiling water, transfer immediately to 70% ethyl alcohol, and then, after 24 hours, change the alcohol. Color notes must be made before killing. Or the following preservative may be made up and carried in the field and the specimens dropped directly into it, left in it for not more than 24 hours, then transferred to 95% alcohol for preservation: kerosene — 1 part; ethyl alcohol (95%) — 10 parts; glacial acetic acid — 1 part; dioxin — 1 part. This prevents blackening and shriveling. Store preserved larvæ and pupæ in vials; and keep the vials in tight, wide-mouthed jars with some preservative in each jar. This is good insurance against drying out of corks and specimens. As previously noted, outfits for "blowing" larvæ can be purchased from dealers. Pupal shells from which the butterflies have emerged can be dried, fastened to a small card and either pinned beneath the butterfly or placed alongside it, with an identifying label. So can egg shells.

CHAPTER THREE

The Butterfly and its Environment

IN THIS CHAPTER we shall try to outline the chief points of the study of the relationships between butterflies and their environments — what is scientifically known as *ecology*. This, very aptly called "scientific natural history," is almost the most recent major branch of biology. It is also in many ways the most interesting, for it includes everything an animal or plant does, its effects on the other living things around it, and their effects on it. It also includes the effects of such physical features as climate, soil, terrain, and water. Let us first consider some of the major physical features of our area, and see how these affect the butterflies. Then we shall look at the relations of the butterflies with other forms of life: first with plants; then with other animals; finally with other butterflies.

WORLD FAUNAL REGIONS

Studying the distribution of life in the world, we see a number of major divisions, corresponding roughly with the great continental areas. In each of these divisions, which for animals are called *faunal regions*, the living things show closer relationship to each other, as a whole, than to those of other regions. These regions are: (1) *Holarctic*, Arctic and Temperate regions of both Old and New Worlds. (2) *Neotropical*, including Central and South America. (3) *Ethiopian*, most of Africa. (4) *Indo-Australian*, the tropical Asiatic lands, from India and Malaya through the Australian area.

Of these we are concerned with the Holarctic and Neotropical; for it is to the former that North America belongs, and it is from the latter that many animals and plants have migrated northward into our area.

The Holarctic Region includes all of Europe; a thin strip along the northern edge of Africa; Asia south to northern India and Burma; and North America south to Mexico and, in central Mexico, some areas south of the border. It is subdivided into two subregions: (a) *Palæarctic* (from the Greek *palæos* — old) in Europe and Asia, and (b) *Nearctic* (Greek, *neos* — new) in North America. These Old and New World areas are much more alike than most people realize. A major part of our butterflies belong to genera that also occur in the Palæarctic, and a rather large number of species are common to both subregions. Many times, in the text that follows, you will see a butterfly described as "Holarctic"; many such species range from Spain across Europe, Asia, and North America to eastern Canada and the eastern United States.

The Neotropical Region is very rich in butterfly life, containing many distinctive groups. Many such butterflies have pushed northward into our area from the Antilles into Florida or from Mexico into Texas. Most of these are, of course, essentially southern in our area; but some of them range far northward, even to Canada.

Knowledge of the original home of a butterfly is a great help in understanding things about it. Knowing whether its relationships are Holarctic or Neotropical, we can recognize its closest relatives, and study them, too. Then we can understand many things about it that might be unintelligible if we considered it alone.

Surprisingly few groups of butterflies are of North American origin, i.e. *endemic*. One such is the group of Swallowtails to which *Papilio glaucus* and *rutulus* belong; but this is only a small part of the whole *Papilio* group. Another, apparently distinct from relatives in the Palæarctic, is the genus *Speyeria*, the Large Fritillaries.

CLIMATIC DIVISIONS

In our area we can distinguish two sets of divisions, both dependent on *climatic* features. One is the *Life Zones* (see p. 23), a series of belts running across the continent, ranging from the Arctic Zone in the North to the Subtropical Zone in the South. Temperature is the major factor here. The other is the *Rainfall Zones*, a series of east-west divisions in which water (chiefly rainfall) is the determining factor. These range, in our area, from the humid east coast, with heavy rainfall, to the dry, central Great Plains where the rainfall is too light to support much but short grasses.

LIFE ZONES

(1) *Arctic-Alpine Zone* (see p. 16). This, the northernmost zone, is characterized by plants and animals adapted for life in extremely cold regions where there is a short growing season. These are characteristic Arctic conditions; but they also occur far to the south of the Arctic on high Alpine mountaintops. Here occur isolated "islands" of Arctic plant and animal life, their nearest relatives in the true Arctic perhaps hundreds of miles northward. In our area, such islands of Alpine Zone occur on the highest mountains of the Gaspé Peninsula in Quebec, on Mt. Katahdin, Maine, and on Mt. Washington and its neighbors in New Hampshire. Lesser, partly Arctic-Alpine areas occur on Mt. Lafayette, New Hampshire, and to a slight degree in the Green Mountains of Vermont and the Adirondacks and Catskills of New York.

Plants are more clearly zonal in distribution than most animals. *Learn the index plants if you wish to recognize life zones.* In Arctic-

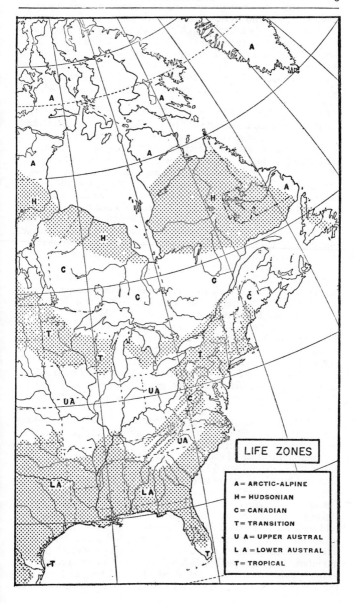

LIFE ZONES

A = ARCTIC-ALPINE
H = HUDSONIAN
C = CANADIAN
T = TRANSITION
U A = UPPER AUSTRAL
L A = LOWER AUSTRAL
T = TROPICAL

Alpine there are no trees. Characteristic plants are low, shrubby Willows, some only a few inches high; various Heaths, other flowering plants, grasses, sedges and lichens. Truly Alpine butterflies of our area are few: there are two of the genus *Œneis* and one *Boloria* in New England, and a couple more *Œneis* in Gaspé. There are many more species in the Arctic, chiefly *Œneis* and *Erebia* (*Satyridæ*), *Boloria* (*Nymphalidæ*), *Plebeius* and *Lycæna* (*Lycænidæ*), and *Colias* (*Pieridæ*).

(2) *Hudsonian Zone* (p. 23, H). Not a major life zone in itself, but rather a broad borderline or "tension" area between Arctic and Canadian zones, marked by an average midsummer temperature of 50–57° F. Characteristic trees are Firs, Spruces, Tamarack, Jack Pine (*P. banksiana*) and Willows. For the most part these are greatly stunted and form low, tangled, almost mat-like growths (*krumholz*). The zone runs along the southern edge of the Arctic, and also occurs as a belt at the lower edge of Alpine Zone on mountains. It also occurs on some peaks which do not quite get up to true alpine conditions. Few, if any, butterflies occur in Hudsonian Zone alone. Perhaps *Papilio machaon* is most representative. Many Arctic species range down, and Canadian zone species range up, into the Hudsonian zone; and some of these range far southward in the acid "muskeg" bogs.

(3) *Canadian Zone* (see p. 16). This is the zone of the great northern forest area, with an average midsummer temperature of 57–64° F and a luxuriant growth of Fir, Spruce and Tamarack. This *coniferous* forest readily gives way under local conditions to Aspen and the Beech-Birch-Maple *deciduous hardwood* forest; and White and Red Pines and Hemlock are common trees in southern areas. Characteristic shrubs and herbaceous plants occur in open areas. Many butterflies characterize Canadian Zone. A few such are: *Colias interior; Pieris napi; Cœnonympha tullia; Erebia epipsodea; Speyeria atlantis; Polygonia gracilis, faunus, and satyrus; Erora læta; Everes amyntula; Plebeius sæpiolus; Carterocephalus palæmon;* and *Hesperia laurentina*.

True Canadian Zone runs far southward at high elevations along the Appalachians, not, of course, in a continuous strip. It is thus recognizable as far south as Georgia.

A marked feature of Canadian Zone is the presence "in it, but not of it" of extensive acid bog areas (see p. 17). These are characterized by Black Spruce (*Picea mariana*), Tamarack (*Larix*) and a dense, low growth of intermingled Sphagnum Moss, Lichens, Cranberry (*Vaccinium*), Labrador Tea (*Ledum*) and other Heaths, Pitcher Plant (*Sarracenia*) and Sundew (*Drosera*). Such bogs are cold and, for this reason as well as because of their characteristic plants, are really extensions of Arctic and Hudsonian zones down in the lowland Canadian areas. In this way they are much like the mountaintops, representing isolated islands of more northern life forms. Typical such bogs are those at Mer Bleue and many in the Laurentides Park, Quebec; Passadumkeag, Orono, and near

Mt. Katahdin, Maine; and numerous smaller ones occurring, sometimes in diluted form, in Michigan, northern Indiana, southern Vermont, McLean, New York, southern New Jersey, and even in West Virginia and south into the Carolinas. Some characteristic butterflies are: *Cænonympha tullia* subspecies; *Œneis jutta; Boloria eunomia, titania,* and *freija; Incisalia lanoraieensis;* and *Lycæna epixanthe.*

(4) *Transition (Alleghanian) Zone.* The Transition Zone is, like the Hudsonian, not well marked in itself, but rather a borderline or tension zone where Canadian and Austral zones meet and mingle. Its plants, as well as its animals, are mostly clearly derived from Canadian and Austral sources. Sometimes they are differentiated as subspecies or minor species. A few butterflies found mostly in the Transition Zone are: *Pieris virginiensis, Euptychia mitchellii, Boloria selene myrina* and *toddi ammiralis, Melitæa harrisii, Euphydryas phæton, Lycæides melissa samuelis, Strymon edwardsii* and *acadica, Pyrgus centaureæ wyandot, Hesperia sassacus, Polites mystic,* and *Poanes hobomok.*

(5) *Austral Zone.* South of the Transition Zone, and extending to nearly our whole southern boundary, are the two Austral Zones. Sometimes these are combined with the Transition as the "Austral Region." They are what we mean when we speak of "The South"; and the Lower Austral is often called "The Deep South."

The Upper Austral has an average summer temperature range of 72-79° F. Primarily it is the region of temperate deciduous forests with no such mixtures of White Pines, Hemlocks, etc. as characterize the Transition Zone. Characteristic trees are Beech, Maples, Oaks, Gums, Hickories, Tulip Tree and Sassafras; but there are also large areas of the more southern hard pines. The Upper Austral reaches farthest northward along the coast, in very diluted form even to Mt. Desert Island, Maine. Southward it blends widely with the Lower Austral. East of the Appalachians it is the zone of the "Piedmont" — the area between the Transition Zone forest of the real mountains and the Lower Austral of the flat coastal plain.

The Lower Austral Zone, with an average summer temperature over 79° F., is the zone of the eastern Coastal Plain and of the low, rich, often swampy country of the deep south. Like the Upper Austral, it extends well northward along the coast, entering eastern Virginia. Southward it extends to Lake Okeechobee in Florida, and to the subtropical areas in the lower Rio Grande Valley of Texas. It is the area of the southern hard pine forests (see p. 33), *Pinus tæda, echinata, palustris* and *caribæa,* and of the Magnolias, Live Oak (*Quercus virginiana*), Bald Cypress (*Taxodium*), "Spanish Moss" (*Tillandsia*) and (southward) of Palmetto (*Sabal*).

A great many butterflies characterize the Austral Zones. A few characteristic ones are: *Papilio palamedes, Phœbis eubule, Eurema nicippe, Euptychia areolata* and *hermes sosybia, Agraulis vanillæ, Lephelisca virginiensis, Atlides halesus, Strymon cecrops* and *m-album, Autochton cellus, Urbanus proteus, Atalopedes campestris, Polites vibex, Problema byssus,* and *Megathymus yuccæ* and *cofaqui.*

(6) *Subtropical and Tropical Zones.* There is doubt that we should speak of any North American areas as truly tropical; at best we have only rather dilute tropical areas in southern Florida and Texas, not comparable to the true tropical fauna and flora farther south. However, within our tropical area are a great many plants and animals that differ in no essential from their relatives of the true tropics. Some details of the plants are discussed below under "hammocks" (see also p. 33). The butterflies add up to a surprisingly large total. In Florida there are fewer than in Texas, but nearly all are, as one would expect, breeding residents. Of the species in southern Texas a large number are casuals, merely occasional strays from contiguous Mexico. A few butterflies are: *Papilio polydamus, Phœbis philea* and *agarithe; Eurema proterpia; Danaus berenice; Heliconius charitonius; Phyciodes frisia; Anartia jatrophæ; Dryas julia; Eunica monima* and *tatila; Marpesia petreus; Strymon martialis, acis, pastor, columella,* etc.; *Phocides batabano; Polygonus lividus; Astraptes fulgerator; Heliopetes laviana* and *macaira; Cobalus percosius, Lerodea edata,* etc.

RAINFALL ZONES

As we have seen, we cross the various Life Zones in passing from north to south. Another important series of divisions runs along an east-west axis. The differences between these are determined primarily by rainfall. In this respect the continent has a dry interior, with regions of heavier rainfall along both West and East coasts where run the mountain chains; and another region of heavier rainfall somewhat west of the center where runs the chain of the Rockies. If we were to cross the Appalachians and travel westward we would find ourselves approaching the central region of aridity. Just after leaving the mountains we might note little change; but after crossing the Mississippi we would notice the trees becoming more and more confined to river and creek bottoms; while the intervening areas, lacking trees, tended instead to be covered with tall grasses. This is *Savannah* or *Prairie.* Still farther west we would find the trees disappearing almost entirely, except for cottonwoods along watercourses, and the long grasses giving way to short "bunch grasses." We would be at the eastern border of the Great Plains (*steppe*) which stretch westward from about the longitude of the 100th meridian all the rest of the way to the Rocky Mountains. (See p. 32.)

Where rainfall is heavy a forest can exist and occupy most of the terrain. Where it is lighter the forest cannot exist in the drier areas, which will be occupied by long grasses; a still lighter precipitation will permit no forest at all. Where the rainfall is so light as not to permit even the tall grasses to flourish, the short, water-conserving grasses take over the land. And in regions of even less rainfall even the short grasses cannot survive; here grows the *desert scrub* such as is found in the extremely arid Great Basin west of the Rockies.

Such a pattern has, of course, profoundly influenced the distribution of the animal life of the continent. The chief effect has been the virtual isolation from each other of the three essentially humid regions, the *West Coast*, the *Rocky Mountains*, and the *Eastern area*. Separated by arid barriers, each has tended to develop a characteristic flora and fauna.

Several factors complicate this essentially simple pattern. The first and chief is the broad Mississippi Valley lying between the arid plains and the humid Appalachian Mountains. This valley and that of the Ohio River have acted as pathways for the northward extension of southern species which therefore range farther northward (even into Ontario) than they do along the coastal strip. The second is the high, cool ridge of the Appalachians which, as we have seen, carries northern species far to the south of their otherwise normal ranges.

The third factor is the isolation of the Mississippi Valley from the Eastern coastal strip by the intervening mountain barrier, preventing the intermingling of forms from the two regions and therefore enabling them to become different from each other. Other factors are: the presence of the Ozark Plateau in Arkansas and southern Missouri, introducing a cooler, more humid area in an otherwise more arid region; the mollifying climatic influence of the Great Lakes, permitting the spread of even Upper Austral species far northward; and the general southward thrust of the Laurentian Shield, bringing large areas of Canadian Zone southward into northern Wisconsin, Minnesota, and Michigan.

To summarize, we might see what we would pass through if we were to travel westward from some point on the central Atlantic seaboard. In succession we would encounter:

(1) *Southeastern Coniferous Forest* — the region of hard Pines extending up the coastal strip even, in dilute form, to New York and Cape Cod.

(2) *Eastern Temperate Deciduous Forest* — the region of broad-leaved trees of the inner coastal plain and the lower "piedmont" or foothills.

(3) *Mixed Coniferous and Deciduous Forest* — the Transition Zone forest of the upper "piedmont" and the main mountain chain.

(4) *Northern Coniferous Forest* (and Northern Hardwoods) — the Canadian Zone of the highest Alleghany peaks and ridges.

(5) *Mixed Coniferous and Deciduous Forest* again, as we descend the western side of the mountains.

(6) *Temperate Deciduous Forest* — the original plant cover of much of the Ohio and Mississippi River valleys, now largely destroyed and replaced by agriculture.

(7) *Savannah* — the mixed forest and tall grasslands of the central and western Middle West.

(8) *Prairie* — tall grasslands, with forest only in the most favorable lowlands and river bottoms.

(9) *Steppe* (Great Plains) — short grasslands with trees, mostly cottonwoods, only along wet river bottoms.

ENVIRONMENTS AND HABITATS

Within the major north-south and east-west divisions of the life and climatic zones occur a great many different local *environments*, caused by variations in altitude, slope, exposure to wind or sunlight, presence of rocks, type of soil. If we are to be successful collectors and field students we must learn to recognize these in any area in which we are working. It is to these local environmental conditions that most plants and animals are strongly adapted. Some species have very limited environmental ranges but, if their special environment occurs in a number of life zones or climatic belts, they may have a wide geographic range. These are referred to in the text as *local* species. We may find one such from Maine to Florida; but in small, separated colonies, each only in just the right environment.

Ocean Beach and Dunes. These are characterized by very specialized plants, adapted to life with a minimum of water due both to saltiness and to fast run-off of rain in the sand. No distinctive butterflies; but important as migration routes.

Salt and Brackish Marshes (see p. 32). Here we find a few distinctive butterflies, notably *Panoquina panoquin*, and to some degree *Brephidium pseudofea* and *Problema bulenta*. There is good general collecting along the landward side.

Waste Places and Roadsides are *recently cleared* areas, perhaps burned or plowed, growing up to the particular plants that immigrate fastest to bare places. They are very special collecting places for many butterflies, because of these special plants. Do not confuse them with stable, long-existing *meadows*, or with *old fields* which are still more stable.

Dry Meadows contain a great variety of grasses (and so, of Skippers), herbaceous plants, and butterflies. Look for meadows with a variety of plants — cultivated hayfields are much poorer, and farmers have a very justifiable dislike for people who trample them.

Dry Hillsides may be fundamentally meadows, but with different plants because of the faster run-off of water; or may be growing up to shrubs and young trees, and thus be still different.

Old Fields are distinctive. They are meadows that are beginning to grow up to shrubs and small trees; eventually they may return to forest conditions. Many distinctive shrubs such as Sweet Fern and Bayberry (*Myrica*), Blueberry and Huckleberry (*Vaccinium* and *Gaylussacia*), Sheep Laurel (*Kalmia*), Shrubby Cinquefoil (*Potentilla*), Hardhack and Steeplebush (*Spiræa*), Hawthorns (*Cratægus*), and others attract or support a great variety of butterfly species.

Wet Meadows have special grasses, run more to sedges, and have many special herbaceous plants — hence many special butterflies. They are a step between dry meadows, on higher ground, and marshes on lower.

Marshes (see p. 17) have considerable standing water, but no heavy tree or shrub growths. *Swamps* on the other hand have trees and shrubs, which shade out the lower grasses, sedges and rushes. So, in general, marshes are richer in butterflies. But, especially in the South, shaded swamps have some species not found elsewhere.

Acid Bogs (see p. 17) have been much confused with marshes and swamps; and this confusion has retarded and confused our knowledge of them. Bogs are strongly acid, and so have very special plants, i.e., Pitcher Plants (*Sarracenia*), Sundew (*Drosera*), Sphagnum Moss (in mats or carpets), Cranberry (*Vaccinium*), Leatherleaf (*Chamædaphne*), Labrador Tea (*Ledum*), Tamarack or Larch (*Larix*), Black (*not* Red or White) Spruce (*Picea mariana*), and White (*not* Red) Cedar (*Chamæcyparis*). See under Canadian Life Zone (p. 16).

Savannahs are mixed growths of tall grasses and sedges, interspersed with limited patches of forest. They are really a borderline between forest and prairie. Poplar and Oak Savannah is a dominant feature of much of the western Middle West. Much of the Florida Everglades is a Grass Savannah (e.g. Sawgrass, *Mariscus*) interspersed with clumps (hammocks) of tree growth.

Prairies are areas of tall grasses and herbs, especially of the western Middle West. Distinguish between "wet" and "dry" prairie.

Steppe is the technical name for the short-grass Great Plains. It enters our area only along the western edge. It has many distinctive species (see p. 32).

Forests or Woodlands are of many distinctive types, basically caused by soil, rock, and water run-off differences, and by past histories of clearing, lumbering, and burning. Chief types are: Northern Coniferous, Mixed Coniferous-Deciduous (see p. 16), Temperate Deciduous, and Southern Coniferous (see p. 33). As noted above, wooded swamps occur, with distinctive water-loving trees; such as, in the South, the *Bayheads* (Magnolia and Bay) and Cypress Swamps. The great Pine forests of the South (now mostly butchered and burned) have been divided into the "*High Pine*" forests on higher, dryer soil; the *Pine Flatwoods* on lower, wetter ground; and the *Miami-Rockland Pine* growing in southern Florida on nearly bare rock base. Southern Pine Forests have far more butterflies than one would expect; they are more open, shading the ground less, than the Northern Coniferous Forest. The latter is deep-shaded and damp; in it butterflies occur chiefly along roads and trails and stream banks.

Hammocks are special forest types in southern Florida. They are islands of broad leaved trees. Most interesting are the subtropical hardwood hammocks (see p. 33) containing a great variety of tropical trees. Here, alone, are found certain tropical butterflies.

Mangrove Thickets are characteristic forests along low-lying coasts of the far South. The three Mangroves (Red, White and Black), with Buttonwood (*Conocarpus*), form almost impenetrable tangles. Some butterflies occur chiefly here (e.g., *Phocides bala-bano*).

BUTTERFLIES AND CLIMATE

Broad, climatic effects on butterflies are evident in many species. They range from (1) the production of *seasonal forms* where, for example, the butterflies emerging from overwintering pupæ are different from those that develop during the summer; to (2) the appearance of different northern and southern *subspecies* of the same species.

Seasonal Variation. Many of our butterflies show marked seasonal variation, of which much, at least, can be attributed to the effects of temperature. These effects are not necessarily the same in different families, but usually tend to conform to pattern within a family. In *Pieridæ*, for example, the "spring forms" tend to be paler, with reduced dark borders or spots (*Colias philodice, Pieris napi*, and *Pieris rapæ*). Spring specimens of *Papilio glaucus* are small and pale; so are spring specimens of *Papilio marcellus*, the Zebra Swallowtail. On the other hand the spring brood of the Spring Azure, *L. argiolus*, shows a great increase in the dark markings beneath, while summer forms are far paler. In the Angle Wings (*Polygonia*) are several striking examples. In *P. interrogationis* the overwintering adults are mostly paler above, with shorter tails on the HW and a smoother wing outline in general; while the summer brood specimens have heavy, dark borders and hindwings, and much more pronounced apices, angles, and tails. Similarly, in the Pearl Crescent, *Phyciodes tharos*, the cold weather brood has more extensive dark markings.

Experimental work in rearing butterflies under controlled temperature conditions has shown, in many cases, that such effects are due directly to temperature. It is not all as simple as that, however. In one European *Polygonia* (*c-album*), the production of light and dark forms has been shown to result from the lengthening or shortening of the larval period, rather than from the direct temperature effect.

In addition to temperature, *variations of humidity* may have a marked result; and this can be so intermingled with the temperature effects that in studying collected specimens we cannot tell what results from which. Clear-cut, dry and wet season forms are known in many butterflies. The tropical Leaf Wings (*Anæa*) are outstanding examples; and our species show this well. Austin Clark has recorded observations on the Buckeye (*Precis lavinia cœnia*) around Washington, D.C., that suggest the occurrence there of dry and wet environment forms which differ not only in appearance but also to some degree in habits. Migratory and non-migratory phases of *Precis* are well known from the tropics, where temperature variation is slight from one season to another.

GEOGRAPHIC VARIATION

To what degree much of the recorded geographic variation is a matter of temperature and humidity differences, is something which we can only infer. In *Papilio glaucus*, as we have noted, spring specimens tend to be small and pale. Now, as we go northward we find that in central Canada, where there is only one generation a year, the whole population looks similarly small and pale. In Canada this population has been named as a *geographic subspecies*, "*canadensis*," i.e., a part of the species limited to a certain area and showing distinctive characteristics. The temptation is strong to attribute the whole thing to lowered temperatures alone. But suppose we brought a batch of eggs of *canadensis* down to Florida, and reared the butterflies in the conditions under which the very large, richly colored subspecies *australis* develops there. Would our *canadensis* eggs develop as *australis*, under the mollifying influences of the Citrus State, or would they develop into the same small, pale specimens that their parents were? I do not know; and until someone does this sort of thing I will not even hazard a guess. Scores of our butterflies have similar, distinct northern and southern subspecies; and at present we can do no more than guess at the factors that have brought them into being.

Lest a wrong impression be gained, let it be emphasized that a great many geographic subspecies exist which have, as far as we know, little if any direct connection with temperature and humidity factors. Desert subspecies tend to be markedly paler and lighter colored than forest-dwelling populations on other regions. Perhaps a humidity factor is involved. The selective effect of the generally lighter colored desert environment must play a part, but cannot be a basic cause. Many other subspecies vary according to no rules at all that we can infer, differing in such things as changes in pattern, or in proportionate lengths of structures. At present we are little beyond the stage of cataloging such variations.

BUTTERFLIES AND PLANTS

The relationships between butterflies and plants are as intimate as possible, and more complex than generally supposed. On the one hand, butterflies are almost entirely plant-eating insects, and thus may be considered harmful to the plants. On the other hand, the existence of the butterflies is of extreme importance to very large numbers of plants which are dependent upon flower-visiting insects for cross-pollination. In this vital activity the butterflies, along with bees and flower-visiting flies, play a major part. The very flower itself is an organ of the plant that attracts insects for

Beach, Dunes, and Salt Marsh (*upper picture*). This scene might be almost anywhere along the coast from Canada to Florida. A narrow barrier strip of beach and dune fronts the ocean. Behind it is a belt of salt marsh, and usually a lagoon. A few butterflies characterize the salt (and brackish) marshes. Chief is the Salt Marsh Skipper (*Panoquina panoquin*); and quite consistent are the Eastern Pygmy Blue (*Brephidium pseudofea*) and the Rare Skipper (*Problema bulenta*). The plants of the marshes are very numerous. Tall Marsh Grasses (*Spartina*) and Rushes (*Juncus*) form the chief cover. Shrubs such as Bayberry (*Myrica*), Groundsel Tree (*Baccharis halimifolia*) and Salt Marsh Elder (*Iva oraria*) form sometimes dense growths. The fleshy Glassworts (*Salicornia*) and (southward) Saltwort (*Batis*) are characteristic. Good butterfly collecting may be had on such flowers as the Goldenrod (*Solidago sempervirens*), Salt Marsh Fleabane (*Pluchea camphorata*), Coast Blite (*Chenopodium rubrum*), Marsh Rosemary (*Limoneum carolineanum*), Sabatia (*Sabatia angularis*), and many others.

No distinctive butterflies occur on the beaches and dunes, although many special and characteristic plants grow there. But these are major migration routes or "flyways," not only for birds but also for the famous Monarch (*Danaus*) and other butterflies such as the Painted Lady (*Vanessa cardui*) and the Buckeye (*Precis lavinia cœnia*). The big Dragonflies (*Anax junius* and *Epiæschna heros*) migrate here, too, and in the autumn you may see them being chased by migrating Merlins, the finest fliers of our small Hawks. A visit to the beach during the September migrations will repay you well, especially if you can get to such a famous locality as Cape May, N.J. where great swarms of the Monarch sometimes assemble.

Yucca Flowering on the Great Plains (*lower picture*). No photograph could do justice to the limitless sweep of the rolling plains, so I have shown one of the characteristic and most interesting plants. The main short-grass plains lie west of our area, but many plains butterflies range eastward consistently. Some of our eastern butterflies, too, are represented by different subspecies in the plains and westward. The borderline between the eastern and western butterflies is, perhaps, most clear from Oklahoma to the Dakotas; but southward and northward it becomes more diffuse and hard to place.

So many western butterflies range eastward across the plains and more or less deeply into our area that it is impossible to list them here. They are all described in the text in Part 2, following. Nor would it be possible to describe the multitudinous, characteristic plants of the plains. The region exists as it does chiefly because of lack of rainfall. This makes natural growth of trees impossible and limits the vegetation to short, water-conserving grasses and other plants. It is this that makes the plains and the prairie regions east of them the great grain belt of the continent.

The Yucca or Spanish Bayonet (*Yucca glauca*) is not, of course, solely a western plant but occurs in dry places all over the south and, in cultivation and as an escape, north to Canada. In it bore the larvæ of the Giant Skippers (*Megathymidæ*). If you will look inside its blossoms you will almost surely see the little, white Yucca Moths (*Tegeticula*). The female of this extraordinary insect collects a ball of pollen from the stamens and jams it down on the stigma, thus cross-pollinating the flower. She also lays eggs in the flower. Without her activity the flower could not form a fruit and seeds; and without the seeds, on which they feed, her larvæ would not be able to develop into the next generation of Yucca Moths.

Plate 4   33

SOUTHERN PINES AND TROPICAL HARDWOODS

Southern Pine Forests (*upper picture*) cover great areas below the Mason and Dixon Line, characterizing much of the Upper and Lower Austral Zones. The chief Pines are the Loblolly (*Pinus Tæda*), Yellow (*P. echinata*), Longleaf (*P. palustris*), and Caribbean or Slash (*P. caribæa*). The southern pine forests, being more open than the northern coniferous forests, admit much more light to the ground beneath. As a result, there is a rich undergrowth of shrubs, herbs and grasses; and as a result of this, collecting in the "pine flats" is very profitable for the butterfly hunter. The area shown here (in central Florida) is, I am sorry to say, all too typical of much of the southern pineland, which is annually ravaged by severe fires. Such burning may actually seem to benefit such of the butterflies as feed on quick-growing herbs or shrubs that do best on burned land; but it is a deplorable waste of one of our most important natural resources.

Tropical Hardwood Forest in the Florida Keys (*lower picture*). Compare this picture, with its riot of vegetation, with the one of Arctic-alpine Zone on Mt. Katahdin. Little light reaches the ground through such a dense tree canopy. Many typical tropical butterflies occur chiefly or entirely in such environment, in our area, or around its edges. Some characteristic ones are: Zebra (*Heliconius charitonius*), Julia (*Dryas julia cillene*), Purple Wings (*Eunica monima* and *tatila*), Ruddy Dagger Wing (*Marpesia petreus thetys*), Florida Leaf Wing (*Anæa floridalis*), Schaus' Swallowtail (*Papilio aristodemus ponceanus*), Florida White (*Appias drusilla neumægenii*), Nise Sulphur (*Eurema nise*) and Hammock Skipper (*Polygonus lividus savigny*).

Among such vegetation collecting is not easy at best. It is rendered even slightly hazardous by the abundance of the Poisonwood Tree (*Metopium*), a close relative of Poison Ivy. The best results will be obtained along roadsides and shaded trails. Some characteristic trees of the tropical "hammocks" are: Gumbo Limbo (*Elaphrium simaruba*), Torchwood (*Amyris elemifera*), Tamarind (*Lysiloma bahamensis*), Mastic (*Sideroxylon fætidissimum*), Mahogany (*Swietenia mahogani*), Manchineel (*Hippomane mancinella*), Strangler Fig (*Ficus aurea*), Lignum Vitæ (*Guiacum sanctum*), Jamaica Dogwood (*Ichthyomenthia piscipula*), and a host of others. In the larger, more humid hammocks Orchids and Pineapple-like Bromeliads grow thickly on the trunks and branches of the trees; and the beautiful and variegated tropical Tree Snails (*Liguus*) may be seen in numbers. The Black Whiskered Vireo sings monotonously in the treetops, and Swallow Tailed Kites wheel overhead. The best remaining tropical hammocks are in the Florida Keys and in the Everglades National Park. For the latter, butterfly hunters should "check in" at Park Headquarters at Homestead, Fla. Here they will meet with ready cooperation and friendliness from the authorities of this, our outstanding "natural history" National Park.

this purpose; and the sucking mouthparts of the butterflies, and the whole attunement of their responses to flowers, are developments by the insects to the same end.

Flower Visiting. In their choice of flowers, butterflies differ widely. Some species are very catholic in their tastes, visiting almost any available blossom. Others, extremely specialized, visit the flowers of only a few species of plants, or of only one or two. Nor is there necessarily any correlation between the kind of plant eaten as a larva and the kind visited as an adult. The Baltimore (*Euphydryas phæton*), for example, has been noted as shunning the flowers of the Turtlehead, its food as a larva.

Food Plants of Larvæ. Most butterfly species are limited to one, or a very few related species of plants as larval food. Sometimes only plants belonging to a certain family will be eaten. In many cases the original "choice" is made by the mother, who lays the eggs on the plant. But the larvæ will not eat any plant that is handy, and so there are multitudes of records of larvæ starving to death when leaves of the right plant were not available. In many species the specialization extends even to strong preference or requirement of the right part of the plant, or the right type of leaf.

Thus, some of the *Lycænidæ*, which regularly feed on flower buds of certain plants, may refuse to eat even young, tender leaves, or may do so only as a last resort. There is certainly an inherited factor here, whether we call it an "instinct" or a "behavior pattern."

In some cases, changes of food plant may occur during larval life. These may be quite a normal thing, as in some species which may feed on quite a number of different plants anyway. Sometimes, however, they occur only under certain conditions. Larvæ of the Baltimore (*Euphydryas phæton*) will feed only on Turtlehead during their first season. They then hibernate, partly grown. The next Spring they may return to eating Turtlehead, or may change over to such plants as Ash, Viburnum, or Honeysuckle.

Most larvæ are leaf eaters. Some species, however, regularly eat leaf and flower buds; others, seed pods and seeds; and others bore into fruits. The larvæ of the Giant Skippers (*Megathymidæ*) live only as borers in *Yucca* and *Agave*.

Nearly any of the seed plants may be eaten by some butterfly larva, ranging from Pines and the very primitive Cycads (*Zamea*) to Grasses and Sedges, Mints, the poisonous Milkweeds and the Oaks, rich in tannic acid. I do not, however, know of any that eats Poison Ivy!

CONSERVATION

We are coming to realize that conservation is a far more complex thing than merely protecting "useful" animals and plants and killing "harmful" ones. A true program of conservation for an area may be the most far-reaching thing imaginable. It consists of working out a method of attaining a reasonably stable "balance of nature," so that the life in the area will *maintain itself in equilibrium* with a minimum of human attention (and expense). Be it understood that this does not mean only a balance of wild plants and animals, or refer to an equilibrium only in wild and uncultivated areas. Before European man came to North America, every area had attained, more or less, its own equilibrium. We cannot ever go back to such conditions, nor should we try to. Primeval conditions are gone beyond recall. We must strive today to bring about a new set of balances, consonant with man's presence in, and use of each area. It may be a matter of preventing soil erosion for agricultural reasons; or of watershed protection to prevent either floods, or the silting of streams used for power, water supply, or navigation. It may be concern for the timber value of a forest, or for a recreational area. Or it may be the protection of the topsoil in the vacant lot next door, to prevent growths of ragweed and poison ivy. In any event, the modern biologist and ecologist is coming to realize, more and more, how greatly the lives of every plant and animal in an area affect every other plant and animal there, and play their parts in the local dynamic "balance of nature." In such an equilibrium anywhere, the part played by the butterflies, bees, and flies, essential as they are for the survival of the majority of the flowering plants, cannot be overemphasized.

BUTTERFLIES AND
OTHER ANIMALS

In nearly all cases, relationships between butterflies and other animals are at the expense of the butterflies; since in all stages of their lives butterflies are preyed upon and "parasitized" by an enormous assemblage of enemies. There are, however, a few exceptions to this which we will note first.

BUTTERFLY PREDATORS

In our area one butterfly, the Harvester (*Feniseca*) is a true predator. Its larvæ feed on woolly aphids (*Schizoneura, Lanigera,* or *Prociphilus*) which occur in masses on stems of Alder and other plants. Other members of the same group of butterflies in other parts of the world have the same habit.

The older larvæ of a Blue (*Maculinea arion*) of England feed on ant larvæ in the ant nests, to which they are carried by the ants themselves. During their first three instars the Blue larvæ feed on plant tissues in the normal way. Perhaps some of our Blues have a similar habit.

Larval cannibalism in a state of nature is not uncommon among butterflies of several families. Examples are the larvæ of the Baltimore and of a number of *Lycænidæ*. In captivity, butterfly larvæ are more liable to be cannibalistic, because of the abnormal conditions. It may be noted that quite a number of moth larvæ show marked cannibalistic or predatory tendencies; and that at least one moth larva lives as an internal parasite of other insects.

PREDATORS AND BUTTERFLIES

In all stages, butterflies are liable to attack from predators. Vertebrate animals such as monkeys, birds, lizards, frogs, and toads catch the adults. So do predatory insects such as dragonflies, robberflies, and various bugs. It is not at all uncommon to see butterflies with badly torn wings resulting from attack by a bird. A large toll is taken by Spiders, both the web weavers and the Crab Spiders that lie in ambush on flowers. Every season the smaller insectivorous mammals, as well as birds, must kill countless millions of larvæ and pupæ and probably eggs.

Protection against predators is very largely a matter of either escape or concealment. Rapid and erratic flight, dodging ability, and hiding are all escape devices. Perhaps the spininess of many larvæ is a protection against some birds, as is the hairiness of the Tent Caterpillar (Moth) larva.

Many larvæ lie well concealed during daylight hours. Some build nests of leaves or fold a single leaf; others depart from the food plant entirely and hide many feet away. Possibly, however, the chief protection of butterflies comes from various types of protective form and coloration. This is a complex subject which we had better consider separately.

PROTECTIVE FORM AND

COLORATION

Nearly every known way in which an animal can secure protection from its enemies by adaptations of its form and color is known among our butterflies. The chief types, with a few examples, are:

    (1) *Object Resemblance.* Resemblance to some specific object of no interest to predators, such as a dead leaf (*Anæa, Polygonia* adults; *Limenitis, Polygonia* pupæ; *Limenitis* larvæ); or a bud (*Lycænid* larvæ and pupæ); or a bird dropping (young *Papilio* and *Limenitis* larvæ).

    (2) *Background Resemblance.* Merging into the general background, e.g., dull colored adults of many genera, especially *Satyridæ*; green undersides that blend with leaves (*Mitoura gryneus*); green larvæ and pupæ (especially *Pieridæ*); merging into Pine needles (*Incisalia niphon* larvæ).

    (3) *Flash and Dazzle Coloration.* Dull coloration when resting, then brilliant, flashy colors exposed in flight, then a sudden return to

dull coloration by dropping suddenly. This confuses the pursuer. E.g., adults with bright upper sides and duller undersides, *Polygonia, Cercyonis, Vanessa, Eunica, Anæa*, etc.

(4) *Ruptive Coloration*, i.e., breaking up the outline by bold, contrasting color patches; e.g., adults of many groups; larvæ of *Papilio cresphontes* and *polyxenes, Limenitis*, etc.

(5) *Warning Coloration*, i.e., bright, distinctive, highly visible colors and patterns that actually attract attention. This occurs among those species which, by eating poisonous and bad-tasting plants, are really inedible. By "advertising," they "warn off" predators. E.g., *Danaus* adults and larvæ; *Heliconius; Dione, Dryas*.

(6) *Mimicry*. The Monarch (*Danaus*) is genuinely inedible, since it feeds on milkweed. It advertises this fact (warning coloration) by distinctive orange-brown color, and slow, lazy flight. The Viceroy (*Limenitis archippus*) which feeds on willow and poplar is perfectly good bird food. But it has the colors and habits of the Monarch. Without doubt it gains much protection from birds which have learned to leave alone anything that looks like a Monarch. This is our best example of butterfly mimicry. In the tropics there are dozens more striking, *Danaiidæ* and *Heliconiidæ* being the chief "models" for "mimics" of nearly all butterfly families and many moth families, too.

PARASITES AND BUTTERFLIES

Much greater than the danger from predators is that from "parasites," chiefly other insects. These are mostly members of two other insect orders, *Diptera* (Flies) and *Hymenoptera* (Wasps, Bees, etc.). In the *Hymenoptera* a number of families, chiefly the *Ichneumonidæ, Braconidæ* and *Chalcididæ;* and in the *Diptera* mainly members of one family, the *Tachinidæ*, are the major parasites on butterflies. A female parasite, finding a butterfly caterpillar, lays her egg or eggs on or in it. Her larva then lives inside the caterpillar, gradually eating its tissues. Frequently the caterpillar lives long enough to pupate; but seldom if ever can it transform to the adult butterfly. Instead, from the pupa emerges the parasite, which may have pupated inside the butterfly pupa; or the parasite larva bores out, drops to the ground, and pupates there. Butterfly larvæ are the stage chiefly attacked, but some egg parasites are known. Anyone who finds larvæ and brings them home to rear them is liable to hatch out a parasitic wasp or fly instead. Such material is very valuable, when the name of the butterfly host is known. Send the parasites, and what is left of the butterfly larva or pupa, with full data, to the Department of Entomology, United States National Museum, Washington, D.C. Many parasitic wasps and flies are of enormous value to man, being our best means of defense against many harmful insects. Many have been introduced from abroad for this purpose. Such beneficial parasites are reared by the millions in laboratories, and distributed in the field where harmful insects are threatening. Many of the parasites are very specific in their choice of host species, attacking only certain insects. Probably the wasp that you rear from a *Papilio* larva is a parasite on *Papilio* larvæ only. Nor does the tale stop there; there are still other parasites that attack the parasites.

> Now, greater fleas have lesser fleas
> Upon their backs to bite 'em;
> And on those fleas are other fleas;
> And so ad infinitum.

REPRODUCTIVE CAPACITY

It would give a very false impression if we implied that the various means of defense against predators and parasites which have been discussed above were the only or even the chief means of survival that butterflies have. Of far greater importance is their reproductive ability. A single female may lay hundreds of eggs; and if, from these, only two of her offspring survive to become adults and reproduce in turn, her species is secure for another generation as far as her efforts are concerned. In general the reproductive capacity of butterflies is much smaller than that of many other animals which have fewer other defenses against enemies and harmful natural forces. But it is still quite large, as befits a group so much preyed upon and parasitized.

BUTTERFLY HABITS AND

BEHAVIOR

What butterflies do, and how they do it, may be of as great interest as the butterflies themselves. Far too many collectors are interested only in getting specimens, and so notice actions and activities only as these help them to collect. They thus miss much of the most interesting part of butterfly study; for activities may vary, from species to species, as greatly as the structures and appearance of the butterflies themselves. There is here an almost untouched field for interesting work and observation that will richly repay the intelligent observer.

Light and Shade. The forest-loving butterfly stays in the forest, where dark, shaded areas abound. It may fly into a patch of light in a small clearing and rest there; but there must be shadows near by. Take it or chase it into a brightly lit field, where there are no shadows, and it will fly, fast and continually, until it again finds itself in a shaded area. Its whole system is attuned by inheritance to a certain balance of light and shade. The same, in reverse, is true of a species of open country. The inherited behavior pattern rigidly determines the general environment which a butterfly will seek, and in which it will stay. When it is in that environment, other inherited factors take over, and determine its further reactions to minor differences of light and shade so as to lead it to flowers or mates. Smell and taste are important factors, too, and the perception of motion of small objects. Out of their reactions to such stimuli are built the behavior patterns of the butterfly.

Flight Habits differ widely. Compare the easy, lazy, sailing flight of a Monarch with the fast, erratic darting of a Skipper, and the weak, jerky fluttering of a Grass Nymph, never far from the shelter of long grass and ever ready to dodge into it. Or compare the actions of a male of such a species as the Pearl Crescent, darting after every passing shadow, with the purposeful flight of a female working her way through the foliage in search of the right plant on which to lay her eggs. Every species has its characteristic flight habits, sometimes recognizable as far as a specimen can be seen. If two or more people are collecting together, try running a contest on flight recognition (but catch the specimen for identification, or it doesn't count). You will be surprised after a while to see how distinctive the species are on the wing.

Migration is more common than supposed. The Monarch's autumnal mass flights southward are famous; but many more of our butterflies migrate, although not so spectacularly. Some of these are the Painted Lady (*Vanessa cardui*), the Buckeye (*Precis lavinia*), the Purple Wing (*Eunica monima*), the Great Southern White (*Ascia monuste*), the Cloudless Sulphur (*Phœbis sennæ*) and the Little Sulphur (*Eurema lisa*). Migration records are valuable and should be carefully kept (when identification is sure) and published. *The Migration of Butterflies* is the authoritative reference book on the subject (see p. 306). We still know almost nothing about the effect of such factors as "population pressure" and "parasite pressure" in causing true migrational flights.

Sleeping Assemblies have been noted in a number of species; *Heliconius* are known to gather together in groups in the late afternoon and spend the night together. There have been interesting reports of some of our Swallowtails (*Papilio palamedes*, *troilus*, and *glaucus*) apparently doing the same thing. Good observations are badly needed.

Flyways. A number of kinds of butterflies have been observed using various local routes consistently, perhaps only at certain times of day and in certain directions. Possibly some such records are of gathering sleeping assemblies, but others seem not to be so. Sometimes these local flights are confused with true long-distance migrations. The field observer should keep a sharp watch for such consistent flyways.

Mud Puddle Clubs are familiar sights. Who has not seen a swarm of butterflies, sometimes packed close together by the hundreds, gathered at a puddle or damp place on a country road. Some species are consistent visitors; most are merely casuals. There is evidence that in some species it is the young bachelor males who gather peaceably at the puddles; after some days they forsake the habit and scatter, seeking mates. We need many observations on the species involved, the sexes represented, and the subsequent behavior. Some constant puddle visitors are the Sulphurs (*Colias, Eurema lisa, Phœbis eubule*), the Pearl Crescent (*Phyciodes tharos*), the Tailed Blue (*Everes comyntas*), the Zebra and Tiger Swallowtails (*Papilio marcellus* and *glaucus*), and the Buckeye (*Precis lavinia*).

Courtships are in some species consistent performances, but there are very few good records of detailed observations. In many species the female merely flutters on a flower or plant while the male hovers over her before they pair. In others, the two may fly straight up, high above the trees, in a complex "dance." The duration of time when the male and female remain together, held by the grip of the male's harpes, also varies widely in different species. Pairs taken fastened together should be preserved carefully and labeled "in copula." They may be valuable where there is doubt as to what males in an area belong to the same species as what females. Any records of males and females of *different* species either courting or mating are exceedingly valuable.

Butterflies and Odors. Many species have been recorded as possessing distinctive odors recognizable by man. Examples in males are *Speyeria cybele, Boloria myrina,* and *Euptoieta claudia,* "strong and spicy"; *Lycænopsis pseudargiolus,* "delicate, like crushed violet stems"; *Colias eurytheme,* "strong, like sweet heliotrope"; and *Phœbis eubule,* "very strong, like violets, musk." In females, *Speyeria, Boloria, Limenitis, Papilio,* "disagreeable odors when pinched"! Further records of this nature, made and checked by more than one observer at the time, would be very interesting.

The prominent scent scales (*androconia*) of many male butterflies undoubtedly function very largely in recognition and courtship. In some courtships (i.e. that of the Monarch) the male has been noted acting so as to scatter over the female the scales from special scent pouches.

Butterflies are strongly attracted to some odors. *Papilio glaucus* has been recorded as attracted to tobacco smoke. The odors of carrion, excrement, urine, and fermentation are very attractive to many species. High-flying butterflies which normally never come near the ground can be brought down by such odorous baits. What part the odors of flowers play in attracting butterflies is a question.

Pugnacity and Territory. Certain of our butterflies are notoriously pugnacious, chasing and driving away not only other butterflies, sometimes of species many times their own size, but also insects of other orders, birds, and even dogs and people. Particularly noted for this is the Pearl Crescent (*Phyciodes tharos*); others are the Buckeye (*Precis l. cœnia*), American Copper (*Lycæna p. americana*), and Silver Spotted Skipper (*Epargyreus clarus*). One writer records an apparently inherent feud between the Pearl Crescent and the Buckeye, and also notes that the Monarch (*Danaus*) seems to have a special aversion for the Ruby-Throated Hummingbird! The pugnacity of the Pearl Crescent has more than once cost me a specimen of some other species which I was stalking, only to have it chased away before I could net it.

Males of the Pearly Eyes (*Lethe*) have been noted as adopting favorite perches on a tree trunk, from which they dart out from time to time to drive away other males. Such records are very suggestive. During the last generation we have learned much about the important part that *territorial instincts* play in the life cycles of many animals, ranging from salamanders and toads to mammals and birds. Such instincts are far more widespread than formerly believed, and are almost a dominating force in the lives of nearly all of the birds. Very little thought has been given to insects in this respect. It is my belief that we may find territorial instincts better evolved in some of the butterflies than we might expect. A series of thorough observations and checks will prove extremely interesting and valuable.

Resting Positions and Actions. Many butterflies have very characteristic resting positions, sometimes correlated with peculiar activities. Thus we see that most Hairstreaks and Coppers (*Lycænidæ*) on alighting on a leaf, hold the forewings together over the back, spread the hindwings slightly out at the sides, and then rub the hindwings forward and back alternating them with each other. Or we note the characteristic resting position of many Skippers, with the forewings together over the back but the hindwings held out straight to the sides. Many observations have been made of the way in which some butterflies (e.g. the Arctics, *Œneis*) alight on the ground, hold the wings over the back, and then turn to the proper direction and lean to one side or the other, in such a way that the shadow they cast is minimized. Other observations have indicated that the long, slender tails on the hindwings of Hairstreaks (e.g. *Atlides halesus*) may look enough like a pair of antennæ at the rear to puzzle, for the critical moment, an attacker. Longstaff's *Butterfly Hunting in Many Lands* is a most worthwhile book, replete with such observations. We need many such studies on our butterflies, for very few have been made and published.

CHAPTER FOUR

Life Histories and Growth

DURING ITS life a butterfly undergoes a complex series of changes, collectively known as its *metamorphosis* (Greek — change of form). In this development four distinct stages occur: *egg, larva* (caterpillar), *pupa* (chrysalis) and *adult*.

Growth, like that of other insects and their relatives, is not gradual and continuous, but progresses by a series of jumps following periods of no change of form or size. This basically stems from the presence of the *exoskeleton* which, unyielding and unstretchable, surrounds all parts of the insect. Encased in this, the insect cannot materially increase in size; periodically it moults the old shell, briefly increases very rapidly in size, and then forms a new, larger shell. For a time there is no further growth; the insect concentrates on eating, digesting, and storing food. Then comes another moulting, another rapid but short growth period, and so on. The act of moulting is termed *ecdysis*; the period between moults is called an *instar* or *stage*.

The series of instars continues until the larva is full grown. It then transforms into the inactive *pupa*, which neither eats nor moves about. Within the pupal shell most of the larval tissues break down, then build up again into the organs of the adult butterfly. The structural reorganization completed and the adult fully formed, the pupal shell splits and the adult emerges. It spreads and hardens its wings and flies away. Thereafter it grows and moults no more — little butterflies do not grow up into larger ones. The function of the adult is *reproduction;* that of the larva *nutrition;* of the pupa, *structural reorganization.*

THE EGG

Butterfly eggs differ enormously in appearance, but all have (1) a thick shell, excellent protection against drying out and enemies, and (2) an opening at one end, the *micropyle*, through which the egg is fertilized. The shape varies greatly, but is somewhat characteristic for various groups; examples are the tall, thin, spindle-shaped eggs of the Whites and Yellows, or the flat, "turban-shaped" eggs of the Blues. In most of the true butterflies the surface of the egg is ornamented with raised or sunken ribs, grooves, knobs, pits or other sculpturing; but some groups tend to have smooth, unornamented eggs.

The egg is a very valuable stage in the life cycle, being a small, compact unit of life that can be produced economically in large numbers, placed in a suitable environment and left to fend for itself. It is well protected against drought or cold, and thus can serve to carry the species through periods of harmful weather.

The eggs are usually placed very deliberately by the female, in a way characteristic of her species, for example only on the under-surface of a leaf, or only at the tip of a leaf. Sometimes they are laid singly; in other species large masses may be piled up more than one layer deep. Almost always the egg is laid on or near the specific food plant of the species — a useful fact for the field worker to keep in mind.

THE LARVA (CATERPILLAR)

A butterfly larva is simple, primitive, and "wormlike" com-pared with the adult. Nevertheless it possesses some specialized structures, and may have very specialized habits.

The *head* is distinct. On it are two semicircles of tiny, simple eyes, the *ocelli*; a pair of very short, simple *antennæ*; a small *labrum* or upper lip; a pair of short, jointed *palpi*; and a pair of strong biting jaws or *mandibles*. The openings of silk glands are on a small projection called the *spinneret*, on the lower lip or *labium*.

Each of the next three segments, those of the *thorax*, bears a pair of short, *jointed legs* each ending with a single claw. On the dorsal side of the prothorax may be a chitinous shield (Skippers), the *prothoracic shield*. Then on each of the third, fourth, fifth and sixth of the ten abdominal segments is one pair of short, fleshy *prolegs*, each with a series of minute hooklets (*crotchets*) at its tip. The number and arrangement of the hooklets are of some impor-tance in classifying larvæ. The last abdominal segment bears another pair of prolegs, the *anal prolegs*.

On each side of the first thoracic, and of each abdominal segment is a *spiracle* (or *stigma*), an opening into the respiratory passages. Many larvæ have color stripes along the sides; a stripe above the row of spiracles is *suprastigmatal*, one below the row is *substigmatal*.

The newly hatched larva has a disproportionately large head, and is usually clad only in simple bristles or hairs, not in the elaborate vestiture that it may develop later. In some groups (*Pieridæ*) the bristles are tubular, connected to glands that secrete a sweet liquid (honeydew) very attractive to Ants.

As the larva grows it sheds its old exoskeleton ("skin") at inter-vals, developing a larger one shortly afterward. Characteristic color patterns, hairs, spines, or fleshy filaments develop, until the full-grown larva is quite different in appearance from the newly hatched one. Larvæ are usually quite distinctive; some may be identified more easily than the adults. We illustrate a number of distinctive types, and in the text following give short diagnoses of all known last-stage larvæ.

Many larvæ have special protective adaptations. Some are very hairy or spiny. Others, especially those which feed on such plants as Milkweeds and Passion Flowers which have bitter or poisonous juices, are distasteful or poisonous. Most such adaptations tend to conceal the larvae from enemies, or, in the cases of "protected" poisonous or distasteful ones, actually to advertise them. The larvae of the Swallowtails (*Papilio*) have a Y-shaped scent organ, the *osmaterium*, which they protrude from the first thoracic segment (behind the head). Others, especially those of *Lycaenidae*, have large "honeydew" secreting glands opening to the exterior either over the general body surface (Coppers) or by a single, large opening (Blues). This makes the larvae very attractive to ants, which attend them eagerly. As a result the ants attack enemies of the larvae. In one Blue the ants carry the larva into the ant nest where it feeds on ant larvae — a fair exchange for the honeydew which it produces!

Cannibalistic habits have been observed among the larvae of a number of the Blues. The larvae of the Harvester (*Feniseca*) a related species, go beyond this, and are regularly predatory, feeding on certain types of aphids ("plant lice").

The majority of butterfly larvae are solitary, but a few are sociable. The larvae of the Baltimore (*Euphydryas phaeton*) live in a communal web during their first season; and other related Nymphalids are to a lesser degree sociable. None of our butterflies approach in this respect the larvae of a Mexican White (*Eucheira*) which spin a firm, gourd-like nest in which the colony spends the winter.

Many of our species hibernate in the larval stage. Most of these do so when about half grown; but a surprising number spend the winter as newly hatched larvae, without eating until the spring.

Not all members of one larval brood grow at the same rate. Sometimes some of the larvae grow quickly and transform to adults in normal time, while others of their brethren slow down their larval life and may pass into an inactive state (*diapause*) even in midsummer, that lasts until the next spring. They then finish growth and transform into adults at the same time as the offspring of their speedier brothers and sisters, their nephews and nieces. Sometimes such partially retarded generations cause confusion when we try to figure out how many broods there are annually in a given locality.

The larval stage has become specialized, biologically speaking, as the *nutritive* part of a butterfly's life cycle. Undisturbed by thoughts of sex or travel (in fact, undisturbed by thoughts) a larva eats, and eats, and then eats some more. It transforms incredible amounts of plant material into tissues and stored foods which it will use during the succeeding pupal and adult stages.

THE PUPA (CHRYSALIS)

After larval growth has finished comes the last larval moult. The next stage is entirely different. The *pupa* is an inactive, mummy-like object with appendages tightly fastened down. It may have some power to wriggle its abdomen, but that is all. It remains in one spot (see *Megathymus* for the exception) and apparently does nothing. Internally, however, a drastic reorganization is taking place. The larval structures mostly break down and disappear; and in their place there are built up the complex organs of the adult. When the transformation is completed the last moult occurs, and the adult emerges from the old pupal shell. After that, no more growth changes occur.

Butterfly pupæ are often called "chrysalids"; but the term *pupa*, being used for this reorganization stage in other insects as well, is preferred.

Butterfly pupæ are exceedingly varied in shape and color. Some are plain, oval, and mummy-like. Others have elaborately sculptured shapes, or long spiny or knobby projections. Some are dull and plain, brown or green; others are brilliantly colored, perhaps with metallic gold or silver markings. Each species, however, holds very true to its own pattern.

A characteristic pupal structure is a spiny process at the end of the abdomen, the *cremaster*. This is usually caught into a silk button spun by the larva, and so holds the pupa in place. There may in addition be a silk girdle passed around the thorax. Most butterfly pupæ are not enclosed in silk cocoons, as are so many moth pupæ, but hang from the cremaster, and the girdle if this is present. A few true butterfly larvæ prepare a crude sort of cell, in which they pupate. Nearly all Skipper pupæ are enclosed in a rather crude, loosely woven cocoon.

The pupal period may be of very short (eight to ten days) or of very long (more than a year) duration, depending on the specialization of the species or on the time of year. Many species hibernate in the pupal stage, and in some species part of the pupæ may not emerge the next year but may wait over another winter.

As pupal life progresses the colors change markedly. In many species the colors and patterns of the adult can be seen through the "shell" over the wings for some days before its emergence.

THE ADULT

We will discuss the structures of the adult in the next chapter, and have covered adult habits and behavior in Chapter 3.

CHAPTER FIVE

Structures of the Adult Butterfly

LIKE OTHER insects the adult butterfly consists of three main regions, *head*, *thorax*, and *abdomen*, each composed of a number of segments. As we have seen, the "skeleton" is largely external, forming a hard covering over the skin. The basic substance of this is a horny material, *chitin* (pronounced "kie-tin"). A "heavily chitinized" part is tough and strong; a "lightly chitinized" one, thin and weak.

Five convenient descriptive terms constantly used are:

dorsal — the upper side, that usually away from the ground; the "back"
ventral — the lower side, that usually nearer the ground; the "belly"
lateral — the sides, between dorsal and ventral
basal — of an appendage (leg, wing), the end fastened to the body
distal — of an appendage, the free end, outward from the basal

THE HEAD

The head bears the following parts: (1) A pair of *antennæ*, long, many jointed sensory organs with an enlarged club at or near the tip. In Skippers there is often a slender portion beyond the club, the *apiculus* (Fig. 5; 3 & 4). (2) A pair of large *compound eyes* composed of thousands of *ommatidia*. Each eye is more or less hemispherical. When its upper edge is concave or notched it is *emarginate*. (3) One pair of jointed sensory organs, the *palpi*, on each side of the mouth, thickly clothed with scales and hairs. (4) The *proboscis* ("beak" or "tongue"), slender, tubular, and flatly coiled, through which liquids are sucked into the mouth.

THE THORAX AND ABDOMEN

The thorax consists of three segments, the *prothorax*, *mesothorax*, and *metathorax*. Each bears a pair of jointed legs; and the meso- and metathorax each bears a pair of wings. The five main divisions of a leg, from the base out, are *coxa*, *trochanter*, *femur*, *tibia*, and five-jointed *tarsus* or foot. The long, first tarsal joint is the *metatarsus*. Fig. 4, p. 47.

Near the middle of the fore tibia (i.e., the tibiæ of the first pair of legs) may occur (Swallowtails) a small, movable *epiphysis* (EP.). On the hind tibiæ are sharp, basally jointed *spurs*; in true butterflies one pair, in Skippers usually two pairs. A series of sharp *spines* may be present. A pair of *claws* (CL.) tips the last tarsal segment; between

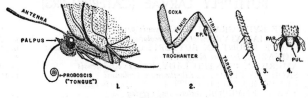

Fig. 4

these is a pad, the *pulvillus* (PUL.); and outside their bases may be a pair of delicate *paronychia* (PAR.). Organs on the hind tarsus enable the butterfly to taste sweet liquids with its feet. Contact of these organs with the petals of a flower sets off a reflex activity that uncoils the proboscis.

The abdomen consists of eleven segments, not all visible externally. At its tip are the external sex organs, the *genitalia*. These are of great importance in classification.

In respiration, air is admitted through paired openings, called *spiracles* or *stigmata*, along the sides of the body. It passes into a system of delicate air-tubes, the *tracheæ*, which branch to all parts of the body.

THE WINGS

Characteristics of the wings such as color, pattern, shape, and venation are of major importance in classification. The wings are joined to the thorax by small, basal structures to which in turn fasten internal muscles. The wings may be moved not only by these but by changes of the shape of the thorax. They begin development in larval life as internal organs, which grow throughout the larval and pupal stages. At emergence from the pupa they are for the first time fully external. They are then soft, thin-walled sacs into which run branches of tracheæ. Rapidly expanded, they

Fig. 5

1, 2–True Butterflies   **3, 4–Skippers**

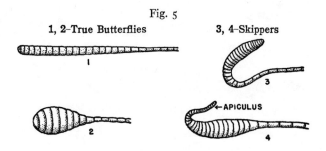

BUTTERFLY LARVAE (CATERPILLARS)

Most of the larvæ have been re-painted after Scudder's illustrations
in *The Butterflies of New England* . . .

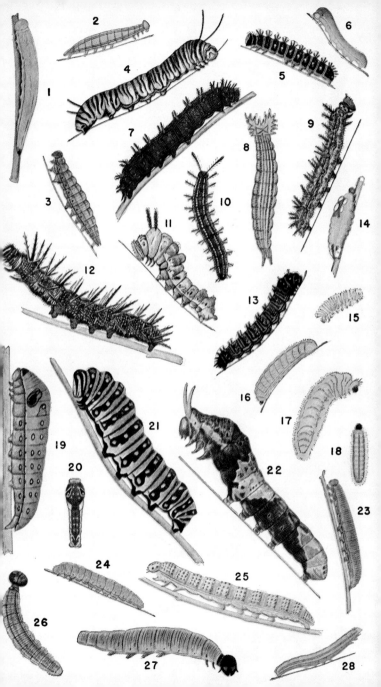

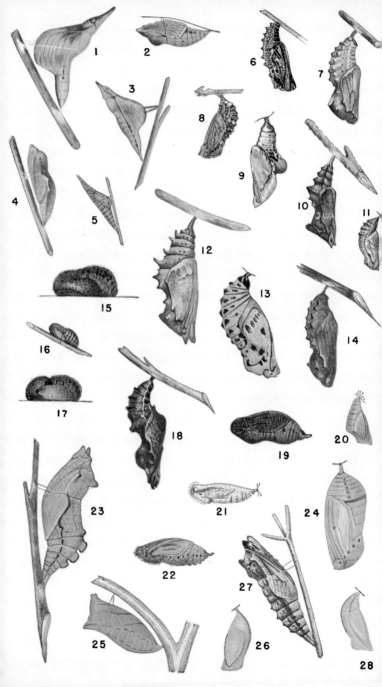

BUTTERFLY PUPAE (CHRYSALIDS)

flatten so that the upper and lower surfaces touch each other and fuse except along the tracheæ. The pathways of the tracheæ, the so-called *veins*, become tubular and develop thickened walls.

The wings are transparent and membranous, but in most butterflies are completely covered with tiny, flat scales, "shingled" in overlapping rows. In addition to the normal scales, special "scent scales" or *androconia* occur on the wings of males. In some groups (*Pieridæ*, Blues) these are scattered among the regular scales; but in many other groups (*Danaidæ*, *Satyridæ*, *Hesperiidæ*) they are concentrated in patches, called *stigmata* (singular, *stigma*) or "brands or sex-patches." The costal margin of the forewing (*Hesperiidæ*, *Pyrginæ*) or the anal margin of the hindwing (*Papilio*) may be expanded and rolled over, enclosing a long pocket of androconia, the *costal fold* and *anal fold*.

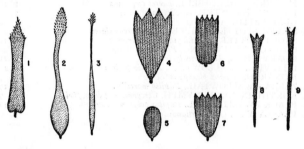

Fig. 6

1–3, ♂ scent scales; 4–9, wing and body scales.

The names of the angles and margins of the wings are important. The front edge is the *costal margin*, or *costa*. The angle at its outer end is the *apex*. The *outer margin* is called just that. The outer, posterior angle is the *anal* or *outer angle* or, in the forewings, the *tornus*. The posterior margin is the *anal margin* or *inner margin*. The central part of a wing is the *disc* or *discal* area, and the outer region is the *limbal* area. In condensed descriptions in this book the term "above" has been consistently used to refer to the upper sides of the wings, the term "beneath" for the lower sides.

Note the system of referring to the position of markings as "basal," "postbasal," "submedian," "median," "postmedian," as illustrated. These terms are important, for they are constantly used. See Fig. 7, p. 51.

WING VENATION

The veins are of the greatest importance in classification. There are various systems for designating them. I here follow the "Com-

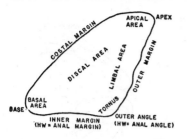

Fig. 7

stock-Needham" system because of its wide use in this country. Older writers and writers in other countries have used different systems.

Basically there are eight main veins. Let us consider a forewing first. Since some of the main veins branch a number of times, as many as twelve major veins and branches may reach the margin.

Nearest the front of the wing is *Costa* (C), running out from the base along the margin. It does not branch.

Next is *Subcosta* (Sc), shortly behind the costal margin. In butterflies this is likewise unbranched.

Next is *Radius* (R). When all of its branches are present there are five, designated R_1, R_2, R_3, R_4, and R_5. In Skippers all branches of radius arise from the discal cell. In the true butterflies there is always some "stalking" of radial branches, either with other radial branches or with a branch of the next vein, Media. In the wing of *Cercyonis alope* (Fig. 4), R_3, R_4, and R_5 are thus stalked, with R_3 "shorter stalked" than R_4 and R_5. In *Lycæna thoë* (Fig. 5) there are only four radial branches, R_4 and R_5 having completely fused together. In other cases (*Nathalis*) R_3, R_4, and R_5 have all completely fused, so that there are only three radial branches. Note also how in *Pieris* (Fig. 3) R_3 and R_4 have fused together and their product, R_{3+4} is stalked with R_5.

Next is *Media* (M). In the butterflies the basal part of this vein has disappeared (it is present in some other insects and moths) so that we see only the branches. These are three in number, M_1, M_2, and M_3. In most butterflies all arise from the discal cell; but M_1 may have moved forward and become stalked with the radial system as in *Pieris* (Fig. 3).

Next is *Cubitus* (Cu), two-branched (Cu_1 and Cu_2) in all our butterflies. Its branches arise separately from the posterior part of the discal cell.

Next are the three *Anal veins*, 1st A, 2d A, and 3d A. Of these, only 2d A is fully present in the forewings of all of our butterflies, though 1st A and 3d A may be present as short spurs or rudiments. See the figures of the venation of *Papilio* (Fig. 1) and *Epargyreus*

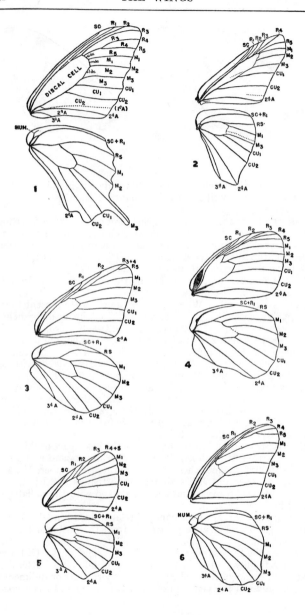

(Fig. 2). Some authors call 1st A *post-cubitus* and call the other anal veins *vannal veins.*

Cells. In addition to the discal cell, the other areas bounded by veins are specifically named, each taking the name of the vein anterior to it. Thus the space between vein R_2 and R_3 is called cell R_2; the space between Cu_1 and Cu_2 is called cell Cu_1. Actually the matter is more complex than this, but for our purposes the foregoing will suffice. We illustrate a Swallowtail wing with both the veins and the cells designated.

The venation of the hindwing is easily understood when that of the forewing has been mastered. Its chief differences are: (1) There may be a small accessory vein, the *humeral vein,* in the expanded area at the base of the costa. (2) The first branch of radius always fuses completely with Sc, the result being known as $Sc + R_1$. The remaining parts of radius are unbranched and run to the margin as a single vein, called *radial sector* (Rs). (3) There tend to be more anal veins than in the forewing, only our Swallowtails (*Papilio*) having only 2d A. In the others both 2d A and 3d A are present and well developed.

Mention has been made of the *discal cell* or, simply *the cell,* the area in the central part of the wing between the stems of R and Cu. It is important to note whether this cell is *closed* at its outer (distal) end by cross veins (the three *discocellulars*) or whether it is *open.* The closing cross veins are often quite weak. The open condition is well illustrated by *Limenitis* (Fig. 6). A spur of a vein sticking back toward the base from the distal end of the cell is called a *recurrent vein.*

In most butterflies the veins can be seen better on the lower surface. Wetting the area lightly with 95 per cent alcohol helps for close examination; or the scales can be carefully scraped off from a small area. For critical study wings can be broken off and bleached in Laborraque's solution or strong Clorox.

THE GENITALIA

At the end of the abdomen are located the openings of the digestive tract and sex ducts. Here have evolved sets of rather complex organs concerned with reproduction, the *genitalia,* usually heavily chitinized. In the majority of butterflies they differ consistently from one species to another, and are thus of the greatest value in classification. They often serve to distinguish species otherwise so similar that they can hardly be told apart. In some groups, particularly in the Skippers (i.e., *Erynnis*) they are the only truly reliable means of identification.

THE MALE GENITALIA

Our illustration shows an imaginary species, designed to illustrate the chief structures most simply. It represents the genitalia

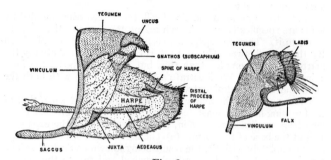

Fig. 8

Left-usual butterfly type. Right—Lycænid.

as if removed from the abdomen and seen from the butterfly's left side. The left (nearer) *harpe* has been removed, so as to show the inner face of the right harpe and the central structures.

Basic structure is a firm, chitinized ring, jointing and fastening the whole apparatus to the abdomen. The dorsal (upper) part of this ring is the roof-like *tegumen*. Extending down around each side from this, and across the bottom, is the U-shaped *vinculum*. At the ventral (lower) side of this the *saccus* extends forward into the abdomen.

Extending mid-dorsally to the rear from the tegumen is the *uncus*. This may be broad basally and usually has a single prong; but in many groups it bears two prongs, and is then *bifid*. Beneath the tegumen and uncus runs the *rectum*, the posterior end of the digestive tract, ending in the *anus*. Below this and supporting it may be a more or less strongly chitinized structure, the *subscaphium*. Arms may extend down on either side from the tegumen or the base of the uncus, also supporting the anal region. These form a *gnathos*.

Particularly in *Lycænidæ* occurs a pair of strong, curved, sharp rods, the *falces* (sing. *falx*) which arise as described above for a gnathos; and in place of the normal uncus are a pair of rounded, hairy pads, the *labides* (sing. *labis*). See Fig. 8.

At each side, with its upper basal corner more or less articulated to the tegumen, and its lower basal corner to the saccus or vinculum, is one of the pair of *harpes* (also called *claspers* or *valves*). These often bear elaborate spines or teeth; we illustrate a harpe with one internal, subdorsal spine and a finely toothed distal process. Spread apart or pulled together by internal muscles, they grip and hold the end of the female's abdomen. In this they are assisted by the uncus above.

In the middle, between the harpes, is the tubular *œdeagus* or penis, supported beneath by a U- or Y-shaped *juxta*. Inside this

runs the *ejaculatory duct,* along which flows seminal fluid from the
testes and storage sacs in the abdomen. In this duct may occur
strong, barbed or thornlike structures, the *cornuti.*

To list even the major types of variation in these organs would
require many pages, since many butterflies differ more in genitalia
than in color and pattern. Every one of the parts mentioned shows
characters of importance in some species. Probably the harpes
show most variation.

The characters of the uncus, gnathos, and harpes can often be
studied without dissection by merely clearing away the long hairs
and scales that usually cover the genitalia, with a fine brush.
Dissection is done after first soaking the abdomen in a weak (3
per cent) solution of potassium or sodium hydroxide over night and
then cleaning and dissecting under a dissecting microscope or
powerful lens. The whole abdomen may be broken from the
specimen, or just the posterior part may be cut away.

Far too little work has been done on the female genitalia of butterflies. In some groups, at least, there are good distinguishing
characteristics; there is a wide-open field for valuable research here.

BUTTERFLY COLORS

The colors of butterflies are so prominent and play so important
a part in their classification that we should know at least a little
about them. The matter is not as simple as you might think.

Butterfly colors are of two types, *pigment* and *structural.* Often
these are combined in one individual. They occur almost entirely
in the scales and hairs.

A *pigment* is a specific substance with a definite chemical composition. We are all familiar with pigment colors in paints, dyes, and
inks. Without going into the terrifying complexities of organic
chemistry we can say little in detail about butterfly pigments. It
is worth noting that the white, yellow, and orange pigments of the
Pieridæ are derived from the urea, a waste product, and that pos-
session of such pigments sets these butterflies apart from all others.
The blacks, browns, and reds of other butterflies, known as *mela-
nins,* are of an entirely different chemical nature; and the part
played by pigments eaten by larvæ, such as the whole series of
chlorophyll pigments of green plants, has yet to be evaluated. It
has recently been shown that in at least one group of butterflies
(*Œneis*) distinctions between closely related species may be made
by simple chemical tests of certain of their pigments. The whole
study is yet in its infancy, but it may have far-reaching results.

Structural colors are produced in a purely "mechanical" way without the necessity of any pigment being present. They are thus like
the colors produced by a glass prism, the blue of the sky, the spec-
trum of the rainbow, and an oil film on water. The structural,
usually iridescent, colors of butterflies are produced in three chief
ways: (1) fine, parallel ridges or grooves on a flat surface, (2) fine

granules (or ends of fine rods) in a medium of a different refractive index, and (3) very thin, superimposed films of different refractive indices.

Thus the blue of butterfly wings or markings is always structural. So are metallic or pearly effects, such as the "silver" of the Fritillaries and the "copper" of the Coppers. Some of the green colors are undoubtedly structural (*Mitoura*) while others are very possibly due to pigments (*Anthocaris*). Often both structural and pigment colors are present, one underlying the other; this produces very striking effects.

A fairly useful, rough test of color type is to wet the area with a liquid such as alcohol or carbon tetrachloride. If the visible color disappears or changes to a markedly different hue, but reappears on drying out, the chances are that there is structural color. A pigment color, on the other hand, will darken, that is, change in intensity, but will not change in hue. We can actually dissolve out a pigment with the right solvent but we cannot do this with a structural color.

CHAPTER SIX

Butterfly Classification

The Order Lepidoptera. Butterflies are members of the great insect order *Lepidoptera*. The detailed classification of this and of the other orders of insects is complex and not appropriate to this book. References to several adequate books on general entomology will be found in Part III. The *Lepidoptera* derive their name from the presence of scales on the wings (Greek: *lepis* — a scale and *pteron* — a wing). The order is divided into a number of *superfamilies*, containing a total of more than seventy-five families. Two superfamilies containing a total of eleven families constitute the Butterflies and Skippers of our area. The remainder of the order are the Moths, which range from tiny species with a wing expanse of less than one thirty-second of an inch up to the giant Saturniids with an expanse of several inches.

Butterflies and Moths. There is no single, absolutely trustworthy character by which all Butterflies (including the Skippers) and Moths can be separated. Some families of Moths (*Castniidæ*) are closer to the popular conception of Butterflies than are some of the Butterflies. The following comparisons, then, will not hold true in every instance.

Moths. At the base of the costal margin of the hindwing of most Moths is a long, strong bristle or bunch of bristles, the *frenulum*, which locks onto the forewing and holds the wings together. Butterflies and Skippers do not have a frenulum, the expanded edge (*humeral angle*) of the hindwing at this point serving the same function. The *antennæ* of Moths are either simple, hairlike, and tapering, or else they are set with teeth like a comb and are tapering and feathery. A few Moths have a clublike swelling at the tip of the antenna, but all of these have a frenulum. In Butterflies and Skippers the antennæ have a clublike swelling at or near the tip; in some this is very gradual and inconspicuous, but in others it is very large and abrupt. Most Moths rest with the wings flat, either out at the sides or over the back, but some do not. Most butterflies and Skippers tend to rest with the wings held upright over the back; but there are a number of exceptions. The Moths are typically nocturnal or "*crepuscular*" (flying at dusk or dawn), but some families are day-flyers. Nearly all Butterflies are strictly diurnal; in fact the majority are inactive even on cloudy days. There are, however, a few exceptions, such as the Giant Skippers which have been described as holding mating flights and courtships at dusk; and occasional Butterflies are collected at lights at night.

While the majority of Moths tend to be dull colored, some, especially of the diurnal groups (e.g., *Urania*), vie with the brightest of the Butterflies in brilliant and iridescent colors. Finally, the larvæ of most of the Moths weave a silken covering, the *cocoon*, in which they change to the pupal stage; but in many groups, especially those which pupate underground, there is no cocoon. Moth pupæ are mostly brown and unornamented. In the True Butterflies there is practically no trace of a cocoon, but a few species pupate in a silken larval nest which is almost cocoonlike. In the Skippers there is regularly a loose cocoon, inside which the pupa may be fastened or suspended by silk bands. The pupæ of many of the Butterflies are often ornamented with bright colors and bizarre shapes and projections. Those of the Skippers are plainer and more mothlike.

Butterflies and Skippers. For all practical purposes the "True Butterflies" and the "Skippers" are usually considered together and collected by most people interested in either. Sometimes they are collectively called *Diurnal Lepidoptera*, a convenient term. There is a popular, largely incorrect, idea that Skippers are much more primitive than Butterflies and so connect them with the moths. Actually each group is of different ancestry, and each has its different, closest relatives among the moths. There is no exact usage of the common names "Butterfly" and "Skipper." Most people, like myself, mean to include the Skippers when they use the term "Butterfly." Like many "common name" situations, it is a bit awkward. If we wish to be exact we should use the superfamily names, *Papilionoidea* and *Hesperioidea*. These are characterized and differentiated as follows:

(1) *Papilionoidea — True Butterflies.* Head, thorax, and abdomen are relatively slender. Wings are proportionately large. Antennæ arise close together on the head. Club of antenna extends to its distal (outer) end, and is never followed by a slender tip. At least one of the veins arising from the discal cell of the forewing is forked or branched, sometimes with three, or even four, branches. Flight, while often swift, is not powerful with fast, blurring wing strokes. The prothorax of larva is not notably slender so as to look like a "neck." Larvæ of many groups are brightly colored and ornamented with spines and tubercles. Pupæ of practically all species are not enclosed in a silken cocoon, at most they are fastened to a solid surface by a silk girdle and button.

(2) *Hesperioidea — Skippers.* Head, thorax, and abdomen are relatively stout and massive, wings proportionately smaller. Antennæ arise far apart on the head. Club of antenna usually ends some distance short of the distal end, often followed by a more slender part, the *apiculus*, which is often bent backward into a hook. All veins arising from discal cell of FW are simple and unbranched. Flight is swift and darting, with fast-beating, often blurring wings. The prothorax of larva is so much more slender than either head or rest of thorax that it looks like a neck. Larvæ

tend to be duller colored and unornamented, without prominent spines and bristles. Pupæ are typically plain and unornamented (some have a single prominent horn), suspended by a silk girdle inside a loosely woven silk cocoon (absent in Giant Skippers, *Megathymidæ*).

The following key will serve to distinguish the families of *Papilionoidea* in North America, but will not hold true for all other regions. The technical terms used in it have been explained in Chapter 5.

The Families of the True Butterflies.

1. Front legs of both males and females greatly reduced in size, functionless for walking, carried folded close to the thorax; radial vein (R) of FW with five branches 2
1. Front legs of females normal, not reduced in size, functional for walking; front legs of males sometimes reduced, but usually only slightly; radial vein of FW with only three or four branches[1] 6
2. Palpi much longer than thorax, protruding beaklike in front

Snout Butterflies *Libytheidæ*, p. 120
2. Palpi not nearly as long as thorax 3
3. One or more veins of the FW greatly swollen at base; small to medium-sized butterflies, without blue or green iridescent colors; cell of HW closed; club of antenna gradual and not greatly swollen . . . . Wood Nymphs and Satyrs, *Satyridæ*, p. 66
3. None of the veins of the FW greatly swollen at base; the few exceptions (*Mestra*, *Callicore* and *Eunica*) have the cell of the HW open or weakly closed and have brighter colors, with blue, green, or purple iridescence in *Callicore* and *Eunica*; antennal club more abruptly swollen 4
4. Antennæ without scales; male with a scent pouch on each HW below vein Cu$_2$ halfway out from base; females with end of front tarsus knobbed and spined

Monarchs, *Danaidæ*, p. 77
4. Antennæ scaled, at least on upper surface; males without such scent pouches; females with front tarsus not knobbed at tip 5
5. FW more than twice as long as wide; butterflies of a characteristic tough, rubbery structure, containing disagreeable tasting and smelling or poisonous body fluids

Heliconians, *Heliconiidæ*, p. 79
5. FW less than twice as long as wide; butterflies not noticeably tough and rubbery, not containing disagreeable or poisonous body fluids . . . . . . Brush Footed Butterflies, *Nymphalidæ*, p. 83
6. HW with only one anal vein . . . . Swallowtails, *Papilionidæ*, p. 171
6. HW with two anal veins 7
7. FW with vein M$_1$ stalked on the radial stem for a considerable distance out from discal cell; face between eyes as wide as long; predominantly white, yellow or orange

Whites and Sulphurs, *Pieridæ*, p. 181
7. FW with vein M$_1$ arising either at or near the apex of the

[1] The Orange Tips (*Anthocaris* and *Euchloë*) are an exception, having five branches of radius.

discal cell;[1] face between eyes much narrower than long... 8

8. HW with a humeral vein and a vein along costal margin; forelegs of male greatly reduced, less than half the size of the middle legs, and without spines....Metalmarks, *Riodinidæ*, p. 121

8. HW with neither costal nor humeral vein; forelegs of male not greatly reduced, more than half the size of the middle legs, and bearing spines

Gossamer Winged Butterflies, *Lycænidæ*, p. 125

The Families of the Skippers.

1. Head narrower than thorax; hind tibia with only one pair of spurs; palpi small; size large, body very robust; larvæ boring in Yucca stems and leaves

Giant Skippers, *Megathymidæ*, p. 274

1. Head nearly as wide, to wider than thorax; hind tibia usually with two pairs of spurs; palpi not noticeably small; size averaging much smaller, body not so robust; larvæ external feeders on plant leaves, usually in a leaf nest

Skippers, *Hesperiidæ*, p. 203

[1] The Harvester (*Feniseca*) is an exception, having vein M_1 well stalked on the radial stem.

Part 2

Resident Butterflies of Eastern North America

ALL SPECIES of butterflies known to breed in Eastern North America, no matter how rarely, are described in this part. Others of casual or accidental occurrence and those believed wrongly recorded are treated separately (p. 275).

Headings, Abbreviations and Symbols. ♂ — male, ♀ — female. FW — Forewing, HW — Hindwing. "Above" is used consistently only to mean the upper surface of the wings, "beneath" to mean the lower surface. TL means "type locality."

Larval descriptions are necessarily greatly condensed. **Food** refers to larval food plants. I have tried to list all those recorded except where a species is a general feeder. Some evidently wrong records have been eliminated or queried. Those preceded by *also* are probably of secondary importance — larvæ in captivity will sometimes eat abnormal plants. I hope that omissions will be called to my attention. I have followed *Gray's Manual* 7th edition and Small's *Flora of the Southeastern United States*, changing old names where necessary as indicated by these.

Dates are merely for general guidance. Those in the mountains may be two or three weeks behind those a few miles away in the lowlands. Dates in the far south may run two to three months ahead of those in the north. The dates help to establish a general sequence, details of which must be worked out in each locality. *Number of broods* is, again, an average that may vary widely from south to north. There are often partial or overlapping broods.

Range refers to the range *in our area* of the whole species. The borders of ranges are not only diffuse because of straying and irregular because of topography, but also change from time to time. Many published distribution records are untrustworthy because of misidentifications.

Under **Subspecies** are listed essential facts about the geographic subspecies of our area, whether these are discontinuous ones or intergrading forms in a "cline." "Race" is treated as synonymous with "geographic subspecies." Considerable liberality has been shown in recognizing the worth of many named subspecies, even though some are really no more than distinct "local forms." Far too many very minor or imaginary "races" have been named. Exact data on the ranges of subspecies are badly lacking; this book is the first attempt for our area to bring these data together. Remember that in clinal (see p. 297) conditions there are often no sharp boundaries between subspecies.

SATYRS AND WOOD NYMPHS
Family *Satyridae*

All illustrations are × 1 (natural size)

1. LITTLE WOOD SATYR, *Euptychia cymela*   p. 69
   Upper & under sides,♂ (Sharon, Conn.).   Larger than *sosybia;* FW
   beneath with 2 eyespots; eyespots above large; postmedian crosslines
   beneath concave outwardly. Can. s. to Fla. & Tex.

2. CAROLINA SATYR, *Euptychia hermes sosybia*   p. 69
   Under side,♂ (Orlando, Fla.).   Small & dark; eyespots above small or
   absent; postmedian crosslines beneath straight or convex outwardly.
   N.J. southward.

3. MITCHELL'S SATYR, *Euptychia mitchellii*   p. 69
   Under side,♂ (Wakelee, Cass Co., Mich.).   Small; FW beneath with
   4 eyespots, HW with 6, the central ones largest.   Mich., Ohio, N.J.

4. GEMMED SATYR, *Euptychia gemma*   p. 70
   Under side,♂ (Coosawhatchie, S.C.).   No eyespots on FW beneath;
   HW with large violet-gray patch, eyespots small, silvery. Va. to Ill.,
   s. to central Fla. & Mex.

5. BLUE EYED GRAYLING, *Cercyonis pegala alope*   p. 72
   Upper & under sides,♂ (Bedford, N.Y.).   Orange patch on FW, the
   lower eyespot in this large. Va. & N.J. n. to Me.

6. SOUTHERN WOOD NYMPH, *Cercyonis p. pegala*   p. 72
   Upper side,♂, (Currituck Co., N.C.).   Lower eyespot of FW smaller
   or absent; HW with anal eyespot large; size large, colors bright.   N.J.
   & Va. southward.

7. GEORGIA SATYR, *Euptychia areolata*   p. 70
   Upper & under sides,♂ (Deenwood, Waycross, Ga.).   Long, thin eyespots; red lines; N.J. southward, coastal plain.

8. PEARLY EYE, *Lethe portlandia*   p. 66
   Upper side ♂ (Sharon, Conn.).   Large size, prominent eyespots; ♂
   with no sex scaling on FW. Can. s. to Fla. & Gulf States.   Woodlands.

9. CREOLE PEARLY EYE, *Lethe creola*   p. 67
   Upper side, ♂ . Coosawhatchie, S.C.).   Large size, prominent eye-
   spots; ♂ with sex scaling between veins of FW; long, thin FW. Va. &
   Ill. southward. Woodlands.

10. CHRYXUS ARCTIC, *Œneis chryxus strigulosus*   p. 73
    Upper side,♂ (Grayling, Mich.).   Medium size; bright orange-brown
    above; ♂ with sex scaling on FW.   Ont. & Que.

11. MACOUN'S ARCTIC, *Œneis macounii*   p. 73
    Upper side, ♂ (Didsbury, Alberta).   Large size; bright orange-brown
    above; prominent eyespots on FW; ♂ with no sex scaling.   Ont.,
    Minn., Mich.

12. WHITE VEINED ARCTIC, *Œeneis taygete*   p. 74
    Under side, ♂ (Wolstenholme, Que.).   Dull brown above; HW be-
    neath with contrasty markings and white-lined veins. Labrador &
    Gaspé. Open spaces, mountaintops.

Plate 8   65

SATYRS AND FRITILLARIES
Families *Satyridae* & *Nymphalidae*
All illustrations × 1 (natural size) except *Speyeria diana*

1. JUTTA ARCTIC, *Œneis jutta*   p. 74
   Upper side, ♂ (Passadumkeag, Me.). Above with submarginal
   orange-brown; prominent eyespots on FW. Subarctic s. to Me. &
   N.H. Black Spruce — Sphagnum Bogs.
2. MT. KATAHDIN ARCTIC, *Œneis polixenes katahdin*   p. 74
   Upper side, ♂ (Mt. Katahdin, Me.). Above with light submarginal
   band rather prominent; varying number of dark or ocellate spots. Mt.
   Katahdin, Me.
3. WHITE MOUNTAIN BUTTERFLY, *Œneis melissa semidea*   p. 75
   Upper side, ♂ (Mt. Washington, N.H.). Wings dull, unmarked
   above, thinly scaled. See text. Alpine summits, N.H.
4. GREAT SPANGLED FRITILLARY, *Speyeria cybele*   p. 87
   Upper & under sides, ♂ (Mashipicong, N.J.). FW above with no
   black spot below cell near base (see No. 6 below). HW beneath with
   broad, light yellow-brown, submarginal band. Can. s. to N.C. &
   Okla.
5. GORGONE CHECKERSPOT, *Melitæa gorgone carlota*   p. 95
   Under side, ♂ (Douglas Co., Kan.). Postmedian and submarginal
   lines and crescents of HW beneath deeply angled and scalloped inwardly. Mex. n. to Mich. & westward, e. to Ga.
6. APHRODITE, *Speyeria aphrodite*   p. 87
   Upper & under sides, ♂ (Mashipicong, N.J.). FW above with black
   spot below cell near base; HW beneath with narrow, light submarginal
   band. Canada s. to N.C. & Kans.
7. DIANA, *Speyeria diana*   p. 86
   Upper side, ♂ (Tarry, Ark.). Reduced to ⅔ natural size. Dark base;
   light, lightly marked outer area; no silver spots beneath. W.Va. to Ga.,
   w toArk. Woodland roads.
8. ATLANTIS FRITILLARY, *Speyeria atlantis*   p. 86
   Upper & under sides, ♂ (Scranton, Pa.). FW above with dark margins; HW beneath very dark, with narrow light submarginal band.
   Can. s. to W. Va., Mich. & Minn.
9. DIANA, *Speyeria diana*   p. 86
   Upper side, ♀ (L. Toxaway, N.C.). See No. 7 above. Reduced to
   ⅔ natural size.

Synonyms have been given only when they have had such wide or recent use that their omission would cause confusion. Complete synonymies are found in the latest check lists and catalogs by various authors (see Part III, Appendix 2).

Form and *Variety* names are given only for prominent forms that have possible biological significance, or for those the omission of which would cause confusion in identification. There is a great host of such forms and aberrations that cannot be covered practicably in this book. I have treated such names as having no status in official specific and subspecific nomenclature.

Family Satyridæ: The Satyrs and Wood Nymphs

THE SATYRIDS are not a large family in our area, but include some common, widespread species encountered nearly everywhere. They are medium sized, with characteristic jerky and fluttering, although at times rapid, flights. Most fly low and seek cover when alarmed, dodging through tall grasses and shrubs, and hiding. They are then not easily caught. When hiding they fold the fore-wings inside the hindwings, and may alight on the ground and crawl under leaves and trash. They do not visit flowers avidly. Characteristically Satyrs are some shade of brown with at least some "eyespots" (ocelli) on the wings. The front legs are very greatly reduced, more so in the males than in the females. The antennal club is very weak; and from one to three of the main wing veins are swollen basally. The egg is more or less spherical, sometimes somewhat elongated, with a raised network. The larvæ are spindle shaped, thicker at the middle and tapering to the ends, and have the last segment somewhat forked. They are clothed with very short hairs and are usually striped lengthwise. Growth is slow, so that larval life is long and many species are single brooded. The larvæ feed on grasses or sedges. The pupæ are plain, brown or green, unornamented. Sometimes they are suspended by the cremaster alone, or pupation may take place in a shallow cell on the earth, among trash or under rocks. The family has also been known as the *Agapetidæ*.

PEARLY EYE. *Lethe portlandia* Fabricius   pp. 49, 64
1.6–2.0 in. A typically woodland and woods-edge species. Its quick flight and habit of alighting on tree trunks often make it difficult to catch. It is very local; a colony may occupy a small area perhaps miles from the next colony. It often occurs in the same areas as *L. creola*, with which it has been much confused. Males are quite likely to adopt a particular tree trunk as a "territory," return to it day after day and chase other butter-

flies away from it. Combats between males are thus frequent.

There appears to be no great generic distinction between *Lethe* and *Enodia*, a generic name formerly used for *portlandia* and *creola*, and *Satyrodes*, the name formerly used for *eurydice*. *Enodia* can be used as a subgeneric name for our species.

Similar Species: — Males of *creola* have the FW much narrower, with sex scaling between veins. Females of *creola* have the wing shape of *portlandia*, but have five well-developed eyespots on the FW beneath (*portlandia* has four, the one below vein Cu$_2$ being tiny or absent); and also on the FW beneath have the dark postmedian line more irregular, protruding abruptly outward in cell M$_1$ (it is straighter in *portlandia* and protrudes farthest out in cell M$_2$). *Eurydice* has more rounded wings than *portlandia* and *creola*, with smoother, less wavy margins; has a lighter, more yellowish and washed out coloration; has rounder, more distinctly ringed eyespots; and a consistently different pattern of the transverse lines beneath.

Larva: — Yellowish green, anal fork red-tipped; two red-tipped horns on head, a longer pair on last segment. **Food:** — Grasses. One brood in North, two in South. Adults in early June (Lat. 40°). Hibernation as part grown larva.

Range: — Quebec and Manitoba s. to Florida and Gulf States.
Subspecies: — *L. p. portlandia* (TL "America Meridionalis") Florida and Gulf States, n. in coastal plain to s. New Jersey. Large, brightly colored, and boldly marked. *L. p. borealis* A. H. Clark (TL Hymers, Ontario) Maine, Quebec w. to Manitoba. Smaller, darker, dark border of HW above broader; dark submarginal band of HW beneath broader. *L. p. anthedon* A. H. Clark (TL Lava, Sullivan County, New York) central New England w. to Minnesota and Kansas, s. in mountains to Georgia; the white markings beneath much reduced; eyespots of FW beneath in a straight, not a curved, line; eyespots of HW beneath with white pupils. The species as a whole represents something of a "cline," although there is doubtless some habitat (ecotypic) segregation due to isolation of colonies. The subspecies, not well marked, intergrade greatly, especially northward.

CREOLE PEARLY EYE. *Lethe creola* Skinner   p. 64
2.0 in. Like *portlandia*, *creola* is a forest butterfly, with a fast flight and a habit of alighting on tree trunks. The males are active and belligerent. It flies in the shade, and at dusk after other butterflies have gone to sleep. It has been noted associated with Cane (*Arundinaria*). Much more work is needed on its life history, distribution and relationships with *portlandia*. **Food:** — Presumably Grasses.
Similar Species: — see *L. portlandia*.
Range: — Manitoba, Illinois, Michigan, eastern Virginia s. to Texas, Louisiana, Florida (rare) (TL — Opelousas, Louisiana)

EYED BROWN. *Lethe eurydice* Johannson (*canthus* L.)   p. 81
1.8 in. Like its congeners, *eurydice* is very local; but unlike them
it favors open, marshy meadows. Its flight is weaker, dancing,
and close to the ground. It is often locally common.

Similar Species: — see *L. portlandia.*

Larva: — Minutely hairy, pale green, striped lengthwise with
narrow, darker bands; head and last abdominal segment each
with a pair of red-tipped horns. Unlike most Satyrs it feeds
by day. **Food:** — Grasses. One brood. Adults in early June.
Hibernation as part-grown larva.

Range: — Quebec, Ontario, and Manitoba s. to n. Florida
(southward chiefly in mountains).

Subspecies: — *L. e. eurydice* (TL Philadelphia, Pennsylvania)
Canada s. to New Jersey, Pennsylvania and West Virginia;
ground color lighter, dark postmedian band serrate and irregular.
L. e. appalachia R. L. Chermock (TL Brevard, North Carolina)
West Virginia to Georgia in the mountains, to northern Florida
(swamps?), not typical in piedmont in the South; darker ground
color, coloration less contrasty; postmedian band straighter,
less jagged and irregular. *L. e. transmontana* Gosse (TL Compton, Quebec) has been suggested as a race name for the most
northern part of the population, on the basis of a lighter ground
color; but the name seems hardly warranted.

Genus Euptychia *Huebner:*
The Wood Satyrs

A VERY large genus, chiefly Neotropical, of which six species
occur in our area. All are of small to medium size, brown or gray,
with prominent eyespots ("ocelli") on the wings. They occur
mostly in woods, usually along the edges, in brushy openings along
sunlit forest trails, or in open, woodland glades; but they often stray
out into grasslands, and one species, *areolata*, consistently occurs in
the open. Other generic names that have been used are *Megisto*
Huebner, *Neonympha* Huebner, *Cissia* Doubleday and *Cyllopsis*
Felder. Of these *Cyllopsis* may be used as a subgenus for *gemma*
Huebner. The following table will serve for our species:

rubricata — ground color reddish, FW & HW above with one ocellus
  each; FW beneath with one large ocellus, and HW with two; Texas
  and Oklahoma
cymela — ground color brownish gray, much lighter beneath; FW &
  HW both above and beneath with two large ocelli each, on the FW
  beneath that below vein Cu_1 the larger; postmedian cross lines of FW
  beneath concave outwardly
hermes sosybia — ground color darker than *cymela*, especially beneath;
  wings above with ocelli very small or absent; FW beneath with ocellus

below vein Cu₁ very small; postmedian cross lines of FW beneath straight or convex outwardly; discocellular veins beneath prominently outlined with dark scales

mitchellii — FW beneath with four ocelli, HW beneath with six, the central ones of each series the largest, not those toward the costal and anal margins as in *cymela* and *sosybia*

areolata — ocelli of HW beneath elongate; crosslines of wings beneath brick red to orange red

gemma — HW beneath with a large, submarginal, violet gray patch, ocelli small, brightly silvered

LITTLE WOOD SATYR. *Euptychia cymela* Cramer ("*eurytus*")
p. 64

1.75 in. Like its congeners, *cymela* flies near the ground, expertly twisting through tall grasses and shrubbery. Though a slow flier, it is unexpectedly difficult to net, dodging into cover to reappear ten feet away on the other side of a bush. It favors rather open, deciduous woods and wet meadows surrounded by woods, especially if there is considerable shrubbery. It is common in most of its range.

Similar Species: — *mitchellii* and *hermes sosybia*, see genus discussion.

Larva: — Pale, greenish brown, finely hairy, with narrow, lengthwise stripes; head, its tubercles, and body tubercles, whitish. Food: — Grasses. One brood in north, at least a partial second in south. Adults in mid-May. Hibernation as part grown larva.

Range: — s. Canada w. to Nebraska, s. to n. Florida, Gulf States and Texas.

Subspecies: — *E. c. cymela* (TL "Cape of Good Hope") is northern, occupying most of the range. *E. c. viola* Maynard (TL Central Florida), that of the far South, is brighter, almost violet gray, especially beneath. Along the southern borders of its range *viola* is extremely distinct.

CAROLINA SATYR. *Euptychia hermes sosybia* Fabricius   p. 64

1.5 in. With practice the smaller, darker *sosybia* can be distinguished even in flight from *cymela*. It has the same habits and flight but prefers damp woods and wooded swamps a bit more.

Similar Species: — *cymela, mitchellii*, see genus discussion.

Larva: — Light green with darker green, lengthwise stripes, and many fine, yellow, hairy tubercles. Food: — Grasses. Two broods. Hibernation probably as part-grown larva.

Range: — Upper and Lower Austral Zones, s. New Jersey s. through Florida, Gulf States, and Texas. Northern limits in Mississippi Valley uncertain.

MITCHELL'S SATYR. *Euptychia mitchellii* French   p. 64

1.6 in. Little is known about *mitchellii*, which occurs in south Michigan (TL Cass County) and Ohio, and has been recorded from northern New Jersey (Dover, Woodport). The New Jersey records are a bit dubious. Look for it in boggy, wet meadows. The greater number of large ocelli distinguishes it.

GEORGIA SATYR. *Euptychia areolata* Abbot & Smith pp. 48, 64
1.7 in. Far more than its congeners, *areolata* prefers open, marshy or boggy areas, although southward it also occurs in grassy areas in open pine woods. I have never noticed it alighting upon trees. For many years its northern limit has been the railroad station at Lakehurst, New Jersey. Collecting in the long grass to the south of the station we always get *areolata;* but I have seen very few to the north! In the South it prefers drier ground than in the north.
Larva: — Yellow green with darker stripes; head green, tubercles brownish, anal tubercles red tipped. **Food:** — Grasses. One brood in the north, two or more in the south. Adults in mid-June. Hibernation as part-grown larva.
Range: — Southern New Jersey s. to southern Florida, Gulf States, and Texas. Distribution northward in Mississippi Valley uncertain.
Subspecies: — *E. a. areolata* (TL Georgia) Florida n. to Virginia. *E. a. septentrionalis* Davis (TL Lakehurst, New Jersey) Virginia n. to New Jersey, ocelli of HW beneath less elongate, red of the ocelli yellower; FW with apex rounder and outer margin more convex. The distribution is clinal; a broad blend zone extends from Virginia through North Carolina.

RED SATYR. *Euptychia rubricata* Edwards
1.75 in. Easily recognized by its red coloration, *rubricata* is a species of the Southwest which enters our area only in w. Texas and Oklahoma (TL Waco, Texas).

GEMMED SATYR. *Euptychia gemma* Huebner   p. 64
1.75 in. A widespread but local species, recorded as most likely to be found in tall grass meadows, especially near running water.
Larva: — Dimorphic; green (early brood) or brown (later broods) with darker lengthwise stripes, and long, paired tubercles on head and last abdominal segment. **Food:** — Grasses. Two or more broods.
Range: — Virginia to Illinois, s. to central Florida and into Mexico.
Subspecies: — *E.g. gemma*, range as above, except for: *E.g. freemani* Stallings & Turner (TL Pharr, Texas) tropical areas of southern Texas into Mexico; ground color more reddish brown; striations of wings beneath darker red brown, but transverse lines not as well marked as in *g. gemma*. The summer brood is less distinct from *g. gemma*.

THE RINGLETS. *Cænonympha tullia* Muller   p. 81
1.2–1.8 in. A number of Ringlets occur in North America.

Most of them were long considered to be distinct species, but recent work has shown that nearly all are best considered as subspecies of the Palæarctic *tullia*. The genus as a whole is Holarctic, and northern or montane. The butterflies are small, of pastel shades, densely haired, with naked eyes, and with the bases of veins Sc, Cu, and 2d A of the forewing swollen. The species as a whole forms at least a partial cline, and some of the subspecies intergrade greatly with each other in their "blend zones." The larva is long and slender, tapering but slightly at the ends, is clothed with many short hairs, and has two very short projections on the last abdominal segment. Apparently all subspecies are single brooded, and feed on grasses in the larval stage. The adults, found in open grassy meadows, have a weak, low flight.

INORNATE RINGLET. *C. tullia inornata* Edwards   p. 81
Wings above ochreous brown, lighter basally and discally; FW beneath darker, with a lighter postmedian band, and one ocellus; HW beneath grayer, with an irregular, broken, light, postmedian band consisting of an angulate streak on the costal half of the wing and a small, isolated patch below that; ocelli usually absent except one or two in anal region.
Range: — Western Ontario (TL Lake Winnipeg) e. through Ontario, northern Minnesota, northern Michigan, Quebec, and Labrador. Labrador specimens average darker. Possibly *quebecensis* Barnes & Benj. (TL Chelsea, Quebec) is a valid subspecies.

PRAIRIE RINGLET. *C. tullia benjamini* McDunnough
Brighter, lighter ochreous than *inornata*, but with the same reduced markings on the wings beneath.
Range: — Prairie regions (TL Waterton Lakes, Alberta), entering our area in the Dakotas and, perhaps, Wisconsin and Minnesota.

McISAAC'S RINGLET. *C. tullia mcisaaci* dos Passos
Much darker, greener gray than *inornata*, especially in the male; the female paler and more buffy. Ocelli of the HW beneath completely absent.
Range: — Newfoundland (TL Doyle's Station). Specimens from northeastern Newfoundland resemble *inornata* more closely.

OCHRE RINGLET. *C. tullia brenda* Edwards ("*ochracea*")
Bright ochreous above; HW beneath heavily marked with whitish as follows: three postbasal patches, a complete, zigzag postmedian band and a complete row of submarginal ocelli.
Range: — *Brenda* (TL Los Angeles, California) enters our area in South Dakota, Nebraska and (doubtfully) Kansas. It intergrades in blend zones with both *inornata* and *benjamini*.

MARITIME RINGLET. *C. tullia nipisiquit* McDunnough
Upperside deep brown, nearly as dark as *mcisaaci;* HW beneath
with the apical ocellus (lacking in *mcisaaci*) present in many
males and in all females; pale postmedian band more prominent
than in *inornata* and *mcisaaci;* size large.
Larva: — Adults in early August.
Range: — Maritime provinces (TL Bathurst, New Brunswick
in a salt marsh).

THE WOOD NYMPH (GRAYLING). *Cercyonis pegala* Fabricius
pp. 48, 49, 64
2.0–2.75 in. The Wood Nymph, although essentially a woodland species, often occurs in meadows as well. The butterflies
frequently alight on tree trunks; and this, with their fast, very
irregular flight and skill at dodging, makes them sometimes difficult to catch. A number of the forms here placed under the
one species, *pegala*, have heretofore been treated as separate
species. *Alope*, in particular, has been separated from *pegala;*
and *nephele, maritima,* and *carolina* placed as either subspecies
or forms of *alope*. It seems best, however, to "lump" all into
one broadly distributed, clinal species. Actually no clear-cut
boundaries exist between contiguous forms, but instead, blend
zones of varying width in which many intermediate forms occur.
The generic name will remain in some doubt until there has been
a thorough revision of the Old World forms as well as those of
the New World. Both *Satyrus* Latreille and *Minois* Huebner
have been widely used.
Larva: — Downy, yellowish green with four lighter, lengthwise
stripes; the anal fork reddish. **Food:** — Grasses. One brood
(perhaps two in south). Adults in late June. Hibernation as
newly hatched larva.
Range: — Hudsonian Zone in Canada s. throughout our area
into Mexico.
Subspecies: — *C. p. pegala* (TL "America") Florida and Gulf
States n. to North Carolina and (blend zone with *alope*) New Jersey in coastal plain; northern limits in Mississippi Valley uncertain; large, brightly colored, with tendency to reduce or lose lower
ocellus in orange FW patch; ocellus of HW above prominent.
C. p. texana Edwards Southwest, Texas, n. to Kansas; like *pegala*
but markings beneath more clear cut and distinct; paler colored.
C. p. carolina Chermock & Chermock (TL Conestee Falls,
North Carolina) southern Appalachian Mountains; paler brown
than *alope* and *pegala;* a minor form. *C. p. alope* Fabricius (TL
"India") Virginia (mountains) and New Jersey n. to Maine and
Quebec (coastal plain) and New York (inland); blends with
maritima along its eastern limits, with *nephele* northward, with
carolina and *pegala* southward; smaller, not so richly colored as
pegala, both ocelli in orange patch of FW well developed. *C. p.
maritima* Edwards (TL Martha's Vineyard, Massachusetts)
coastal edge, Maryland to Maine; like *alope*, but with FW patch

deeper orange. *C. p. nephele* Kirby (TL "Canada") FW dark, lacking yellow orange patch (but ocelli present); New York and New England (mountains) n. and w. through northern Mississippi Valley and Canada to Hudsonian Zone. Note: the above forms represent merely averages. Intermediates not only occur abundantly in blend zones but also may occur anywhere in an area. Sometimes in blend zones local colonies of one form or another seem to be segregated out. A terrific amount of work is needed on the distributional problems of this clinal species.

Genus Œneis *Huebner:*

The Arctics

LIKE *Erebia*, *Boloria*, and *Colias*, this is a genus of predominantly Arctic (and Alpine) butterflies. Drab colors, extreme hairiness, and ability to withstand the most rigorously cold climate mark the "Arctics." The larvæ are stout bodied, thickly covered with short hairs, and conspicuously marked lengthwise with broken stripes. All species are single brooded, feed on grasses and hibernate as larvæ. The adults are sometimes difficult to identify by color and pattern. The genitalia of both sexes offer good grouping characters; but no thorough work on these has yet been published, so that we are a little vague about some relationships.

MACOUN'S ARCTIC. *Œneis macounii* Edwards p. 64
2.2 in. The largest of our species, *macounii* is the only one in which the males lack a darker sex patch along the lower part of the cell of the FW above. Grassy, Canadian Zone meadows, perhaps favoring wet or boggy ones.
Range: — Subarctic w. and central Canada s. to northern shore of Lake Superior (Nipigon), Isle Royale, northern Minnesota and Michigan. Adults in early July. (TL Lake Nipigon)

CHRYXUS ARCTIC. *Œneis chryxus* Doubleday p. 64
1.8 in. Like *macounii*, *chryxus* is subarctic rather than truly Arctic. The presence of a darker sex patch and the bright, orange-brown coloration distinguish it in our area. It occurs in meadows and grassy, open hillsides. A fairly accessible place to find it is in the grassy, Alpine Zone on Mt. Albert, Gaspé Peninsula, Quebec. I have found it here in early to mid-July, associated with *Papilio brevicauda*, *Œneis taygete*, and similar northern forms.
Range: — Arctic, s. to Gaspé (mountains), south-central Canada, northern Michigan.
Subspecies: — *O. c. calais* Scudder (TL James Bay) the eastern and northern subspecies, larger; wings duller and darker colored,

especially basally. *O. c. strigulosus* McDunnough (TL Gull
Lake, Minden, Ontario) late May-early June, the central and
western subspecies of our area; smaller, brighter colored. Other
subspecies occur westward.

WHITE VEINED ARCTIC. *Œneis taygete* Geyer   p. 64
1.75 in.   Dull, grayish brown above, lacking ocelli; boldly
marked on the HW beneath with black, gray and white, the
veins white-lined; dark band on HW beneath abruptly produced outward below M_1.
Range: — Arctic Canada s. to Labrador and Gaspé (mountains),
also Rocky Mountains and Alaska.
Subspecies: — *O. t. taygete* (TL Hopedale, Labrador) Baffin
Island s. to Gulf of St. Lawrence, w. to e. side James Bay and Hudson Bay; smaller; less mottled and lighter, yellow-brown above;
median band narrower on HW beneath; white areas and lines of
HW beneath more contrasting. *O. t. gaspeensis* dos Passos
(TL Mt. Albert, Gaspé, Quebec); larger; wings above darker,
chocolate brown, more mottled; HW beneath with median band
wider but light areas and veins less extensive and contrasting.

JUTTA ARCTIC *Œneis jutta* Huebner   p. 65
1.9 in.   A wide ranging, circumpolar species of both Old and
New Worlds, *jutta* extends farther south than most other *Œneis*,
occurring in Maine and New Hampshire in acid, "muskeg"
bogs.   Grayish brown; wings above with a more or less interrupted, submarginal, orange-brown band; ocelli of FW above
prominent.   Adults have a strong, erratic flight and are very
wary and hard even to approach, let alone to catch. They often
alight on tree trunks.   When you have chased one through a
bog, sinking to your knees at every step in saturated sphagnum
moss, hurdling small tamaracks and black spruces, and dodging
around larger ones, tripping over clumps of heaths, and boring
through a cloud of bloodthirsty blackflies, you have earned your
specimen — if you catch it. Adults in mid to late June.
Range: — Arctic s. to Newfoundland, Nova Scotia, Maine and
New Hampshire, perhaps northern Michigan.
Subspecies: — *O. j. jutta* (TL Lappland) does not occur in
North America.   *O. j. terra-novæ* dos Passos (TL Doyle's Station,
Newfoundland) Newfoundland; larger, darker; with wider, sub-
marginal, cadmium yellow band on wings above. *O. j. ridingiana*
Chermock and Chermock (TL Riding Mountains, Manitoba)
Manitoba and eastward; submarginal band of wings above deeper
ochreous than *j. jutta*, more distinctly broken into spots.

POLIXENES ARCTIC. *Œneis polixenes* Fabricius   p. 65
1.6 in.   Widely distributed in the Arctic; one isolated colony on
Mt. Katahdin, Maine.   Wings above broadly shaded submarginally with yellowish brown, ocelli reduced; a series of indistinct, light submarginal dots between veins, stronger on HW.

Beneath, HW and apex of FW yellowish brown, shaded with whitish, marbled and scrawled with dark brown; dark transverse band fairly well defined basally, its outer edge more regularly scalloped than in *melissa*. The race on Mt. Katahdin occurs above timberline.

Subspecies: — *O. p. polixenes* (TL "America Boreali," probably Labrador) Arctic s. to Labrador; larger, darker, submarginal light areas above darker, orange brown, not prominent, with darker, diffuse spot-row between them and margin, especially on HW. *O. p. katahdin* Newcomb (TL Mt. Katahdin, Maine) Mt. Katahdin only; smaller, lighter colors more contrasty; submarginal dark ocellate spots on FW above more prominent.

MELISSA ARCTIC. *Œneis melissa* Fabricius   pp. 48, 65
1.7 in. Widely distributed in the Arctic of both Old and New Worlds, s. to Labrador and, in one isolated colony, to New Hampshire. Wings dull, dark brown above, with no ocelli. Beneath smoky to blackish brown, the HW and apex of FW marbled and reticulated with blackish; transverse blackish band of HW margined both basally and outwardly with whitish, its outer edge more irregularly and finely scalloped than in *polixenes*. The race of the White Mountains, New Hampshire, is famous as the "White Mountain Butterfly."

Subspecies: — *O. m. melissa* (TL Newfoundland) very rare in Newfoundland, less rare in Labrador; large, wings pale brownish, wings fairly heavily scaled; *O. m. assimilis* Butler (TL Repulse Bay–Northern Hudson Bay); northern Arctic; smaller than *m. melissa*, very blackish gray above and very heavily scaled. *O. m. semplei* Holland (TL Little Cape Jones R., east coast, Hudson Bay); east coast Hudson Bay and Churchill, Manitoba; smaller than *m. melissa*, very brownish above with more tendency to orange brown in ♀ ♀; heavily scaled. *O. m. semidea* Say (TL White Mountains, New Hampshire); Alpine summits of White Mountains; smaller than *m. melissa*, larger than *m. assimilis* and *m. semplei;* brownish; wings thinly scaled; dark basal area of HW more set apart by postmedian light shade outwardly. Because of a good motor road, Mt. Washington in early July is one place where anyone can catch an *Œneis*.

Genus Erebia *Dalman:* The Alpines

LIKE *Œneis*, this is chiefly a genus of far northern species; but some Western species range southward at lower elevations. In the East, however, no *Erebia* occur southward even on Alpine summits, as do some *Œneis*. Adults are characteristically brownish black, with ocelli and other markings of brownish orange to red. Veins R_3–R_4

are typically stalked and, because of a considerable basal projection of M_2, the cell of the forewing often looks forked terminally. The larvæ are rather plain, usually unmarked or lightly striped, the head large and the body tapering. In some species the pupa is enclosed in a rudimentary cocoon of a few strands of silk. All appear to be one-brooded.

RED DISKED ALPINE. *Erebia discoidalis* Kirby p. 81
1.8 in. Brownish black above; FW with costal margin, and a broad, central shade from base to apex and outer margin, brownish red; HW with whitish marks along costa; wings beneath brown, shaded and irrorated outwardly with gray.
Range: — Arctic and subarctic America, chiefly from Hudson Bay westward, s. to central Minnesota (Itasca Park, 31 May). One brood, adults mid-May to mid-June. (TL Cumberland House, Lat. 57° N.)

ROSS' ALPINE. *Erebia rossii* Curtis p. 81
1.6 in. Wings brownish black above and beneath; FW with one or two subapical ocelli in male, two or three in female, brownish red. HW beneath with a pale, often indistinct, postmedian grayish band.
Range: — Arctic and subarctic Asia and America, e. to Baffin Island.
Subspecies: — *E. r. rossii* (TL Boothia Peninsula) Arctic North America; *E. r. ornata* Leussler (TL Churchill, Manitoba) Churchill, probably other subarctic localities; the two subapical ocelli on the FW above almost always fuse into one large ocellus.

THEANO ALPINE. *Erebia theano* Tauschenberg
1.5 in. Wings above brown; FW with no ocelli, but a well-defined, prominent, postmedian band of elongated, orange red patches; HW with this band prominent on costal half, reduced or absent on posterior half. FW beneath with upper side pattern more or less repeated, paler; HW beneath with one cellular and a number of postmedian spots, creamy white. Widely distributed in the Old and New World Arctic, *theano* (TL Altai Mountains, Siberia) enters our area only in Manitoba, where it occurs south to at least the central part of the province as subspecies *canadensis* Warren (*sofia* Strecker). (TL north of Churchill, Manitoba.)

COMMON ALPINE. *Erebia epipsodea* Butler
1.8 in. Wings above sooty brown, with three or four prominent ocelli, broadly surrounded by red, forming postmedian bands on both FW and HW. A common species of the north and of the Rocky Mountains, where it occurs in meadows at lower elevations than other Erebias.
Range: — Alaska and western Canada, e. to Manitoba and per-

haps western Ontario, s. in mountains into New Mexico. (TL "Rocky Mts.")

DISA ALPINE. *Erebia disa* Thunberg
The subspecies *mancina* Westwood (TL "Rocky Mts.") of disa circumpolar species has been taken as far southeastward as Smoky Falls, Mattagami R., Ontario (29 June). Wings above blackish brown, more or less suffused basally with reddish; FW with three or four ocelli broadly surrounded with dark red; HW with no ocelli or spots. FW beneath deep reddish brown; HW beneath dusted with gray, a more or less distinct, post-median, gray band, a white spot on costa and another in cell near outer end.

Family Danaidæ: The Monarchs

ALTHOUGH only one species occurs over most of our area, that one is the familiar (and famous) Monarch. Typically Danaids are large butterflies, with a slow, deliberate flight as befits insects so "protected" by bad tasting body fluids that they have little to fear from birds. The family is large and worldwide, but chiefly tropical. They are, perhaps, the most specialized of our butterflies. The forelegs, greatly reduced in both sexes, end in peculiar spiny knobs in the females. The males of our species possess a patch of scent scales (*androconia*) on each hindwing below vein Cu₂, and an extensible hair pencil on each side of the last abdominal segment that can be rubbed on the scent scales to disperse odors. The antennæ are naked with the club weakly swollen. The eggs are stout, elongate, truncate cones, with many ribs and crosslines. The larvæ are naked, usually brightly colored, with paired, fleshy filaments. The pupæ are stout, taper rapidly to the end of the abdomen, and are suspended by the cremaster alone. The larvæ feed on *Asclepiadaceæ* (Milkweeds) and *Solanaceæ* (Nightshades), plants with milky, acrid, poisonous juices, and are therefore highly "protected" from predatory enemies. The family has also been called the *Lymnadidæ*.

MONARCH or MILKWEED BUTTERFLY. *Danaus plexippus*
Linnæus pp. 48, 49, 81
3.5–3.9 in. No butterfly is more familiar to more people than the Monarch, because of its large size, bright colors, fondness for flowers and wide distribution. Its flight is slow and sailing, but powerful as befits a long-distance champion. Perhaps it is best known for the great swarms of thousands of individuals that gather for the night during the autumn mass migrations southward. The northward migration in spring, a more protracted and individual affair, is less noticed. The adults overwinter in

the most southern parts of our area, but then do not all make the entire trip north; instead they fly part way, lay eggs, and die. Their progeny then fly north, even far into Canada, and breed in turn. Perhaps a few adults or pupæ hibernate in the north. Monarchs have been recorded hundreds of miles out in the Atlantic or Pacific. That they cross these oceans unaided is improbable; but the species has occupied Ascension Island, the Canaries, and the Azores, and occurs frequently in western Europe. It has spread across the entire Pacific from Hawaii, where it was presumably introduced about 1850, to Formosa and the Andaman Islands.

The scientific name of the Monarch has caused as much discussion as that of any other butterfly; even today authorities differ strongly. I follow the ruling of the International Commission on Zoological Nomenclature. You may find the Monarch referred to as *Anosia*, *Danaus*, or *Diogas*, *archippus*, *plexippus*, or (southern) *nigrippus*. His androconia doubtless smell just as sweet to his lady, no matter what we call him.

The "protected," conspicuous Monarch is "mimicked" by the Viceroy, *Limenitis archippus*.

Larva: — The early stages, all figured here, are found on Milkweeds (*Asclepias*) of various species, sometimes on Dogbane (*Apocynum*) or Green Milkweed (*Acerates*). Adults may be expected (Lat. 40°) in late April or early May, the southward migration in mid September.

Range: — North America, n. to central Canada in the east.

Subspecies: — Our Monarch is *D. p. plexippus* Huebner. The subspecies of Central and northern South America is *D. p. megalippe* Huebner (*nigrippus* Hænsch) with shorter (46mm), broader forewing with white subapical spots. Specimens resembling this occur as far north as New Jersey. We are dealing with a "cline," with an enormous "blend zone" between northern and southern forms. We should refer to *all* North American specimens as race *plexippus*, no matter what their appearance.

QUEEN. *Danaus gilippus* Cramer   p. 81
3.1–3.3 in. Easily distinguished from the Monarch by its darker brown ground color (so tnat the veins are less prominent) and its lack of the darker, apical shading and the dark inner margin of the FW. A common species of the far south, with the same habits and slow, soaring flight as the Monarch, the Queen is not migratory. In Florida, where the Queen is the dominant "protected" Danaid, the "mimicking" Viceroy is also a darker brown, while in the north, where the lighter colored Monarch is dominant, the Viceroy is lighter colored too.

Similar species: — *Danaus eresimus* has a proportionately shorter cell; is paler limbally than basally; the black veins of the HW beneath are not bordered with white except to about half way between cell and outer margin, making a postmedian series of whitish marks.

Larva: — Brownish-white, cross striped with brown and yellow; a greenish yellow stripe along the side; paired, fleshy filaments on mesothoracic and second and eighth abdominal segments.

Food: — Milkweeds, (*Asclepias*), *Nerium, Funastrum, Vincetoxicum, Philabertia, Stapelia.* Three broods (Florida), adults in late March.

Range: — s. Georgia, Florida, Gulf Strip, Mississippi Valley n. to Kansas (uncommon) and Nebraska (accidental).

Subspecies: — *D. g. berenice* Cramer, (TL "Jamaica") veins of HW above not white edged; white spots in HW border above much reduced; southeastern United States (and Cuba). *D. g. strigosus* Bates (TL Guatemala), HW veins above white-edged; spots in HW border larger; Mexico into Texas and Mississippi Valley, w. to Arizona and California. *D. g. gilippus* (TL Rio de Janeiro, Brazil) not in our area.

Danaus eresimus Cramer   p. 81

3.1–3.3 in. Occurring only in the extreme southern part of our area, *eresimus* is common in southern Texas (Pharr), September to December.

Similar Species: — see *D. gilippus*

Subspecies: — *D. e. montezuma* Talbot, Panama to Texas, postmedian paler patches on HW beneath conspicuously white scaled along veins, sometimes reduced to their white edges, spots at end of cell similar, often large; no postmedian spots on FW below vein M_3. *D. e. tethys* Forbes, Antillean, has been recorded from Florida; one safe record is near Royal Palm State Park (R.L.C.) postmedian patches of HW beneath evenly colored, those at end of cell small; FW with pale or white spots in cells below veins M_3, Cu_1, sometimes Cu_2.

Family Heliconiidæ: The Heliconians

THERE IS no more interesting group of butterflies than the tropical Heliconians. Brilliant colors and patterns characterize the group in a riot of mimicry. Not only are the Heliconians mimicked by dozens of species of butterflies and even moths of many families, but they mimic each other! A number of species will, in one locality, converge on a common pattern, but in another locality the same species will be found all looking the same as each other, in different guise. This makes it easier for predators to learn to leave all *Heliconius* alone but drives the entomologist crazy when he tries to classify the various forms. This is termed *Müllerian mimicry.* Our Zebra is a worthy representative of this great genus.

Some authorities place Heliconians as a subfamily of the *Nymphalidæ;* others recognize the family rank of *Heliconius* and its

BUTTERFLY STRUCTURES AND EARLY STAGES

1. **EGG OF VICEROY** (*Limenitis archippus*) on the tip of a Willow leaf. Greatly magnified. See also Nos. 7 & 8 below.   p. 114
2. **ADULT FEMALE, ATLANTIS FRITILLARY** (*Speyeria atlantis*) with the legs extended. Note the tiny, almost useless front leg, characteristic of the Family *Nymphalidæ*.   p. 86
3. **ADULT and PUPA SHELL of GREAT SPANGLED FRITILLARY** (*Speyeria cybele*). The pupa was found among dead leaves on the ground. The butterfly has just spread and hardened its wings. Note that it uses only the middle and hind legs (see No. 2, above).   p. 87
4. **LARVA OF SILVER-SPOTTED SKIPPER** (*Epargyreus clarus*) preparing its "cocoon" just before changing to the pupa stage. Skippers like this make the nearest to a cocoon of any of our butterflies.   p. 206
5. **YOUNG LARVA OF SPICEBUSH SWALLOWTAIL** (*Papilio troilus*). At this age the brown and white larva looks very much like a bird dropping. It may escape the notice of birds and other enemies because of this.   p. 178
6. **FULL GROWN LARVA OF SPICEBUSH SWALLOWTAIL** (*Papilio troilus*). At this age the green and yellow larva, which lives in a one-leaf nest, bears a striking resemblance to the head of the common Green Snake. Perhaps it derives some protection from enemies because of this.   p. 178
7 & 8. **VERY YOUNG LARVA and "HIBERNACULUM" OF VICEROY** (*Limenitis archippus*). In the autumn the larva makes its "hibernaculum" by eating away the terminal part of a Willow leaf, and folding the basal part to make a tube. This is lined with silk and fastened firmly to the twig. In it the tiny larva spends the winter. You can find them by inspecting upland Willow bushes after the leaves have fallen.   p. 114

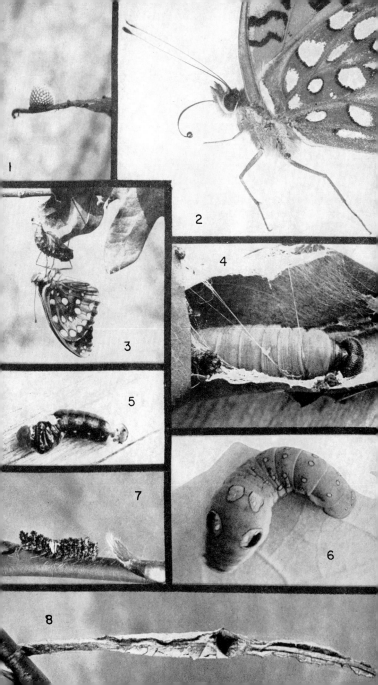

1

2

3

4

5

7

6

8

Plate 10   81

MONARCHS, SATYRS AND HELICONIANS
Families *Danaidae, Satyridae & Heliconiidae*
Some illustrations reduced to ¾ natural size

1. **MONARCH,** *Danaus plexippus*   p. 77
   Upper side, ♂ × ¾ (Scranton, Pa.). Orange brown with black borders
   and veins; spots mostly white. Entire continent n. to centr. Can.
2. **QUEEN,** *Danaus gilippus berenice*   p. 78
   Upper side, ♂ × ¾, (Key Largo, Fla.). Dark reddish brown; black
   borders & veins; white spots. Fla. to Tex., straying n. to Nebr.
3. **ERESIMUS,** *Danaus eresimus*   p. 79
   Upper side, ♂, × ¾ (Brownsville, Tex.). Orange brown, darker &
   more reddish basally. See text. S. Tex. & (accidental?) Fla.
4. **EYED BROWN,** *Lethe eurydice*   p. 68
   Upper & under sides, ♂, × 1 (Sharon, Conn.). Above brown with
   lighter shades; beneath lighter brown, dark brown lines; eyespots
   with lighter rings. S. Can. s. to n. Fla.
5. **ROSS' ALPINE,** *Erebia rossii*   p. 76
   Upper side, ♂, × 1 (Churchill, Man.). Brownish black; eyespots
   ringed with brownish red. Arctic & Subarctic.
6. **RED DISKED ALPINE,** *Erebia discoidalis*   p. 76
   Upper side, ♂, × 1 (Edmonton, Alberta). Brownish black; costal
   margin & discal shade of FW brownish red. Arctic & Subarctic.
7. **INORNATE RINGLET,** *Ceononympha tullia inornata*   p. 71
   Upper & under sides, ♂, × 1 (Charlton, Ont.). Olive brown above,
   FW basally and discally ochre brown. Canada, see text.
8. **ZEBRA,** *Heliconius charitonius tuckeri* Comstock & Brown   p. 82
   Upper side, paratype ♂, × ¾ (Sandspur, Winter Park, Fla.). Black
   with yellow stripes. S.C. through Fla. & Tex. southward.
9. **JULIA,** *Dryas julia cillene*   p. 83
   Upper side, ♂, × ¾ (Key Largo, Fla.). Bright, satiny orange brown
   with dark brown markings. Female much duller colored. Southern
   Fla. & (*delila*) Tex.
10. **GULF FRITILLARY,** *Agraulis vanillæ nigrior*   p. 82
    Upper side, ♂, × ¾ (Key Largo, Fla.). Bright orange brown with
    dark brown markings. HW beneath with very large, bright silvery
    spots. N.J. Minn. & Iowa southward.

tropical relative *Eueides* but place *Dryas* and *Agraulis* as Nymphalids. Inclusion of all in the *Heliconiidæ* seems warranted primarily on the basis of larval and pupal characters, as well as on genitalic structures.

All have large heads and long, slender forewings; and most are brilliantly colored and marked with black, red, yellow, blue, or orange brown. All are "protected" butterflies with poisonous body juices, and are left alone by predators. The cell of the hindwing is closed by cross veins in *Heliconius*, open in the other genera. The humeral vein of the hindwing is simple, curved towards the base. The front legs are reduced and nonfunctional as in *Nymphalidæ*. The egg is long, slender, and subcylindrical. The larva is slender, with several rows of extremely long, branching spines. The pupa is most bizarre, with protruding wing cases, a highly irregular shape, and many tubercles. The larvæ feed on various species of Passion Flowers (*Passiflora*).

ZEBRA. *Heliconius charitonius* Linnæus   p. 81
    Field Marks: — 3.0–3.4 in. Cannot be confused with any other butterfly in our area. Flies in deep woods or around their edges, never far from cover. The flight is slow and fluttering with extremely shallow wing beats. A Zebra can, however, dodge into cover very expertly and can make good speed when alarmed. Zebras gather to sleep in colonies at night, scattering to feed during the day.
    Larva: — White, with transverse brown or black spots and six rows of slender black, branching spines. Pupa brown, angular, with two flat projections from the head and numerous gold-tipped spines. By wriggling the pupa is able to make a distinct creaking sound. **Food:** — Passion Flowers (*Passiflora*). Two, three or more broods.
    Range: — Southern South Carolina s. through Florida; also Texas, straying n. to Kansas; occurs in most of tropical America.
    Subspecies: — *H. c. charitonius* (TL St. Thomas, Virgin Islands) does not occur in our area. *H. c. tuckeri* Comstock & Brown (TL Winter Park, Florida) has the yellow bands much narrower than in any other race; the band above Cu₂ of the FW is broken in about ninety per cent of the specimens. Fewer Florida females show a rusty orange tinge of the yellow. In *H. c. vazquezæ* Comstock & Brown (TL Campeche, Campeche, Mexico) the yellow markings are broader, the band above Cu₂ is never broken, and the females more frequently are orange tinged. *Tuckeri* is the race of the Eastern part of our area; *vazquezæ* occurs in the western (Texas to Kansas) part.

GULF FRITILLARY. *Agraulis vanillæ* Linnæus   pp. 49, 81
2.6–2.8 in. In coloration and pattern *vanillæ* is distinctive. Wings above, bright orange brown with dark brown and black markings; FW beneath deepening to crimson basally; HW beneath with *large, elongated spots of brilliant, metallic silver.* Female darker, with

heavier dark markings. A common, fast-flying butterfly of open spaces, quite addicted to flower visiting.

Larva: — Brownish yellow, striped with brownish; six rows of branching spines on body, and a pair of longer ones, curving backward on head. **Food:** — Various Passion Flowers (*Passiflora*). Three (or more?) broods in South. First adults in February–March (Florida).

Range: — Argentina n. to New Jersey, Minnesota and Iowa, rare in northern states.

Subspecies: — Eastern area specimens are *A. v. nigrior* Michener (TL Upper Matecumbe Key, Florida). In the Southwest and California is *A. v. incarnata* Riley (TL Durango City, Mexico), with which our eastern specimens intergrade in Texas, Arkansas, Missouri, etc.

JULIA. *Dryas julia* Fabricius   p. 81

3.2–3.7 in. Wings above bright brownish orange (♂) or light olivaceous brown (♀); beneath pale, dull brown. The flight is strong, rapid, and wide-ranging. The butterflies are strongly addicted to flower visiting. In November, 1946, I saw a swarm of this species which lined the roadsides in the Florida Keys for many miles.

Larva: — poorly known; possesses long, branching spines.

Food: — Passion Flowers (*Passiflora*). Two or more broods.

Range: — In our area, southern Florida (*cillene*) and southern Texas (*delila*).

Subspecies: — *D. j. julia* is South American. *D. j. cillene* Cramer (TL "Surinam") Cuba and southern Florida (chiefly in the Keys); as illustrated. *D. j. delila* Fabricius (TL Jamaica) and form *moderata* Stichel, Jamaica and Central America n. into southern Texas; dark markings of wings above greatly reduced, sometimes absent.

Family Nymphalidæ: The Brush-Footed Butterflies

THIS IS the largest family of the true butterflies. It includes many familiar species, most of them medium-sized to large. The front legs are greatly reduced in both sexes, as in the *Satyridæ*, *Danaiidæ*, and *Heliconiidæ*, and are often hairy and brushlike (hence the common name). Except in one small subfamily, the *Ergolinæ*, no wing veins are swollen basally as in Satyrs. The cell of the hindwing is usually open. The antennæ are scaled and definitely, often very strongly, clubbed. The larvæ do not bear fleshy filaments, but many have branching spines. The pupæ, which have conspicuous projections, hang from the cremaster alone. So numerous and varied are the members of the family that few generalizations can be made about appearance, habits, and environments. In many of our species the colors run to a rich, orange brown with dark markings. The majority are fast, strong fliers, and visit flowers freely. Most are more than one-brooded. Few are very rare, excepting those which barely reach our area. Some are rather restricted in habitat, but others range over a wide variety of environments. One, the Painted Lady (*V. cardui*), is the most cosmopolitan of butterflies.

The classification within the family is rather confused, what with "splitters," "lumpers," and various workers who attach great importance to larval characters, or venation or genitalia alone. The following is somewhat of a compromise. Our knowledge is too incomplete to warrant any extreme classifications.

SUBFAMILY NYMPHALINÆ:

Tribe Argynnidi:	*Euptoieta, Speyeria, Boloria*
Tribe Melitæidi:	*Euphydryas, Melitæa, Phyciodes, Chlosyne*
Tribe Nymphalidi:	*Hypolimnas, Polygonia, Nymphalis, Vanessa, Precis, Anartia, Metamorpha, Hypanartia*

SUBFAMILY ERGOLINÆ: *Myscelia, Dynamine, Diæthria, Eunica, Mestra, Hamadryas, Biblis*

SUBFAMILY LIMENITINÆ:

Tribe Liminitidi:	*Limenitis, Adelpha, Smyrna, Historis*
Tribe Charaxidi:	*Anæa*
Tribe Apaturidi:	*Chlorippe, Asterocampa*

VARIEGATED FRITILLARY. *Euptoieta claudia* Cramer

pp. 48, 49, 96

2.25 in. The *Euptoietas* are closely related to *Speyeria*, the true Northern Fritillaries, but always lack silver spots beneath. *Claudia* is a wide ranging fast flyer, not easily caught except at flowers. It prefers open fields and roadsides.

Similar Species: — *E. hegesia* lacks the dark basal area of the wings above followed by a paler band, and has the basal half of the HW above nearly unmarked.

Larva: — Orange red; two dark stripes on each side enclosing white spots; six rows of dark spines, the front pair of the dorsal row larger, longer and pointing forward. **Food:** — Violets and Pansies (*Viola*), sometimes destructive; Passion Flower (*Passiflora*), May Apple (*Podophyllum*), Beggar Ticks (*Meibomia*), Purslane (*Portulaca*), Stonecrop (*Sedum*), Moonseed (*Menispermum*). Two or three broods, adults in early Spring; hibernation as adult.

Range: — Eastern United States, uncommon or rare north of Virginia, Illinois, and Minnesota, common southward (Tl Jamaica).

MEXICAN FRITILLARY. *Euptoieta hegesia* Cramer   p 96

2.25 in. A common tropical species, breeding in our area in southern Texas (Pharr, Brownsville).

Similar Species: — see *E. claudia*.

Subspecies: — *E. h. hegesia* (TL Jamaica), the subspecies of Cuba, the Bahamas and Jamaica, apparently does not occur in the United States. *E. h. hoffmanni* W. P. Comstock (TL Escuinapa, Sinaloa, Mexico) is the mainland subspecies, northward into Texas; larger, greater tonal contrasts in coloration, basal area deeply colored, followed by paler band.

Genus Speyeria *Scudder:* The Greater Fritillaries (Silverspots)

MEDIUM SIZE to large. Most of the species are orange brown with blackish, transverse, zigzag lines and rows of spots, and metallic silver spots beneath. Most females have paler ground color and heavier dark markings and basal suffusion. The cell of the HW is closed by a fine cross vein. The flight is swift and powerful. Most species, occurring chiefly in open meadows, are eager flower visitors. The larvæ are velvety, dark brown or black, with six rows of blackish, barbed spines, those of the dorsum of the prothorax shorter. As far as is known all feed only at night, on various species of violets, hide by day away from the food plant. All hibernate as newly hatched larvæ and are technically single-brooded. However, from the time of the first emergence of adults there is a more or less uninterrupted sequence of others emerging for two to three months, so that this so-called "single brood" is very extensive. In one (*cybele*) there is something of a break in the sequence of emergences, so that in a way this species is partially double brooded.

Until recently all our Nearctic species were placed in the genus *Argynnis* with related Old World species. They are now classed in *Speyeria* with two subgenera *S.* (*Speyeria*) and *S.* (*Semnopsyche*), the latter "having a secondary bursa copulatrix in the female." If, as many workers prefer, our species are to be kept in *Argynnis*, *Speyeria* and *Semnopsyche* should still be used as subgenera. There are many North American species, most of them wide-ranging and geographically varied. The subspecific classification is puzzling, particularly in the west, since in most of the species the distribution is partly "discontinuous" with formation of isolated subspecies, and partly "continuous" with intergrading, clinal forms. I have followed very largely the only recent major work, that of dos Passos and Grey (American Museum Novitates No. 1370, 1947).

REGAL FRITILLARY. *Speyeria idalia* Drury   pp. 49, 96
3.4–3.6 in. *Idalia* with its velvety, blue-black hindwing cannot
be mistaken for any other species. The marginal row of spots
of the HW above of the male is typically fulvous; of the female
creamy white like the submarginal row. *Idalia* favors open,
grassy fields near wet meadows or marshy areas, is likely to be
quite local, occurring in rather restricted colonies. Adults fly
from mid June to mid September. The flight is a bit slower
and more gliding than that of its congeners. The females deposit
the eggs on a variety of plants, but probably always near violets.
Early Stages: — see the genus description.
Range: — Maine to Nebraska and South Dakota, s. to North
Carolina, Georgia (?) and Arkansas (TL New York City, N.Y.).

ATLANTIS FRITILLARY. *Speyeria atlantis* Edwards pp. 65, 80
2.7–2.9 in. A more northern, Canadian Zone species, *atlantis*
is sometimes confused with *aphrodite*. It has the outer marginal
border of the FW above more nearly solid black, not consisting
largely of a fulvous line between two black ones; has a darker
ground color above; and on the HW beneath has the ground
color a dark purplish brown (not reddish brown as in *aphrodite*)
with somewhat more extensive silver spots. Adults June to
September.
Similar Species: — *S. aphrodite,* see above.
Early Stages: — see genus description.
Range: — Maritime Provinces s. in mountains to Virginia w.
to Michigan, Minnesota, Alberta, Oregon, California and s.
through Rocky Mountains.
Subspecies: — *S. a. atlantis* (TL Catskill Mountains, New
York) Maritime Province s. to Virginia, w. to Wisconsin. *S. a.
canadensis* dos Passos (TL Doyle's Sta., Newfoundland) New-
foundland, darker, dark markings heavier. *S. a. hollandi*
Chermock and Chermock (TL Riding Mountains, Manitoba)
Manitoba, marginal border of FW above consistently black,
ground color of HW beneath darker black brown than *a. atlantis.*
See also *S. lais* in the section on Casual Species (p. 276).

DIANA. *Speyeria diana* Cramer   p. 65
3.7–3.8 in. The female departs radically from the usual coloration of the genus, being black basally and marked with blue
outwardly, the FW markings pale, almost white. This is cited
as a case of mimicry, the supposed model being the black and blue
Papilio philenor, a Swallowtail supposedly distasteful to birds.
Diana is essentially a woodland species. The Chermocks, who
found it in large numbers near Brevard, North Carolina, describe
the males as occurring only along woodland roads, where they
alight on sunlit patches of red clay. The females keep to the woods
and thickets. A strong, gliding flier, it is very wary, and little
attracted to flowers, but may be baited with manure or dung.

Early Stages: — see genus description.

Range: — Chiefly in mountains and piedmont, West Virginia s. to Georgia, w. to southern Ohio, Indiana, Missouri and Arkansas (TL Jamestown, Virginia).

GREAT SPANGLED FRITILLARY. *Speyeria cybele* Fabricius
pp. 48, 65, 80

3.3–3.7 in. The most familiar of our Silverspots, *cybele* is marked by its size, its somewhat less reddish ground color, the heavy, black sex scaling of the veins of the central area of the FW above in the males, the greater width of the light, submarginal band of the HW beneath, and the lack of a submedian, dark spot below the cell on the FW above. *Cybele* favors wet meadows, open spaces and roadsides, but strays widely, visiting flowers avidly. It appears earlier than its congeners, flies from mid May to October.

Similar Species: — *S. aphrodite, atlantis.*

Early Stages: — see genus discussion.

Range: — Maritime Provinces s. in our area to North Carolina and Georgia (mountains), Tennessee, Arkansas and Oklahoma.

Subspecies: — *S. c. novascotiæ* McDunnough (TL White Point Beach, Queens Co., Nova Scotia) Nova Scotia, New Brunswick, Quebec, northern Maine; small, light submarginal band of HW beneath reduced in width. *S. c. cybele* (TL New York, N.Y.) New England s. to Georgia, w. to Great Plains except for northern Middle West and Manitoba; larger, colors bright, light submarginal band of HW beneath broad. *S. c. krautwurmi* Holland (TL Mackinac Co., Michigan) appears to be somewhat geographic, being most marked in the northern Mississippi Valley, but far from being a valid subspecies; is characterized by paler fulvous ground color of the females, contrasting strongly with darker basal areas. *S. c. pseudocarpenteri* Chermock & Chermock (TL Sand Ridge, Manitoba) likewise characterized by paler females, is also of slight subspecific value.

APHRODITE. *Speyeria aphrodite* Fabricius
p. 65

3.25 in. Somewhat more northern than *cybele, aphrodite* is also a common and familiar butterfly, ranging widely from the wet meadows that are, perhaps, its favorite haunt. It appears somewhat later in the season than *cybele*, flying from late June through September. Its flight is quicker than that of *cybele*, but it is less wary.

Similar Species: — see discussions under *atlantis* and *cybele*.

Early Stages: — see genus discussion.

Range: — Southern Canada s. to Georgia, Tennessee, Illinois, Indiana and Kansas; southward uncommon or rare and only in the mountains.

Subspecies: — *S. a. winni* Gunder (TL St. Calixte de Kilkenny, Quebec) eastern Canada; small, light submarginal band of HW beneath narrow; fringes black and white checkered, submarginal spots of FW above light colored in females; not a sharply marked "subspecies." *S. a. aphrodite* (TL New York, N.Y.) New England s. to North Carolina and Tennessee (mountains), w. through northern Ohio and other Middle West states to Nebraska, dark markings above not unduly heavy, light, submarginal band of HW beneath well defined. *S. a. alcestis* Edwards (TL Galena, Illinois) appears to be a subspecies of the *southern* belt of *aphrodite's* range across the Middle West, from western Pennsylvania to southern Wisconsin; the light submarginal band of the HW beneath is absent, filled in by the dark red brown basal color. *S. a. manitoba* Chermock & Chermock (TL Sand Ridge, Manitoba) or *mayæ* Gunder, Manitoba westward; smaller, HW beneath with ground color very pale, silver spots more prominently narrowly dark margined. All of these "subspecies" are stages in a cline, and show much intergradation.

Genus Boloria *Moore:* The Lesser Fritillaries

MUCH MORE northern than the closely related *Speyeria,* none of the species range far south, some are among the most arctic of insects. All are small, orange brown with black markings, resembling miniature Greater Fritillaries; but beneath most species lack silvered spots, and have instead complex patterns of red, brown, and white. Females have heavier dark markings.

The flight is normally slow and low, but can be fast and erratic. The variegated pattern seems to blur the outline of the wings, so that it is often curiously difficult to keep sight of an escaping specimen.

The larvæ are cylindrical with six rows of barbed spines on the abdomen, two to four on the thorax, and many short hairs. They feed by night, hide by day, hibernate either when newly hatched or half grown. Violets are the favorite food; but there are reports from other *Violaceæ,* as well as Rock Cress (*Arabis*), Strawberry, Spiræa, *Hedysarum,* Knotweed (*Polygonum*), Nettle (*Urtica*), Primrose (*Primula*), Burnet (*Sanguisorba*), Alpine Goldenrod (*Solidago cutleri*). There is but one brood in the far north; but the more southern species are two or three brooded. The brood sequence is complicated; some larvæ of the first brood finish growth normally, while others of the same brood enter a lethargic state when half grown, hibernate, finish growth the next spring.

Our North American species have long been called *Brenthis* Huebner; but this name should be restricted to a small Old World group, so that ours fall into the genus *Boloria* Moore (type *Papilio pales* Schiffermueller). This need not be split further into separate genera, although subgenera are fully warranted. The species of our area would thus be in the subgenus *Clossiana* Reuss (type *Papilio selene* Schiffermueller).

As would be expected in a group so essentially Arctic, many species occur all around the northern hemisphere from Labrador to Spain, via Alaska. There are a few related species in the colder and mountainous parts of South America and Africa.

SILVER BORDERED FRITILLARY. *Boloria selene* Schiffermueller   p. 112

1.5 in. *Selene* is common in marshy meadows and brushy swamps, strays to dry meadows and roadsides. In our area it and *toddi* extend farther south than any others of the genus.
Larva: Greenish brown, greenish mottled; dorso-lateral barbed spines of prothorax four times as long as others. **Food:** — Violets. Three broods, less in far north, one only in Maryland at southern limit of range in the coastal plain. Adults in mid May. Hibernation as either newly hatched or half grown larva.
Range: — Labrador, Quebec and Newfoundland w. to Alberta, s. to Maryland (coastal plain), North Carolina (mountains) and southern Illinois.
Subspecies: — *B. s. selene* is European. *B. s. terra-novæ* Holland, Newfoundland. Ground color of HW beneath dark, but bright, mahogany brown. *B. s. atrocostalis* Huard (TL Chicoutimi, Quebec) eastern and central Canada, northern New England, Michigan, Minnesota and Wisconsin, has dark markings above heavier, especially along costal and outer margins. *B. s. myrina* Cramer (TL New York) central New England w. to Nebraska, s. to Maryland, North Carolina (mountains) and southern Illinois, is the "average" form, figured here. *B. s. marilandica* A. H. Clark (TL Beltsville, Maryland) "larger, richer in color, dark markings heavier," one-brooded; merely a local form, now perhaps extinct. *B. s. nebraskensis* Holland (TL Dodge Co., Nebraska) much larger (Exp. 1.8–2.0 in.) otherwise much like *myrina*, apparently limited to eastern Nebraska.

BOG FRITILLARY. *Boloria eunomia* Esper   p. 112

1.5 in. The spots of the submarginal row of the HW beneath, and the front two or three of these spots on the FW beneath, are round and white, ringed with black; in other species these are solid black. In some *eunomia* the light spots beneath are silvered, but never as strongly as in *myrina*; and in *myrina* there is an extra row of silver spots, on the HW beneath, just basal of the row of spots mentioned above, not present in *eunomia*. In North America, at least, *eunomia* is primarily an acid bog species. It has a swift, "flickering" flight; is not easily caught when alarmed. Formerly called *B. aphirape* Huebner.
Range: — Arctic America, south to Labrador, Mt. Katahdin,

Maine, Quebec, Ontario and Manitoba; in Rocky Mountains to Colorado.

Subspecies: — *B. e. triclaris* Huebner (TL Labrador) arctic & subarctic; s. to Labrador and Churchill, Manitoba; dark markings narrow, ground color yellow brown, dark spots of HW beneath yellow brown to orange brown. *B. e. dawsoni* B. & McD. (TL Hymers, Ontario) southern Canadian; Mt. Katahdin, Maine, Ontario & southern Manitoba; ground color deeper orange brown, considerably suffused with black, black markings heavier, dark areas of HW beneath darker, richer red brown. Recorded particularly from bogs where collectors in northern states should watch for it in early July.

PURPLE LESSER FRITILLARY. *Boloria titania* Esper p. 112 1.6 in. The light spots of the HW beneath, particularly of the median band, are greatly invaded, sometimes obliterated, by the darker yellow brown or red brown ground color. The ground color above is orange brown, the dark markings tend to be heavy. In the Gaspé Peninsula, Quebec, where the species was first recorded by James Sanford, I have found it along roads through Black Spruce woodland about mid-July. Ontario records are from boggy areas; but the New Hampshire race occurs only at and above timberline in Alpine meadows; and in Minnesota and the Rockies it is common in high, grassy meadows, often wet, but not truly boggy. It may well occur in grassy or boggy meadows in northern New England localities. It appears to be very local.

In the literature most of the divisions of this species will be found called either distinct species or else subspecies of *B. chariclea*. The latter is, however, a probably distinct, more Arctic species with subspecies of its own. Our forms are conspecific with the European *B. titania* Esper. The "subspecies" in the East are not very distinct ones. Most are merely gradations in a cline; and even where there is geographic isolation the differences are relatively slight.

Similar Species: — see *B. chariclea*, below.

Range: — Northern North America, s. to Gaspé Peninsula, Quebec (Cascapedia R., July), Maritime Provinces, New Hampshire (mountains — July), Ontario, northern Minnesota, Manitoba; in Rockies s. to New Mexico.

Subspecies: — *B. t. boisduvalii* Duponchel (TL probably Labrador) Arctic s. to Labrador and Churchill, Manitoba; smaller, dark markings perhaps a trifle lighter; HW beneath with ground color orange brown to red brown. *B. t. grandis* B. & McD. (TL Hymers, Ontario) New Brunswick and Quebec (Gaspé), Ontario, northern Minnesota, s. Manitoba (mid June–July); larger, ground color above deeper, dark markings heavier, ground color of HW beneath rich deep purple brown to red brown, general coloration of HW beneath more contrasty.

B. t. montina Scudder (TL White Mountains, New Hampshire) Hudsonian Zone, Alpine summits, White Mountains; submarginal, triangular spots of wings above tending to fuse less with marginal line than in *grandis*, HW beneath lighter, more orange brown, not as deeply colored, less contrasty looking than in *grandis*, spots of median band and outer margin of HW beneath tending a little more to be white than in *grandis*. There is no great difference between *montina* and the eastern populations of *grandis;* and it is not until we study *grandis* from southern Manitoba westward that we see a form really distinct from the eastern populations.

ARCTIC FRITILLARY. *Boloria chariclea* Schneider p. 112
1.4 in. This is the most Arctic of our butterflies, having been taken at 81° 42′ north latitude. It is circumpolar, occurring in both Old and New Worlds. It is extremely variable, but the variation is largely individual, relatively slightly geographic. It has been, as noted above, much confused with *titania*, to which it is undoubtedly closely related.
Similar Species: — *B. chariclea* is smaller than *titania*, has more pointed forewings, narrower dark markings above, but the basal and median areas of the HW above are more heavily suffused with dark scaling. On the HW beneath the median spot row tends to be less obliterated by the dark ground color, a large costal spot, a long, pointed discal one, and some smaller ones posteriorly being white or silvery; and the postmedian spots also tend to be light, white, or silvery toward the costal half of the wing.
Range: — Arctic, s. to Baffin Island, northern Labrador and Southampton Island, Hudson Bay.
Subspecies: — *B. c. arctica* Zetterstedt (TL Greenland) appears to occupy all of the eastern Arctic, s. to Labrador; white markings of HW beneath more obscure, not greatly silvered if at all. *B. c. butleri* Edw. (TL Cape Thompson, N. W. Alaska) central and western Arctic; markings of HW beneath more clear cut, often silvered.

POLARIS FRITILLARY. *Boloria polaris* Boisduval p. 112
1.25 in. This is another circumpolar species, ranging around the Arctic from northern Norway to Greenland. It is easily identified by the rather narrow FW, the heavy basal and median dark suffusion of the HW above, and the large number of small, white markings on the HW beneath. It occurs farther southward than *chariclea*, being common at Churchill, Manitoba. It is said to have a rapid, somewhat erratic flight.
Range: — Arctic Norway to Greenland, via Alaska.
Subspecies: — I can see no consistent difference between *B. p. polaris* (TL Norwegian Alps, North Cape) and the two so-called "subspecies," *grœnlandica* Skinner 1892 (TL west coast of

Greenland) and *americana* Strand (TL Ellesmere Island, Jones Sound), or between any of the New World populations.

FREIJA FRITILLARY. *Boloria freija* Thunberg   p. 112
1.4 in. *Freija* is another circumpolar species of both Old and New Worlds. It extends farther to the south than either *chariclea* or *polaris*. Above, the ground color is somewhat paler than in most *Boloria*, the dark markings heavy and somewhat suffused, the basal and median areas of the hindwing considerably suffused with dark scales. On the HW beneath are a large, basal spot, a large submedian costal spot and a long, pointed, submedian discal spot, all white; the dark basal area is externally margined with black, followed by a pale, postmedian band; and the marginal spots are white. *Freija* is more easily recognized by its "look" than by details.

Range: — Arctic Regions, Norway and Lapland to Labrador and Quebec (Laurentides Park); s. in Rocky Mountains to New Mexico.

Subspecies: — *B. f. freija* occupies all our part of the above range except the extreme Arctic of North America and the northern Canadian Rockies. I can see no consistent differences between Old World, Rocky Mountain, and subarctic American specimens. *B. f. tarquinius* Curtis (TL Boothia Peninsula) seems to be a northern Arctic subspecies, being above much duller and darker, its black markings enlarged and diffuse. I have seen valid *tarquinius* from Baffin Island; but the name should not be used for occasional dark specimens from farther south within the range of *B. freija freija*.

MEADOW FRITILLARY. *Boloria toddi* Holland   p. 112
1.6–1.8 in. This and the Silver Bordered Fritillary, *selene*, are the two *Boloria* that extend southward well into the eastern states. The shape of the narrow FW, somewhat "truncate" or cut off diagonally at the apex, is distinctive. The underside of the HW is variegated with brown, gray, lilac and purplish; the basal area is distinctly yellowish; and only one spot, that on the costa, is distinctly light colored. The marginal and submarginal dark spots of the wings above tend less to fuse so as to form a dark margin. *Toddi* should be sought in damp meadows where *selene* also flies; but may be found visiting flowers in nearly any meadow or roadside area not too far from a marshy spot. For many years it was known as *bellona* Fabricius; but this name, a homonym, has been replaced by *ammiralis*, while *toddi*, the oldest valid name, serves for the whole species.

Similar Species: — *B. frigga* lacks the truncate FW, is darker brown above with heavier dark markings, and has less yellow and more violet gray on the HW beneath.

Larva: — Dark, shining green, with a velvety black band along each side; tubercles and spines dull, yellowish brown. **Food:** —

Violets (*Viola*). Two broods. Adults in early May. Hibernates as young larva.

Range: — Central and southern Canada e. to Quebec, s. to New Jersey and (in mountains) North Carolina, Illinois, Michigan, Minnesota, Wisconsin and northern Nebraska.

Subspecies: — *B. t. toddi* (TL St. Margarets R., N.E. Quebec) is the eastern Canadian Zone race, s. into northern New England; dark markings heavier, wings above somewhat suffused with dark scales, particularly basally. *B. t. ammiralis* Hemming (TL "North America") is the race from central New England southward; wings above less suffused with dark scales, dark markings less extensive. There is a north-south clinal gradation.

SAGA FRITILLARY. *Boloria frigga saga* Staudinger   p. 112
1.6–1.9 in. Related to *toddi*, *frigga* is much more northern, occurring from Lapland to Labrador. *B. f. frigga* Thunberg (TL Lapland) does not occur in North America, our representatives in eastern North America being probably all *B. f. saga* (TL Labrador ?). In western North America other subspecies occur; one (*sagata* Barnes & Benjamin) ranges far southward in the Rockies. *Saga* is common at Churchill, Manitoba, in northern Labrador and Baffin Island.

DINGY ARCTIC FRITILLARY. *Boloria improba* Butler p. 112
1.35 in. The pattern and coloration of *improba* show it to be a close relative of *toddi* and *frigga*, but what a dwarfed, dark, and dull butterfly it is! It is limited to the true Arctic. In North America from Alaska to Baffin Island, except for a far western subspecies that ranges south into British Columbia. It is very rare in collections.

THE BALTIMORE. *Euphydryas phæton* Drury   pp. 48, 96
2.0 in. The Baltimore is widespread but is intensely local. It occurs only where the food plant (Turtlehead) grows, and seldom wanders more than a hundred yards from the plant. Curiously, though, the butterflies seldom visit its blossoms. Turtlehead being a plant of wet meadows, look there for the Baltimore. The butterfly is black, white spotted, with a marginal row of brick red to orange red spots. A number of striking aberrations are known, and there is considerable normal variation.

Larva: — (see Pl. 5) Feed in a communal web until autumn, hibernate in the web; in spring more solitary, finish feeding, pupate. **Food:** — Turtlehead (*Chelone glabra*) also, rarely, *Wistaria*, Ash (*Fraxinus*), Japanese Honeysuckle (*Lonicera japonica*), *Viburnum*, etc. One brood, adults in late May–June, hibernation as part grown larva.

Range: — Maritime Provinces, southern Quebec and Ontario s. to Virginia (coastal plain), Georgia (mountains and piedmont), Illinois, Michigan, Minnesota, Wisconsin, eastern Kansas, Iowa.

Subspecies: — *E. p. borealis* Cherm. & Cherm. (TL Lincoln, Maine) Maritime Provinces, northern New England, Quebec and Ontario; jet, almost glossy black above, marginal spots larger, redder, forming a wider band, size larger. *E. p. phæton* (TL New York), from range of the above southward. These poorly differentiated subspecies are really statistical gradations in a cline, and are still less noticeable because of variability.

Genus Melitæa *Fabricius:* The Checker Spots

THE GENERIC classification of *Euphydryas*, *Melitæa*, and *Phyciodes* has changed greatly in recent years, due chiefly to a thorough study of male genitalic characters. *Euphydryas* now consists of relatively few species, mostly western. These were removed from the old *Melitæa*; but *Melitæa* has gained some species formerly in *Phyciodes* (*nycteis*, *ismeria*, and *carlota*); and to *Phyciodes* have been added various species of other genera such as *Anthanassa* and *Eresia*. The classification here follows that of Forbes (*Entomologica Americana*, 1945, Vol. 24, No. 4) in which details can be found.

None of our *Melitæa* belong to the typical subgenus, which is Old World, but to the subgenus *Microtia* Bates. Generic names formerly used for some of the species are *Cinclidia* Huebner and *Charidryas* Scudder.

HARRIS' CHECKERSPOT. *Melitæa harrisii* Scudder　　p. 97
1.4–1.7 in. Wings above, light orange brown with brownish black markings. HW beneath with prominent, whitish, blackedged basal and median spots as well as submarginal row of crescents. Essentially northern and very local, in small colonies. Very variable. Look for it in damp meadow areas, especially if they are somewhat brushy; the presence of Blue Flag (*Iris*) is a good indicator of the possibility of *harrisii;* that of the food plant is a better one.
Similar Species: — *M. nycteis* lacks, on the basal two thirds of the HW beneath, the strong contrast between dark ground color and light spots of *harrisii*.
Larva: — Orange, black banded; a black dorsal stripe, six rows of short, black, barbed spines. Larvæ feed communally in early life. **Food:** — *Aster* (*Doellingeria*) *umbellatus*, a common, whiteflowered, northern Aster of moist thickets. One brood. Adults in early June. Hibernation as part-grown larva.
Range: — Maritime Provinces w. to Manitoba, s. to New Jersey,

Pennsylvania, West Virginia, Georgia (!), northern Ohio, Indiana, Illinois, Michigan, and Wisconsin.

Subspecies: — *M. h. albimontana* Avinoff (TL White Mountains, New Hampshire) eastern Canada and northern New England; "dark markings reduced, orange brown areas correspondingly larger, especially on HW." *M. h. liggettii* Avinoff (TL Slippery Rock, Pennsylvania) Pennsylvania; "larger, dark markings more extensive." *M. h. harrisii* (TL Massachusetts?) as figured here, intermediate; southern New England southward and westward. Neither *albimontana* nor *liggettii* is a well-defined subspecies, both at most representing stages in the general north-south clinal gradation. Specimens typical of either can be taken in many *h. harrisii* colonies. Part of the same clinal gradation is *M. harrisii hanhami* Fletcher of Minnesota and Manitoba, with still more reduced black markings than *albimontana*. None of these so-called subspecies is really distinct.

ISMERIA CHECKERSPOT. *Melitæa ismeria* Boisduval & Leconte

Known only from the ancient figure of a female, probably from southeast Georgia, *ismeria* is one of our greatest problems. It certainly is not *Melitæa harrisii* or *nycteis* nor *Phyciodes phaon*. A few *gorgone* females taken recently in Georgia lean toward *ismeria*. Perhaps it will prove to be an extreme female of the true *gorgone*, with the wings beneath basally very whitish, the postmedian band orange, almost continuous and, in general, the light markings, eyespots and lunules more extensive. Georgia collectors should watch out for it. For the time being we should hold the name *ismeria* in abeyance.

GORGONE CHECKERSPOT. *Melitæa gorgone* Huebner   p. 65
1.3–1.5 in. *Gorgone* (the oldest name) is based on an odd population from eastern Georgia, somewhat resembling *tharos*. Very few have been found. In northern (inland) Georgia it intergrades with the familiar *carlota* Reakirt (TL Colorado) which extends thence westward though uncommon in our area. Beneath, *gorgone* lacks the prominent deep, arrowhead-like, outer lines and lunules of *carlota*, which we figure. We should restrict the name *gorgone* to eastern Georgia specimens. See also *ismeria*, above. Much more material for study is badly needed.

Similar Species: — *M. nycteis* (quite similar above) has the narrow, dark postmedian line on the HW beneath composed of gently curved, inwardly concave elements; in *gorgone* this line is very zigzag, formed of deeply and sharply bent, outwardly concave elements; *gorgone* also has the subterminal markings and crescents deeply scalloped inwardly.

Larva: — Yellowish with three longitudinal black stripes, the

BRUSH FOOTED BUTTERFLIES
Family *Nymphalidae*

All illustrations are reduced in size, $\times \frac{1}{2}$ or $\times \frac{3}{8}$

1. **VARIEGATED FRITILLARY,** *Euptoieta claudia*   p. 84
   Upper side, ♂, $\times \frac{3}{4}$ (Virginia). Dull orange brown, dark brown markings and paler shades. Patterned basal half of HW (see *hegesia*, No. 2). Fla. & Tex. n. to Va. & Minn., scarce northward.
2. **MEXICAN FRITILLARY,** *Euptoieta hegesia hoffmanni*   W. P. Comstock   p. 84
   Upper side, ♂ paratype, $\times \frac{3}{4}$ (Jalapa, Mex.). Brighter orange brown. Unpatterned basal half of HW. S. Tex.
3. **REGAL FRITILLARY,** *Speyeria idalia*   p. 86
   Upper side, ♂, $\times \frac{3}{8}$ (Mt. Kisco, N.Y.). Orange brown FW; blue-black HW with median spots whitish, submarginal ones fulvous in ♂, whitish in ♀. Me. w. to S.D., s. to Ga. & Ark.
4. **BALTIMORE,** *Euphydryas phaëton*   p. 93
   Upper side, ♂, $\times \frac{1}{2}$, (New Jersey). Black with white spots; the marginal spots tawny red. S. Can. s. to Ga., Ill. & Kans.
5. **THE MIMIC,** *Hypolimnas misippus*   p. 278
   Upper side, ♂, $\times \frac{3}{8}$ (Oak Hill, Fla.). Black with large white, purplish rimmed spots. Casual in Fla. See No. 6 below.
6. **THE MIMIC,** *Hypolimnas misippus*   p. 278
   Upper side, ♀, $\times \frac{3}{8}$ (Canefields, Dominica, B.W.I.) Tawny brown; black markings; white subapical spots. See No. 5 above.
7. **COMPTON TORTOISE SHELL,** *Nymphalis j-album*   p. 105
   Upper side, ♂, $\times \frac{3}{8}$ (vicinity Scranton, Pa.). Dark to light orange brown; black patches; white subapical marks on FW & HW. Can. s. to N.C., Mo. & Iowa.
8. **MOURNING CLOAK,** *Nymphalis antiopa*   p. 106
   Upper side, ♂, $\times \frac{3}{8}$ (Northcastle, N.Y.). Deep purplish brown; yellow margins; blue submarginal spots. Entire eastern area except Fla. & far Arctic.
9. **WHITE PEACOCK,** *Anartia jatrophæ guantanamo*   Munroe   p. 110
   Upper side, ♂ paratype, $\times \frac{3}{4}$ (City Point, Brevard Co., Fla.). White with yellow brown marginal spots and dark brown markings. S. Fla. & Tex., strays northward.
10. **RUDDY DAGGER WING,** *Marpesia petreus thetys*   p. 114
    Upper side, ♂, $\times \frac{1}{2}$ (Royal Palm State Park, Fla.). Orange brown with dark brown markings; long tails. Fla. & Tex.
11. **GOATWEED BUTTERFLY,** *Anæa andria*   p. 117
    Upper side, ♂, $\times \frac{1}{2}$ (Ranken, Mo.). Bright red-orange-brown, shading to grayish brown margins. Mostly lacks dark pattern above (see *floridalis*, below). Tex. n. to Nebr., e. to Ga.
12. **FLORIDA LEAF WING,** *Anæa floridalis*   p. 118
    Upper side, ♂, $\times \frac{3}{4}$ (Biscayne Bay — Slosson). Colors as in *andria;* more patterned above; see text. S. Fla.

Plate 12   97

CHECKERSPOTS, CRESCENTS, ETC.
Family *Nymphalidae*

All illustrations are × 1 (natural size)

1. HARRIS' CHECKERSPOT, *Melitæa harrisii*   p. 94
   Upper & under side,♂, (Litchfield, Conn.). Yellow brown with black
   markings; light spots beneath yellowish white to white. Very variable. Canada s. to N.J., Ill. & Wis.

2. SILVERY CHECKERSPOT, *Melitæa nycteis*   p. 98
   Upper & under side,♂ (Woodlands, N.Y.). Yellow brown with black
   marks; HW beneath very whitish, with some satiny luster. Can. s. to
   N.J., Ill. & Kans.

3. PAINTED CRESCENT, *Phyciodes picta*   p. 99
   Under side, ♂ (Jemez Springs, N.M.). Above, yellow brown with
   heavy black pattern. Beneath, apex of FW and whole HW light,
   creamy; Summer brood (*pallescens*) figured here. Nebr. to Okla. &
   westward.

4. VESTA CRESCENT, *Phyciodes vesta*   p. 99
   Under side, ♂ (Cuantla, Mor., Mex.). Yellow brown above with
   blackish borders and markings; HW beneath with transverse bands
   definite, these orange brown, narrowly black-edged. Complete
   transverse marks on FW beneath; see text. Mex. n. into Kans.

5. CAMILLUS CRESCENT, *Phyciodes camillus*   p. 99
   Under side, ♂ (Grand Canyon, Colo.). Above, yellow brown with
   extensive dark markings; a light bar in end of cell of FW beneath;
   little or no marginal dark patch on HW beneath. Western, straying
   into Nebr. & Kans.

6. TEXAN CRESCENT, *Phyciodes texana*   p. 101
   Upper side, ♂ (Kerr Co., Tex.). Blackish brown with white spots
   and indistinct orange brown markings; shape of FW. Tex. & Fla.

7. SCUDDER'S PATCHED BUTTERFLY, *Chlosyne lacinia adjutrix* p. 101
   Upper side, ♂ (Jalapa, Mex.). Dark brown; median spot band
   orange brown, paler toward costa of FW; other spots whitish. Tex.,
   straying northward.

8. AMYMONE, *Mestra amymone*   p. 111
   Upper side,♂ (Tex.). Gray and white, broad marginal border of HW
   orange brown. Base of vein Sc of FW swollen. Tex., straying
   northward.

9. DINGY PURPLE WING, *Eunica monima*   p. 111
   Upper side,♂ (Key Largo, Fla.). Brownish black with faint purple
   sheen except on borders; larger spots whitish. S. Fla. & Tex. Rare, in
   hammocks.

10. FLORIDA PURPLE WING, *Eunica tatila tatilista*   p. 111
    Upper side,♂ (Key Largo, Fla.). Brownish black with purple sheen
    more pronounced than in *monima*; spots whitish. Note shape of FW.
    Southern Fla. & Tex.

11. *Myscelia ethusa*,   p. 278
    Upper side, ♂ (Presidio, V.C., Mex.). Purplish blue; blackish
    transverse bars; subapical spots of FW white. s. Tex.

barbed spines black. **Food:** — Aster, Sunflower (*Helianthus scaberrimus*) and, questionably, Oak (*Quercus chrysolepis*). One brood northward, more southward.
Range: — Mexico n. through Mississippi Valley to Michigan, Minnesota & westward; e. to Georgia, perhaps throughout Gulf States.

SILVERY CHECKERSPOT. *Melitæa nycteis* Doubleday   p. 97
1.5–1.6 in. Widespread northward, *nycteis* is less local than *harrisii*, occurs widely in open meadows, along lake shores and roadsides. Its large size and more clear-cut, checkered markings separate it from the *Phyciodes* species, as do its male genitalic characters (ventral edge of harpe with a projecting spine).
Similar Species: — see *M. harrisii* and *M. gorgone*, above.
Larva: — Black, on each side a dull orange stripe; barbed spines black. **Food:** — Various sunflowers (*Helianthus*), Asters (*Aster*) and *Actinomeris*. One brood in north, two in south. Adults in early June. Hibernation as part-grown larva.
Range: — Southern Canada, Maritime Provinces w. to Manitoba, s. to New Jersey and (in mountains) North Carolina, Ohio, Indiana, Illinois, Missouri, and Kansas.
Subspecies: — *M. n. nycteis* (TL "Middle States") the eastern subspecies, as figured here. *M. n. drusius* Edwards (TL Colorado & Arizona) west of the Mississippi River, upper side darker, dark markings more extensive. *M. n. reversa* Chermock & Chermock (TL Riding Mts., Manitoba) Manitoba; upper side with dark markings greatly reduced, light areas more extensive.

Genus Phyciodes *Huebner:* The Crescents

ALL OF OUR species are small; most are orange brown above with dark markings and have on the outer margin of the HW beneath one or more crescent-shaped spots, sometimes bright and pearly. In the tropics many *Phyciodes* are incredibly varied, mimicking *Heliconiids* and *Danaids*. Most of our species are two or more brooded. Some are difficult to identify without studying the genitalia. The very considerable differences in some species between lighter summer broods and darker winter broods must be kept constantly in mind. Crescents are familiar butterflies of open fields and roadsides. Our Crescents fall into three subgenera *P.* (*Phyciodes*), *P.* (*Eresia*) Doubleday and *P.* (*Tritanassa*) Forbes, characterized largely by genitalia characters.

PAINTED CRESCENT. *Phyciodes picta* Edwards   p. 97
1.0–1.2 in. On the upper side, *picta* resembles *phaon*, from which it may be told by the comparatively unmarked apex of the FW beneath; in the summer brood *pallescens* (figured) also by its nearly immaculate, cream colored HW beneath; and in the spring brood *picta* also by the much lighter, chocolate-brown markings of its HW beneath. In *phaon* the apex of the FW beneath is crossed by fine, brown lines; and in both broods *phaon* has heavier, darker markings on the HW beneath. It has been suggested that *picta* and *phaon* are conspecific; but their distributions overlap very widely.
Similar Species: — *P. phaon*, see above.
Larva: — Mottled yellowish or greenish brown, with seven chief rows of short spines; these are brown in summer larvæ, yellow in autumn ones. **Food:** — Various Asters.
Range: — Western states, s. into Mexico, e. into Nebraska, Kansas, and Oklahoma (TL "Nebraska Territory").

PHAON CRESCENT. *Phyciodes phaon* Edwards   p. 112
1.0–1.2 in. *Phaon* is a common species of the Southeast, flying in company with *P. tharos*. Its flight seems to me to be a trifle faster and more erratic than that of *tharos*. The lighter, summer form is *phaon*, the darker, winter brood is *hiemalis*.
Larva: — Olivaceous, with longitudinal dark brown lines and mottled bands; many branching spines in rows; head creamy white with large brown spots on sides and dorsum. **Food:** — Fog Fruit and Mat Grass (*Lippia lanceolata* and *nodiflora*) — data from California.
Similar Species: — *P. picta*, see above. *P. tharos: phaon* has checkered fringes, which *tharos* lacks; has the ground color of the HW and apex of FW beneath lighter, cream colored; and has a distinctly two-toned appearance of the light areas of the wings above, the median spots being lighter.
Range: — Florida to Texas, n. to Georgia (TL St. Simon's Island, Georgia) and Kansas; s. into Mexico.

VESTA CRESCENT. *Phyciodes vesta* Edwards   p. 97
1.1–1.3 in. *Vesta* is best known by its finely checkered appearance above; and by the presence on the FW beneath of a *complete*, transverse black line, between the postmedian and subterminal lines, connected by black bars along the veins so as to enclose some tawny spots.
Range: — Mexico n. to Kansas (TL Texas).

CAMILLUS CRESCENT. *Phyciodes camillus* Edwards   p. 97
1.3–1.5 in. *Camillus* is a widespread, common species of the west which enters the western edge of our area.
Similar Species: — *P. tharos: camillus* has the upper side gen-

erally darker with smaller pale markings; always has a cream-colored bar in the outer part of the cell of the FW beneath; and usually lacks the marginal dark patch which *tharos* has on the HW beneath.

Range: — Western states, e. into Nebraska and Kansas (TL Colorado).

TAWNY CRESCENT. *Phyciodes batesii* Reakirt   p. 112
1.3–1.5 in. Although very similar to *tharos*, *batesii* is a distinct species, northern, single-brooded, and co-existing with *tharos*. It has probably been overlooked in many regions where it occurs. Many published records are untrustworthy. I have found it quite local in dry, open hillside fields. We badly need information about its habits and distribution and possible relationship with *camillus*.

Similar Species: — *P. tharos*: *batesii* has the HW beneath comparatively unmarked yellow; the black patch in the middle of the inner margin of the FW beneath is comparatively large, as high as an interspace between veins and twice as long, and much larger than the black subapical patch on the costa of the same wing beneath. *Batesii* tends to have the median row of light spots of the FW above lighter in color than the other light areas.
Larva: — Incompletely known; said to be somewhat gregarious.
Food: — Aster ("Blue Wood Aster, *A. undulatus*"). One brood. Adults in late May–June. Hibernation as larva.

Range: — Quebec, Ontario, and northern New England, w. to Nebraska, s. (rare) to Virginia (TL Gloucester, New Jersey).

PEARL CRESCENT. *Phyciodes tharos* Drury   pp. 49, 112
1.3–1.5 in. Ranging from Canada into Mexico, and abundant throughout most of its range, *tharos* is one of our most familiar butterflies. It occurs nearly everywhere in open spaces, in meadows, and along roadsides, and is a most consistent puddle visitor. Some authors have recorded it as a slow and sluggish flier; but to me it seems just the opposite. It is active and pugnacious, darting after other butterflies that come near its perch, and driving them from the area. Many times has a butterfly which I was stalking or watching been put to flight by the attack of a *tharos*, or of that other aggressive midget, the American Copper. *Tharos* is an eager flower visitor, but also alights much on leaves, stones, or bare ground. A good field recognition character is the way in which, on alighting, it holds its wings out at the sides and saws them up and down a few times. The spring brood, subjected to cold in the pupal stage, has more extensive dark markings. This cold weather form was named *marcia*, but is the typical form of the name *tharos*. The hot weather form is known as *morpheus*. The lack of major geographic variation over most of the range is quite remarkable.
Similar Species: — *P. batesii*, *camillus*, *phaon*, see above.

Larva: — Black with yellow dots; a yellow band along each side, and eight rows of yellow-brown spines; feeds sociably, sluggish, spins no web. Eggs laid in masses of 20–200, sometimes two or more layers deep, on leaves of food plant. **Food:** — Asters, particularly New England Aster (*A. novæ angliæ*), Crownbeard (*Verbesina helianthoides*). One brood in Canada, two in northern United States, up to five in far south. Adults in mid-April. Hibernation as part-grown larva.

Range: — Throughout eastern area from Canada (Canadian Life Zone) into Mexico.

Subspecies: — *P. t. arctica* dos Passos (TL Port au Port, Newfoundland) Newfoundland; dark marginal bands of upper side black and broad; ground color of under side deeper, more orange yellow. *P. t. tharos* (TL New York) remainder of our area; lighter than the above.

CUBAN CRESCENT. *Phyciodes frisia* Poey   p. 112
1.0–1.2 in. The *concave* outer margin of the FW marks the Cuban Crescent from the other *Phyciodes*. *Frisia* enters our area in both Florida and Texas. I have found it common along roadsides in the Florida keys in winter, visiting flowers freely. There must be at least two broods.

Range: — Tropical America n. into southern Florida, southern Texas, and westward.

Subspecies: — *P. f. frisia* (TL Cuba) southern Florida; ground color above bright orange brown, HW above with extensive areas of this color. *P. f. tulcis* Bates (TL Guatemala) Guatemala into southern Texas and westward; ground color above paler, cream colored to pale tawny; HW above mostly black.

TEXAN CRESCENT. *Phyciodes texana* Edwards   p. 97
1.5–1.7 in. Largely black above, with white spots, *texana* cannot be confused with other *Phyciodes*. From the somewhat similar *Chlosyne* species (see below) it is distinguished by its lack of broad, brown or whitish patches on the HW above; and by its having but one subterminal white spot on the FW, below vein Cu_2. The Chlosynes either have this spot plus another above it, below vein Cu_1; or else only the spot below vein Cu_1.

Range: — Florida n. into Georgia (*seminole*); Mexico into Texas, casual n. to Kansas (*texana*).

Subspecies: — *P. t. texana* (TL Texas) ground color of FW wholly or mostly brownish black. *P. t. seminole* Skinner (TL Bainbridge, Ga.) basal area of FW above largely orange brown.

SCUDDER'S PATCHED BUTTERFLY. *Chlosyne lacinia adjutrix* Scudder   p. 97
1.7 in. This is the only "Patched Butterfly" that consistently occurs in our area; other species that stray in are listed in the section on Casual Species. Wings brownish black above, with white

outer spots; a broad median orange-brown band, and orange-brown basal spots. **Food:** — Sunflower (*Helianthus*).

Range: — Mexico into Texas (TL Texas), casual to Kansas and Nebraska. A few of the specimens taken at Pharr, Texas, resemble the western race, *californica* Wright, with much more extensive light brown markings.

Genus Polygonia *Huebner:* The Angle Wings

THE "ANGLE Wings" well deserve their name. The ragged outlines and mottled brown colors of the under sides make them "dead leaf mimics" beyond compare, a feature on which they often capitalize by sitting with the wings held together over the back. They also doubtless gain a certain protection because of the surprise element involved when the brighter, upperside colors (flash color) suddenly appear or disappear. All are essentially northern, this being a Holarctic genus. All are primarily forest species, to be sought along roads and trails through the woods, although some range out into open spaces. In the more northern species there is one brood annually; in those which extend farther southward there are two. The winter is passed as the adult, as is likewise true in the next genera, *Nymphalis* and *Vanessa*. You can collect butterflies in midwinter if you have the patience to go around prying into all sorts of hollow trees, old barrels and boxes, and tin cans. I once found six species of *Polygonia* and *Nymphalis* in a rubbish dump in an afternoon in February. Sometimes a warm winter sun will bring out a few "hibernators," presenting the spectacle of butterflies flying over the snow.

Polygonias show considerable seasonal dimorphism, adults of the autumn (overwintering) brood being usually lighter in color. However, some individuals resembling the autumn brood may be produced among the summer populations. There is also some sexual dimorphism, females being somewhat paler above and much more evenly and dully colored beneath. The larvæ are mostly brownish and bear many spines. The pupæ are greatly angulate and irregular in shape, resembling dried, twisted leaves. The adults are quite pugnacious. They have fast, erratic flights, and are quite wary. They are extremely fond of sap and fruit juices, and may be baited with these; they do not visit most flowers very freely.

QUESTION MARK. *Polygonia interrogationis* Fabricius

pp. 48, 113, 144

2.4–2.6 in. The largest of the genus, and the species with the greatest southward range, the Question Mark is distinguished as well by its less irregular wing margins. It also has a dark spot, in cell M_2 of the FW, lacking in other species. On the HW beneath, the silvery discocellular mark consists of a curved line and a separate dot (hence the name "Question Mark"); in other species only the "comma" line, curved or angled, is present. The tail of the HW and a narrow edge on both wings are violet gray, more marked in the pale "winter" form (typical *interrogationis*, also called *fabricii*) than in the darker summer form (*umbrosa*).

Larva: — Reddish brown, with irregular, lighter dots and patches; many branching spines, one pair of them on the head.
Food: — Elm (*Ulmus*), Hackberry (*Celtis*), Nettle (*Urtica*), Basswood (*Tilia*), Hops (*Humulus*), False Nettle (*Bœhmeria*). Two broods in North to five in South. Adults (hibernators) in April–May.
Range: — Maritime Provinces, Quebec, and Ontario, s. throughout our entire area into Mexico (TL "Boreal America").

HOP MERCHANT or COMMA. *Polygonia comma* Harris p. 113
1.7–1.9 in. Next to the Question Mark, *comma* is our commonest and most widespread Angle Wing. It emerges from hibernation somewhat earlier than the others, often in March. Its flight is fast and erratic; and it is very pugnacious. At times the larvæ are destructive to Hops. The summer form, *dryas*, has the dark marginal borders greatly widened; that of the hind wings may cover the outer two thirds.
Similar Species: — *P. faunus* and *satyrus* are brown beneath like *comma*; *P. progne* and *gracilis* are gray beneath. *Comma* lacks the green marbled spots on the HW beneath of *faunus*, and has smoother, less jagged wing margins. From *satyrus*, *comma* is distinguished by its broader HW border, twice as wide as that of the FW, and by the small size (or absence) of the inner of *two* dark spots in cell Cu_1 of the FW. The lighter forms of *comma* have prominent violet-gray edging.
Larva: — Vary from dark brown or greenish brown to nearly white, with darker blotches and crosslines; numerous thorny spines, one pair of these on the head. Makes a rough nest on the food plant. **Food:** — Hops (*Humulus*), Elm (*Ulmus*), Nettle (*Urtica*), False Nettle (*Bœhmeria*). Two broods in North, three in South.
Range: — Maritime Provinces, Anticosti Island, Quebec, & Ontario, s. to North Carolina (in mountains), w. to Kansas, Nebraska, and Iowa. There are old records from Texas (?).

SATYR ANGLE WING. *Polygonia satyrus* Edwards pp. 49, 144
1.7–1.9 in. Essentially western, *satyrus* enters our area in southern Canada as the form *marsyas*, brighter in color and pattern than typical *satyrus*; this does not, however, seem to be a geographic race.

Similar Species: — *P. comma, faunus;* see under *comma,* above.
Larva: — in the West, feeding on Nettle (*Urtica*), making a crude nest as *comma* does. It appears to be one-brooded.
Range: — Western North America, e. to northern Minnesota, Michigan, New York, Ontario, Quebec and Newfoundland (TL Colorado).

GREEN COMMA. *Polygonia faunus* Edwards   p. 113
1.7–1.9 in. Even dull specimens of *faunus* can be recognized by the slightly greenish luster of the wings above, the two rows of submarginal green spots on the wings beneath, and the greater irregularity of the margins. It is essentially a Canadian Zone species, ranging southward in the mountains in association with the northern forests, and is strongly limited to forest environments.
Similar Species: — *P. comma, satyrus;* see under *comma,* above.
Larva: — Reddish or yellowish brown with a large, dorsal, white saddle behind the middle, and a broken, dull orange, lateral band; spines mostly white, anterior ones light brownish. Solitary, feeding only on the lower surfaces of leaves. **Food:** — Black Birch (*Betula lenta*), Willow (*Salix humilis*), Alder (*Alnus*), Currant and Gooseberry (*Ribes*). The Birch is the favorite. One brood only. Adults (hibernators) in early spring.
Range: — Canada s. to Georgia and Iowa.
Subspecies: — *P. f. faunus* (TL Catskill Mts., New York) the northern race, smaller and lighter. *P. f. smythi* A. H. Clark (TL Mt. Rogers, Grayson County, Virginia) West Virginia aud Virginia to Georgia (mountains) is larger and darker.

GRAY COMMA. *Polygonia progne* Cramer   pp. 113, 144
1.6–1.8 in. *Progne* and *gracilis* are much grayer beneath than the other species, and in both the ends of the silvery comma on the HW beneath either taper or at least are not enlarged. *Progne* is not so northern as *faunus* and *gracilis*. It is double-brooded, and quite dimorphic. The summer form *l-argenteum* is much darker above, and has the lower arm of the silvery comma shorter than the upper arm, so that the mark resembles an L. *Progne* flies a little more slowly than other *Polygonias*, but even at that is difficult enough to catch. It is not so strongly limited to forests.
Similar Species: — *Progne* lacks the contrasty, broad, light gray postmedian band on the wings beneath that characterizes *gracilis*, but intermediate specimens occur. The *upper* arm of the silvery comma is blunter at the tip in *gracilis*, more tapering and pointed in *progne*.
Larva: — Yellowish brown with darker spots and lines; lighter on the sides; spines blackish. When disturbed, the larvæ throw both ends out from the leaf, holding on only at the middle.
Food: — Currant and Gooseberry (*Ribes*), less often Elm (*Ulmus americana*). Two broods. Hibernates as adult.

Range: — Canada s. to Virginia (mountains), Illinois, Missouri (Willard, Ozarks); w. in eastern area to Kansas and Nebraska (TL New York)

HOARY COMMA. *Polygonia gracilis* Grote & Robinson   p. 113
1.4–1.6 in. *Gracilis* is a Canadian Zone species; like *progne* it is a somewhat slower flier than other Angle Wings. The life history is almost wholly unknown. Females might be induced to lay eggs on one of the food plants of other northern species, such as Black Birch, Currant, Gooseberry, or Willow. It is certainly one-brooded. Adults often alight on Everlasting (*Gnaphalium*) flowers.
Similar Species: — *P. progne*, see above.
Range: — Canada s. into northern New England, New York, Michigan, and Minnesota.

Genus Nymphalis *Kluk:* The Tortoise Shells

CLOSELY related to the Angle Wings, the Tortoise Shells are another essentially northern, Holarctic group. Their generic nomenclature is quite complicated; the names *Vanessa*, *Aglais*, *Euvanessa*, *Eugonia*, and *Hamadryas* having been variously used for them. The inner margin of the FW is straight, not concave as in *Polygonia*. See also *N. californica* in the section on Casual Species, page 278.

COMPTON TORTOISE SHELL. *Nymphalis j-album* Boisduval & Leconte   pp. 96, 113
2.5–2.7 in. Of our three species, this most deserves the name "Tortoise shell," its colors being a lovely blending of black, deep orange brown, yellow browns, and white. Beneath, it is marbled gray, paler outwardly, usually with a tiny white J at the lower end of the cell of the HW. It is a woodland species. It is a swift flyer but, folding its wings above its back, "mimics" a dead leaf or a bit of bark to perfection. Like the *Polygonias*, it is addicted to visiting sap, rotting fruit and mud puddles.
Larva: — Light greenish, somewhat speckled and striped with lighter shades; head and body with black, bristly spines; feeding socially. **Food:** — Northern White Birch (*Betula alba*), Willows (*Salix*), perhaps Poplars (*Populus*). One brooded. The adults live for nearly a year. Hibernates as adult, probably to some degree, also, as pupa. Quite noted for its periodicity, being extremely abundant one season, nearly absent the next.
Range: — Canada, s. in Canadian and Transition Zones to North Carolina, Missouri (Ozarks, A.E.B.), northern Michigan, Minnesota, and Iowa.

MILBERT'S TORTOISE SHELL. *Nymphalis milberti* Latreille

p. 113

1.7–1.8 in. Much smaller than its relatives, *milberti* is, like *j-album*, essentially northern and a woodland species, often common in New England and Canada; but sometimes it ranges southward in years of extreme and abnormal abundance. It often occurs in open fields and roadsides.

Larva: — Black, the sides greenish yellow; with many raised, whitish dots and bristly spines; head black with two whitish papillæ (raised "bumps"). Feed in colonies. **Food:** — Nettle (*Urtica*). Three broods. Adults in early April. Hibernation as both adult and pupa.

Range: — Newfoundland, and central & southern Canada, s. chiefly in mountains and piedmont to West Virginia.

Subspecies: — *N. m. viola* dos Passos (TL Doyle's Sta., Newfoundland) Newfoundland; light band deeper orange, not paler toward its basal edge. *N. m. milberti* (TL perhaps Philadelphia, Pa.), remainder of the range in eastern area.

MOURNING CLOAK. *Nymphalis antiopa* Linnæus

pp. 48, 49, 96, 113

2.75–3.25 in. The Mourning Cloak with its dark, light-bordered wings is a very widely ranging species of the temperate parts of the Holarctic region. It is one of our most familiar butterflies, ranging, unlike its congeners, in open country as well as in woodlands. In most of its range it is probably the first butterfly on the wing in the Spring, frequently emerging from hibernation before the snow has left the ground. As the "Camberwell Beauty" it is a famous and greatly prized species in England, where it occurs only as a rare migrant from the Continent. It is subject to great, although rare, individual variation, chiefly caused by temperature; one such (*hygeia*) has the light marginal borders very wide and "smeary."

Larva: — Velvety black, peppered with raised white dots; a row of red, mid-dorsal spots; head without spines, body with several rows. **Food:** — Elm (*Ulmus*), Willow (*Salix*), Poplar (*Populus*), Hackberry (*Celtis*), Rose, etc. Two broods, perhaps three southward. Hibernation as adult, possibly also as pupa.

Range: — Entire eastern area except for Arctic Zone and southern Florida.

Subspecies: — The true *a. antiopa* (TL Sweden) is a northern form, smaller, with a narrow, light border, such as occurs in North America only in northern Canada. The form of most of our area tends to be larger, with a wider border. This agrees with the parallel clinal variation in Europe, where the southern form has been named *creta* Verity (TL Tuscany, Italy). I question the propriety, and deny the advisability, of using this name for our southern population, which is not the same thing biologically. Similar cases occur in *Vanessa atalanta* and *cardui*, below.

Genus Vanessa *Fabricius:* The Thistle Butterflies

THIS IS another genus of world-wide distribution. The relationship between Old and New Worlds is close, for two of our three species occur in both hemispheres with only minor differences. One of these, the Painted Lady, occurs in so nearly all of the possible places in the world that it well deserves its other name of "The Cosmopolite." All three species are frequent flower visitors, but their fondness for those of Thistles is proverbial. Some of the species have pronounced migratory habits. All are fast flying and wide ranging. In our area the species are at least double brooded, hibernate as adults and, to some degree, as pupæ.

RED ADMIRAL. *Vanessa atalanta* Linnæus   pp. 49, 113, 144
1.75–2.2 in. The general dark ground color, bright orange-red bands across the FW and at the outer margins of the HW, and the prominent, white apical spots of the FW mark an *atalanta* as far as one can see it. There is some seasonal variation, early specimens averaging a little smaller and lighter colored; while later (wet environment ?) ones are larger and darker, with the red band of the FW more or less broken.
Larva: — Extremely variable; some are black with rows of yellow spots and many raised, white warts along sides, and with black, orange-based spines; others have the entire body whitish mottled, or light greenish, or brownish; the larvæ live singly, in a leaf lined with silk and folded together, may pupate in this "nest." **Food:** — Nettles (*Urtica*), Hops (*Humulus*), False Nettle (*Bœhmeria*), Pellitory (*Parietaria*), all being *Urticaceæ* (Nettle Family). Two broods (perhaps more in South?). Hibernation as adult and pupa. Adults in late spring.
Range: — Central & southern Canada and Newfoundland s. through Florida and Texas to the Antilles and Guatemala.
Subspecies: — Our *atalanta* have been identified with the subspecies *italica* Stichel (TL central and southern Italy) (apical white spots smaller, red band of FW narrower, black spots in orange band of HW smaller). As with *N. antiopa* (see above) I doubt the propriety of using the name of one subspecies for another population in a far distant area.

PAINTED LADY (COSMOPOLITE). *Vanessa cardui* Linnæus
    pp. 49, 113
2.0–2.2 in. As befits such a wide ranging species, the Painted Lady occurs in nearly all environments, so long as they are open and brightly lighted, even on alpine summits. At times it is strongly migratory during periods of great abundance that may

be followed by periods of great scarcity. The fluctuations are probably caused by parasites and exhaustion of available food supply, as well as by emigration. Some seasonal or "wet-dry" form variation occurs, and much individual variation.

Similar Species: — *V. virginiensis* has the postmedian black spots of the HW above larger, and the front and rear of these larger than the others; on the HW beneath, *cardui* has all four of these spots repeated and ocellate; *virginiensis* has only two very large ocellate spots here.

Larva: — Head dark, hairy, not spiny; body yellowish green, black mottled, with a yellow lateral stripe; spines yellowish. Lives singly in a compact nest of leaves, buds, fragments, silk, etc. **Food:** — chiefly *Compositæ:* Thistles (*Cirsium, Carduus, Centaurea*), Burdock (*Arctium*), Groundsel (*Senecio*), Sunflowers (*Helianthus*), Pearly Everlasting (*Anaphalis margaritacea*), Sage or Wormwood (*Artemisia*), Everlasting (*Gnaphalium*), etc.; and on Hollyhock (*Althaea*), Borage (*Borago officinalis*), etc. Two broods in North, doubtless more in South where it flies all winter. Hibernation as adult or pupa.

Range: — North America, except for Arctic, southward.

Subspecies: — Our *cardui* have been identified with the subspecies *carduelis* Cramer (TL Africa) lighter colored and with less black than the typical *cardui* of northern Europe. As noted above under *Nymphalis antiopa* and *V. atalanta*, I question the propriety of this.

AMERICAN PAINTED LADY. *Vanessa virginiensis* Drury
pp. 48, 113

1.7–2.1 in. Like its near relative *cardui*, *virginiensis* occurs throughout our area except in the far north, and is a common, active, and wide-ranging butterfly. Like *cardui* it is subject to great periodic fluctuations in abundance. It was known for many years by the specific name *huntera* and was then called "Hunter's Butterfly."

Similar Species: — see *V. cardui*.

Larva: — Velvety black; narrow, yellow cross bands; a row of white spots on each side of the abdominal segments; spines blackish. Lives singly in a compact nest of silk, leaves, plant fragments, etc., encloses the blossoms in the web; often pupates in nest. **Food:** — chiefly the Everlastings (*Gnaphalium, Antennaria,* and *Anaphalis*), also many other Composites, and Mouse Ear (*Myosotis*), etc. Two broods in North, probably more in South. Hibernation as adult or pupa.

Range: — Central and southern Canada s. throughout our area to Cuba and Guatemala (TL New York, Maryland, and Virginia).

THE BUCKEYE. *Precis lavinia* Cramer   pp. 49, 113
2.2–2.5 in. The Buckeye (*cœnia*) is common and widespread in

the United States. It has a rapid, nervous flight, is wary, and an expert dodger. Fortunately for collectors it is fond of visiting flowers and mud puddles. In autumn it may be seen migrating southward along beach and dune areas in considerable numbers. It is noticeably quarrelsome; Austin Clark has noted its particular persecution of the large, black-and-white winged Carolina Locust (*Dissosteira carolina*).

We do not yet fully understand the relationships of the various forms of this butterfly, or of its close relatives. Conventional ideas of "subspecies" as geographically distinct populations, sometimes "clinal" or geographically graded, do not fully apply. In Florida, for example, we have two so-called "subspecies" occurring in the same area! At some time during the past these must have been isolated, and during that time have become different enough so that now they do not interbreed. In other regions, however, they do intergrade. In addition to this sort of thing, there are both "static" and "migratory" phases; sometimes one or the other, but not both, will occur in an area. Again, there are "dry season" and "wet season" forms, respectively pale and dark colored, or similar differences between specimens from dry and wet environments. The "dry" forms may tend to be active and migratory; the "wet" ones, sluggish and static. To top all this there is considerable individual variation. A great deal of careful study and thorough analytical work is needed.

Larva: — Dark olive gray, striped and spotted with yellow or orange; numerous short, branching spines, one pair of them on the head. **Food:** — Plantain (*Plantago*), Gerardia (*Gerardia*), Toadflax (*Linaria*), Snapdragon (*Antirrhinum*), False Loosestrife (*Ludvigia*), Stonecrop (*Sedum*), *Lippia* (*zonalis* in Cuba). One to two broods in North, several in South. Hibernates as adult. In the northernmost parts of its range it may not survive the winter, the population being annually renewed by northward migration.

Range: — Tropical America n. to southern Canada.

Subspecies: — *P. l. cœnia* Huebner (TL Cuba) all of the above range; eyespots of HW above large, the anterior one from two to three times as large as the posterior one, with red or red-orange area within it extensive; light markings of FW above tending to creamy white; wings shorter. *P. l. zonalis* Felder, Florida (chiefly coastal) and southern Texas (Pharr, rare); anterior eyespot of HW little larger than posterior one, with little or no red internally; light patch of FW orange brown to salmon pink, often much reduced; outer margin of FW tending to greater concavity; wings longer. *P. l. genoveva* Cramer has been listed as occurring in the United States, but I doubt it. The figures in Holland (Butterfly Book, rev. ed., Pl. XX, fig. 8 & 9) of "*lavinia*" and "*genoveva*" may both be referred to *zonalis*.

WHITE PEACOCK. *Anartia jatrophæ* Johannson   p. 96
1.9–2.3 in. Very widespread in the tropics, *jatrophæ* enters our
area only in the far South. Its habits resemble those of the
Buckeye, but it is not so fast-flying or wary. In the tropics it
forms many subspecies and local forms. I once caught four of
these in two days: *guantanamo* Munroe in Florida, *semifusca*
Munroe in Puerto Rico, *saturata* Staudinger in Haiti and
jatrophæ in Brazil. This is characteristic of twentieth century
entomology in more ways than one! *Jatrophæ* also tends to produce different seasonal forms.
Larva: — Head shiny black with large, branching spines; body
black with large, silvery spots and four rows of black branching
spines. **Food:** — "*Jatropha manihot*" in Brazil, *Lippia* in Cuba,
Bacopa in Puerto Rico.
Range: — Tropics to s. Florida and s. Texas, straying to Massachusetts and Kansas.
Subspecies: — *A. j. guantanæmo* Munroe (TL Guantanamo,
Cuba), Fla.; ground color light (winter form) to darker with
more brownish suffusion (summer form); outer marginal border
of HW above not noticeably yellow. *A. j. luteipicta* Frueh-
storfer (TL Honduras) Texas; outer marginal border of HW
above yellow, this often extending far basad; general color
yellower.

FATIMA. *Anartia fatima* Fabricius
2.0 in. *Fatima* enters our area only in southern Texas, where it
is well established and at times common. (March–May, October–November). Wing shape of *jatrophæ*. Ground color dark
gray brown. FW with a light spotband about ⅛ in. wide from
mid costa to about ⅔ way out on inner margin, continued across
HW, slanting outwardly nearly to outer angle (cell M₃) then
bent in toward anal angle. On FW also three larger, two smaller,
subapical light spots. HW with an incomplete red spotband
of two spots at end of cell and two below them in cells M₃ and
Cu₁. Fringes white-spotted. In typical *fatima* the light spots
are cream-colored; in the form "*venusta*" Fruhstorfer they are
white.

Genus Eunica *Huebner:* The Purple Wings

MEDIUM SIZED to small butterflies of the tropics, barely entering
our area. There are many tropical species, some brilliantly iridescent. Ours are deep brown to black above, with light spots on
the FW and a purple iridescence; are somewhat mottled and

marbled beneath with lighter browns and greys. If you wish to find *Eunicas*, go into the dense shade of a tropical hardwood forest or "hammock." There you will see them flitting about in the dappled light and shade, and alighting on tree trunks where their underside coloration protects them well. How to net them without damaging their wings is a problem that I have never fully solved. I have never seen our species congregating at mud puddles and stream banks in the open, as tropical forms are said to do, although I have occasionally taken *tatila* along roadsides near woods.

FLORIDA PURPLE WING. *Eunica tatila* Herrich-Schæffer p. 97
1.6–2.0 in. *Tatila* is not uncommon in southern Florida in the right environment and season. Its habits are noted above.
Similar Species: — *E. monima.* *Tatila* is larger; has seven (instead of six) larger, more prominent, white spots on the FW; has a much more intense, bluer iridescence; and has the apex of the FW more produced and the outer margin more concave.
Range: — Tropical hardwood hammocks of southern Florida. I have seen no authentic specimens from southern Texas, but it may well occur there.
Subspecies: — *E. t. tatila*, if the mainland subspecies according to W. P. Comstock, is the one that would occur in Texas; it has white scales centering the postmedian black spots of the HW beneath. *E. t. tatilista* Kaye (TL Jamaica), the Antillean subspecies, lacks these white centers, occurs in Florida.

DINGY PURPLE WING. *Eunica monima* Cramer p. 97
1.2–1.4 in. In both Florida and Texas *monima* is rare. I have seen but a half-dozen authentic Florida specimens (Miami, May, June, August; Key Largo, May and July) and know but one authentic Texas record (Pharr, July). Like *tatila* it favors shaded woods. There is a most interesting record of a series of migratory specimens caught on a ship between Cuba and Hispaniola; and a windblown stray was taken in Kansas (Caldwell, 30 May).
Similar Species: — See *E. tatila*, above. Males lack white spots on the FW.
Larva: — Dull orange; an irregular, black lateral band; scattered tubercles bearing long, dark, black bristles. **Food:** — (Mexico) a Tropical Prickly Ash (*Zanthoxylum pentamon*).

AMYMONE. *Mestra amymone* Menetries p. 97
1.4–1.6 in. *Amymone* is easily recognized; the FW is pale gray basally and terminally; the HW has a pale, yellowish-brown outer margin. See also the section on Casual Species.
Larva: — Two long spines on the head with crests of small spines at their tips. **Food:** — *Tragia*.
Range: — Southern Texas (common) strays to Kansas and Nebraska (TL Nicaragua).

LESSER FRITILLARIES AND CRESCENTS
Family *Nymphalidae*

All illustrations are × 1 (natural size)

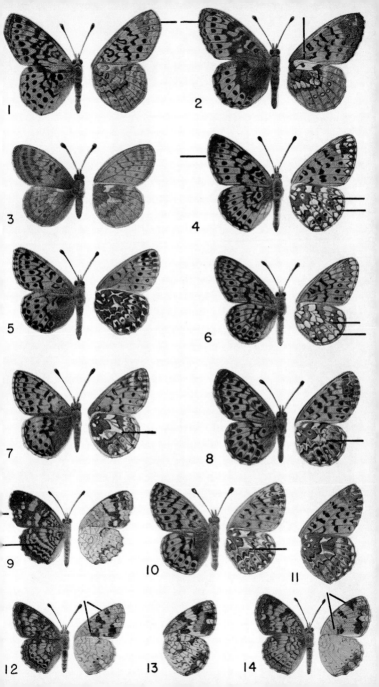

Plate 14   113

BRUSH FOOTED BUTTERFLIES
Family *Nymphalidae*

All illustrations are × ¾ natural size

1. **HOP MERCHANT,** *Polygonia comma*   p. 103
   Upper side, ♂, (Bedford, N.Y.) Brown beneath, no greenish; see text. Can. to N.C. & Kans.
2. **GREEN COMMA,** *Polygonia faunus*   p. 104
   Upper & under sides, ♂, (Jefferson H'lands, N.H.) Greenish marks beneath; very irregular margins; Can. to S.C. & Iowa.
3. **GRAY COMMA,** *Polygonia progne*   p. 104
   Upper side, ♂, (Stowe, Vt.) Grey beneath; cf. *gracilis* fig. 5; see text. Can. to Va., Mo. & Kans.
4. **QUESTION MARK,** *Polygonia interrogationis*   p. 102
   Upper side, ♂, (Manahawken, N.J.) Large; longer tails; smoother margins; HW beneath with silver dot below comma. Can. southward.
5. **HOARY COMMA,** *Polygonia gracilis*   p. 105
   Under side, ♂, (Laggan, B.C.) Grey beneath, much paler outwardly; see text. Northern.
6. **COMPTON TORTOISE SHELL,** *Nymphalis j-album*   p. 105
   Upper side, ♂, (W. Bridgewater, Vt.) Large; white spots on FW & HW. Northern.
7. **MILBERT'S TORTOISE SHELL,** *Nymphalis milberti*   p. 106
   Upper side, ♂, (Somers, N.Y.). Small; orange band. Northern.
8. **MOURNING CLOAK,** *Nymphalis antiopa*   p. 106
   Upper side, ♂, (N.Y. City, N.Y.) Large; yellow edges. Nearly entire eastern area.
9. **RED ADMIRAL,** *Vanessa atalanta*   p. 107
   Upper side, ♂, (Port Sewall, Fla.) Orange red bands. Can. southward.
10. **PAINTED LADY,** *Vanessa cardui*   p. 107
    Upper side, ♂, (Manzanilla, Mex.) Five all-black submarginal spots on HW above; beneath these are all present, small, subequal. Can. southward.
11. **AMERICAN PAINTED LADY,** *Vanessa virginiensis*   p. 108
    Upper side, ♂, (Flushing, L.I.) Submarginal spots of HW above contain blue; beneath there are only two of these, very large. Can. southward.
12. **BUCKEYE,** *Precis lavinia cœnia*   p. 108
    Upper side, ♂, (Chapel Hill, N.C.) Upper eyespot of HW very large, with red or purple. S. Can. southward.
13. **TROPICAL BUCKEYE,** *Precis lavinia zonalis*   p. 108
    Upper side, ♂, (Titusville, Fla.) Upper eyespot of HW small; see text. Fla. & s. Tex. southward.
14. **TAWNY EMPEROR,** *Asterocampa clyton*   p. 119
    Upper side, ♂, (Maplewood, N.J.). No large, black eyespot on FW; cf. *celtis*, fig. 15; spots of FW tawny. S. New England southward.
15. **HACKBERRY BUTTERFLY,** *Asterocampa celtis*   p. 12c
    Upper side, ♂, (Greene, Ala.) Large black eyespot on FW; spots of FW white or whitish. S. New England southward.

RUDDY DAGGER WING. *Marpesia petreus* Cramer   p. 96
2.6–2.8 in.   Dagger Wings may be recognized by the produced apex of the FW; and the long tail on vein M₃, and the shorter one at the anal angle, of the HW.   Three species enter our area but only *petreus* is an established, breeding resident.   For the other two (*coresia* and *chiron*) see the section on Casual Species. *Petreus* is bright orange-brown above, with dark brown and black markings.

Larva: — Reddish brown, ventral surface and dorsal surface from third abdominal segment backward yellow; sides with round black spots, and, posteriorly, oblique, black, mostly white edged lines.   A dorsal filament on each of 2d, 4th, 6th, and 8th abdominal segments, that of 8th longer and curved backward apically. Head dull yellow, with two black streaks and a black spot, two long, strong, hairy horns.   **Food:** — Figs (*Ficus*) and *Anacardium*.   Above data from Brazilian records.   Two or three broods.

Range: — Not uncommon in southern Florida n. to Indian River; casual northward.   Southern Texas, rare; casual to Kansas.

Subspecies: — *M. p. petreus* (TL Surinam) is South American, does not enter our area.   Our subspecies is *M. p. thetys* Fabricius (TL "Central America").

Genus Limenitis *Fabricius:* The Viceroys and Admirals

THESE ARE large butterflies, comprising a widespread genus of both Old and New Worlds.   One of our species is famed as a "mimic." The larvæ hibernate when part grown in a characteristic tube (*hibernaculum*) made of the rolled up basal part of a leaf, that is fastened to the twig of the food plant, exposed to all the forces of the winter weather.   Larvæ and pupæ are distinctively grotesque in form.   Recent work has changed the names of some forms by combining what were formerly called separate species.   The genus name, too, may seem strange to those who have known the group as *Basilarchia* Scudder.

VICEROY or MIMIC. *Limenitis archippus* Cramer pp. 48, 80, 144.
2.6–2.8 in.   The Viceroy departs radically from the colors of its relatives to "mimic" the Monarch.   Thereby it presumably gains protection, for the distasteful Monarch is seldom attacked by predators   The Viceroy is common over most of the eastern area, preferring open spaces, meadows, and roadsides.   Its flight is quite different from that of the Monarch, being a faster-beating flapping alternated with glides in which the wings are held horizontally and not slanted upwards as in the Monarch.   It is very

fond of flowers; and I have often seen it sipping the sweet honeydew secretions of aphids on leaves, or the apparently tasty juices, probably of fungi, on decaying wood. Many aberrant specimens and supposed "hybrids" have been recorded and named. One of these (*lanthanis*) lacks the narrow postmedian line across the HW and thus looks even more like the Monarch.

Similar Species: — *Danaus plexippus* and *D. gilippus;* the Viceroy is smaller than the Monarch (*D. plexippus*), or the Queen (*D. gilippus*), has heavier black along veins, and a black postmedian line across the HW.

Larva: — (see Pl. 5) Feeds largely at night, rests by day on twigs or exposed midribs of eaten leaves. **Food:** — Willows (especially *Salix nigra* & *sericea*), Poplars, and Aspens (*Populus balsamifera, tremuloides, deltoides, nigra*, etc.), Plum, Cherry, Apple, *Chrysobalanus*, etc. Two broods in north, three or more in south. Hibernation as part-grown larva. Adults in late May–early June.

Range: — Central Canada s. through Florida and Texas into Mexico (*L. a. hoffmani* R. L. Chermock); less common westward to Great Plains.

Subspecies: — *L. a. archippus* (TL "Island of Jamaica in North America"), northern, s. to South Carolina, Georgia, and Louisiana; ground color orange brown. *L. a. floridensis* Strecker; Florida straying (or occurring as isolated specimens) northward into North Carolina, perhaps in small colonies into Virginia; color very dark brown, almost dark mahogany in southern Florida; *L. a. watsoni* dos Passos (TL Alexandria, Louisiana) Louisiana, Alabama, Arkansas, & northern Texas; FW dark brown with light spots large, HW lighter brown. The species forms a double cline, with north-south gradation, and a large "blend zone" along the eastern coastal plain, another one through the Gulf States. *Watsoni* is an intermediate, blend zone form.

WHITE ADMIRAL or BANDED PURPLE. *Limenitis arthemis* Drury   pp. 49, 128

2.8–3.2 in. The prominent white band across the wings is distinctive of the northern White Admiral. In the Red Spotted Purple, which is now regarded as a subspecies of more southern range, the band is missing. The White Admiral is a common Canadian Zone butterfly of the northern United States and Canada. It is primarily a denizen of open hardwood forests and forest edges. A strong flier, it sails up and down a glade or road, or may spend much time on a favorite perch, often high in a tree. It frequently visits flowers and is also addicted to carrion, excrement, and the secretions of aphids. Sometimes it occurs in great abundance in small areas, hundreds of specimens jostling each other good-naturedly on a wet spot.

Larva: — Very similar in habits and appearance to that of *L. archippus* (Pl. 5); differs chiefly in that the smaller tubercle behind the largest on each side of the top of the head is shorter, broader, and more fused basally with the larger one. Both differ from the larva of *astyanax* (see below) in having fewer (less than 20) minute warts on a body segment above the line of the spiracles. **Food:** — Black and Yellow Birch (*Betula lenta* & *lutea*), Willow (*Salix*), Aspen, and Balsam Poplar (*Populus tremuloides* & *balsamifera*), less often Hawthorn (*Cratægus*); perhaps also Shadbush (*Amelanchier*) and Basswood (*Tilia*). One and a partial second brood northward, two southward. Hibernation as young larva. Adults in mid-June.

Range: — Forested areas of Canada, s. in Canadian Zone into northern New England, New York, Pennsylvania, Michigan, and Minnesota.

Subspecies: — *L. a. rubrofasciata* Barnes & McDunnough (TL Saskatchewan); western Ontario, Manitoba, and westward; HW above with a submarginal row of large, brick red spots; wings beneath with red spots forming distinct bands. *L. a. arthemis* (TL New York, probably Catskill Mountains), range e. and s. of the above; red spots both above and beneath reduced, sometimes absent above. See also *L. a. astyanax*, below.

RED SPOTTED PURPLE. *Limenitis arthemis astyanax* Fabricius   p. 128

3.1–3.4 in. Although long considered a separate species, the Red Spotted Purple is now regarded as a subspecies of the White Admiral. Its range begins where the range of the more northern form ends, and extends south into northern Florida and central Texas. In the narrow zone where *arthemis* and *astyanax* occur in contact there appear various "hybrids" between them. This suggests strongly a former geographic separation of the two, now eliminated by recent extensions of their ranges. One such form, with more or less of the white band of *arthemis* but with greenish blue markings and red spots like those of *astyanax*, is *albofasciata;* another, with essentially no white band but otherwise the general coloration of *arthemis*, is *proserpina* ("spots brick red, not orange red as in *astyanax*"). Except in New York, Pennsylvania, and New Jersey, the "contact zone" of the subspecies is narrow. *Astyanax* favors open, scrubby woods and woods edges, but is not such a high flier as *arthemis*, or so limited to the forest. It visits flowers freely, is also much addicted to carrion, manure, and excrement.

Larva: — Characterized under *arthemis*. **Food:** — Willows (*Salix*), Poplars (*Populus tremuloides* and *grandidentata*), Plum, Apple, Quince, Wild Cherry, Hawthorn (*Cratægus*), Gooseberry (*Ribes*), Deerberry (*Vaccinium stamineum*), Hornbeam (*Carpinus*), Scrub Oak (*Quercus ilicifolia*) (!), etc. Three broods. Hibernation as part-grown larva. Adults in mid-May (much earlier southward).

Range: — Central and southern New England, New York, Pennsylvania, Ohio w. to Nebraska, s. to central Florida, and central Texas (TL "America").

Genus Anæa *Huebner.* The Leaf Wings

MEDIUM SIZED to large butterflies, the Leaf Wings have the apex of the FW pointed and more or less hooked, so that the outer margin is concave; and a slender, sharp tail on vein M_3 of the HW. The colors of the upper side are usually brilliant orange-red, orange-brown, or blue; the undersides are plain, dead-leaf brown or grayish. The butterflies have a swift, erratic flight, from which they alight suddenly on a twig or tree trunk, sit with the wings folded above the back, and thus look like a dead leaf. The protective value of this, increased by the "surprise" factor of the sudden vanishing of the bright colors, makes them outstanding examples of *protective resemblance.*

The adults are greatly attracted to sap, rotting fruit, manure, etc. In some species "dry season" and "wet season" forms are very marked, differing in wing shape as well as color. Females have the ground color above paler and the dark markings heavier and more outstanding. The New World tropics have a bewildering array of species. Five occur in our area, two of them as strays (see section on Casual Species, p. 280).

GOATWEED BUTTERFLY. *Anæa andria* Scudder   p. 96
2.2–2.6 in. Above, bright orange, paler in the female; beneath, pale brown with fine mottlings and marblings. The female has a wide, irregular, lighter, postmedian band across the upper side of both wings, narrowly margined with darker brown. The summer ("dry season") form, *andriæsta*, has the apex of the FW less produced; the outer margin of the HW less rounded and the anal angle more obtuse; and a somewhat duller ground color above. Since the broods overlap greatly, both forms often fly together; it is the "wet," or winter season, form that hibernates.
Similar Species: — *A. floridalis, aidea,* and *glycerium. Glycerium* has the outer margin of the FW strongly swollen outward at vein Cu_2, so that the margin is very sinuate. In both *floridalis* and *aidea* the wing margins are finely serrate or jagged, not smooth as in *andria;* both these species have more decided patterns above than *andria,* especially in the males.
Larva: — Grayish green, tapering posteriorly, covered with many fine, raised points; head gray green with small tubercles. lives, when older, in a folded leaf. Food: — Crotons or Goatweeds (*Croton capitatus* and *monanthogynus*). Two broods. Hibernates as adult. Adults in early April.
Range: — Georgia, Tennessee, Ohio, Illinois, southern Michigan, and Nebraska, s. to Gulf States and Texas, not in peninsular Florida; rare northward (TL probably Illinois or Missouri).

FLORIDA LEAF WING. *Anæa floridalis* Johnson & Comstock

p. 96

2.6–2.9 in. Formerly considered a subspecies of *A. aidea*, the Florida Leaf Wing seems to be a close, but distinct species. It is not uncommon in southern Florida, where it is the only *Anæa*. Records there of *A. portia* refer to this species. Like its congeners it is at least two brooded, with considerable difference in appearance between the broods; the summer form has the wing shape smoother, the apex of the FW less produced. I have taken it only in woodlands or around their edges.

Similar Species: — *A. andria*, see above. *A. aidea* occurs in Texas n. to Kansas; males of *aidea* tend to have a stronger dark pattern above, especially with regard to the lighter, postmedian band and the dark edges inside and outside this. The dark, inner edge of this band is, in *aidea*, less irregular and more evenly scalloped, tending somewhat to break the band into partly separate spots. *A. glycerium* (stray in Texas) has very different wing shape.

Larva: — Green, dotted with many fine, white tubercles; a pair of yellow lateral stripes; head light green with seven orange and two black tubercles. Pupa pale green, shaped much like that of the Monarch (*Danaus*). **Food:** — Croton (*Croton linearis*). At least two broods.

Range: — Southern Florida (TL Florida City).

TROPICAL LEAF WING. *Anæa aidea* Guerin

1.9–2.2 in. *Aidea* occurs widely in the tropics, but in our area is regular only in Texas, whence it ranges rarely to Kansas. In the tropics the usual two seasonal forms occur; but in our area only the summer form, *morrisonii* has been recorded.

Similar Species: — *A. andria* & *floridalis;* see above. *A. glycerium* has very sinuate outer margin of FW, strongly produced outward at Cu_2; also has stronger dark apical markings on FW above, and a definite subapical band, often only slightly interrupted, from costa to outer margin.

Range: — In the eastern area: southern Texas (May, Sept.–Oct.) n. to Oklahoma and Kansas (rare) (TL on shipboard, Campeche Bay, Mexico).

Genus Asterocampa *Ræber:* The Hackberry Butterflies

HACKBERRY BUTTERFLIES are most commonly seen flying around Hackberry trees, alighting on the twigs and leaves; but they also visit mud puddles. They have a fast, erratic flight, and are vigorous dodgers. They often alight on tree trunks. They also, peculiarly enough, not infrequently alight on people! The larvæ are striped, taper characteristically from the middle to both ends, have the last segment forked, and bear a pair of large, heavily barbed horns on the head. Females are larger, lighter colored, and broader winged than males. In the south the species run greatly to geographic variations, showing clinal gradation in this; intergradation along the line makes identification of intermediate specimens difficult. Only two species occur widely in our area, one other entering it in southern Texas. Until recently our species were placed in the genus *Chlorippe* Boisduval, a very large group of the tropics of which one species is a stray into our area (see section on Casual Species, p. 280).

TAWNY EMPEROR. *Asterocampa clyton* Boisduval & Leconte
pp. 48, 113
1.9–2.6 in. Widespread in our area, *clyton* is probably overlooked in many regions. Look for it around Hackberry trees, especially around the edges of woods. Rare northward, often locally common in the south.
Similar Species: — *A. celtis* and *leilia*. On the FW above, *clyton* lacks the prominent, submarginal, round, black or ocellate spot in cell Cu$_1$ that both *celtis* and *leilia* have. In some *celtis* and *leilia* forms there is another similar spot above this in cell M$_3$. Also on the FW above, *clyton* has two solid, zigzag, dark bars. So does *leilia;* but in *celtis* the basal bar is broken into two spots, and both these and the other bar frequently have light centers. Larva: — (see genus description) Striped with yellow, green and white, gregarious when young. Food: — Hackberry (*Celtis*). Perhaps only one brood in northern part of range, two or more southward. Hibernates as half-grown larva. Adults in mid-June.
Range: — Southern New England and New York, w. to Nebraska, southward.
Subspecies: — *A. c. clyton* (TL "American Meridionale") northern, most of the above range; ground color darker and more suffused with dull, dark clouding, especially basally. *A. c. flora* Edwards (TL Palatka, Florida) Coastal Plain, Georgia s. through Florida and Gulf States; larger, ground color much lighter and brighter, dark markings reduced. *A. c. texana* Skinner (TL Round Mountain, Texas) central Texas n. into Kansas; large; postmedian and subterminal rows of light spots of FW creamy white; in *flora* on the HW above, the very thin, dark line between the black spots and the dark marginal border is very faint or absent; in *texana* this line is usually noticeably present. *A. c. louisa* Stallings & Turner (TL Pharr, Texas) southern Texas; apical region of FW above with ground color very

dark; ground color of rest of wings duller brown; light spots of FW above white. All of these forms appear to stray and to intergrade in blend zones.

HACKBERRY BUTTERFLY. *Asterocampa celtis* Boisduval & Leconte   p. 113
1.9–2.4 in. Like *clyton*, *celtis* has a wide range in our area, and is associated everywhere with Hackberry in woodland areas.
Similar Species: — *A. clyton* & *leilia*; see above under *clyton*.
Larva: — Like that of *clyton*, less pale dorsally. Food: — Hackberry (*Celtis*). Two broods northward, three southward. Hibernation as half-grown larva. Adults in late May–June.
Range: — Southern New England, New York, Pennsylvania, Ontario, Illinois, Michigan, and Minnesota, and southward.
Subspecies: — *A. c. celtis* (TL Georgia) northern, s. to ranges of others (below); ground color above darker, more suffused with dull brownish. *A. c. alicia* Edwards (TL New Orleans, Louisiana) South Carolina through Florida and Gulf States into eastern Texas; larger, ground color lighter and brighter; white spots of FW larger; in general much more boldly and contrastingly marked. *A. c. antonia* Edwards (TL Texas and Arizona) central and southern Texas southward and westward; much like *c. celtis*, smaller with duller ground color, but with two, fully ocellate spots on FW above (in cells M_3 & Cu_1). *A. c. montis* Edwards (TL Mt. Graham, Arizona) of the Rocky Mountains, has been recorded from Kansas; in it the upper of the two ocellate spots of *antonia* is imperfectly developed. Perhaps the *montis*-like specimens from Kansas, Oklahoma, and Texas should be referred to *antonia*.

LEILIA. *Asterocampa leilia* Edwards
2.0–2.3 in. *Leilia* is a Mexican and western species which, as the subspecies *cocles* Lintner (TL Hidalgo, Texas) occurs, common to abundant, in southern Texas (Hidalgo, Del Rio, Laredo, Pharr, Feb.–May, Sept.–Oct.). Its general appearance resembles that of the other species. In addition to the characters cited (above, under *clyton*) it has the ocelli of the FW beneath centrally pupiled with blue, not with white as in *A. celtis antonia*.

Family Libytheidæ: The Snout Butterflies

THIS IS a small family, with but one species in our area. The most distinctive characteristic is the extreme length of the palpi, which project in front like a long snout or beak. The front legs of the males are reduced in size, but those of the females are normal and functional; in this the *Libytheidæ* are intermediate between the Skippers, *Pieridæ*, *Papilionidæ*, etc. with fully normal legs; and the Nymphaloid series with the legs greatly reduced in both sexes. In the Old World, too, *Libytheidæ* have the same general appearance, their color, pattern and wing shape being distinctive.

SNOUT BUTTERFLY. *Libytheana bachmannii* Kirtland

pp. 48, 49, **144**

1.75 in. At times not uncommon in the South and Middle West, but rare northward, the Snout Butterfly is found in both open country and woods, and along roadsides. It visits flowers, but seems more attracted by muddy stream and lake margins. The flight is swift and erratic. The wings above are dark blackish brown, with orange brown patches and subapical white spots on the FW. It is "dimorphic," there being one form dark beneath with little mottling, and another light beneath with much mottling.

Larva: — Head small; two thoracic segments enlarged, rising above head as a hump which bears a pair of dull black tubercles basally ringed with yellow; last abdominal segment sloped abruptly down; dark velvety green, a yellow mid-dorsal and a pair of yellow lateral stripes. **Food:** — Hackberry (*Celtis occidentalis*) and, in west, Wolfberry (*Symphoricarpos occidentalis*). Three or four broods. Adults in early April. Hibernation as pupa.

Range: — Entire eastern area n. to Canadian Zone, i.e. central New England, southern Ontario; rare and erratic northward and in Florida.

Subspecies: — *L. b. bachmannii* (TL northern Ohio) range as above except for southern and western Texas. *L. b. larvata* Strecker (TL Southwestern Texas) in our area, in Rio Grande Valley, Texas (August–October.); and in Oklahoma and Kansas as a stray; light markings above less extensive; wings less angulate, and outer margin of HW less undulate; size larger.

Family Riodinidæ: The Metalmarks

METALMARKS are small to small-medium sized butterflies. Only a few occur in the eastern area, but in the New World tropics there are hundreds. The popular name comes from the usual presence of small, metallic looking spots or lines on the wings. The front legs of the males are usually greatly reduced but those of the females are normal. The head is very narrow; the eyes are more or less emarginate around the bases of the antennæ; and the palpi are very short. On the HW the humeral vein is present and in our species the costa is thickened out to the humeral angle. The eggs of our species are somewhat flat and turban shaped. The larvæ are either more or less cylindrical or else flattened, broad and "slug-shaped," and bear numerous hairs, sometimes a dense covering. The pupa is short, stout, and well rounded with no prominent projections. It is suspended by the cremaster and, nearly always, a girdle; and is covered with short hairs and a few long, bristle-like ones.

The adults very frequently alight with their wings spread out at the sides and, in many species, pitch up onto the under side of a leaf. Our species are rather plainly colored; but in the tropics occurs nearly every imaginable combination of colors, patterns, and wing shapes. A peculiarity of tropical Metalmarks is that although there are hundreds of species, very few are at all common; so that one catches many species but very seldom many specimens of any one.

The family is also known as the *Erycinidæ* or *Lemoniidæ*.

Our really native species belong to the genus *Lephelisca* (formerly called *Charis*, *Calephelis*, or *Nymphidia*) but a number of essentially tropical species occur in southern Texas. Many are very difficult to identify, but the genitalia seem to have good characters. The key given below will work fairly well for most specimens, but some of the species run very close.

KEY TO THE *RIODINIDÆ* OF EASTERN NORTH AMERICA

1. Costal margin of FW distinctly concave at about its middle   2
1. Costal margin of FW not distinctly concave.............   3
2. Wings above dull orange brown, somewhat brighter along costal region of the HW, crossed by a number of obscure, irregular, broken, dark transverse lines; on FW just beyond costal concavity is a whitish and yellowish, three-parted mark extending down to below vein M_3; Texas.....*Emesis emesia*
2. Dark brown above with an incomplete, postmedian line of metallic spots extending down from costa of FW; outer margins of wings lighter yellowish brown with broken metallic lines; Texas.........................*Caria domitianus*
3. Wings above greenish blue with dark markings; Texas
                                                    Lasaia sessilis
3. Wings above brown or orange brown   4
4. Wings above dark brown, checkered with irregular bands of squarish, light gray-brown spots; Texas....*Apodemia walkeri*
4. Wings above dark brown to orange brown; markings dark, or of lines of metallic spots and dashes; without prominent light spots.............................Genus *Lephelisca*   5
5. Fringes, especially of FW, checkered (not always prominently)   6
5. Fringes not checkered   8
6. Size large (exp. 0.85–1.15 in.)..........................   7
6. Size small (exp. 0.75–0.85 in.); Texas ....*L. perditalis*
7. Coloration above dark and dull, with a central, suffused, dark shade across wings; fringes more checkered; metalmarks of FW above forming a rather uninterrupted line;

wings beneath with more reddish flush; chiefly northeastern
L. borealis

7. Darker above, red-brown, lighter than the above; little
central, dark suffusion across wings; fringes definitely
checkered; metallic spots less prominent, thinner and more
crescent-shaped; outer margin of FW slightly concave; Texas
L. rawsoni

7. Lighter and brighter above, rich mahogany brown when
fresh; little central, dark shade across wings; fringes little
checkered; metalmarks of FW forming a more irregular,
broken line; less reddish flush on wings beneath; chiefly
north-central................................... *L. muticum*

8. Wings above darker, markings less distinct; metallic spot-
lines less conspicuous; FW of ♂ very slender and pointed;
wings beneath light yellow brown, contrasting lighter and
paler than upper side; Texas...................... *L. nemesis*

8. Wings above lighter and brighter, markings distinct; metallic spot-lines more conspicuous; FW blunter and more
rounded in both sexes; color beneath not so contrastingly
lighter and paler than upper side; widespread, southern
and eastern .... *L. virginiensis*

LITTLE METALMARK. *Lephelisca virginiensis* Guerin   p. 128
0.70–0.80 in. The Little Metalmark is locally common in the
South, but becomes rare northward. It occurs mostly in open
grassy fields and wet meadows. I have found it common in
Florida both in grassy, salt-marsh meadows, and in dry, grassy
savannah in the Everglades. Its small size, uncheckered fringes
and bright colors distinguish it. The life history needs to be
worked out. There appear to be a number of broods in the
South.
Range: — Southern Florida, Gulf States and southern Texas
n. to Virginia and Ohio.

NORTHERN METALMARK. *Lephelisca borealis* Grote & Robinson   p. 128
1.0–1.15 in. Limited to the northeastern part of our area, *borealis* is usually scarce and local. Records of *"borealis"* from Ohio
westward appear to be really of the next species, *muticum*, with
which it was long confused. *Borealis* occurs in dry, hilly meadows and open woods where its food plant grows, not, as sometimes recorded, in low, wet meadows and swamps.
Similar Species: — *L. muticum, rawsoni* (see key above).
Larva: — Green with a number of black dorsal spots; covered
with long, white hairs. **Food:** — Ragwort or Groundsel (*Senecio
obovatus*). One brood. Adults in early July. Hibernation as
part-grown larva.
Range: — Southern New England, s. to Virginia, w. to Ohio.

SWAMP METALMARK. *Lephelisca muticum* McAlpine   p. 128
0.9–1.0 in. Prior to 1937 *muticum* was unnamed and confused
with *borealis*. Its range overlaps that of *borealis* in Ohio, whence

it extends westward. It occurs in wet meadows and swamps
where the food plant grows, has been recorded from a tamarack
bog in Michigan. Its flight is rather weak.

Similar Species: — *L. borealis, rawsoni* (see key above).

Larva: — Green with long white hairs, those of the anterior seg-
ments projecting forward, of the posterior segments, backward.
Pupa pale green, abdomen somewhat yellower; suspended by a
girdle and covered with a mat of the larval hairs. **Food:** —
Swamp Thistle (*Cirsium muticum*). One brood. Adults in late
July and August. Hibernation as part-grown larva.

Range: — Pennsylvania, Ohio, Illinois, Missouri, Michigan (TL
Willis, Washtenaw Co.), Minnesota, Wisconsin. Records of
borealis from this area probably refer to *muticum*.

RAWSON'S METALMARK. *Lephelisca rawsoni* McAlpine

0.85–1.0 in. Recently named from Texas, Rawson's Metalmark
most resembles *muticum* but may be told by its more checkered
fringes and less prominent metalmarks. It may be a subspecies
of *L. guadeloupe* Strecker.

Range: — Southern Texas (TL Kerrville) westward; July–Sept.

FATAL METALMARK. *Lephelisca nemesis* Edwards   p. 128

0.75–0.80 in. *Nemesis* differs from *virginiensis* in its dark coloration and general indistinctness of pattern above; and from the
other dark species in its small size, lack of checkered fringes, and
very pointed wing shape in the ♂. Common in southern Texas.

LOST METALMARK. *Lephelisca perditalis* Barnes & McDunnough   p. 128

0.75–0.85 in. The little, dark *perditalis* is known by its small
size, general dark and dull coloration with rather narrower,
metalmark lines, and the checkered fringes of the FW. In particular the checkered fringes and broader, more rounded FW of
the ♂ distinguish it from *nemesis*. Common in southern Texas
and westward, flying throughout the year.

WALKER'S METALMARK. *Apodemia walkeri* Godman &
Salvin

0.70–0.90 in. Ground color dark brown, checkered with irregu-
lar, broken bands of lighter, gray brown, squarish spots; beneath
paler, somewhat ochreous tinged, markings much as above.
Superficially it resembles a small *Melitæa* or *Phyciodes*.
Southern Texas (Pharr, Brownsville) May–June, October–
December.

EMESIA METALMARK. *Emesis emesia* Hewitson

1.1–1.2 in. Both *Emesis* and the next genus, *Caria*, have the
costa of the FW distinctly concave at about the middle. This is

most marked in *emesia*, which is dull orange brown above, brighter along the costal region of the HW, with a number of irregular and broken, somewhat obscure, transverse dark lines. On the FW just beyond the costal concavity is a three-part, yellowish and white mark extending down to below vein M_3. *Emesia*, which has been taken at Pharr, Texas in October and November, is rare there, commoner in Mexico. I have found no records from our area of *E. ares* Edwards or *E. cleis* Edwards, listed in Holland.

DOMITIAN METALMARK. *Caria domitianus* Fabricius
0.8–1.0 in. Wings above dark brown; an incomplete postmedian line of metallic spots extending down from costa of FW; borders lighter yellow brown with broken, metallic lines. *Domitianus*, *melicerta* Schaus, and *ino* Godman & Salvin may be variations in a single, clinal species. *Domitianus* has a large amount of iridescent green near the center of the costa of the FW; *ino* has merely a small amount; *melicerta* has very little or none at all. I have seen specimens from Brownsville, Texas that could be referred to either *ino* or *melicerta*. The species is common throughout the year in the Brownsville–Pharr region.

BLUE METALMARK. *Lasaia sessilis* Schaus   p. 145
0.8–0.9 in. Wings above dull greenish blue, with transverse, broken, dark lines forming a somewhat checkered pattern. *Sessilis* has been confused with *Lasaia narses* Staudinger and *sula* Staudinger, both of Mexico. *Narses* has a distinct, dark, mid-costal patch on the FW above. *Sula* is duller colored. *Sessilis* is common at Pharr and Brownsville, Texas, September–November, April.

Family Lycænidæ: The Gossamer Winged Butterflies

THIS IS a very large, world-wide family. All are small (one, in fact, is our smallest butterfly), but many are rapid fliers. Our members of the family fall naturally into four subfamilies, the Hairstreaks (*Theclinæ*), Harvesters (*Gerydinæ*), Coppers (*Lycæninæ*), and Blues (*Plebeiinæ*). The majority of the species have at least some iridescent blue, green or coppery; some are among the most brilliant of butterflies. The head is very narrow and the eyes emarginate. The males' front legs are slightly reduced (lacking tarsal claws and pulvilli), but those of the females are fully developed and functional. Our species all lack one or two branches of radius in the forewing, and have no humeral vein in the hindwing. The egg is usually strongly flattened, decorated with pits, raised knobs or lines. The larva is usually short, broad and oval, quite flattened and "sluglike," and covered with fine hairs. Many of the larvæ possess glands that secrete "honeydew"; this attracts ants with which the larvæ have mutually beneficial (symbiotic) relationships. The larvæ of some, in fact, live in ant nests, feeding on debris or on the ant brood. Many larvæ show strong cannibalistic tendencies. In one of our species (*Feniseca*) the larva is an out-and-out predator, feeding on plant lice (Aphids). The pupa is short and rounded, its lower surface nearly flat, is usually covered with short hairs, and is fastened by the cremaster and a silk girdle.

Subfamily Theclinæ: The Hairstreaks

OUR HAIRSTREAKS are small to medium sized (most species with fine hairlike "tails" on the hindwings) and have only three branches of radius in the forewing. The common name comes from the fine, transverse, streaky lines on the wings beneath. Most of our species are relatively plain brownish, but among the hundreds of species in the tropics many are iridescent blue, green and gold, as beautiful as any butterflies.

Hairstreaks have swift, darting flights, sometimes too fast to follow with the eye. They occur mostly in open spaces, in meadows, and along roadsides, although a few are forest species. Nearly all are great flower visitors, best collected by watching Milkweed, New Jersey Tea (*Ceanothus americana*), Spanish Needles (*Bidens*), etc. Many habitually perch on leaves or twigs and when startled will, if not too frightened, return to the same perch after a short flight. Some larvæ are attended by ants, and may be found by watching concentrations of ants on bushes and trees. A number bore into fruits or buds, although the majority are leaf feeders.

The generic arrangement is rather uncertain. The name *Thecla* was originally used for most of the species. Many other names have been proposed, some doubtless valid. There has never been, however, a large scale, world-wide study using structural characters such as the genitalia. As a result we must for the present "lump" most of the species in one genus. The name *Strymon* is probably preferable for this inclusive grouping.

Many Hairstreaks are far from easy to identify. A "key" is therefore given below that will aid when used with the illustrations and the diagnoses. *Eumæus* and *Incisalia* are omitted from the key. The tropical *Strymon* recorded in Florida and Texas (see section on Casual Species, p. 281) are included.

TROPICAL SPECIES (F = Florida only, T = Texas only) *acis* (F), *azia* (T), *bazochii* (T), *beon* (T), *calanus* (F), *cestri* (T), *clytie* (T), *columella, endy-*

mion (T), *facuna* (T), *laceyi* (T), *martialis* (F), *mæsites*, *pastor* (T), *simæthis* (T), *spurina* (T), *xami* (T), *yojoa* (T), *echion* (T), *rufofusca* (T), *zebina* (T.).

MORE WIDELY RANGING IN OUR AREA (N = northern) *acadica* (N), *alcestis*, *caryævorus* (N), *cecrops*, *edwardsi*, *falacer*, *favonius*, *gryneus*, *hesseli* (N), *halesus*, *læta* (N), *liparops*, *m-album*, *melinus*, *ontario*, *titus*

KEY TO THE SPECIES, BOTH SEXES (*Atlides, Erora, Mitoura,* and *Strymon.*)

1. Upper side solid blue or with extensive blue areas 2
1. With only small blue areas above, at anal angle of HW, or none 12
2. Solid blue above; green beneath. . . . .*S. mæsites*
2. Not solid blue above 3
3. Males with base and disc of wings brilliant, shining blue; females with only basal parts of wings thus brilliant; large, exp. 1.2 in. or more 4
3. Blue above not brilliant and intensely iridescent. 5
4. Wings light brownish beneath with a narrow postmedian line on FW, an irregular postmedian line and a submarginal line on HW, and an orange submarginal patch in cell Cu_1 of HW; abdomen bluish above, whitish beneath. . . . . . .*S. m-album*
4. Wings deep brown beneath with orange red basal spot; the FW of male with metallic blue-green central ray; the HW with large blue-green and orange red spots at anal angle; abdomen orange red beneath; anal angle of HW much produced . . . . *Atlides halesus*
5. Wings green beneath 6
5. Wings brown or gray beneath 7
6. HW with a short tail on Cu_2; anal angle more projecting; HW beneath with distinct postmedian line of white bordered spots; and beyond that a submarginal orange brown band below vein M_3, beyond that large patches in cells Cu_1 and Cu_2 and 2dA; tropical . . . .*S. pastor*
6. HW with no tail, anal angle less projecting; HW beneath with indistinct postmedian line of spots not outwardly white bordered; tropical. . . . .*S. facuna*
6. HW with no tail, beneath with transverse rows of red spots; northern . . . .*Erora læta*
7. Postmedian transverse lines of wings beneath bright red to orange red inwardly, especially on HW. 8
7. Postmedian transverse lines beneath not bright red inwardly 9
8. Red of transverse lines broad; submarginal spots of HW below vein Cu_1 and at anal angle large, largely dark. . . . . . .*S. cecrops*
8. Red of transverse lines narrow, especially on FW; submarginal spots of HW below vein Cu_1 and at anal angle largely orange red, with small, external black pupils; wings above with more blue, especially in males. . . . .*S. beon*
9. HW with no tails; FW above with no blue; HW beneath with a mottled pattern, the transverse lines indistinct
   [1] *S. bazochii*
9. HW with tails; FW above with some blue; wings beneath with clear-cut transverse lines. 10

[1] Note: *cestri* females might run here, for some of them have a very pale, bluish white above. They have a very prominent, black, submarginal spot on the HW in cell Cu_1 both above and below, which *bazochii* lacks.

ADMIRALS, METALMARKS AND HAIRSTREAKS
Families *Nymphalidae, Riodinidae* and *Lycaenidae*

Illustrations of the Admirals are × ⅔.   The others are natural size

1. RED SPOTTED PURPLE, *Limenitis arthemis astyanax*   p. 116
   Upper & under sides, ♂ (Savannah, Ga.) × ⅔.   No white band.   Cf.
   fig. 2.   New England s. to Fla. & Tex.
2. WHITE ADMIRAL, *Limenitis arthemis arthemis*   p. 115
   Upper & under sides, ♀ (Charlton, Ont.) × ⅔.   Broad white band;
   cf. fig. 5.   Can. s. into centr. New England & Pa.
3. NORTHERN METALMARK, *Lephelisca borealis*   p. 123
   Upper & under sides, ♀ (Blacksburg, Va.) × 1.   Dark median shade
   across wings; checkered fringes; see text.   Northeast, w. into Ohio, s.
   to Va.
4. SWAMP METALMARK, *Lephelisca mulicum*   p. 123
   Upper side, ♂ (Oakland Co., Mich.) × 1.   Little median dark shade;
   fringes less checkered; see text.   Ohio. to Minn. & Mo.
5. HYBRID ADMIRAL, *Limenitis arthemis* f. *albofasciata*   p. 116
   Upper side, ♂ (Scranton, Pa.) × ⅔.   See text; more or less of the white
   band of *arthemis arthemis*.
6. LITTLE METALMARK, *Lephelisca virginiensis*   p. 123
   Upper & under sides, ♂ (Gainesville, Fla.) × 1.   Small; uncheckered
   fringes; bright coloration.   Va. & Ohio southward.
7. FATAL METALMARK, *Lephelisca nemesis*   p. 124
   Upper side, ♂ (Pharr, Tex.) × 1.   Small; dark; uncheckered fringes;
   pointed FW of ♂.   S. Tex.
8. LOST METALMARK, *Lephelisca perditalis*   p. 124
   Upper side, ♂ (Brownsville, Tex.). × 1.   Small; dark; checkered
   fringes; S. Tex.
9. GREAT PURPLE HAIRSTREAK, *Atlides halesus*   p. 133
   Upper side, ♂ (Monticello, Fla.) × 1.   Large; brilliant color; long
   tails; ♀ is duller.   N.J. & Ill. s. to Fla. & westward.
10. MÆSITES HAIRSTREAK, *Strymon maesites*   p. 139
   Under side, ♂ (Miami, Fla.) × 1.   Small; beneath, green; above
   (fig. 13) iridescent blue; S. Fla. & S. Tex.
11. BARTRAM'S HAIRSTREAK, *Strymon acis bartrami*   p. 138
   Under side, ♂ (Miami, Fla.) × 1.   Plain brown above; basal spots
   & bolder pattern of HW beneath.   Cf. fig. 14.   S. Fla.
12. RED BANDED HAIRSTREAK, *Strymon cecrops*   p. 133
   Upper & under sides, ♂ (Monticello, Fla.) × 1.   Red median band
   beneath; see text.   N.Y. & Mich. southward.
13. MÆSITES HAIRSTREAK, *S. maesites*, upper side, see fig. 10.
14. MARTIAL HAIRSTREAK, *Strymon martialis*   p. 138
   Upper & under sides, ♂ (Biscayne Bay, Fla.) × 1.   Much blue above;
   HW beneath lacks basal spots (cf. fig. 11).   S. Fla.

Plate 16   **HAIRSTREAKS AND ELFINS**   129

Family *Lycaenidae*

All illustrations are × 1 (natural size)

1. GRAY HAIRSTREAK, *Strymon melinus*   p. 134
Upper & under sides, ♂ (Cape May, N.J.) Grey; no basal or discal
marks beneath; orange lunule above and beneath. Can. southward.

2. SOUTHERN HAIRSTREAK, *Strymon favonius*   p. 135
Under side, ♂ (Jupiter, Fla.) Orange patches above; HW beneath
with extensive orange band; long tails; N. to W.Va. & N.J.

3. COLUMELLA HAIRSTREAK, *Strymon columella*   p. 140
Under side, ♂ (Homestead, Fla.) HW beneath with prominent
round spots below costa. Fla., Gulf States, s. Texas.

4. NORTHERN HAIRSTREAK, *Strymon ontario*   p. 135
Under side, ♂ (Mobile, Ala.) Above with orange patches; HW beneath with less orange (cf. fig. 2). Can. s. to Texas.

5. ALCESTIS HAIRSTREAK, *Strymon alcestis*   p. 135
Under side, ♂ (Caldwell, Kans.) Beneath, lines sharp & clear; bars
at ends of cells; FW with some orange. Tex. to Kans.

6. CORAL HAIRSTREAK, *Strymon titus*   p. 134
Under side, ♂ (Yaphank, L.I.) No tails; prominent coral-red submarginal spots. Can. s. to Ga. & Tex.

7. ACADIAN HAIRSTREAK, *Strymon acadica*   p. 136
Under side, ♂ (Gravenhorst, Ont.) Pale beneath; round, well
separated spots; orange spot on HW above. Can., northern States.

8. STRIPED HAIRSTREAK, *Strymon liparops*   p. 138
Under side, ♂ (Putnam, Conn.) Lines beneath very far apart and
"offset." Can. to Ga.

9. FLORIDA HAIRSTREAK, *Strymon calanus*   p. 137
Under side, ♂ (Ocoee, Fla.) Large; dark; long tails; orange spot on
HW above; long blue spot on HW beneath. Fla.

10. BANDED HAIRSTREAK, *Strymon falacer*   p. 137
Under side, ♂ (Canadensis, Pa.) Shorter tails; lines beneath not
broken into separate spots; no orange above; Can. southward.

11. EDWARD'S HAIRSTREAK, *Strymon edwardsii*   p. 136
Under side, ♂ (Omaha, Nebr.) Lines beneath broken into separate,
oval spots; lighter; Can. to Ga. & Kans.

12. HICKORY HAIRSTREAK, *Strymon caryævorus*   p. 137
Under side, ♂ (Johnstown, N.Y.) Bands beneath wider, more
broken and "offset." S. Can. & n. N.Y.

13. OLIVE HAIRSTREAK, *Mitoura gryneus*   p. 141
Under side, ♂ (Suffold Co., Va.) Beneath, green; tail; see text. New
England to n. Fla. & Tex.

14. EARLY HAIRSTREAK, *Erora læta*   p. 142
Upper & under sides, ♂ (Sherburne, Vt.) No tails; grey-green
beneath with red spots; ♀ has much blue above. Que. to Ky.

15. BROWN ELFIN, *Incisalia augustinus*   p. 146
Under side, ♂ (Coram, L.I.) Beneath, much orange-brown, no grey
clouding. Can. to Va., Ill. & Mich.

16. HOARY ELFIN, *Incisalia polios*   p. 147
Under side, ♂ (Lakehurst, N.J.) Much grey clouding beneath.
Can. s. to N.J., Ind. & Mich.

17. HENRY'S ELFIN, *Incisalia henrici*   p. 147
Under side, ♂ (Greenwood Lake Glens, N.J.) Less grey clouding
beneath; contrast between basal and outer areas on HW; see text; ♂
lacks stigma. Que. to Fla. & Tex.

18. FROSTED ELFIN, *Incisalia irus*   p. 148
Upper & under side, ♂ (Blairstown, N.J.) Long narrow stigma of
♂; less contrast between basal and outer areas of HW. Can. to Ga.
& Tex.

19. PINE ELFIN, *Incisalia niphon*   p. 149
Upper & under sides, ♀ (Tryon, N.C.) Above, with orange-brown;
HW beneath strongly patterned. Can. to Fla. & n. Tex.

20. BOG ELFIN, *Incisalia lanoraiensis*   p. 148
Under side, ♂ (Lincoln, Me.) Small; less distinct pattern beneath;
Black Spruce bogs, Que. & Me.

10. Large, exp. 1.1 in. or more; male above nearly all dark, dull blue with very narrow, indistinct, dark borders; female grayish brown above; ground color beneath dark, transverse lines narrow; orange-red and black spot in cell Cu₁ of HW very little longer than wide, if any..........................*S. spurina*

10. Smaller, exp. seldom over 1.0 in.; blue above light, dark borders and apices widely black; transverse lines beneath prominent, inwardly white.................................... 11

11. Transverse lines beneath much broken into spots and dashes, bright red, margined outwardly with white; submarginal spot in cell Cu₁ of HW beneath nearly round; ground color beneath very pale..*S. clytie*

11. Transverse lines beneath distinct and continuous, narrowly dark gray, outwardly broadly white; submarginal spot in cell Cu₁ pale orange-yellow and black, much longer than wide...*S. martialis*

12. HW with no tail..................................... 13

12. HW with tail.. 14

13. HW beneath brown with a submarginal row of orange red spots..*S. titus*

13. HW beneath strongly mottled whitish and brown, with a prominent black submarginal spot in cell Cu₁; no submarginal row of red spots...............................*S. cestri*

13. HW (and apex of FW) beneath greenish, with transverse rows of red spots................................*Erora læta*

14. Wings above with no orange or orange-brown spots or patches except occasionally a trace of a lunule in cell Cu₁ of the HW, or a small patch at anal angle................ 23

14. Wings above with definite areas or patches of orange or orange brown in the discal area, in addition to a submarginal, orange and black lunule on the HW in some species ... 15

14. Wings above with no discal areas or patches of orange or orange-red, but with a large orange and black submarginal lunule on the HW in cell Cu₁........................... 20

15. Wings largely green beneath........................... 16

15. Wings brown beneath................................. 17

16. Postmedian lines beneath broad and prominent, that of the HW very deeply and squarely looped outward at its middle; colors rich and bright.........*Mitoura hesseli* & *gryneus*

16. Postmedian lines beneath narrower and less conspicuous, that of the HW straight from costa to cell M₃, projecting outward in two long points along veins Cu₁ and Cu₂ which connect with the submarginal light markings; colors pale and "washed out" looking above and beneath......*Mitoura xami*

17. Postmedian lines beneath inwardly red.......*S. endymion cyphara*

17. Postmedian lines beneath inwardly black or brownish black 18

18. Transverse lines beneath greatly broadened, and broken by segments being "offset"............................*S. liparops*

18. Transverse lines beneath normal and narrow............ 19

19. HW beneath with a prominent, submarginal, orange-red band, widest in cells M₃ and Cu₁, extending strongly toward costa to ve in R₄....................................*S. favonius*

19. This band on HW beneath much narrower, tending to be broken into separate spots; wings above with smaller orange patches...*S. ontario*

20. Postmedian lines of wings beneath broken into widely separated, round spots, ringed with white; northern . . . . . *S. acadica*
20. Postmedian lines not broken into separated, round spots. . . 21
21. Transverse lines beneath very straight and unbroken, very widely white externally; two round, white spots in basal area of HW beneath. . . . . *S. acis*
21. Transverse lines beneath narrower and more irregular. 22
22. Wings beneath light gray; postmedian line of FW not extending below vein Cu₂; no bars or marks on basal half of wings beneath. . . . . *S. melinus* & *buchholzi*
22. Wings beneath brown; postmedian line of HW extending to anal vein; basal parts of wings with transverse bars   *S. calanus*
23. Wings beneath green. . . . .*S. simœthis*
23. Wings beneath gray or brown. 24
24. Transverse markings of wings beneath margined internally with orange-red or red. 25
24. Transverse markings of wings beneath not margined internally with orange-red or red. 29
25. Wings beneath pale, very mottled, with a transverse, white, postbasal shade on the HW, and white shades outside the postmedian transverse lines. . . . .*S. yojoa*
25. Wings beneath not mottled, without such transverse, whitish shades. 26
26. FW beneath with definite bar at end of cell; HW beneath with postbasal spots above, in and below cell; postmedian lines irregular and broken. 27
26. FW beneath with at most a very faint bar at end of cell; HW beneath unmarked out to postmedian line; postmedian lines more even and unbroken. 28
27. Wings beneath with transverse postmedian lines and postbasal spots clear orange-red. . . . .*S. clytie*
27. Wings beneath with transverse postmedian lines and postbasal spots, though more or less inwardly red, essentially dark brown and white. . . . .*S. laceyi*
28. Small, exp. 0.6–0.8 in.; pale and "washed out" looking beneath; no discocellular bars beneath; postmedian line of HW beneath irregular, broken into more or less separate spots; submarginal spot of HW in cell Cu₁ largely pale orange with small black pupil. . . . .*S. azia*
28. Larger, exp. 0.8–1.1 in.; wings beneath dark, with bold, bright markings; a red bar at end of each cell; postmedian line of HW continuous, black, white and red; spot in cell Cu₁ large and black, with very little, if any, orange . . . .*S. cecrops*
29. Postmedian line of FW beneath extending only to vein Cu₂, not below it; HW beneath with no blue, submarginal patch in cell Cu₂, and with two prominent, round, ocellate spots below costa: one postbasal, the other postmedian. . . . . .*S. columella*
29. Postmedian line of FW beneath extending strongly below vein Cu₂; HW beneath with a blue, submarginal patch in cell Cu₂, and with no prominent, round, subcostal spots. 30
30. Transverse lines beneath thin and clear-cut, dark inwardly and white outwardly, rather even and continuous; that of HW forming a connected VW below veins Cu₁, Cu₂ & 2d A;
S. alcestis

30. Transverse lines beneath broad and irregular, or offset and broken into separate spots or patches; no connected VW mark as above....................................... 31

31. Transverse lines beneath, particularly of HW, broken into separate, narrow, oval, white-edged spots............*S. edwardsi*

31. Transverse lines not thus broken into separate, oval spots, although sometimes very irregular..................... 32

32. Transverse lines beneath greatly broadened and broken by segments being "offset"; blue submarginal patch of HW in cell Cu₂ usually capped inwardly with orange..........*S. liparops*

32. Transverse lines not so greatly broadened and "offset"; blue patch in cell Cu₂ of HW usually not capped inwardly with orange.. 33

33. Transverse lines beneath narrower, more smooth and continuous, none of their segments deeply "offset" inwardly from the rest....................................*S. falacer*

33. Transverse lines beneath broader, more irregular due to some segments being offset inwardly; this is especially so in FW below vein M₃ and on HW below veins Sc+R₁ and M₃; orange submarginal lunules on HW beneath smaller *S. caryævorus*

ATALA. *Eumæus atala* Poey $\qquad$ p. 145

1.75 in. This distinctive tropical visitor occurs in southern Florida as the subspecies *florida* Roeber. It has the FW above iridescent blue-green except for the blackish border and veins. HW above brownish black with a border of brilliantly iridescent blue-green spots. Wings beneath brownish black, FW unmarked; HW with a large, orange-red spot near the base of the anal margin, and three rows, median, postmedian and subterminal, of iridescent, blue-green spots. Abdomen orange. *E. minyas* Huebner probably does not occur in the United States despite old records. *Atala* has a deceptively slow and lazy-looking flight, keeps to the edges of brushy areas and hammocks, visiting freely such flowers as Spanish Needles (*Bidens*) and Scrub Palmetto (*Serenoa*). Food: — "Coontie" (*Zamea integrifolia*), a common plant in Florida, once the staple food of the Seminole Indians.

Atala has been common in southern Florida, but at present is either extremely rare or extinct. The last records I know are of specimens taken about 1933 in an inland hammock near the Royal Palm State Park. The reasons for this decrease are not known. Certainly the real estate developments around Miami and the fires in the Everglades were major features.

Dr. Frank N. Young, Jr., who has especially studied *atala*, assures me that larvæ of a moth, *Seirarctia echo* Abbot & Smith were harmful competitors with *atala* larvæ for food, and also were somewhat cannibalistic. Enormous numbers of these appeared at the time *atala* was becoming scarce. The 1926 hurricane also hurt *atala* considerably. Perhaps overenthusiastic collecting played a part. Let us hope that this, one of our most beautiful butterflies, will "stage a comeback." Collectors who may find it should release females and keep at most only a very few males.

GREAT PURPLE HAIRSTREAK. *Atlides halesus* Cramer p. 128
1.4 in. *Halesus* has the most brilliant, changeable coloring of any of our butterflies. Hold a specimen between your eyes and the source of light, and look at the wings at a sharp angle; then turn slowly so that the light is coming from your back and look at the wings at right angles. The flight is erratic but not very swift. It is best taken at flowers. I have noticed that it seems to prefer Spanish Needles (*Bidens*) and, in Florida, Star Jasmine (*Trachelospermum*), especially near Live Oaks on which Mistletoe is growing.
Larva: — Slightly downy, green; nine oblique, darker green bands on sides, a narrow middorsal stripe, a yellowish lateral stripe above bases of legs. **Food:** — Mistletoe (*Phoradendron flavescens*) perhaps also Live Oak (*Quercus virginiana*). Two broods. Adults (Florida) April, September–November.
Range: — Florida, n. to New Jersey, Illinois, w. to California; very rare northward.
Subspecies: — Specimens from the Mississippi Valley and Texas appear to have a deeper ground color, and darker, sootier color beneath. In this they resemble the West Coast subspecies *estesi* Clench.

WHITE M HAIRSTREAK. *Strymon m-album* Boisduval & Leconte p. 145
1.2 in. The species receives its name from the white M (or W) formed by the postmedian line on the HW beneath. It is widespread, although essentially southern, but nowhere abundant; it seems quite broad in its choice of habitats. Its flight is fast and erratic.
Larva: — Downy, light yellowish green, head black; a middorsal stripe and seven oblique lateral stripes are duller, darker green. **Food:** — Oaks, "Milk Vetch or Locoweed (*Astragalus*)." I wonder if the Vetch record is accurate; it is a strange foodplant for the species. Three broods in south. Hibernates as pupa.
Range: — South America n. to New Jersey, Pennsylvania, Ohio, and Kansas; uncommon to rare northward. Records from Texas are curiously lacking.

RED BANDED HAIRSTREAK. *Strymon cecrops* Fabricius p. 128
1.0 in. Upper side dark, slightly brownish black. Females may have considerable blue basally, especially on the HW, males a little. Very common in the South, ranging northward. Life history unpublished. **Food:** — *Croton* (C. L. Remington) and (New Jersey) *Rhus copallina* (Rawson & Ziegler).

Similar Species: — *S. beon* — see couplet 8 of Key.
Range: — Florida, Gulf States and Texas n. to New York (Long Island), Indiana, Missouri, and Michigan.

BEON HAIRSTREAK. *Strymon beon* Cramer
1.0 in. *Beon* has been much confused with *cecrops* in the past. It is common in Mexico and southern Texas, has strayed northward to Kansas. Mr. Otto Buchholz tells me that it prefers to alight near the bases of tree trunks. See couplet 8 of Key.

CORAL HAIRSTREAK. *Strymon titus* Fabricius   pp. 48, 129
1.3 in. Our only common, widespread Hairstreak lacking tails on the hindwings. In this it resembles the Elfins (*Incisalia*); but its pattern is unmistakable. Its flight is rapid, but it is easily caught on flowers. It frequents open meadows and roadsides.
Larva: — Flat, slug-shaped, downy, yellowish green; head black; dorsal rosy areas on thorax and posterior part of abdomen.
Food: — Wild Cherry, Plum. One brood. Adults in July and August. Hibernation as egg.
Range: — Georgia, Gulf States and Texas n. to Ontario, Manitoba, and westward.
Subspecies: — *S. t. titus* is the northern subspecies, s. to Virginia and Kansas. *S. t. mopsus* Huebner (TL Georgia) Virginia and Kansas s. to Oklahoma and Texas; ground color beneath lighter; markings beneath brighter and more distinct; black spots on HW conspicuously ringed with white. *S. t. watsoni* Barnes & Benjamin (TL Kerrville, Texas) southern Oklahoma and Texas; larger; still lighter beneath with spots smaller, black, ringed very clearly with white; red submarginal markings of HW beneath very pale, almost orange.

GRAY HAIRSTREAK. *Strymon melinus* Huebner   p. 129
1.1 in. Probably our commonest Hairstreak, *melinus* is easily recognized by its clear, blue-gray color, light underside, and the prominent orange spot both above and beneath at the anal region of the HW. Its flight is often extremely swift. It visits flowers freely. At times its larvæ have been reported as seriously damaging crops of beans or hops.
Larva: — Naked, unmarked reddish brown, head very small.
Food: — Hops (*Humulus*), Mallow (*Malva*), Knotweed (*Polygonum*), St. Johnswort (*Hypericum*), Cultivated Beans (*Phaseolus*), Hounds Tongue (*Cynoglossum*), Scarlet Mallow (*Sphæralcea*), Hawthorn (*Cratægus*). Larva bores in fruits and seeds. Two broods in north, three or more in south. Adults in June. Hibernation as pupa.
Similar Species: — *S. buchholzi* (southern Texas, rare, see p. 282) is darker.
Range: — Southern Canada, s. through Florida and Texas into Central America.

Subspecies: — *S. m. melinus* (TL Georgia) Florida, Gulf States, eastern Texas n. to North Carolina and Arkansas; larger, pale gray beneath, orange red markings of HW large both above and beneath, postmedian lines beneath rather straight. *S. m. humuli* Harris (TL Massachusetts) Canada s. to North Carolina, Tennessee, Missouri and Nebraska; smaller, darker above and beneath, more brownish beneath, orange red markings of HW smaller, postmedian lines beneath rather straight. *S. m. franki* Field (TL Lawrence, Kansas) Kansas, Oklahoma, central and western Texas, westward; larger, ground color beneath whitish, not brownish, submarginal row of dark bars indistinct, lighter and smaller; orange red marks smaller than in *m. melinus;* postmedian line of HW more irregular.

SOUTHERN HAIRSTREAK. *Strymon favonius* Abbot & Smith
p. 129
1.1 in. *Favonius* chiefly occurs in the southeast, but strays northward. The oval, gray stigma of the male is quite conspicuous. The orange patches on the upper side of the brown wings, especially on the HW, are distinctive.
Similar Species: — *S. ontario*, see couplet 19 of key and below.
Food: — Oaks (*Quercus*)
Range: — Gulf States n. to West Virginia and New Jersey, rare northward. TL Georgia.

NORTHERN HAIRSTREAK. *Strymon ontario* Edwards p. 129
1.1 in. Most resembling *favonius*, *ontario* has much less extensive orange on the HW beneath, and the postmedian and subterminal lines correspondingly farther apart. It is nowhere common, usually rare. Like other northern Hairstreaks it is best sought on flowers, particularly of New Jersey Tea (*Ceanothus americana*).
Similar Species: — *S. favonius*, see couplet 19 of key.
Early Stages: — Very poorly known. Food: — Hawthorn (*Cratægus*), Oak (*autolycus*).
Range: — Ontario and Quebec s. to Gulf States and Texas.
Subspecies: — *S. o. ontario* (TL Port Stanley, Ontario) south to Oklahoma and Texas. *S. o. autolycus* Edwards (TL Dallas, Texas) Texas and Oklahoma; ground color lighter both above and beneath; orange brown patches above larger; postmedian line of HW beneath more irregular; submarginal orange patches of HW beneath larger; submarginal line of FW beneath less distinct. Intergradation of the two forms occurs in a blend zone in Missouri, Arkansas, eastern Oklahoma and northern Texas. Northern *o. ontario* may entirely lack orange on the FW above. A good clinal distribution.

ALCESTIS HAIRSTREAK. *Strymon alcestis* Edwards p. 129
1.1 in. Essentially western. The stigma of the ♂ is extremely

small. The markings beneath are sharp and clear-cut; the bar at the end of each cell is white, with a thin black line bordering it both basally and distally. The HW beneath has the postmedian line forming a clearcut VW; and the orange submarginal markings of the HW beneath extend up on the FW for some distance. The life history is unpublished. **Food:** — Chinaberry (*Melia*). **Similar Species:** — *S. falacer*, see couplet 30 of key.

Range: — In the eastern area, Texas, Oklahoma and Kansas (April–June) rarer northward (TL Dallas, Texas).

ACADIAN HAIRSTREAK. *Strymon acadica* Edwards   p. 129
1.2 in. As its name implies, the Acadian Hairstreak is northern. It is easily recognized by the pale ground color beneath, the reduction of the postmedian lines to rows of round spots, and the presence of an orange spot on the HW above. The adults fly in wet meadows, especially along streams where there are willows. **Similar Species:** — see *S. edwardsii*, below.

Larva: — Very broad, grass green; head brown, two yellowish stripes on sides, in these a row of short, oblique, yellowish bars. **Food:** — Willows (*Salix*).

Range: — Central and southern Canada w. to Pacific, s. in the eastern area to New York, Pennsylvania, Michigan, Illinois, Iowa, and Kansas.

Subspecies: — *S. a. acadica* (TL London, Ontario) from southern Canada southward. *S. a. watrini* Dufrane (TL Saskatchewan) a not very distinct subspecies of more northern Canada (Port Hope, Bobcaygeon, Gravenhorst and Ottawa, Ontario, Aylmer, Norway Bay and Meach Lake, Quebec) with darker ground color beneath.

EDWARDS' HAIRSTREAK. *Strymon edwardsii* Grote & Robinson   p. 129
1.0–1.15 in. *Edwardsii* can be confused with *falacer* and *acadica;* from the former, it can be told by the postmedian lines beneath, which are broken into separate, oval, dark spots ringed with white. In *acadica* these spots are still more separate, rounder, and more contrasted with a lighter ground color. *Acadica* also has more extensive submarginal orange markings on the HW beneath. *Edwardsii* is very active and pugnacious, has a fast flight. Look for it around scrub oak thickets, resting on the leaves and twigs; and on flowers. **Similar Species:** — *S. falacer* & *acadica*, see above, also couplets 20 & 31 of Key.

Larva: — Brown with pale brownish markings; head black with a small white band; numerous blackish warts with brown hairs. **Food:** — Oaks, especially Scrub Oak (*Quercus ilicifolia*). One brood, adults in late June and July. Hibernation as egg or young larva.

Range: — Maritime Provinces w. to Manitoba (TL Queenstown, Ontario) s. to Georgia and Kansas, rare southward.

BANDED HAIRSTREAK. *Strymon falacer* Godart pp. 49, 129
1.0–1.15 in. This and *melinus* are our commonest and most widespread hairstreaks. The postmedian lines beneath are not clearly broken into separate, oval spots, as they are in *edwardsii*. It has in the past been confused with *caryævorus*. The latter usually has the postmedian lines wider and more irregular, but an occasional specimen will be found that cannot be determined by pattern. There are genitalic differences, however.
Similar Species: — *S. edwardsii* (see above); *S. caryævorus*, see above and couplet 33 of Key.
Larva: — Dimorphic, either grass green or brown, with lengthwise lighter and darker lines. Food: — Oak, Hickory (*Carya*), Butternut (*Juglans cinerea*). One brood. Adults in mid June. Hibernation as egg.
Range: — Southern Canada w. to Manitoba, s. to Georgia, Gulf States and Texas.
Subspecies: — None in our area; some in the west.

FLORIDA HAIRSTREAK. *Strymon calanus* Huebner p. 129
1.1–1.25 in. For long considered rare or possibly extinct, *calanus* is now known to be not uncommon in central Florida. It is distinguished by its large size, dark brown ground color, orange lunule in the anal region of the HW above (sometimes reduced or absent), very long blue spot in the anal region of the HW beneath, and long tails. The HW beneath has more extensive orange submarginal markings than *falacer;* and the black mark at the outer edge of the largest orange lunule is a definite bar, not a spot or crescent. For long this species was known as *wittfeldii* Edwards but, as recently shown, we must call it *calanus*, really an older name. This is confusing, since the name *calanus* has long been used for the common and widespread species which we now must call *falacer*. However, we must follow the rules.
Similar Species: — *S. falacer*, see above.
Range: — Northern and central Florida. TL Georgia.

HICKORY HAIRSTREAK. *Strymon caryævorus* McDunnough
p. 129
0.0–1.1 in. This is a northern and a recently described species, formerly confused with *falacer*. It is genitalically distinct from *falacer*, but cannot always be told from it by pattern. It appears to be quite rare and local.
Similar Species: — See. *S. falacer* above, and couplet 33 of Key.
Early Stages: — Imperfectly known; larva said to be more evenly pale green without much trace of darker dorsal or lateral

markings. **Food:** — Hickory (*Carya*). One brood. Adults in July.

Range: — Ontario, Quebec, New York (Johnstown), and Minnesota (Lake Jefferson, Lesuer Co.).

STRIPED HAIRSTREAK. *Strymon liparops* Boisduval & Le-conte   p. 129

1.15 in. All races are easily distinguished by the underside pattern, the lines being very far apart and strongly broken and "offset." Despite its wide range of food plants, *liparops* is quite local and never very common anywhere.

Larva: — Bright grass green, with indistinct, yellower green, oblique stripes on the sides. **Food:** — Oak (*Quercus*), Willow (*Salix*), Shadbush or Juneberry (*Amelanchier*), Apple (*Malus*), Plum and Wild Plum (*Prunus*), Blueberry (*Vaccinium*), Blackberry (*Rubus*). The larva may bore into fruits as well as eating leaves. One brood. Adults in July. Hibernation as egg.

Range: — Maritime Provinces w. to Manitoba, s. to Georgia, Missouri, Kansas, and Arkansas.

Subspecies: — *S. l. liparops* (TL Screven Co., Georgia); orange-brown patches above, at least on the FW; excessively rare. *S. l. strigosus* Harris (TL Massachusetts) Arkansas and Tennessee n. to central Canada; almost or entirely lacks orange brown patches on wings above, has the white streaks on wings beneath narrow, but conspicuous. *S. l. fletcheri* Michener & dos Passos (TL Manitoba) FW above with prominent orange brown patches as is in the southern race; wings beneath much darker brown with purplish or greenish gloss, the white streaks inconspicuous.

MARTIAL HAIRSTREAK. *Strymon martialis* Herrich-Schaeffer   p. 128

1.0 in. FW above deep brownish black to black; below the cell, a light blue basal patch which may extend less than half to more than two thirds out to outer margin. HW light blue, costal margin black, more broadly beyond cell; fringe white; a narrow, black terminal line; a small, deep orange-red patch at anal angle; submarginal lunules black, the one in cell Cu_1 (between tails) much the largest. Beneath, *martialis* resembles *S. acis bartrami;* but the latter is brown above, has an orange and black submarginal lunule on the HW in cell Cu_1.

Larva: — Dull, unmarked green, its upper surface covered with short, white hairs. **Food:** — *Trema floridana* (*micrantha*). At least two broods, perhaps more.

Range: — Florida, Miami district southward, not uncommon, rather local. Also in Bahamas, Cuba (TL), and Jamaica.

BARTRAM'S HAIRSTREAK. *Strymon acis bartrami* Comstock & Huntington   p. 128

1.0 in. Easily distinguished from *martialis* by its plain, brown color above, and from all species by the distinctive underside pattern. Not rare, but decidedly local in southern Florida, *bartrami* is the mainland representative of a species widely distributed in the Antilles. The adults visit flowers eagerly, particularly those of Wild Croton.

Larva: — Apparently unknown. **Food:** — "Wild Croton" (?).

Range: — Florida from Miami area (TL) southward; not rare, decidedly local. Other subspecies in Antilles to Antigua and Jamaica.

SARITA HAIRSTREAK. *Strymon simæthis sarita* Skinner

0.8 in. Wings above light brown, basally slightly lighter and faintly blue-tinged. Wings beneath light, bright, yellow-green. FW below Cu gray, fading to white on inner margin; a silvery white, transverse postmedian line; an orange-brown patch, chiefly beyond this line, in cells Cu_1 & Cu_2; HW with similar postmedian line, somewhat broader and pointed outwardly below M_2, forming a sharp V on vein 2d A; a broad, green band beyond the line; then a broad, brown-red submarginal band, narrow at its beginning at vein $Sc + R_1$, then broadening, thickly dusted with white scales, with a number of internal, iridescent, pearly lunules.

Range: — Though widely distributed in the Antilles, does not occur in Florida. The subspecies *sarita* (TL Comal Co., Texas) is well established around Brownsville, Pharr, and McAllen, Texas (September–December), differs little from *s. simæthis*.

PASTOR HAIRSTREAK. *Strymon pastor* Butler & Druce

0.8–1.0 in. Male deep, dull blue above, costal and outer margins of FW black. Female duller, greenish blue, costa and outer third of FW black; beneath, both sexes, yellowish green, costa with some brown shading, inner margin broadly pale, brownish gray; HW with postmedian band broken into small, widely separated, brown and white spots; two large brown, red-brown and white patches below veins Cu_1 and Cu_2, and 2d A. Well established around Brownsville, rather rare at Pharr, Texas (April–May and October–December). The specimen figured by Holland as "*pastor*" is probably *longula* Hewitson, a tropical species.

MÆSITES HAIRSTREAK. *Strymon mæsites* Herrich-Schæffer

p. 128

0.8–0.9 in. The gemlike *mæsites* cannot be confused with any other of our Hairstreaks. The wings above are brilliantly iridescent, purple-blue in the male, duller and darker in the female. In southern Florida it occurs rarely but consistently. In southern Texas it is extremely rare. All Florida specimens of which I know have been taken at flowers, especially Spanish Needles (*Bidens*).

Subspecies: — *S. m. mæsites,* southern Florida (Miami s. and Keys) as illustrated. *S. m. telea* Hewitson, Brazil to Texas (Laredo, June), brown patch on HW beneath smaller, not extending below Cu₁; W mark of postmedian line of HW strongly angulated.

COLUMELLA HAIRSTREAK. *Strymon columella* Fabricius p. 129
0.9–1.0 in. Wings above brown; stigma of male much darker. HW above with prominent dark spots in anal region, especially below vein Cu₁ (above base of tail). The very plain coloration and pattern beneath, and the prominence of the two dark spots along the costal edge of the HW beneath are distinctive. A widespread tropical species.
Subspecies: — *S. c. modesta* Maynard (TL Florida) Florida n. into Gulf States; larger, browner, markings beneath more distinct. *S. c. istapa* Reakirt (TL vicinity Vera Cruz, Mex.) Panama into Texas (very common, lower Rio Grande valley throughout year) smaller, paler, and grayer, with less distinct markings beneath.

BAZOCHII HAIRSTREAK. *Strymon bazochii* Godart
0.9 in. Above, FW brown, HW blue with wide costal, and narrow outer marginal, brown borders. No tails on HW, anal angle projecting little. A row of submarginal brown spots on HW, those below veins Cu₁ and Cu₂ the largest. Wings beneath much mottled with brown and whitish; a large, round or oval, ocellate, postbasal spot below costa of HW, HW with a dark brown, basal, and a larger, apical patch. Fringes white. Well established around Pharr, Texas. (March–May, Oct.–Dec.), ranges thence to Brazil (TL). Occurs in Cuba (subspecies *gundlachianus* Bates) but has not been recorded from Florida
Similar Species: — See *S. cestri,* p. 281.

CLYTIE HAIRSTREAK. *Strymon clytie* Edwards
0.75–0.85 in. Male nearly solid brown on wings above, with faint, light blue, basal tinges. Female with FW brown above, inner margin broadly light blue to three quarters way out; HW light blue with costa and apex broadly light brown, and a series of small submarginal brown spots. Wings beneath, both sexes, very pale gray with light, orange brown markings as follows: a bar at end of cell of FW; a postbasal, transverse line of four dashes on HW; the usual postmedian lines, much broken and offset. Below vein Cu₁ of HW is a submarginal, pale orange, black-pupiled spot; and another spot, darker and more complex, at anal angle. The very pale underside is quite diagnostic. *Clytie* might be confused with *S. azia;* but the latter is smaller and darker, lacks the discocellular bar of the FW and the postbasal marks of the HW, and has the postmedian lines straighter and less broken.

Clytie is common in southern Texas (Brownsville, Pharr) ranges thence southward (TL San Antonio, Texas). A darker winter form occurs October–February, a lighter summer form, with more and darker blue above, throughout the rest of the year.

AZIA HAIRSTREAK. *Strymon azia* Hewitson

0.60–0.75 in. As noted above under *clytie*, *azia* is somewhat similar to that species but is distinguished by its underside pattern and its small size. It occurs in southern Texas (Pharr, March–May), well established but never common.

OLIVE HAIRSTREAK. *Mitoura gryneus* Huebner   pp. 49, 129

0.9–1.0 in. Sometimes not uncommon, and widely distributed, the Olive Hairstreak is quite local. It should be sought near Red Cedar, the food plant. Its flight ¡is swift and darting; but a flushed specimen, if not too alarmed, will usually return to the spot from which it took off. Cedar groves on dry hillsides, and flowers near them, are most likely. Females have more orange coloration above than males; and some females are very dark above, all or nearly all sooty brown.

Similar Species: — *M. xami* in Texas — see couplet 16 of Key; *M. hesseli* — see next species.

Larva: — Slug-shaped, dark green, with a row of very light green, oblique bars on each side. **Food:** — Red Cedar (*Juniperus (Sabina) virginiana*) and (*very* dubious) "Green Brier (*Smilax rotundifolia*)." Two broods in north, probably more in south. Adults in late April, again in July. Hibernation as pupa. The darker summer brood is *smilacis* Boisduval & Leconte. The specific name *damon* Stoll, apparently an invalid homonym, has been widely used in the past.

Range: — New England w. to Ontario, Minnesota and Nebraska, s. to northern Florida and Texas.

Subspecies: — *M. g. gryneus* Huebner (TL Virginia) range as above except for Florida and Texas. *M. g. sweadneri* F. H. Chermock (TL St. Augustine, Florida) Florida; lacks orange-brown discal shading of *g. gryneus* above, HW beneath with larger black patch at anal angle and patch in cell Cu1 lacking orange. *M. g. castalis* Edwards (TL Waco, Texas) Texas and westward; like *g. gryneus* in pattern but with colors lighter and more faded looking; less orange-brown or yellow-brown on wings above.

HESSEL'S HAIRSTREAK. *Mitoura hesseli* Rawson & Ziegler

0.85–0.95 in. Confused with *M. gryneus* until 1950, *hesseli* is now known to be a distinct species. Its discovery is a fine example of the close field observation and untiring collecting that marks the best work of our amateur collectors. On the HW beneath the white postmedian dash at the anal margin is concave externally and convex internally, while in *gryneus* it is concave internally and convex externally; and the spot of this same row just below the costa is set more inwardly than the one below it, while in *gryneus* the two spots are more in line. On the FW beneath the white postmedian spot nearest the costa is set much more outwardly than the one next below it, while in *gryneus* the two are more in line with each other and with the others of the row. The green beneath is deeper and less yellowish than that of *gryneus;* and the ocellate submarginal spot of the HW beneath (below vein Cu₁) is less prominent and lacks much or all of the orange of *gryneus*.

Larva:—Shining green, very like that of *M. gryneus*. Feeds at tips of branches. **Food:** — White Cedar (*Chamæcyparis thyoides*). Two broods, May and July (Cyril dos Passos).

Range:—At least New Jersey (TL Lakehurst) to North Carolina.

XAMI HAIRSTREAK. *Mitoura xami* Reakirt
0.85–1.0 in. As noted in the Key (couplet 16) *xami* is easily told from *gryneus castalis*, the Texas race of that species. In the eastern area *xami* (TL vicinity Vera Cruz, Mexico) is well established in southern Texas (Corpus Christi, October; San Benito, June; Pharr, September–December).

EARLY HAIRSTREAK. *Erora læta* Edwards   p. 129
0.8–0.9 in. *Læta* is perhaps the greatest prize of northern collectors. It should be sought (and never expected) along rather shaded trails and "woodroads" in Canadian Zone forest where Beech trees occur. The butterflies alight on bare ground along the trails, and (females) may be seen around the Beeches. They have a fast flight and are not easily seen in the dappled light and shade. The lack of tails and the bluish-green ground color beneath are distinctive. Females have much more blue above than males, look thus rather like *S. martialis*.

Early Stages: — Largely unknown. **Food:** — Probably Beech (*Fagus americana*). One brood, perhaps a partial second one. Adults in May, June, and July. Hibernation as pupa.

Range: — Eastern Canada and New England, s. to Kentucky (!). Chiefly Canadian Zone forest, in mountains southward. (TL London, Ontario). One record from Atlantic City, New Jersey, seems very peculiar.

Genus Incisalia *Scudder:* The Elfins

ELFINS ARE medium to small sized, gray-brown to orange-brown, the females above much more tinted with orange-brown than the males. The hindwings lack the "tails" of many Hairstreaks, but have a more or less scalloped outer margin, often with projections at the vein tips, especially of the cubitals. The inner margin is concave above the anal angle, which is somewhat prolonged outward and bent downward at right angles. The flight is not so fast as in most Hairstreaks. A peculiar action, common to Hairstreaks, is emphasized by some Elfins; on alighting the butterfly holds the wings above the back, keeps the forewings still, and rubs the hind wings forward and back in alternation with each other. The strongly flattened eggs are profusely studded with tubercles connected by ridges. They are laid on new shoot tips. The larvæ resemble those of other Hairstreaks, but are somewhat wider anteriorly, and have the hairs of the laterodorsal ridges and the folds below the spiracles somewhat longer than the others. All are single brooded. The adults are among the earliest butterflies of Spring.

Elfins often prove hard to identify. The following Key, used with the illustrations, should serve for any from our area. There are apparently constant genitalic differences between the species, but not all of these have been worked out.

KEY TO *INCISALIA* OF EASTERN NORTH AMERICA

1. Basal half of HW beneath much darker than outer half, suffused, with no clear-cut markings; submarginal dark spots of FW beneath round, oval or irregular, not sharp, inward-pointing angles.. **3**

1. Basal half of HW beneath not noticeably dark and suffused; markings of this area and of rest of lower surface transverse and clear-cut; submarginal dark spots of FW beneath tending to form inward pointing, angulate lines.............. **2**

2. Size large (exp. 0.80–1.2 in.); outer margin of HW deeply scalloped; markings beneath more contrasty and clear-cut; HW beneath with a narrow, violet-gray, submarginal diffusion; dark line basad of this irregular but unbroken; range extensive, Canada to Georgia and Arkansas..............*niphon*

2. Size small (exp. 0.65–0.80 in.); margin of HW less deeply scalloped; markings beneath less contrasty, more merged into ground color; HW beneath with broader, violet-gray, submarginal suffusion, dark line basad of this more broken and obscure; only in Black Spruce-Tamarack-Sphagnum bogs in northern United States and Canada..............*lanoraieensis*

3. Outer half of HW beneath yellow-brown to orange-red-brown with very little, if any, gray clouding; outer margin of HW very little scalloped...............................*augustinus*

3. Outer half of HW beneath with some, usually much, gray to violet gray dusting or clouding; outer margin of HW usually more deeply scalloped, sometimes with tail-like projections at ends of cubitals.................................... **4**

4. Gray clouding of outer area of HW beneath bright and very extensive, extending up to apex of wing at tip of R_5; FW beneath with a distinct terminal gray band; outer margin of HW never deeply scalloped with short tail-like projections at ends of cubitals....................................*polios*

4. Outer gray clouding on HW beneath duller and less ex-

ANGLE WINGS, OTHER NYMPHALIDS AND THE SNOUT BUTTERFLY

Families *Nymphalidae* and *Libytheidae*

Note that the reductions of the illustrations vary

1. **HOP MERCHANT**, *Polygonia comma*, "winter" form   p. 103
   Upper & under sides, ♀ (Clayton, N.Y.). × ⅔. Brown beneath, not gray; lacking green submarginal spots; above, only one large dark spot in cell Cu₁ of FW; Can. s. to N.C. & Kans. See also Pl. 14.
2. **RED ADMIRAL**, *Vanessa atalanta*   p. 107
   Upper side, ♂ (Essex Co., N.Y.). × ⅔. See also Plate 14. Orange red bands, white spots. Entire eastern area, common.
3. **GRAY COMMA**, *Polygonia progne*, "summer" form   p. 104
   Upper & under side, ♀ (Andover, N.J.). × ⅔. Gray, not brown, beneath; silver "comma" has tapering ends. See also Pl. 14. Can. s. to Va., Mo. & Kans.
4. **SATYR ANGLE WING**, *Polygonia satyrus* (f. *marsyas*)   p. 103
   Under side, ♂ (Charlton, Ont.). × ⅔. Brown beneath, not always as strongly mottled as shown. FW above has two large dark spots in cell Cu₁; no green spots beneath; wing margins smoother than in *faunus*. Can. & northern edge of U.S.
5. **QUESTION MARK**, *Polygonia interrogationis* (f. *umbrosa*) p. 102
   Upper side, ♂ (Northcastle, N.Y.). × ⅔. Large size; dark HW; see also No. 6 and Plate 14. Can. s. through entire eastern area.
6. **QUESTION MARK**, *Polygonia interrogationis*, winter form   p. 102
   Upper side, ♀ (N.Y. City). × ⅔. Lighter HW and longer tails than summer form (No. 5 above).
7. **MALACHITE**, *Metamorpha stelenes biplagiata*   p. 278
   Upper side, ♂ (Shovel Mt., Tex.). × ⅔. Large size; brown-black with light green to greenish white markings. Tex. & s. Fla.
8. **VICEROY**, *Limenitis archippus*   p. 114
   Upper side, ♂ (Englewood, N.J.). × ⅔. Orange brown, black markings & white spots. "Mimics" the Monarch (Pl. 10). Can. s. through entire eastern area.
9. **SNOUT BUTTERFLY**, *Libytheana bachmannii*   p. 121
   Upper side, ♂ (Coosawhatchie, S.C.). × 1 (natural size). Blackish brown, white spots on FW, other marks orange brown. Note wing shape and long, beaklike palpi. N. to Can., rare northward.

Plate 18   145

CHIEFLY HAIRSTREAKS, COPPERS AND BLUES
Families *Nymphalidae, Riodinidae & Lycaenidae*

Note that the reductions of the illustrations vary

1. WHITE SKIRTED CALICO, *Hamadryas feronia*   p. 279
   Upper side, ♂, (Sierra de Tezonapa, Mex.). × ⅔. Bluish gray;
   crosslines and marks blackish and brownish gray. Strays into Tex.

2. FLORIDA ATALA, *Eumæus atala florida* Rœber   p. 132
   Upper & under sides (Miami, Fla.). × 1. Iridescent green on black;
   abdomen orange. S. Fla., very rare, perhaps now extinct.

3. WHITE "M" HAIRSTREAK, *Strymon m–album*   p. 133
   Upper & under sides, ♂ (Royal Palm State Park, Fla.). × 1. Brilliantly iridescent blue above, black borders; beneath brown with
   black-edged, white lines; on HW submarginal spots orange red, spots
   at anal angle blue & black. Note the "M" indicated. N. to N.J., Ohio
   & Kans., rare northward.

4. BLUE METALMARK, *Lasaia sessilis*   p. 125
   Upper side, ♂ (Compostela, Nay., Mex.). × 1. Dull iridescent
   greenish blue with dark markings. S. Tex. southward.

5. SPRING AZURE, *Lycænopsis argiolus pseudargiolus*   p. 169
   Upper side, ♀ (Lakehurst, N.J.). × 1½. Heavy dark borders; this
   being summer form *neglecta*, ground color is largely white above. See
   also Plate 21 (♂).

6. DORCAS COPPER, *Lycæna dorcas*   p. 154
   Upper & under sides, ♂ (Riding Mts., Man.). × 1½. Above, brown
   with purplish tints; HW beneath very dark; see *L. epixanthe*, Plate 21,
   No. 4. Can. s. into Mich. & Me.

7. ARCTIC BLUE, *Plebius aquilo*   p. 167
   Upper & under sides, ♂ (Battle Harbor, Labr.). × 1½. Above
   gray-blue, heavily dusted; beneath, ground color of HW is very dark.
   Arctic.

8. HARVESTER, *Feniseca tarquinius*   p. 150
   Upper side, ♂ (Putnam, Conn.). × 1. Orange brown with black
   borders & spots. Can. s. to Fla. & centr. Tex.

9. CASSIUS BLUE, *Leptotes cassius theonus*   p. 157
   Upper & under sides, ♂ (Miami, Fla.). × 1½. Heavy banding beneath, but note blank area on FW — see text. S. Fla. & Tex.

10. CASSIUS BLUE, *Leptotes cassius theonus*   p. 157
   Upper side, ♀ (Port Sewall, Fla.). × 1½. Heavy dark borders and
   much white above; beneath like ♂.

11. EASTERN PIGMY BLUE, *Brephidium pseudofea*   p. 163
   Upper & under sides, ♂ (Indian River, Fla.). × 1½. Above, brown
   with little if any blue; beneath, ground color dark; row of scintillant
   spots on HW; very small size. Ga., Fla. & Gulf States.

tensive, more limited to posterior part of wing; FW beneath
outwardly brown with no gray terminal band............. 5

5. Basal area of HW beneath dark, strongly contrasting with,
and usually sharply delimited from, outer area; outward projection of this dark basal area below vein M_3 quite square,
its lower angle running out as far as its upper angle; its
upper angle sometimes broadened and double; FW beneath
with outer third tending to light, clearer yellow-brown;
postmedian line of FW usually unbroken and quite clear-cut;
male with no stigma.....................................*henrici*

5. Basal area of HW beneath lighter, much less contrasting
with outer area; outward projection of basal area below
vein M_3 narrower, its upper portion projecting farther
than its lower angle; FW beneath with outer third more
clouded and suffused, less contrasting with basal area; postmedian line of FW beneath more broken into dashes and
less clear-cut; male with a stigma...................... 6

6. Stima of male very long and slender, more or less spindle-
shaped; outer margin of HW deeply scalloped; outer area of
HW beneath with gray clouding extending out to marginal
line.......................................*irus* (and *hadros*)

6. Stigma of male short, oval; outer margin of HW less deeply
scalloped; outer area of HW beneath with gray clouding
chiefly along outer edge of dark basal area, beyond that
(distad) a series of six large, red-brown patches; terminal
line double, white inwardly and brown outwardly; eastern
records dubious...................................*mossii*

BROWN ELFIN. *Incisalia augustinus* Westwood   p. 129
0.9–1.0 in. A locally common, sometimes abundant, northern
species, found in early spring in brushy areas, and in and along
the edges of open woods where its food plants occur. It normally
flies slowly near the ground, but when excited can fly fast and
erratically. It often alights on rocks and twigs where its coloration is highly concealing.
Larva: — Vivid, intense green, with yellowish green markings; a
thin mid-dorsal line, broader latero-dorsal and supra-stigmatal
lines and oblique dashes on sides of segments; thoracic shield
anteriorly whitish or yellowish, posteriorly rosy-tinged; head
gray-green or brownish yellow; spiracles yellow-brown. Previous descriptions of *augustinus* larvæ as "red" are erroneous.
Food: — Blueberries (*Vaccinium vacillans*, probably also *corymbosum* and *pennsylvanicum*), Sheep Laurel (*Kalmia angustifolia*).
One brood. Adults in early April. Hibernation as pupa.
Range: — Newfoundland w. to Manitoba, s. to Virginia, West
Virginia, Illinois, and Michigan.
Subspecies: — *I. a. augustinus* (TL Cumberland House, Lat.
54° N, Saskatchewan) Canada and northern New England, w. to
Alberta; wings above very dark basally, dark brown to ferrugi-
nous brown discally, fringes distinctly checkered. *I. a. croesioides*
Scudder (TL (neotype) Lakehurst, New Jersey) central New
England southward; wings lighter brown to gray brown, not

much darker basally, fringes less checkered. *I. a. helenæ* dos Passos (TL Doyles Station, Newfoundland) Newfoundland and Cape Breton Island; wings golden brown above, markings and contrasts of colors beneath more distinct; fringes checkered. Possibly the Western *I. iroides* Boisduval (TL San Francisco, California) is conspecific with *augustinus.* The species forms a broad cline with much intergradation of forms. The blend zone between *augustinus* and *cræsioides* appears to be wide, covering much of New England and New York.

HOARY ELFIN. *Incisalia polios* Cook & Watson   p. 129
0.9–1.0 in. Rather easily distinguished by the greater extent of the hoary, gray clouding beneath. It is rather local, but likely to be common in its particular haunts. It occurs in open, dry areas, where either rocks or sandy soil cause fast run-off of surface water, favoring the growth of Heaths such as the food plant. *Polios* and *augustinus* are the first Elfins of the spring.
Larva: — Apparently unknown in detail. **Food:** — Bearberry (*Arctostaphylos Uva-ursi*). One brood. Adults in mid April. Hibernation as pupa.
Range: — Subarctic Canada (Hudsonian Zone) s. in our area to central Michigan, northern Indiana and southern New Jersey (TL Lakehurst, New Jersey).

HENRY'S ELFIN. *Incisalia henrici* Grote & Robinson   p. 129
0.9–1.1 in. *Henrici* is widely distributed, but very local, rare and a good catch. Like *irus*, it has very prominent, short, tail-like projections at the ends of the cubital veins of the HW. The males have no stigma on the FW. It is also distinguished by the distinct contrast between the basal and limbal areas of the wings beneath, and by the shape of the outward projection of the basal area of the HW beneath. (See couplet 5 of Key.) It flies in brushy areas, along the edges of woods, in open pine and deciduous woods. I was once studying a colony in northeastern Connecticut, in shady, swampy, deciduous woods with a sparse undergrowth of High Bush Blueberry and Huckleberry (*Vaccinium* and *Gaylussacia*). The hurricane of 1938 blew down about half the trees, and *henrici* has not been seen there since — which shows how exact may be its choice of habitat. It visits flowers freely, especially those of Blueberry, Huckleberry, and Redbud.
Similar Species: — *I. irus* and *polios*, see couplets 4 and 5 of Key.
Larva: — Light green, dorsal, dorso-lateral and lateral stripes paler; or deep red brown with lighter red brown stripes. One brood. Adults in late April. Hibernation as pupa. **Food:** — Blueberry (*Vaccinium vacillans*), Wild Plum (*Prunus pennsylvanicus* and *cuneatus*). See note on this under *I. irus.*
Range: — Quebec, Ontario, Michigan, Nebraska s. to central Florida, Missouri, and Texas.

Subspecies: — *I. h. henrici* (TL Philadelphia, Pennsylvania) Canada s. to North Carolina and Nebraska; "tails" on Cu₁ & Cu₂ of HW short; wings above dark brown with some discal and limbal orange brown, especially in ♀ ♀ ; beneath as figured. *I. h. margaretæ* dos Passos (TL Deland, Florida) known from type locality only; somewhat larger; "tails" of HW very long; dark, grayish brown above with very little orange brown; wings beneath with less contrast between basal and limbal areas; fringes perhaps not checkered. *I. h. turneri* Clench (TL Cowley Co., Kansas) Kansas to northern Texas, somewhat larger; "tails" short; wings above with more orange brown than *h. henrici;* pale and washed-out looking beneath with less contrast between basal and limbal areas; marginal area of FW beneath light; dark, basal area of HW beneath definitely delimited outwardly by a white line. *I. h. solatus* Cook & Watson (TL Blanco Co., Texas) central Texas; "tails" short; wings above dark gray with very little orange brown; very little contrast between basal and limbal areas of wings beneath; basal area of HW not defined outwardly by white line. Considerable intergradation between these subspecies may be expected.

FROSTED ELFIN. *Incisalia irus* Godart   p. 129
0.9–1.45 in. Although widely distributed, the Frosted Elfin is uncommon to rare. Note the long stigma of the ♂, the long "tails" on Cu₁ and Cu₂ of the HW, the gray frosting on the HW beneath, and the lack of contrast between basal and limbal areas beneath. It flies in open, brushy fields, along the edges of open woods, and along roadsides.
Similar Species: — *I. henrici* & *polios.*
Larva: — Slug-shaped; head very small; yellowish green with brownish hairs, turning brownish red just before pupation.
Food: — Lupine (*Lupinus perennis*), False Indigo (*Baptisia tinctoria*). Records of "Plum" appear to be false, based on failure to recognize *irus* and *henrici* as distinct species. Records of "*Vaccinium*" also may be erroneous. The larva bores into the flowers. The pupa is formed in a definite, loose cocoon of silk, leaves and trash. One brood. Adults in April. Hibernation as pupa.
Range: — Southern Canada s. to Georgia, Illinois, Arkansas, and Texas.
Subspecies: — *I. i. irus* (TL "America") range as above except Texas. *I. i. hadros* Cook & Watson (TL near Houston, Texas) central Texas; larger (exp. 1.20–1.45 in.); coloration and pattern beneath very dull and indistinct; rare. There is strong opinion for considering *hadros* a separate species.

BOG ELFIN. *Incisalia lanoraieensis* Sheppard   p. 129
0.60–0.85 in. The recently described Bog Elfin is still poorly

known. Its small size, dull color above, and underside pattern resembling that of a dark, smudged *niphon*, are distinctive. It is known only from acid, Black Spruce-Tamarack-Sphagnum bogs in eastern Canada (TL Lanoraie, Quebec) and Maine, where it occurs in association with *Œneis jutta, Boloria eunomia, Lycæna epixanthe*, etc. It flies in May and June.

Larva: — Feeds on Black Spruce (*Picea nigra*) at first mining in the needles of a young shoot-tip.

PINE ELFIN. *Incisalia niphon* Huebner   p. 129

0.8–1.2 in. The Pine Elfin larva feeds on Pine, a far departure from its congeners. Look for it in and around the borders of open Pine Woods, especially where there are many young trees. It also frequents the vicinity of Red Cedars. Adults visit such flowers as Lupine, Everlasting, and Locust. Females may be flushed by jarring the Pines. The flight, normally slow, is fast and erratic when the butterfly is alarmed.

Larva: — Head yellow, body transparent green with two whitish stripes along each side and a transverse, white patch on the first thoracic segment; thinly covered with short, yellow brown hairs. Its bold striping is highly concealing among the pine needles.

Food: — Pines, probably only "hard" pines, i.e. *virginiana, rigida*, etc., not White Pine (*P. strobus*); perhaps also Red Cedar (*Juniperus virginiana*) or (doubtful) Lupine. One brood. Adults in April. Hibernation as pupa.

Range: — Nova Scotia, Quebec, and Ontario s. to Florida, Arkansas, and northern Texas.

Subspecies: — *I. n. niphon* (TL Florida) n. to New York and southern New England, as illustrated. *I. n. clarki* T. N. Freeman (TL Constance Bay, vicinity Ottawa, Ont.) northern states and Canada; ground color above much paler; ground color beneath golden brown, markings less contrasting; postmedian transverse line (⅔ out from base) of FW beneath very narrowly dark brown, outwardly edged with white, inwardly with golden brown. A blend zone between the subspecies seems to occupy most of central New York and New England.

Subfamily Gerydinæ: The Harvesters

As in the Blues and Coppers, the forewing has a four-branched radius; but in the Harvesters the vein M_1 is long-stalked with radius for some distance out from the cell. We have only one representative of this small, world-wide subfamily, the curious little *Feniseca*.

Like the other members of the subfamily it is predatory during the larval stage.

THE HARVESTER. *Feniseca tarquinius* Fabricius   pp. 48, 145
1.30 in. The details of the life history were not known for nearly
a century after Fabricius named this species after the Roman ty-
rant, Tarquin; so it must be coincidence that the name is so appropriate. The Harvester has an active and nervous, but not a
strong, flight, and is most commonly found within a few rods of
Alders growing in wet or swampy places. It usually alights on
leaves or on twigs to suck aphid honeydew. Its greatest peculiarity is its habit of feeding, in its larval stage, on the white,
"woolly" plant lice (aphids) of the alder and other shrubs.
Another odd feature is the resemblance of the pupa to a tiny
monkey's head; and still another is the speed up of the larval
period, there being only three molts and the whole stage taking
only ten to eleven days. Perhaps this is caused by the greater
nutritional value of its food — or perhaps it has come about because of the danger to the larva from ants which, tending their
aphid "cattle" for the sweet honeydew which they secrete, attack
any invader and have been known to kill *tarquinius* larvæ. The
larvæ are to be found buried beneath a mass of the aphids, covered with a web in which are entangled fragments of the prey,
frass, etc. They are easily reared in captivity if plenty of aphids
are provided, and do not seem to suffer from the attacks of parasitic wasps or flies.
Larva: — Greenish brown with faint olivaceous stripes, the
joints between the segments very prominent, covered with rather
long hairs which are thoroughly dusted with the waxy secretions
of its prey. Food: — Various species of woolly Aphids of the
genera *Schizoneura* and *Pemphigus*, principally on Alder (*Alnus*),
also on Beech (*Fagus*), Ash (*Fraxinus*), Witch Hazel (*Hama-
melis*), Wild Currant (*Ribes*), Hawthorn (*Cratægus*), "Viburnum"
and "Huckleberry." Pupa pale green beneath, greenish brown
to brown above, with darker patches, very irregular in shape, resembling a "monkey's head" or an "ace of clubs." Two broods
in north (Maine) to four or five in south. Adults in mid May
(40°). Hibernation as pupa, perhaps also as adult.
Range: — Maritime Provinces w. to Ontario, s. to Florida, Gulf
States, and Central Texas.
Subspecies: — *F. t. nova-scotiæ* McDunnough (TL South Mil-
ford, Nova Scotia) southeastern Canada and northern New England; orange brown areas above more extensive, black areas correspondingly reduced, especially the submarginal spots of the
HW. *F. t. tarquinius* (TL "Indiis") remainder of the species'
range; orange brown areas smaller, black more extensive. Specimens resembling *nova-scotiæ* appear in many northern localities.
The species evidently forms a cline

Subfamily Lycæninæ: The Coppers

As THE name implies the Coppers tend to a coppery orange coloring, and in this differ from the Blues and Hairstreaks; but not all are coppery or orange, and one western species is bluer than most Blues. There are always four branches of radius in the forewing, and M_1 is not stalked with the radials but arises from the cell. The undersides of the tarsi bear spines in irregular clusters at the sides, not arranged in lines as in Blues. The Coppers are stouter bodied than the Blues, and have faster flights. They are essentially a northern, Holarctic group, although one species occurs in Central America, a few in Africa and a few in the Indo-Australian region. There are more in western North America than in the east. At present all of our species are included in the single large genus *Lycæna;* most are in the subgenus *Tharsalea* Scudder, the nymotypical subgenus being largely Palæarctic. Coppers have been classified in *Heodes* and *Chrysophanus*, but these names are inapplicable.

Coppers are typically inhabitants of marshes, meadows, and roadsides, and open places in general, although a few prefer woodlands. They visit flowers freely but not avidly.

AMERICAN COPPER. *Lycæna phlæas americana* Harris   p. 176
1.0 in. As with many other very good Americans, this Copper's nearest relatives are in the Old World; for our population is a subspecies of the European *L. phlæas*, and not a very distinct one at that. In the northeastern states it is one of the commonest butterflies, becoming scarce southward and very rare in the west. Its small size and bright colors make it unmistakable. It shows considerable variation, both seasonal and individual. Spring specimens are brighter colored and have smaller black spots than later broods. A number of aberrations have been named: in one (*fasciata*) the black spots of the FW enlarge, may fuse to form a patch; in another (*obliterata*) these spots are small, or nearly all absent; in still another (*fulliolus*) the copper is replaced by yellow. There is some evidence that *fasciata* may be locally more common in certain spots.

The pugnacity of this little butterfly is astonishing. Nothing that moves within its range is safe from being "buzzed"; and nearly all other butterflies are driven away. It even attacks the comparatively gigantic Monarch; nor does it stop there, for it will dart at birds, dogs, and even butterfly collectors!

Larva: — Dull, rosy red with yellowish lateral tints; or green sometimes with a reddish dorsal stripe; slug-shaped, downy

Food: — Field or Sheep Sorrel (*Rumex acetosella*) perhaps also Garden Sorrel (*R. acetosa*) and Yellow Dock (*R. crispus*). Two broods in north, three from New England south. Adults in early May (Lat. 40°). Hibernates as pupa.

Range: — Arctic regions from the northernmost limits of butterfly life s. in our area to Georgia, Gulf States, and Arkansas. Rare southward and westward and in the Arctic.

Subspecies: — *L. p. phlæas* Linnæus is Palæarctic, not in our area; in arctic North America occurs *L. p. feildeni* McLachlan (TL Ellesmere Island, Lat. 81° 41′ N.) coppery red replaced by lighter, brassy orange, with some dark suffusion; black spots of FW smaller; gray of wings above and beneath darker. This must be one brooded. It appears to be limited to Arctic Life Zone, s. to Baffin Island (August) though specimens from the Rocky Mountains resemble it. *L. p. americana* Harris (TL Massachusetts) eastern area, Canadian Zone, and southward. *L. p. hypophlæus* Boisduval (TL California), not in our area.

BRONZE COPPER. *Lycæna thoë* Guerin   p. 176

1.30–1.40 in. *Thoë* is the largest of our coppery Coppers. In the ♀ the purplish orange of the ♂ FW is replaced by light orange, on which the black spots are larger and the dark borders wider. Not uncommon, but quite local. Seek a colony in open, wet meadows, even along the edges of salt marshes. I associate it with the kind of meadow in which one finds clumps of Blue Flag (*Iris versicolor*). Here you will also find *Melitæa harrisii* and good Skipper collecting.

Larva: — Slug-shaped, bright yellowish green with a darker stripe along back. **Food:** — Yellow Dock (*Rumex crispus*), Knotweed (*Polygonum*); also recorded (dubious) Prickly Ash. It may feed on some of the more water-loving Docks. Two broods. Adults in mid-June, again in mid-August. Hibernation as egg.

Range: — Quebec and Ontario w. to Saskatchewan, s. to New Jersey, Pennsylvania, Ohio, Illinois, Indiana, and Kansas (rare northward).

BOG COPPER. *Lycæna epixanthe* Boisduval & Leconte   p. 176

0.85–1.0 in. The Bog Copper is very local, never straying far from the *acid bogs* (not marshes) where the foodplant, Cranberry, grows. The ♂ has a faint purplish gloss on the wings above; the ♀ is grayer and duller. The orange submarginal band of the HW is narrow, often reduced, but always at least the anal lunules are present. The black spots on the HW beneath are clear cut, distinct and round; in dark *helloides* and *dorcas* (see below) not only are the HW beneath much darker colored, usually orange brownish, but the dark spots (usually less prominent) are transverse ovals or bars. *Epixanthe* is much paler and more delicately tinted beneath than these.

Similar Species: — *L. dorcas* & *helloides*, see below.
Larva: — Not known in detail. Eggs laid singly on lower surfaces of leaves near tips of shoots of food plant. **Food:** — Wild Cranberry (*Vaccinium macrocarpon*). One brood. Adults in late June and early July. Hibernation as egg, which is able to withstand being flooded in winter.
Range: — Newfoundland, Maritime Provinces, Quebec, and Ontario, s. to Pennsylvania, New Jersey, northern Indiana, Michigan, Minnesota, also (?) Iowa, Nebraska, and Kansas.
Subspecies: — *L. e. epixanthe* (TL probably New Jersey) New Jersey n. to central New York and New England; as figured, wings beneath distinctly light yellowish. *L. e. michiganensis* Rawson (TL Proud Lake, Oakland Co., Michigan) Michigan and Wisconsin, probably Minnesota; orange submarginal line of HW above more extensive; ground color beneath grayish yellow on FW, pale gray, slightly pearly on HW; black spots beneath more prominent, orange lunules brighter. *L. e. phædra* Hall, Newfoundland and Nova Scotia; pale, very whitish yellow to white beneath, dark spots reduced. Specimens from northern New England (Maine) and central New York (McLean Bogs, vicinity Cortland) are more whitish beneath, appear to connect up *phædra* and *michiganensis*, also intergrade to *e. epixanthe*. There is some local segregation, due to restriction to bogs, and a very interesting clinal distribution.

PURPLISH COPPER. *Lycæna helloides* Boisduval   p. 176
1.15–1.30 in. Essentially western, but occurs in the northwestern part of our area. The ♂ is purplish, orange-brown above as illustrated. The ♀ has the FW orange with larger dark spots and a narrow, black border. It varies greatly. Some ♂♂ (*florus* Edwards) are nearly solid, dark, sooty to purplish brown above, the corresponding ♀♀ similarly dark, grayer brown. These dark forms are correspondingly darker, more richly colored beneath. They are sometimes quite indistinguishable from *L. dorcas;* and, since there seem to be no genitalic differences between *dorcas* and *helloides*, they may be really parts of a single species, varying geographically, as in a "cline," but with some local tendencies to segregated, "ecotopic" (environment) forms. The problem requires a great deal more careful collecting, field notes, and rearing and breeding. It offers a fine research opportunity.
Similar Species: — *L. dorcas*, see below; *L. epixanthe.*
Larva: — Grass green, with many spine-bearing, white elevations, covered with colorless hairs; two broken dorsal lines, two lateral stripes and a number of lateral oblique lines are all yellow; head amber, eyes white. **Food:** — Docks (*Rumex* spp.), Knotweed (*Polygonum*), Baby's Breath (*Galium*). Two broods (perhaps only one northward). Adults in June.

Range: — In the eastern area e. and s. to northern Illinois; northern records confused with *L. dorcas.*

DORCAS COPPER. *Lycæna dorcas* Kirby   p. 145
1.0–1.2 in. Resembling *helloides* strongly, *dorcas* averages smaller and is consistently dark brown above, the ♂ with purplish reflections. The orange submarginal band on the HW above is reduced to a narrow line, or to one or two orange lunules near the anal angle. As noted under *helloides*, *dorcas* cannot always be separated from dark *helloides* (*florus*), especially when one does not look at the locality labels! Whatever its relationships may be, it certainly represents a more northern population.
Similar Species: — *L. helloides, epixanthe.*
Larva: — Largely unknown. One record of a ♀ (*dospassosi*) ovipositing on Cinquefoil (*Potentilla*). One brood.
Range: — Canada (Canadian Zone), s. into Ohio, Michigan, and Maine.
Subspecies: — *L. d. dorcas* (TL near Cumberland House, Lat. 54° N, Saskatchewan) range as above except for Maine and New Brunswick; smaller, darker, brown of upper side duller and sootier, dark spots smaller. *L. d. dospassosi* McDunnough (TL Bathurst, New Brunswick) larger, black spots of upper- and undersides heavy, larger, those of under side particularly very strong; ground color beneath dull ochreous, not orange. A very striking subspecies, from a salt-marsh environment, that almost looks distinct enough to deserve specific rank. *L. d. claytoni* Brower (TL Springfield, Maine) Maine, smaller, much darker and duller, spots reduced in size and number, particularly above; anal orange markings usually faint. Found in a dry, upland "old-field," associated with a bush *Potentilla.*

GREAT COPPER. *Lycæna xanthoides dione* Scudder
1.5–1.7 in. Wings above lustrous, brownish-gray. ♂ with a small dark spot in cell and a bar at end of cell of FW; a row of dark, marginal spots on HW, the one or two nearest anal angle sometimes with a trace of orange. ♀ FW with spots in and at end of cell larger, and an incomplete, postmedian row of dark spots; on HW a narrow, submarginal, orange band with black dots in it; this continues up onto FW to below vein Cu₂. Beneath pearl gray, spots of usual "Copper" pattern black; an orange patch above anal angle.
Larva: — Not known in detail. **Food:** — "Bitter Dock" (*Rumex obtusifolius*). One brood. Adults in late June–July.
Range: — Upper Mississippi Valley, Kansas n. through Nebraska and Minnesota to Manitoba, less common westward.

Subfamily Plebeiinæ: The Blues

ALTHOUGH a world-wide group, the Blues reach their greatest abundance in the Northern Hemisphere, there being relatively fewer tropical species. All are small. In the majority blue is the dominant color above, although some are brown and others whitish. The females consistently have much wider dark borders than the males, sometimes so much so that little or no blue is visible. The radial vein of the FW is always four-branched; and veins R_3, R_{4+5} and M_1 arise separately from the cell. The head is narrow, the eyes emarginate. The tarsi bear relatively few spines which are aligned in fairly regular rows. The eggs are flat and turban shaped. The larvæ have very narrow heads. In the larvæ of some Blues we see the greatest development of the "honeydew" secreting gland which pours out its sweet secretion through an orifice on the dorsum of the seventh abdominal segment. These are the species in which symbiotic (mutual benefit) relationships with Ants are most marked. The pupæ bear hairlike appendages, sometimes simple and tapering, sometimes minutely spiny.

Identification and classification of the Blues are sometimes extremely difficult. In some, identification can be made only by characters of the genitalia; and these are incompletely known. Subspecific classification is also very uncertain in some groups. Again, viewpoints on classification differ greatly. One author, an extreme splitter, will claim that we must recognize the "*Plebeiinæ, Catochrysopinæ, Glaucopsychinæ, Everinæ, Lycænopsinæ,*" etc. as separate subfamilies; another, who believes in "lumping," will insist that all the Blues together form no more than one tribe of the subfamily *Lycæninæ*. I have tried to strike a mid-ground between such extremes.

Many of the Blues are more easily identified by general appearance than by particular details. The following key will serve for the genera of our area; but there will always be unusual specimens to be identified largely by a knowledge of what species are likely to occur in the area. It must be kept in mind that the females usually differ very strongly from the males, being darker with much wider borders and sometimes lacking blue altogether. The underside patterns are far more important than those of the upperside.

ESSENTIALLY TROPICAL SPECIES, not normally ranging far north of Florida, Gulf States, and Texas: *cassius* (*Leptotes*), *exilis* (*Brephidium*), *gaika* (*Zizula*), *hanno* (*Hemiargus*), *marinus* (*Leptotes*), *pseudofea* (*Brephidium*), *thomasi* (*Hemiargus*).

ESSENTIALLY NORTHERN SPECIES, not normally ranging far southward from Canada: *amyntula* (*Everes*), *aquilo* (*Plebeius*), *argyrognomon* (*Lycæides*), *melissa* (*Lycæides*), *sæpiolus* (*Plebeius*).

WIDELY RANGING SPECIES: *acmon* (*Plebeius*), *argiolus* (*Lycænopsis*), *comyntas* (*Everes*), *isolus* (*Hemiargus*), *lygdamus* (*Glaucopsyche*).

KEY TO GENERA, *PLEBEIINÆ* OF EASTERN NORTH AMERICA

1. HW with a delicate tail at tip of Cu_2
   Everes (*amyntula & comyntas*)
1. HW with no tail...................................... 2
2. Size very small (0.45–0.70 in.); ground color above orange-brown; blue, if present, limited to basal half; FW with apex and outer margin rounded; HW beneath with a submarginal row of four large, black and metallic spots in cells M_1, M_2, M_3 and Cu_1; much smaller metallic spots in cells $Sc+R_1$, R_5, Cu_2 & 2dA.....................*Brephidium* (*exilis & pseudofea*)
2. Size larger (0.70–1.5 in.); ground color above with more blue in males, though females may be mostly or entirely fuscous or brown; FW (except *Zizula gaika*) with apex more pointed; HW beneath with or without submarginal, metallic spots, but never with these as described above........... 3
3. HW beneath with at least one or two submarginal, metallic or partly metallic spots.............................. 7
3. HW beneath with submarginal spots and markings lacking metallic scaling..................................... 4
4. Size small (0.7–0.8 in.); FW with apex rounded; wings rather long; dingy blue above with very wide fuscous borders; southwest only................................*Zizula* (*gaika*)
4. Larger (normally 0.8–1.5 in.); FW with apex more pointed.. 5
5. Wings beneath with no clear-cut markings beyond the ends of the cells except a single, transverse, postmedian row of ocellate, round or oval black spots, sharply ringed with white ....*Glaucopsyche* (*lygdamus*)
5. Wings beneath with clear-cut marginal and submarginal markings in addition to postmedian row of spots.......... 6
6. Apex of FW very pointed; wings strong, heavily scaled; body relatively large and markedly hairy; color of males tending to a grayer blue; Canada and extreme northern United States
   Plebeius (*aquilo & sæpiolus*)
6. Apex of FW more rounded; wings delicate, lightly scaled; body relatively small, not markedly hairy; color of males purplish blue to violet blue; HW above frequently whitish discally, sometimes nearly all white; central Canada south into Central America....................*Lycænopsis* (*argiolus*)
7. HW beneath with metallic scales only in the submarginal spots of anal region below vein Cu_1..................... 8
7. HW beneath with metallic scales in submarginal spots above vein Cu_1 as well as below it........................... 9
8. Wings beneath with many transverse, streaky markings of bars and lines, and without round, black and white, ocellate spots other than those in anal region of HW (which are not really black, white ringed ocelli); scaling thin so that markings of underside show through on upperside; blue above tending to be replaced by whitish, especially basally, more in females.................... . . ..*Leptotes* (*cassius & marinus*)

8. Wings beneath with fewer transverse markings, and with some round, black and white, ocellate spots (on HW at least one in cell near base and two below costal margin); scaling of wings denser so that underside markings do not show through; females dark, fuscous above, with some basal blue, but no whitish........*Hemiargus* (*hanno, thomasi, & isolus*)

9. Male, as well as female, with a submarginal row of orange and black spots, usually forming a band, on HW above; submarginal spots of FW beneath with no orange; FW beneath with an ocellate spot in cell about halfway out to bar at end of cell; HW beneath with no postbasal spot immediately below cell..................................*Plebeius* (*acmon*)

9. HW of male above with no orange and black submarginal spots or band (female has some); submarginal spots of FW beneath with some orange (sometimes very little); FW beneath with no spot in cell out to the bar at end; HW beneath with a postbasal spot immediately below cell (as well as the postmedian one below Cu₂)
Lycæides (*argyrognomon & melissa*)

Genus Leptotes *Scudder:* The Tropical Blues

THE TWO species of our area are differentiated as follows:

(1) *Cassius;* smaller (0.50–0.80 in.); blue rather pure, not purplish; males with distinct whitish along anal margins of HW above; transverse dark markings beneath brownish gray, narrow, rather clear-cut, more broken into short elements, particularly on HW; on FW beneath, both the submedian and postmedian transverse dark lines tend to fade out below cell and cubital veins, leaving blank, white areas down to inner margin; large submarginal spots of HW beneath elongate, with deep, cobalt blue iridescence; females above with considerable white on posterior, discal areas of FW and HW.

(2) *Marinus:* larger (0.65–1.10 in.); blue decidedly purplish; males with little if any whitish along anal margins of HW above; transverse dark markings beneath pale brown, wide, more unbroken; on FW beneath the submedian and postmedian transverse lines run down to inner margin, leaving no large, blank areas below cells and cubitals; large, submarginal spots of HW beneath round, with pale blue iridescence; females above with posterior discal areas of FW and HW largely suffused with brownish, not largely white.

CASSIUS BLUE. *Leptotes cassius* Cramer   p. 145
0.50–0.80 in. *Cassius* is a sprightly, rather fast flying little Blue, much given to visiting flowers, especially of trees and shrubs. It is common in southern Florida. The ♀ above is pale brownish

white to white, with a brighter blue reflection than the ♂; the
dark borders are very wide, especially on the FW; the dark markings of the underside are repeated, much more subdued, and the
veins are narrowly dark.

Similar Species: — *L. marinus* — see differentiation above.

Larva: — Green with a russet red overtone, the skin rough, the
"head and legs concealed by overlapping fringe"; it eats flower
buds and flowers. **Food:** — Leadwort (*Plumbago*), Hairy Milk
Pea (*Galactia volubilis*), perhaps *Albizzia*, Lima Beans (*Phaseolus*) and Rattle-box (*Crotalaria incana*) (last two records in
Puerto Rico).   Two broods, perhaps more.

Range: — *L. c. cassius*, South American, not in our area.

Subspecies: — *L. c. theonus* Lucas (TL Cuba), southern Florida,
Cuba, Bahamas, Jamaica; ♂♂ with more white scaling along anal
fold of HW above; ♀♀ with much clear white above; markings
beneath narrow, dark, brownish gray; submarginal eyespots of
HW beneath (cells Cu₁ & Cu₂) large. *L. c. striatus* Edwards (TL
San Antonio, Texas) Panama to southern Texas; ♂♂ more purplish blue; ♀♀ with more white, less blue above; markings beneath paler, brownish; submarginal eyespots of HW beneath
smaller, the anal one frequently reduced or even absent.   See
note under *L. marinus*, below.

MARINE BLUE. *Leptotes marinus* Reakirt
0.65–1.10 in. *Marinus* is common in Mexico (TL vicinity Vera
Cruz), ranges to Kansas, where it breeds but cannot overwinter
(Stallings & Turner in litt.), and westward and northward to
California.   In southern Texas it is common, April – December.
The race of *cassius* (*striatus*) that likewise occurs in southern
Texas, resembles *marinus* in coloring more than it does *cassius
theonus;* but may be told by its white females and the pattern
characters described above.

Genus Hemiargus *Huebner:* The Eyed Blues

THREE SPECIES of this essentially tropical genus enter our area.
They have been much misidentified, and their subspecies attributed frequently to the wrong species.   I am following the specific
synonomy of Nabokov (*Psyche*, 1945, 52:1–61) but do not follow
his generic splitting, which places each species in a separate genus.
The species may be distinguished as follows:

(1) *ceraunus* — ♂♂ above slightly purplish blue; ♀♀ above with
no prominent orange and black, submarginal ocellus on HW in cell
Cu₁ as in *thomasi*.   Both sexes beneath with postmedian row of

spots on FW not much enlarged, as in *isola;* space between post-median and subterminal markings not white, as in *thomasi;* ocellate marking on HW in cell Cu₂ double, if developed at all.

(2) *isolus* — ♂♂ above slightly purplish blue; ♀♀ above with submarginal spot on HW in cell Cu₁ sometimes ocellate but not with large inner orange area as in *thomasi.* Both sexes beneath with postmedian row of spots of FW greatly enlarged and conspicuous; ocellate marking on HW in cell Cu₂ double, if developed at all; space between postmedian and submarginal markings not prominently white, as in *thomasi.*

(3) *thomasi* — ♂♂ above a more true blue than other species; ♀♀ above with a large, orange lunule inside black spot in cell Cu₁ of HW. Both sexes beneath with postmedian row of spots of FW not greatly enlarged as in *isola;* HW with submarginal, ocellate spot in cell Cu₂ large and single; space between postmedian and submarginal markings conspicuously white, especially on HW.

CERAUNUS BLUE. *Hemiargus ceraunus* Fabricius   p. 160
0.65–1.0 in. This species is a common Florida butterfly, but is uncommon to rare in southern Texas. It has generally been referred to as *Lycæna* or *Hemiargus hanno* Stoll; but the true *hanno* is a distinct species that does not occur in the United States.
Larva: — Dimorphic, either green with reddish dorsal stripe, or reddish with a green under shade; feeds on flower buds.
Food: — Partridge Pea (*Chamæcrista brachiata*), Hairy Partridge Pea (*C. aspera*), Crabs Eye Vine (*Abrus precatorius*). At least two broods.
Range: — Georgia, Florida, Alabama (*antibubastus*); southern Texas (*zacheinus*).
Subspecies: — *H. c. ceraunus* (TL probably Jamaica) Antillean, not in eastern area. *H. c. antibubastus* Huebner (TL Georgia) Florida, Georgia, and Alabama; as figured; HW beneath has a large, submarginal, ocellate spot in cell Cu₁, a smaller reduced one in cell Cu₂, none in cell M₃. *H. c. zacheinus* Butler & Druce (TL Cartago, Costa Rica) Central America n. into southern Texas: HW beneath has a large, submarginal ocellate spot in cell M₃, in addition to the one in cell Cu₁; that in cell Cu₂ much reduced.

REAKIRT'S BLUE. *Hemiargus isolus* Reakirt   p. 160
0.75–1.1 in. *Isolus* is a common species of the western part of our area, ranging far northward. It occurs in open spaces generally, visits flowers freely. The enlarged row of submarginal spots on the FW beneath is distinctive. The life history appears to be unknown. **Food:** — Mesquite (*Prosopis*) in Texas.
Range: — Mexico (TL vicinity Vera Cruz) n. to Nebraska almost entirely west of the Mississippi River.
Subspecies: — *alce* Edwards (TL Colorado) has sometimes been placed as a subspecies, but is usually considered to be a syno-

BLUES AND SULPHURS
Families *Lycaenidae* & *Pieridae*

The Blues are all × 1½, the Sulphurs × 1

1. MIAMI BLUE, *Hemiargus thomasi bethune-bakeri*   p. 162
   Upper & under sides, ♂ (Miami, Fla.). × 1½. Large, single eyespot
   on HW beneath in cell Cu₂; transverse white band on wings beneath;
   ♀ with large orange spot near anal angle of HW above. Centr. &
   S. Fla. Common.
2. REAKIRT'S BLUE, *Hemiargus isolus*   p. 159
   Under side, ♂ (Omaha, Nebr.). × 1½. Row of larger spots on FW
   beneath. Mex. n. to Nebr. & westward. Common.
3. CERAUNUS BLUE, *Hemiargus ceraunus antibubastus*   p. 159
   Upper & under sides, ♂ (Tybee I., Savannah, Ga.). × 1½. No row
   of larger spots as in *isolus* nor white bands as in *thomasi*; ♀ lacks large
   orange spot on HW above. Ga. & Fla. to s. Tex.
4. EASTERN TAILED BLUE, *Everes comyntas*   p. 163
   Upper & under sides, ♂ (Suffolk, Va.). × 1½. Tails on HW; markings beneath prominent and clear cut (see *amyntula*, below). S. Can.
   southward. Very common.
5. WESTERN TAILED BLUE, *Everes amyntula*   p. 164
   Under side, ♂ (Riding Mts., Man.). × 1½. Tails on HW; markings
   beneath indistinct and blurry; bars at ends of cells scarcely visible.
   Western, e. in Can. to Ont.
6. CROWBERRY BLUE, *Lycaeides argyrognomon empetri*   p. 165
   Upper & under sides, ♂ (Cape Canso, N.S.). × 1½. HW beneath
   with submarginal iridescent and orange spots; dark markings beneath
   very prominent; see text. Maritime Provinces.
7. NEWFOUNDLAND BLUE, *Lycaeides argyrognomon aster*   p. 165
   Under side, ♂ (Hopedale, Labr.). × 1½. Markings beneath less
   prominent than in *empetri* (No. 6). See text.
8. KARNER BLUE, *Lycaeides melissa samuelis*   p. 165
   Upper & under sides, ♂ (Karner, N.Y.). × 1½. See text. Man. e.
   to Mass. See also Pl. 21, No. 10.
9. MEXICAN SULPHUR, *Eurema mexicana*   p. 196
   Upper side, ♂ (Baboquivari Mts., Ariz.). × 1. HW with short tail;
   wings above creamy white; orange shade along costa of HW; "dog's
   head" outline in border of FW. Mex. n. to Okla., straying further.
10. PROTERPIA ORANGE, *Eurema proterpia*   p. 197
    Upper side, ♂ (Patagonia, Ariz.). × 1. HW with no tail; wings
    above orange, dark borders & vein tips. See text. S. Tex.
11. GUNDLACH'S ORANGE, *Eurema gundlachia*   p. 197
    Upper side, ♂ (Santa Rita Mts., Ariz.). × 1. HW with definite
    tail; orange and black above, veins less black than *proterpia*. See text.
12. BOISDUVAL'S SULPHUR, *Eurema boisduvaliana*   p. 196
    Upper side, ♂ (Prescott, Ariz.). × 1. Wings above yellow with
    orange shade along costa of HW; HW with very short tail or none;
    shallow "dog's head" outline in FW border. S. Fla., rare.

SWALLOWTAILS, SULPHURS AND WHITES

Families *Papilionidae* & *Pieridae*

Note that the reductions of the illustrations vary

1. POLYDAMAS SWALLOWTAIL, *Papilio polydamas* p. 180
Upper side, ♂ (Miami, Fla.). $\times \frac{3}{5}$. No tails; black; spots of FW yellow, of HW greenish yellow; HW with greenish luster. Fla. to Tex. & southward.
2. SHORT TAILED SWALLOWTAIL, *Papilio brevicauda* p. 172
Upper side, ♀, (Newfoundland) $\times \frac{3}{5}$. Black; spots yellow, with orange flush distally in each; short tails; HW has blue spots between the yellow spot rows. Newf. & eastern Can.
3. TIGER SWALLOWTAIL, *Papilio glaucus* p. 175
Upper side, ♂ (Bedford, N.Y.) $\times \frac{1}{2}$. Yellow with black pattern; HW with some blue submarginally; see also ♀ (No. 6 below). Centr. Can. s. throughout eastern area. Very common.
4. IDÆUS SWALLOWTAIL, *Papilio anchisiades idæus* p. 178
Upper side, ♂ (Cordoba, V.C., Mex.) $\times \frac{3}{5}$. Brownish black; paler shade on FW; HW with spots pink discally, white marginally. S. Tex.
5. THOAS SWALLOWTAIL, *Papilio thoas autocles* p. 174
Upper side, ♂ (Cordoba, V.C., Mex.) $\times \frac{3}{5}$. Very like *cresphontes;* see text. Strays into s. Tex.
6. TIGER SWALLOWTAIL, *Papilio glaucus* p. 175
Upper side, dark phase (*glaucus*) of ♀ (Stamford, Conn.) $\times \frac{1}{2}$. Dark brownish black; marginal spots yellow; submarginal blue on HW. See text and ♂ (No. 3 above).
7. MÆRULA, *Anteos mærula* p. 189
Upper side, ♂ (Jalapa, Mex.) $\times \frac{3}{5}$. Yellow, slight blackish markings on FW; ♂ has sex patch at base of costa of HW; ♀ is white. Note angled wings. S. Tex. & s. Fla.
8. CLOUDLESS SULPHUR, *Phœbis sennæ eubule* p. 190
Upper side, ♂ (Gainesville, Fla.) $\times \frac{3}{5}$. Clear, nearly unmarked yellow above. Spots beneath show through. Entire area n. to Can.
9. CLOUDLESS SULPHUR, *Phœbis sennæ eubule* p. 190
Upper side, ♀ (Port Sewall, Fla.) $\times \frac{3}{5}$. Color ranges from pale yellow to nearly solid orange; dark markings also variable.
10. TAILED SULPHUR, *Phœbis neocypris bracteolata* p. 284
Upper side, ♂ (Cochise Co., Ariz.) $\times \frac{3}{5}$. Deep yellow, flushed with orange. Tail on HW. May occur in s. Tex.
11. FLORIDA WHITE, *Appias drusilla neumægenii* p. 199
Upper side, ♂ (Jupiter, Fla.) $\times \frac{3}{5}$. White; pearly iridescence at base of FW; orange at base of HW beneath. S. Fla. & Tex.
12. FLORIDA WHITE, *Appias drusilla neumægenii* p. 199
Upper side, ♀ (Key Largo, Fla.) $\times \frac{3}{5}$. HW varies from creamy white to ochreous orange. See text.

nym. (Larger, ground color beneath light brownish-gray, not dark gray.) It is of dubious worth, appearing to fall well within the normal variation of *isolus*.

MIAMI BLUE. *Hemiargus thomasi* Clench   p. 160

0.80–1.1 in. A common Florida Blue, found in open places generally, visiting flowers (especially Spanish Needles — *Bidens*) freely. The larger eyespot of the HW is particularly large and has much orange. The transverse white shade of the wings beneath, caused by broadening and inward extension of the white edge of the submarginal markings, is distinctive. The full scientific name of the Florida race is really something to make even a hardened entomologist wince a bit: "*Hemiargus (Cyclargus) thomasi bethune-bakeri* Comstock and Huntington." The species has been widely referred to in the literature as *Lycæna* or *Hemiargus ammon* Lucas, really a distinct species of Cuba; and Holland included it twice as "*catilina* Fabricus" and "*filenus* Poey."

Larva: — Very incompletely known. **Food:** — Catsclaw (*Pithecolobium guadaloupensis*); *Guilandina crista*. Two broods, the summer one darker, December–April and June–Nov.

Range: — Florida from Titusville and Merritt Island south.

Subspecies: — *H. t. thomasi* Clench (TL Cat Island, Bahamas) not in the eastern area. *H. t. bethune bakeri* (TL Miami) as above.

Genus Brephidium *Scudder:* The Pigmy Blues

THE SPECIES of *Brephidium* are our smallest butterflies. The FW is long, with rounded apex and outer margin. Vein R_1 of the fore wing arises from the cell, runs to Sc and fuses with it. The species are distinguished as follows:

1. *Exilis:* Southwestern and tropical; size slightly smaller fringes largely white, except for a dark patch on FW at end o cubital veins; wings above with considerable blue basally, some times nearly to halfway out; wings beneath whitish basally.

2. *Pseudofea* (*isophthalma*) Southeast United States & Antilles size slightly larger; fringes uniformly dark; wings with no blu above; wings beneath brown basally.

WESTERN PIGMY BLUE. *Brephidium exilis* Boisduval

0.45–0.65 in. *Exilis* is common, flying all year round, in souther Texas, strays north to Nebraska (July–September). It range west to the Pacific, south to Venezuela. Perhaps the easter population should be recognized as a separate subspecies (*fe*

Edwards, TL Waco, Texas) from the western *e. exilis* (TL California); but this is dubious.   **Food:** — Saltbush (*Atriplex*), *Petunia parviflora* (California records).

EASTERN PIGMY BLUE. *Brephidium pseudofea* Morrison

p. 145

0.55–0.70 in. There are inland records, but I have never found *pseudofea* common far from salt water. Only once have I seen it swarming, on Plantation Key, Florida, in early July. Hundreds of specimens were sharply restricted to a small area of semi-tidal flat at the edge of mangroves, overgrown with Saltwort (*Batis*) and Glasswort (*Salicornia*). Its flight is weak and low. The name *isophthalma* Herrich-Schæffer, formerly used for this species, should be restricted to the Cuban race of *exilis*. Our mainland population is a distinct species.
Similar Species: — *B. exilis* — see above.
Early Stages: — Unknown. Apparently at least three broods.
Range: — Georgia, Florida (TL Florida) and supposedly Gulf States. There is one record from Galveston, Texas, perhaps of a stray.

IMPORTED BLUE. *Zizula gaika* Trimen (*cyna* Edwards)

0.70–0.80 in. In the eastern area *gaika* extends east to Brownsville and Pharr, Texas, flies there March–September. Its flight is low and weak. It is a native of Africa, introduced to the southwest before the middle of the last century. It is said to have been brought in with fodder when Jefferson Davis, then Secretary of War of the United States, had a number of camels brought over for use as Army transport animals. Today the camels are long gone, although some escaped and maintained themselves for many years in the wild, adding materially, by the way, to the folk-tales of the desert. But *gaika* remains. Think of its history when you catch one.

EASTERN TAILED BLUE. *Everes comyntas* Godart

pp. 48, 49, 160, 176

0.9–1.1 in. One of our commonest butterflies, occurring in all parts of our area except the far northland. Its northern limit is uncertain, because of confusion with the western *E. amyntula*. The flight is quick, but low and not long continued. It visits flowers very freely, and is a consistent mud-puddle visitor. There is considerable seasonal variation, spring specimens being lighter beneath, the ♀ ♀ darker and browner above, the ♂ ♂ with narrower dark borders above. Females are often wholly brown above.
Similar Species: — *E. amyntula*, more western, extends in southern Canada to Ontario; it is much chalkier white beneath, with less prominent markings due both to reduction of the dark scales

and to the blending of the circumferential white rings with the ground color; the orange lunules are also smaller and paler.

Larva: — Small, black head; body downy, dark green; a dark, brownish stripe down mid-dorsum and similar, faint, oblique lateral stripes; whole body sprinkled with tiny papillæ each bearing a short hair. Feeds in and on flower heads and buds by preference, also eats leaves. Eggs laid on flower buds, stems and leaves. **Food:** — "*Leguminosæ*" such as Bush Clovers (*Lespedeza hirta* and *capitata*), Tick Trefoils (*Desmodium* (*Meibomia*) *canescens* and *marilandica*), Milk Pea (*Galactia*), Everlasting Pea (*Lathyrus*), Clover (*Trifolium*), False Indigo (*Baptisia tinctoria*), Bean (*Phaseolus*), etc. Three broods, probably more southward. Adults in late April–early May. Hibernation as full-grown larva. **Range:** — Southern Canada w. to Pacific, s. throughout United States into Central America; rare or absent in southern Florida. **Subspecies:** — *E. c. comyntas* (TL "North America") entire range of the species in the eastern area except perhaps northwestern part, and Texas; *E. c. valeriæ* Clench (TL Lead (Black Hills) South Dakota) may enter northwestern part of our area; males lack orange submarginal lunule below Cu₁ of HW above; beneath, dingier; females darker. *E. c. texana* R. H. Chermock (TL San Antonio, Texas) Texas, paler, smaller, ♂♂ more violet blue above; ♀♀ lighter; markings beneath less prominent. Neither is a very good subspecies, especially in a clinal species such as this.

WESTERN TAILED BLUE. *Everes amyntula* Boisduval p. 160 0.9–1.1 in. A common species, largely replacing *comyntas* in the Northwest, *amyntula* appears to extend eastward in our area at least to Smoky Falls, Ontario, perhaps into Quebec, and should be looked for in northern Wisconsin, Minnesota, and Michigan.

Genus Lycæides *Scudder:* The Orange Margined Blues

THE RECENT work of Nabokov has entirely rearranged the classification of this genus. The North American species can be separated almost only by male genitalic differences, chiefly by the varying proportions of the parts of the *falces* (see Chapter 5). The very technical details can be found in Nabokov's latest article (Bulletin, Museum Comparative Zoology, 1949, Vol. 101, No. 4, pp. 479–541, 9 Pl.). The color and pattern characteristics of the species are slight, variable, and hard to express. They must be used with great caution, and with full understanding that the relationships of the forms cannot be expressed accurately by a linear nomenclature.

(1) *argyrognomon* Bergsträsser. Present in our area as races *scudderi, empetri,* and *aster*. HW "high angled" and strongly developed; male above more heavily dusted with fuscous; FW above with a wider, dark marginal border; wings beneath, when fawn colored, more vivid in tone; HW beneath with transverse, submarginal orange marks weaker and narrower; ♀ above with less transverse submarginal orange.

(2) *melissa* Edwards. Present in our area as races *melissa* and *samuelis*. HW shorter and rounder, with proportionately less ground color between the markings; male above with less fuscous dusting; FW above with a narrower, dark marginal border; wings beneath, when fawn colored, duller in tone; HW beneath with transverse, submarginal orange marks more extensive and richly colored; ♀ above with more and wider submarginal orange.

NORTHERN BLUE. *Lycæides argyrognomon* Bergsträsser

p. 160

0.90–1.20 in. The well-known Blue of the northeastern states, that has for so long been known as *scudderi,* is no longer included here (see *L. melissa samuelis,* below). In addition to Old World and western North American races, *argyrognomon* includes three subspecies in our area, chiefly Canadian. Its differences from *melissa* are almost entirely genitalic; the rather vague pattern and color characters are given above. Despite Nabokov's very thorough work, the relationships in the group are still far from clear.

Early Stages: — Unknown except that *L. a. empetri* oviposits on Black Crowberry (*Empetrum nigrum*) and is associated with this plant; perhaps also with Pale Laurel (*Kalmia polifolia*).

Range: — In the eastern area: Manitoba eastward, including northern Minnesota to Newfoundland.

Subspecies: — *L. a. argyrognomon,* European, not in North America; *L. a. scudderi* Edwards (TL mouth of Saskatchewan River between Cedar Lake and The Pas, Manitoba); Manitoba, Minnesota (Pequot, Arrowhead Trail) e. (?) to Labrador and eastern Quebec. *L. a. empetri* T. N. Freeman (TL Prince Edward Island), also Nova Scotia and Cape Breton Island; small (0.80–0.92 in.), ground color beneath darker, dark spots beneath relatively very large and distinct, Canadian Zone; *L. a. aster* Edwards (TL Newfoundland), also Labrador and northern New Brunswick and Quebec; small, dark beneath, markings beneath small and less distinct, Hudsonian Zone.

MELISSA BLUE. *Lycæides melissa* Edwards   pp. 48, 160, 176

0.90–1.20 in. *Melissa* flies quickly, but near the ground, in open spaces, frequents flowers, and is very fond of visiting mud puddles or damp places where the butterflies may gather by the hundreds. As noted above, the northeastern population which has always passed as *scudderi* Edwards, is now known to be one of the races of *melissa*. The best-known colony is in the sandy, oak and pine region west of Albany, New York. There is some evidence that a colony once existed on Manhattan Island.

Larva: — Sparsely covered with short hairs; pea green with a darker dorsal area, a yellowish tinge on sides, substigmatal fold white or livid, very faint oblique stripes on sides; body wall very translucent. Larva seldom eats completely through a leaf, is much attended by ants, is thus best found. **Food:** — Lupin (*Lupinus perennis*), Locoweed (*Astragalus*), Alfalfa (*Medicago sativa*) and *Acmispon americanum*, perhaps also New Jersey Tea (*Ceanothus*). Two broods, adults in late May–mid June and late July (Albany).

Range: — In our area: *m. melissa* apparently strays in from west, Kansas to Manitoba, also in Minnesota *L. m. samuelis* Nabokov, Ontario, Illinois, Michigan, Ohio, New York, Pennsylvania, Massachusetts, New Hampshire and North Carolina.

Subspecies: — *m. melissa* (TL Park Co., Colorado); *m. samuelis* (TL Karner [formerly Center], New York); FW with rounder apex and more convex outer margin; ground color beneath smoother, more grayish fawn; general appearance beneath more uniform due to less contrast between ground color and light rims of the dark spots, and narrowness of the rims; upper side of ♀ with orange submarginal lunules generally restricted to HW.

Genus Plebeius *Kluk*

Two OF THE species here included, *aquilo* and *sæpiolus*, more definitely belong together than the third, *acmon*, which should probably be removed to another genus. *Acmon* is easily distinguished by the orange submarginal bands on the HW, both above and beneath, in both sexes. *Aquilo* and *sæpiolus* are both northern species, distinguished as follows:

(1) *Aquilo* — smaller; color above very gray blue, much suffused with dark scales; veins lined with dark scales; dark discal dashes on both FW and HW; outer margin of HW with a row of submarginal dark spots between veins, inside them a narrow, wavy dark line. Wings beneath with ground color brown, very much darker on HW; spots with their whitish borders much enlarged and fused together, forming white patches and incomplete transverse bands.

(2) *Sæpiolus* — larger; color above much bluer, less suffused with dark scales; outer margin of HW (♂♂) nearly or entirely lacking submarginal dots and line; wings beneath white with small dark markings, the white borders of which are inconspicuous, tending to merge with the ground color. ♀♀ blue with very wide dark borders and some orange lunules on HW, or else brown with prominent orange lunules.

ARCTIC BLUE. *Plebeius aquilo* Boisduval p. 145
0.75–1.05 in. A circumpolar Arctic species that enters the eastern area only in the far north, *aquilo* is most familiar to North American collectors from western material. Its small size, dull colors, dingy appearance and hairiness are very "Arctic" looking.
Early Stages: — Unknown. Females seen ovipositing on *Diapensia lapponica* (Baffin Island) perhaps also *Vaccinium* (T.N.F.).
Range: — Manitoba n. (west of Hudson Bay) to Ellesmere Island, e. (across Northern Hudson Bay) to Labrador.
Subspecies: — *P. a. aquilo* (TL Labrador, also Cape North and Siberia, upon the Altai) Churchill, Manitoba northward, e. to Labrador; smaller (0.75–0.90 in.), wings above lighter, with more blue; dark borders not so extensive. *P. a. lacustris* T. N. Freeman (TL Norway House, Manitoba) central Manitoba, larger (0.90–1.05 in.) dark marginal borders above very broad, sometimes entirely suffusing wing. *P. a. suttoni* Holland (TL Southampton Island, northern Hudson Bay) appears to fall within the normal range of variation of *a. aquilo.* This is a pity, for Dr. George Sutton, for whom the "race" was named, deserves more than most people to have something outstanding named for him. *P. a. megalo* McDunnough of Alberta probably does not enter the eastern area.

SÆPIOLUS BLUE. *Plebeius sæpiolus* Boisduval p. 176
0.90–1.2 in. Just when *sæpiolus* began pushing eastward through southern Canada I do not know, but it must have been quite recently. In Winn's list of the Lepidoptera of Quebec (1912) it is not mentioned. I know that we were surprised when I found it common in the Gaspé in 1929. Now it is quite common in Maine. Perhaps it will continue extending its range southward. It has a rather fast flight, occurs in open fields and along roadsides. The ♀♀ in the west are strongly dimorphic, some being all reddish brown above with strong, orange bands. **Food:** — Alsike Clover (*Trifolium hybridum*); one brood. Adults in early June. Hibernation as larva.
Range: — In the eastern area, all of southern Canada, s. into Iowa, Minnesota, Michigan, and Maine. Early June–July.

ACMON BLUE. *Plebeius acmon* Westwood
0.70–1.0 in. A widespread species of the west that enters the western edge of our area. The ♂♂ are blue above, the ♀♀ brown with slight basal tinges of blue. The orange submarginal bands on the males' upper sides make them unmistakable. ♀♀ may be distinguished from the somewhat similar *L. argyrognomon* and *melissa* by the characters cited in couplet 9 of the Key.
Larva: — Dingy yellowish, irregularly spotted with black, sparsely covered with fine, short hairs and with a narrow, green

dorsal stripe.   Food: — Milk Vetch or Locoweed (*Astragalus*),
Birds Foot Trefoil (*Lotus*), Umbrella Plant (*Eriogonum*), *Acmispon americanum, Hosackia*, etc. (Notes from California specimens).   In eastern area probably two broods.   Adults in June.
Range: — In eastern area Nebraska and (rarely) Kansas and
Minnesota.
Subspecies: — Perhaps the eastern *acmon* should be referred to
subspecies *lupini* Boisduval with broad, not clearly defined, dark
marginal border; and orange band on HW tending to be composed of separated spots.

SILVERY BLUE.   *Glaucopsyche lygdamus* Doubleday   p. 176
0.90–1.20 in.   ♂ shining, silvery blue above; ♀ similar but duller,
with wide, diffuse, fuscous margins.   The lack of markings beneath beyond the postmedian row of ocellate spots, is distinctive.
Lygdamus ranges widely in North America but in our area is essentially northern, although it extends south to Georgia.   A number
of subspecies have been described, of which some in the east are
really merely local forms.   The Silvery Blue has a rather rapid
flight, and occurs in both open woods and fields.   It visits flowers
and damp ground freely.   The larvæ are much attended by ants;
in fact, they are best found by watching for assemblies of ants
on the food plant.
Larva: — Slug-shaped, light green, flecked with white; dorsal
stripes darker green, bordered with light yellow green; head black.
Food: — Everlasting Peas (*Lathyrus ochroleucus* and *carolini-
ana*), perhaps Vetch (*Vicia cracca*).   One brood.   Adults in early
May to June.   Hibernation probably as pupa.   Short flight season.
Range: — Newfoundland and southern and central Canada, s.
into Wisconsin, Minnesota, Michigan, Ohio, New York, Pennsylvania, West Virginia, Georgia, and Alabama (?).   It is practically absent from New England and rare in upper New York
though not uncommon along the shores of the Gulf of St. Lawrence, but has been found common in Pennsylvania, West Virginia, and Virginia.
Subspecies: — *G. l. lygdamus* (TL Screven Co., Georgia);
Georgia and (?) Alabama w. to Arkansas, n. to New York; beneath brown with little gray dusting; spots beneath very large
with large black centers; second spot from costa of HW tending
to be in general line of spots; very rare in south, common locally
Virginia to Pennsylvania; *nittanyensis* F. H. Chermock (TL Bear
Meadows, vic. State College, Pennsylvania) and *boydi* A. H.
Clark (TL Ice Mountain, Hampshire Co., West Virginia) are at
best only local forms; through New York intergrades to next
subspecies.   *G. l. couperi* Grote (TL Anticosti Island); Anticosti,
New Brunswick and Quebec w. to Manitoba, including northern
Illinois, Michigan, Minnesota, and Wisconsin; spots beneath

smaller, especially those of HW; wings beneath much dusted with gray scales, usually finely and evenly; second spot from costa of HW tending to be set inward more than first and third; variable locally. *G. l. mildredæ* F. H. Chermock (TL Baddeck, Cape Breton Island) Cape Breton Island; blue above darker and brighter; spots beneath larger, their white rims broad and conspicuous; wings beneath more coarsely and sparsely gray-dusted. *G. l. oro* Scudder (TL Colorado); not in our area in typical form; wings beneath more thickly dusted with gray, the HW basally with greenish, spots larger; *G. l. afra* Edwards wings beneath gray-dusted, spots, particularly of HW very small; not in our area in typical form. *G. l. jacki* Stallings & Turner (TL Barber Co., Kansas) western Kansas and Oklahoma; blue above bright, more metallic, females with less blue, males with veins above edged distally with black, basally with white; somewhat intermediate between *l. lygdamus* and *l. oro*. Westward *l. couperi* intergrades to both *l. oro* and *l. afra*. A complex clinal species.

SPRING AZURE. *Lycænopsis argiolus* Linnæus pp. 48, 145, 176 0.80–1.25 in. The first Spring Azure of the season never fails to gladden the heart; for it is a sure sign that the long period of cold and torpor is over, and that life is again beginning to renew itself. The first of our native butterflies to emerge from the overwintering pupæ, the Spring Azure may be seen on the wing even while snow still lies on the ground, a blue mite fluttering around Dogwood buds, or seeking the first flowers. The pale, slightly violet-tinged blue of the upper side is frequently, sometimes strongly, whitish on the discs of the wings, particularly the hindwings. The underside is entirely without any orange or iridescent markings, and has a "washed-out" look even though it may be rather heavily marked with brown blotches. The wings are very thinly scaled and delicate looking.

There is great variability, both geographic and seasonal. In the far north, specimens of the single brood are small and heavily marked beneath with large, dark brown patches, constituting a valid *subspecies, lucia* Kirby. Farther south, in southern Canada and the northern and central United States, there appear in the first spring brood specimens resembling *lucia*. Mingled with these, however, are others lacking the central HW patch but possessing the wide, dark border (*marginata*), and still others with no suffusion or coalescence of the spots beneath (*violacea*) thus resembling the summer forms. Spring specimens are small and have a general, gray or brownish tone beneath. On the average the darker specimens (commoner northward) represent earlier specimens, the lighter ones, later ones. In some regions occurs a partial second brood (*neglecta-major*), large, very bright colored above, white beneath, with clear-cut markings. This is "spotty" in its occurrence, but I know some places where it occurs very constantly (e.g. Woodlands, New York, mid-May). In a short time, two to three weeks, this is followed by the full summer brood (*neglecta*- typical *pseudargiolus*) smaller than *neglecta-major* but larger than the spring forms, and the palest of all; above, especially in ♀ ♀, there may be considerable discal white areas; beneath, the wings are clear white with clear-cut, though often small, dark markings. The tendency (clinal) to show more white above as the species progresses southward is carried to its conclusion in the subspecies *gozora* of Central America, much paler and whiter than any of the United States populations. I know no better subject for some experimental work on the effects of season and temperature. The above gives only a very brief and incomplete idea of the variation to be expected.

The adults, which have a rather slow, fluttering flight, are often seen high up around the buds or foliage of trees. They occur in brushy areas, along the edges of woods and most typically in open, deciduous woods. The males visit mud puddles and damp ground, and both sexes visit flowers freely.

Larva: — Whitish, rose-tinted, with a faint, dusky dorsal stripe and very faint, oblique, greenish stripes on the sides; head dark chestnut with black edges; body with short, white hairs; much attended by ants. Eggs laid among flower buds, often tucked down out of sight, or on leaves. **Food:** — Flowering Dogwood (*Cornus florida*), probably other *Cornus*, Black Snakeroot (*Cimicifuga racemosa*), Meadowsweet (*Spiræa salicifolia*), Sumach (*Rhus* sp.), Maple Leaved Viburnum (*Viburnum acerifolia*), New Jersey Tea (*Ceanothus americana*), Blueberry (*Vaccinium corymbosum*), Crownbeard (*Verbesina helianthoides*), *Actinomeris*, etc. Larvæ have been fed on a great variety of plants ranging from Nasturtium and Clover to Willow and Milkweed. One brood in far north, two in much of the eastern area, three southward. Adults in mid-March to April, again in May and June. Hibernation as pupa.

Range: — Hudsonian Zone in Canada southward through the eastern area, absent from Florida (?).

Subspecies: — *L. a. argiolus* is Palæarctic, not in the eastern area. *L. a. lucia* Kirby (TL Cumberland House, Saskatchewan, Lat. 54° N.) and *L. a. pseudargiolus* Boisduval & Leconte (TL "United States") are characterized above in text. *L. a. argentata* Fletcher (TL Cartwright, Manitoba), in eastern area in Manitoba; very white, nearly immaculate beneath; intergrades with *pseudargiolus*.

Family *Papilionidæ:* The Swallowtails

THE SWALLOWTAILS are a large, world-wide family of medium sized to large butterflies. Many species lack the tails on the hind wings that characterize most of ours. In the tropics many are large and incredibly beautiful, such as the great Bird-Winged Butterflies (*Troides*) of the Old World. Our eastern *Papilionidæ* all have fully developed front legs with an epiphysis on the tibia; simple tarsal claws; lack paronychia on the tarsi; and have only one anal vein (2dA) in the hindwing. In the west occurs the tailless genus *Parnassius*. For an interesting popular article on the family, with many illustrations, see "The Swallowtail Butterflies" by Austin Clark in the Smithsonian Report for 1935.

Following general practice, I am including all of our species in the single genus *Papilio* — the original butterfly genus of Linnæus. As subgenera, *Papilio* is used for the "True" (*machaon* group) and "Fluted" Swallowtails; *Graphium* Scopoli for the longtailed, "Kite" Swallowtails; and *Battus* Scopoli for the "Aristolochia" Swallowtails, "protected" species that feed on *Aristolochiaceæ*, have distasteful body juices and a long sex patch along the anal margin of the hind wing of the males. Some authorities consider these to be separate genera, and even split them further.

Genus Papilio *Linnæus:* The Swallowtails

OUR SPECIES are all large, and strong fliers. Most are "tailed," but two southern species are not. They are mostly greatly addicted to visiting flowers, are thus best caught. The larvæ of all possess yellow or orange *osmateria*, scent organs which are protruded from behind the head. These give out a strong odor, probably protective. The angular, rough pupæ are fastened, usually in a vertical position, by a silk girdle as well as by the cremaster.

OLD WORLD SWALLOWTAIL. *Papilio machaon* Linnæus

p. 193

2.75–3.0 in. Band of spots pale yellow, very broad, especially on HW; tails short; outer margin of FW convex. In most of Europe and northern Asia *machaon* is common and widespread, but with us it is chiefly subarctic and western; and North American specimens are rare in collections.

Early stages: — Similar to *polyxenes* (see below); one brood; adults in early July; probably hibernates as pupa. **Food:** — (Europe) *Umbelliferæ* (Parsley, Parsnip, Carrot, Wild Carrot (*Daucus*), etc.).

Range: — Northwest shore of Lake Superior, n. to James Bay and east shore of Hudson Bay, and northwestward; Hudsonian Zone.

Subspecies: — *P. m. machaon*, Europe, not in North America; *P. m. hudsonianus* A. H. Clark (TL Eastern Manitoba) presumably represents the eastern North American populations, as figured.

SHORT TAILED SWALLOWTAIL. *Papilio brevicauda* Saunders
p. 161

2.75–3.0 in. Tails very short; band of spots narrow, yellow with considerable orange, especially in the female. Essentially a Hudsonian and upper Canadian Zone species, ecologically replacing *machaon* in the northeast. Perhaps not fully specifically distinct from *polyxenes*. The various forms around the Gulf of St. Lawrence suggest a cline. Habits as in *polyxenes*. I have seen it eagerly visiting Blueberry and Labrador Tea (*Ledum*) flowers.

Similar Species: — *P. machaon* (wider band); *polyxenes* (longer tails, less or no orange in spotband).

Early stages: — Resemble those of *polyxenes*. **Food:** — *Umbelliferæ*, i.e., Cow Parsnip (*Heracleum*), Parsley (*Petroselinum*), Angelica. One brood. Adults in mid-June–July (Gaspé). Hibernates as pupa.

Range: — Southern Labrador, Newfoundland, Anticosti Island, shores of the Gulf of St. Lawrence, Maritime Provinces.

Subspecies: — All rather poorly distinguished. *P. b. brevicauda* (TL Newfoundland) largest, spotband with most orange (less so in Anticosti); Newfoundland and Anticosti. *P. b. bretonensis* McDunnough (TL Cape Breton Island, New Brunswick) smaller, spots less orange; Maritime Provinces. *P. b. gaspeensis* McDunnough (TL Mt. Lyall, Gaspé, Quebec) still smaller, spots with little or no orange; Gaspé Peninsula, especially in mountains. The Newfoundland form is the most distinct.

BLACK (or PARSNIP) SWALLOWTAIL. *Papilio polyxenes asterius* Stoll (*ajax* Clerck)
pp. 48, 49, 193

2.75–3.5 in. The handsome Black Swallowtail, *polyxenes*, is a very widespread, common species of fields, roadsides, meadows, gardens, and of open spaces generally. Band of yellow spots narrow, the female with these narrower and with more blue in the HW. Several aberrations are known with the spotband greatly enlarged, orange, or greatly reduced. First brood specimens (cold or wet form) are smaller, with larger yellow spots than warmer or dry season forms. There has been much difference of opinion as to the proper specific name, *P. ajax* Linnæus having been used for both this and the Zebra Swallowtail; but the original description of *ajax* is ambiguous. I here use *polyxenes* which is both unambiguous and "official."

Similar Species: — *P. brevicauda* and *bairdii*.

Larva: — When young, brownish black with a white saddle, resembling a bird dropping. Older larva green, each segment crossed by a black band containing small, round yellow spots. This coloration is definitely concealing among the food plant's foliage. Two or more broods in the north, three or more southward. Adults in mid-May. Winters as pupa. **Food:** — Many species of *Umbelliferæ*, cultivated and wild: Caraway, Carrot, Parsley, Celery, Dill, Wild Carrot (*Daucus*), etc. The larvæ are occasional pests in gardens and truck farms.

Range: — North America n. to Hudsonian Zone, rare northwestward.

Subspecies: — *P. p. polyxenes* is Neotropical, not in the eastern area.

GIANT SWALLOWTAIL. *Papilio cresphontes* Cramer

pp. 48, 193

4.0–5.5 in. A common species of the south, rarer northward, extending and contracting its range sporadically. The larvæ ("Orange Dogs") are sometimes injurious to citrus trees. A very strong, high flyer, best caught at flowers. The yellow markings are much more extensive beneath than above. Differs from *thoas* genitalically and in pattern consistently only in the larger size of the large yellow spot below vein M_2 (FW), and the consequent smaller size and more outward position of the small yellow submarginal spot in same cell.

Similar Species: — See *thoas, lycophron, ornythion, aristodemus, andræmon*.

Larva: — Dark brown with creamy white markings; a stripe on prothorax and sides of meso and metathorax, a broad saddle on middle of body and a patch at end of abdomen. Osmateria (scent horns) orange, odor very strong. **Food:** — Various Citrus trees, Prickly Ash, *Zanthoxylum;* Hop Tree, *Ptelea;* Gas Plant, *Dictamnus.* Two broods northward, three in south; adults in early May.

Range: — Massachusetts, New York, Ohio, Michigan, and Minnesota, s. to Key West and Mexican border. Rare and sporadic northward.

Subspecies: — *P. c. cresphontes* Upper and Lower Austral and Tropical Zones. *P. c. pennsylvanicus* Cherm. and Cherm. (TL State College, Pennsylvania) smaller, yellow spots above more regular, those of FW beneath larger, more elongated; yellow of HW beneath more extensive; Transition Zone, and Upper Austral Zone of midwest. Not a very well marked subspecies. Probably the species forms a gradual cline.

THOAS SWALLOWTAIL. *Papilio thoas* Linnæus   p. 161
4.0–5.5 in. A common, widespread tropical species which enters our area rarely in southern Texas; a stray has been reported from Kansas. Florida records are doubtful. Distinguished from *cresphontes* by the characters cited above.
Subspecies: — *P. t. thoas* is South American. The subspecies reaching our area is *P. t. autocles* Rothschild & Jordan (TL Guerrero, Mexico). Probably *P. t. nealces* Rothschild & Jordan (cited from our area) is merely a variety of this.

SCHAUS' SWALLOWTAIL. *Papilio aristodemus ponceanus* Schaus   p. 193
3.5–4.5 in. Wings above brownish, the spot bands narrow, dull yellowish, with diffuse edges. HW beneath with chestnut brown median band inside a postmedian row of blue, lunular spots. *Ponceanus* has led a checkered career. First found in the Brickell Hammock of Miami, Florida, by Dr. Schaus (then attending Spanish War casualties) it was exterminated there by the city's growth. Rediscovered in the Florida Keys it became known as our most desirable *Papilio*, as much as $150 having been paid for a pair. When the colony on Lower Matecumbe Key was wiped out by the 1938 hurricane, *ponceanus* was believed extinct. Later, however, it was found elsewhere on the Keys; and during the early 1940's it built up slowly in numbers. Now, overcollecting by "game hog" collectors has again reduced its numbers seriously in its last stand. NONE BUT MALES SHOULD BE COLLECTED, and then, at most, only one per collector. I believe that most people have enough sportsmanship to help protect the species and to refuse to buy specimens at any price.
Larva: — Brown, with yellow and white markings. **Food:** — Torchwood (*Amyris elemifera*). One brood. Adults in May. Pupæ may overwinter two years. The excellent article "Place of Sorrow" by Florence M. Grimshawe, *Nature Magazine*, 1940, gives a good account of the butterfly and its life history.
Range: — Miami-Rockland and Florida Keys, tropical hardwood hammocks.
Subspecies: — Other subspecies are Antillean, have the yellow banding above broader, the yellow beneath more extensive.

ORNYTHION SWALLOWTAIL. *Papilio ornythion* Boisduval
3.25–4.5 in. Occurs with some frequency in southern Texas (Pharr, September–October, May). A common Mexican species, told from *cresphontes* and *thoas* by its shorter black tails; the yellowish white color of the spots above; and the row of small, submarginal spots on the FW above, which are parallel and close to the outer margin. The median spotband is not narrowed at the inner margin of the FW as in *cresphontes*, but resembles that of *thoas* in this respect.

TIGER SWALLOWTAIL. *Papilio glaucus* Linnæus   p. 161
4.0–6.5 in. The yellow and black Tiger Swallowtail is one of our
most familiar butterflies, from the far north to our southern
boundary. Its strong, sailing flight and addiction to garden
flowers bring it into even large cities, although it is most typically a butterfly of woodlands and savannahs. It well illustrates
a clinal type of distribution, ranging from small, pale yellow
forms in Canada to large, ochreous yellow ones in the deep south.
In the south as many as 50 per cent of the ♀ ♀ are dark brown in
ground color, the remainder yellow like the ♂ ♂; the brown form
is less common to nonexistent northward, and also in the extreme
south. Yellow ♀ ♀ vary considerably in extent of the black
markings and of the blue on the HW, also intergrade to the dark
phase. *Glaucus* is a regular visitor at mud puddles, manure,
and carrion, and has been recorded as attracted by tobacco
smoke. The broods show considerable variation, early spring
specimens strongly resembling the northern *canadensis*. It is
a misnomer, however, to call them *canadensis*, a name which
should be used only for specimens from the area of that subspecies.
Similar Species: — *P. rutulus* & *multicaudatus;* dark ♀ ♀ resemble *P. troilus.* In *rutulus* the submarginal yellow spots of the
FW beneath form a narrow, continuous band, and the FW is
more pointed. In *multicaudatus* the HW is three-tailed, with one
additional shorter tail at the end of Cu_1 and another, still shorter,
at the end of Cu_2. Dark *glaucus* females nearly always show
traces of the dark stripes, and lack the orange costal spot of the
HW of *troilus.*
Larva: — Smooth, green, a pair of large, orange, black-pupiled
eyespots on metathorax, behind these a transverse orange and a
black stripe. Lives in one-leaf nests made by folding the edges
of a leaf over and above it, often high in trees. Pupa rough,
brown, green mottled. **Food:** — A wide variety of trees, i.e., Wild
Cherry (*Prunus*), Tulip Tree (*Liriodendron*), Birch (*Betula*),
Poplar (*Populus*), Ash (*Fraxinus*), Basswood (*Tilia*) etc. Two
broods in north, three in south; Spring adults in early April.
Hibernates as pupa.
Range: — Hudsonian Zone in Canada s. through Florida and
Texas, scarcer at southern limits.
Subspecies: — *P. g. canadensis* Rothschild & Jordan: smaller,
light-yellow, one-brooded; Canada, Newfoundland, northern
New England (mountains); *P. g. glaucus:* larger, deeper yellow;
up to 50% of ♀ ♀ dark, two–three brooded; New England, New
York, Michigan, Wisconsin s. to Georgia, Alabama, Louisiana,
and Texas; *P. g. australis* Maynard: larger still, ochreous yellow,
dark ♀ ♀ scarcer, Georgia through Florida and Gulf States. There
is strong evidence that *P. rutulus*, commonly considered a separate species, is actually conspecific with *glaucus*, forming the western part of a widely distributed cline.

COPPERS, BLUES AND SULPHURS
Families *Lycaenidae* & *Pieridae*

All illustrations are × 1 (natural size)

1. BRONZE COPPER, *Lycæna thoë*   p. 152
   Upper & under sides, ♂ (Flushing, L.I.) Large; light ground color
   beneath; ♀ darker, Can. to N. J. & Kans.
2. AMERICAN COPPER, *Lycæna phlæas americana*   p. 151
   Upper & under sides, ♂ (McLean, N.Y.) Small; bright, metallic
   coppery FW. Arctic (race) to Ga. & Ark.
3. PURPLISH COPPER, *Lycæna helloides*   p. 153
   Upper side, ♂ (Two Harbors, Mich.) HW beneath dull; variable;
   see text. Western, e. to Ill.
4. BOG COPPER, *Lycæna epixanthe*   p. 152
   Upper & under sides, ♂ (Lakehurst, N.J.) Small; dark above; pale
   beneath. Can. to N.J. & Minn. Cranberry bogs.
5. EASTERN TAILED BLUE, *Everes comyntas*   p. 163
   Upper side, ♂ (Suffolk, Va.) Delicate tail; ♀ mostly brown above.
   Can. southward. See Pl. 19, fig. 4.
6. SPRING AZURE, *Lycænopsis argiolus pseudargiolus*   p. 169
   Upper side, ♂ (Putnam, Conn.) Delicate tints; no bright spots on
   HW beneath; Can. southward. See also Pl. 18 (♀).
7. SPRING AZURE, *Lycænopsis argiolus pseudargiolus* "f. *lucia*"   p. 169
   Under side, ♂ (Putnam, Conn. April) Dark markings on HW be-
   neath. See text.
8. SÆPIOLUS BLUE, *Plebeius sæpiolus*   p. 167
   Upper & under sides, ♂ (Baxter St. Park, Me.). Beneath dusted,
   greenish basally; tiny orange spots on HW. s. to Me., & western.
9. SILVERY BLUE, *Glaucopsyche lygdamus couperi*   p. 168
   Upper & under sides, ♂ (Minneapolis, Minn.) Clear, light blue
   above; beneath with round eyespots, no submarginal spots. Can. &
   northern States — see text. ♀ has wide dark margins.
10. KARNER BLUE, *Lycæides melissa samuelis*   p. 165
    Upper & under sides, ♂ (Karner, N.Y.) Prominent orange &
    scintillant spots of HW beneath. Northern States, very local.
11. BARRED SULPHUR, *Eurema daira*, typical winter form   p. 195
    Upper side, ♂ (Winter Park, Fla.) FW above with grey bar; HW
    with *short* dark border; Fla. to Va., w. to Tex.
12. BARRED SULPHUR, *Eurema daira*, typical winter form   p. 195
    Upper & under sides ♀ (Winter Park, Fla.) Lacks FW bar of the
    ♂; beneath, reddish brown. Cf. fig. 14–15 below.
13. DAINTY SULPHUR, *Nathalis iole*   p. 199
    Upper side, ♂ (Louisiana, Mo.) Small; dark bar *on HW;* ♂ with sex
    patch. Fla. & Tex. to Mich. & Nebr.
14. FAIRY YELLOW, *Eurema daira*, summer form *jucunda*   p. 195
    Upper side, ♂ (Winter Park, Fla.). HW with long, dark border
    above, white to pale grey ground color beneath.
15. FAIRY YELLOW, *Eurema daira*, summer form *jucunda*   p. 195
    Upper & under side, ♀ (Winter Park, Fla.). Lacks some or all of the
    dark FW bar of the ♂.
16. PALMIRA, *Eurema daira palmira*   p. 196
    Upper side, ♂ (Habana, Cuba). HW of ♂ white; ♀ has both wings
    white, lacks dark FW bar. Tropical, casual in s. Fla.

Plate 22   177

SULPHURS
Family *Pieridae*

All illustrations × 1 (natural size)

1. **LITTLE SULPHUR,** *Eurema lisa*   p. 198
   Upper side, ♂ (Coosawhatchie, S.C.). Compare with *E. neda* below.
   Wider, more irregular, dark borders; FW above with dark discocellu-
   lar mark and basal dusting; narrower FW with sharper apex. New
   England & Nebr. southward. Common.

2. **LITTLE SULPHUR,** *Eurema lisa*   p. 198
   Upper side, ♀ (Coosawhatchie, S.C.). Dark border different shape
   from male on FW, reduced on HW; paler color common, often white.

3. **NISE SULPHUR,** *Eurema nisa*   p. 198
   Upper side, ♂ (Key Largo, Fla.). Cf. with *lisa* above. Dark borders
   narrower & more even; FW above lacks dark discocellular mark and
   most or all black basal dusting; FW more rounded. S. Fla. & Tex.
   Local, woods edges & brushy areas.

4. **SLEEPY ORANGE,** *Eurema nicippe*   p. 197
   Upper side, ♂ (Pensacola, Fla.). Bright orange; wide, irregular dark
   borders; no tail on HW. N.Y. to Nebr. & southward, common in
   south.

5. **SALOME,** *Eurema salome limoneus*   p. 284
   Upper side, ♂ (Jalapa, Mex.). Short tail on HW; short, square
   "dog's head" in FW border; ♀ is paler yellow with borders much reduced. Casual northward from Mex.

6. **LYSIDE,** *Kricogonia lyside*   p. 194
   Upper side, ♂ (Rio Grande City, Tex.). Sharp apex of FW; basal
   yellow on FW; often has short, transverse, black bar on costa of HW.
   ♀ is whitish, duller. Tex. n. to Kans., also s. Fla.

7. **HECLA ORANGE,** *Colias hecla*   p. 187
   Upper & under sides, ♂ (Shannon I., Cape David Gray, N.W. Greenland, Lat. 75° N.). Orange color; wide dark borders; very heavy dark
   dusting beneath; HW beneath with diffuse, elongate, purplish-pink
   discocellular spot. Arctic & subarctic.

8. **NASTES SULPHUR,** *Colias nastes*   p. 188
   Upper side, ♂ (Gyrfalcon Is., Ungava Bay, Labr.). Greenish yellow
   color, heavily dusted; males have light spots in dark FW border.
   Arctic & subarctic.

9. **BOOTH'S SULPHUR,** *Colias boothii*   p. 187
   Upper side, ♂ (Baker Lake, N.W.T., Can.). Light orange ground
   color, often yellow distally; narrow borders, often almost entirely absent. Arctic.

10. **PELIDNE SULPHUR,** *Colias pelidne*   p. 186
    Upper & under sides, ♂ (Hopedale, Labr.). Wide dark borders;
    wings beneath with much dark dusting; HW beneath with discocellu-
    lar spot ringed with pink. Arctic & subarctic.

SPICEBUSH SWALLOWTAIL. *Papilio troilus* Linnæus

pp. 48, 80, 193

4.0–5.0 in. *Troilus* is another widespread and familiar species. It tends to occur in and near shady woods even more than *glaucus*, although frequently seen in fields and gardens visiting flowers. Its flight is nearer the ground, with less "sailing" than that of *glaucus*, but is not as quick and nervous as that of *polyxenes*. I have seen some notable gatherings at mud puddles in the south. In the ♀ the clouded greenish of the HW is largely or entirely replaced by blue.

Larva: — Like that of *glaucus*, but with another, smaller pair of eyespots behind the large ones; living in a one-leaf nest, seldom high above the ground. Pupa smoother and with more swollen wing cases than in other *Papilios*. Two broods in north, three in far south. Adults in late April–early May (Lat. 40°). Hibernation as pupa. **Food:** — Spicebush (*Benzoin*), Sassafras (*Sassafras*), Sweet Bay (*Magnolia glauca*), Prickly Ash (*Zanthoxylum*), etc.

Range: — Southern Canada, w. to Manitoba, s. through Florida and Texas; rarer w. of the Mississippi River.

Subspecies: — *P. t. troilus*, s. to Georgia. *P. t. ilioneus* Abbot & Smith (TL Georgia) Georgia, Florida, Gulf States; larger, submarginal yellow spots larger, paler; colors brighter; tails often colored. Apparently the species forms a cline.

PALAMEDES SWALLOWTAIL. *Papilio palamedes* Drury

p. 193

4.5–5.5 in. A slowly flying, easily distinguished species, common in the southeast. Occurs most typically in or at the edges of swampy woods. The adults roost high in oaks and palmettos, supposedly communally.

Larva: — "Humpbacked," pale, speckled green, buff below; a pair of eyespots on last thoracic segment, black enclosing an orange ring centered with black; *osmateria* ("scent horns") yellow-brown. Two to three broods. Hibernates as larva or pupa. **Food:** — Red Bay (*Persea*), Sweet Bay (*Magnolia glauca*), Sassafras.

Range: — Coastal Plain from New Jersey (casual) and Virginia s. through Florida and Gulf States into Mexico. In Mississippi Valley uncommon, n. to Missouri (rare).

Subspecies: — In the United States probably only *p. palamedes* occurs. *P. p. leontis* Rothschild & Jordan, with greatly reduced yellow spots above, may not occur in typical form north of Monterrey, Mexico.

IDÆUS SWALLOWTAIL. *Papilio anchisiades idæus* Fabricius

p. 161

2.75—4.0 in. Characterized by a whitish patch on the FW, a pinkish-red patch on the HW, and the absence of tails and of a sex-fold along the anal margin of the HW. Well established along the lower Rio Grande in southern Texas (Sept.–Nov., April–May). An occasional pest of citrus trees in Mexico. A stray has been taken as far north as Kansas.

ZEBRA SWALLOWTAIL. *Papilio marcellus* Cramer pp. 49, 193
3.75–4.5 in. The Zebra can be confused with no other North American species. It shows great seasonal variation. Spring specimens (*marcellus*) of early April (about Lat. 40° N) are small, with short wings, short tails, and restricted dark and extensive light markings. Later spring specimens (*telamonides*) — not a subsequent brood — are larger with longer wings, somewhat heavier dark markings, and more white on the tail-tips. The summer brood (*lecontei*) specimens, emerging in early June, are much larger, with longer wings, longer tails with much more white, heavy dark and restricted light and red markings. This form emerges more or less continually until October, the later specimens being the largest and darkest. Part of the pupæ of each brood either delay emergence until the second regular brood, or else overwinter; so that the brood relationships are complex.
Similar Species: — *Papilio celadon*, see section on Casual Species, page 283.
Larva: — Pea green with narrow, yellow and black cross bands; a wide, black band across the "humpbacked" last thoracic segment; notoriously cannibalistic. **Food:** — Papaw (*Asimina triloba*). Two to four broods, overwintering as pupa.
Range: — Southern New England (rare) w. through southern Ontario, Michigan, Minnesota and Wisconsin, s. through central Florida and Gulf States.
Subspecies: — In central Florida is the weakly distinguished *P. m. floridensis* Holland (similar to *lecontei*) with heavy, dark markings in even the early brood; the southernmost population of a cline.

PIPE VINE SWALLOWTAIL. *Papilio philenor* Linnæus
pp. 49, 193
3.0–4.5 in. Common in the south, less common northward, *philenor* has a fast, erratic flight, but is easily caught on flowers, which it visits avidly. Many specimens will be found stuck all over with the *pollenia* (pollen baskets) of orchids. Most of the HW is shimmering blue to greenish. This iridescence is much more metallic beneath. The male sex pocket of scent scales along the anal margin of the HW, characterizing the *Aristolochia* Swallowtails, is very conspicuous. In the female the submarginal, whitish spots of the FW above are larger. Early spring specimens, smaller and hairier, resemble the California subspecies *hirsuta* Skinner. Of course they should not be called by the name of a subspecies to which they do not belong.
Similar Species: — *P. troilus* has larger submarginal spots, and

orange costal and anal spots on the HW above. *P. devilliers* Godart of Cuba, recorded (probably erroneously) from Florida, resembles *philenor* above, but has larger spots on the HW; on the FW beneath it has a marginal and a submarginal row of white spots; and on the HW beneath it has a submarginal row of brown spots bordered externally with silvery white.

Larva: — Dark purplish brown, with about three paired rows of fleshy tentacles, one anterior pair very long, three posterior pairs longer than the rest. **Food:** — Wild Ginger (*Asarum*), Virginia Snakeroot, and Pipe Vine (*Aristolochia serpentaria* and *macrophylla*), other Aristolochias, Knotweed (*Polygonum*). Two broods, perhaps three in south. Adults in late April. Hibernates as pupa or adult.

Range: — Central New England (rare) w. through southern Ontario, Michigan, Wisconsin, Nebraska, s. through Florida and Texas, to Costa Rica and w. to California.

POLYDAMAS SWALLOWTAIL. *Papilio polydamas* Linnæus

p. 161

3.0–4.0 in. Easily recognizable, as our only tailless *Aristolochia* Swallowtail. Wings above black, spots pale yellow, HW with satiny, greenish iridescence. The HW beneath shows a trace of the postmedian spot row and has a row of narrow, curved, submarginal, pinkish spots. Its flight is fast and erratic, but it is easily captured at flowers. In Winter Park, Florida, I noted it particularly fond of visiting Star Jasmine (*Trachelospermum*). Almost extinct 1920–1933; now quite common.

Similar Species: — Our only other tailless Swallowtail, *P. anchisiades idæus* has a whitish patch on the FW, a pinkish one on the HW.

Larva: — Black, dark reddish purple on segmental junctures; occasional brown-yellow phases occur; two long, fleshy, basally black, red-orange tentacles on first thoracic segment, connected across back by a collar, extend laterally and forward; body with four rows of short, orange papillæ: subdorsal rows, one pair per segment; and lateral rows, black tipped, one pair each on segments 2, 3, 4, 5, 10 and 11. **Food:** — Various *Aristolochia*, both native species (Florida) i.e., *pentandra* and *macrophylla sipho* and introduced species, i.e., *grandiflora gigas* and *ringens*.

Range: — Florida, Georgia, Gulf States, southward into Mexico.

Subspecies: — Perhaps all North American specimens are *P. p. lucayus* Rothschild & Jordan (TL Bahamas), *P. p. polydamas* being Antillean (TL Cuba) and Central American. If the nymotypical subspecies enters the eastern area it does so only in southern Texas.

Family Pieridæ: The Whites and Sulphurs

THIS IS ONE of the major, world-wide families. We owe the very word "butterfly" to the yellow color of common European Sulphurs. In the past the *Pieridæ* have been grouped as a subfamily of the *Papilionidæ*. Modern knowledge shows that they are actually very distinct. Nearly all are white, yellow, or orange, with rather simple patterns. Their pigments, formed from the uric acid wastes of the body, are not found in other butterflies. The front legs show no reduction in either sex, but have no epiphysis as in the *Papilionidæ*. In this respect the *Pieridæ* are the most primitive of butterflies next to the Skippers. Vein M_1 of the FW is nearly always stalked with radial branches; and M_2 is closely associated with the radial system, rather than with the cubital system as in the *Papilionidæ*. From three to five radial branches, some always stalked, reach the margin of the FW. Vein 3d A of the FW is rudimentary; and in the HW there are always two anals.

The eggs are elongate, more or less spindle-shaped, and marked with fine ribs and lines. The larvæ are usually smooth, green, slender, and unornamented, and are not very hairy. Their prothorax is not so much more slender than the head and the mesothorax as to look like a neck, as in *Hesperiidæ*. The pupa typically has a central projection forward from the top of the head, and is suspended by both the cremaster and a girdle. Food plants are varied but favor the *Cruciferæ* (*Brassicaceæ*) (Mustard Family) and the *Leguminosæ*, i.e., the *Cassiaceæ* (Cassias), *Mimosaceae* (Mimosas and Acacias) and *Fabaceæ* (Peas, Beans, Clovers, Vetches, etc.). The larval life tends to be short, so that many species have a number of broods annually. Many species are very common or abundant. Migratory habits are marked in some.

There are three subfamilies, *Pseudopontiinæ*, *Dismorphiinæ*, and *Pierinæ*. All of our species are *Pierinæ*. The *Pierinæ* are divided into three tribes, the *Euchloini* (Orange Tips), *Coliadini* (Sulphurs), and *Pierini* (Whites), all represented in our area.

Sexual dimorphism is marked, the females consistently differing from the males in pattern. Sometimes the dimorphism is in color, too; white females occur in many yellow and some orange species, usually less common or rarer than the normal colored ones. Seasonal dimorphism is also quite pronounced.

FALCATE ORANGE TIP. *Anthocaris genutia* Fabricius

pp. 49, 208

1.30–1.50 in. The "falcate" (hooked) apex of the FW is characteristic. Color above white, the male with an orange patch on the apex of the FW, lacking in females; beneath white, the HW marbled beautifully with yellow-green. *Genutia* is widespread, but very local, found only in or around rich deciduous woodlands (perhaps in more open environments southward). The flight is low and quite erratic, but not fast. Like other woodland butterflies it often flies on cloudy days. Females rarely have some yellow in place of the orange patch of the males.

Larva: — Dull green; finely striped with orange, bluish green, dark blue, white, olive and pale yellow, the orange stripe dorsal, the white ones lateral and widest; head pale, with greenish, inky blotches and black and pale papillæ. **Food:** — *Cruciferæ*, i.e., Rock Cress (*Arabis perfoliatum*), Bitter Cress (*Cardamine*), Winter Cress (*Barbarea vulgaris*), Mouse Ear Cress (*Sisymbrium thaliana*), Shepherd's Purse (*Capsella Bursapastoris*); larva eats flowers, buds and seed pods. One brood in north, two in south. Adults in late March. Hibernation as pupa.

Range: — Massachusetts and Connecticut, s. to Georgia, w. to Illinois and Texas (Dallas).

Subspecies: — *A. g. genutia* Fabricius (TL "Indiis") is the northern race. *A. g. midea* Huebner (TL Georgia) is the southern; larger, with a more extensive orange patch in the male, sometimes extending well basad of the end of the cell. The species forms an evenly graded cline; and data are lacking on any "borderline zone" between the northern and southern populations.

OLYMPIA. *Euchloë olympia* Edwards   p. 208

1.5–1.7 in. *Olympia* is our sole representative of the genus *Euchloë*, a group of the "Orange Tips" that are not "orange tipped." There are others in the west. It is essentially a native of the Middle West, flying in early spring in open woodlands and nearby meadows. The green marbling of the under side of the HW, which "shows through" the upper side, is distinctive.

Larva: — Light green, striped lengthwise with pale slate and bright yellow. **Food:** — Rock Cress (*Arabis lyrata*), Hedge Mustard (*Sisymbrium officinale*), doubtless other *Cruciferæ*. One brood. Adults in April. Hibernation as pupa.

Range: — Pennsylvania, West Virginia, Indiana, Illinois, Michigan and Minnesota s. to Texas; also northwestward.

Subspecies: — *E. o. olympia* (TL Coalburgh, West Virginia) Pennsylvania, West Virginia, Indiana, and Illinois; as figured; subapical black band entire; *E. o. rosa* Edwards (TL western Texas) Texas to Minnesota and westward; black markings less extensive, subapical black band broken at middle; underside of HW with stronger pink flush; not a very valid subspecies, especially in our area.

Genus Colias *Fabricius:* The Sulphurs

AN ESSENTIALLY Holarctic genus containing many northern species in both Old and New Worlds, *Colias* has penetrated a few species into South America, Africa and India. The differences between some of the species are very slight and difficult to characterize. Some appear to be in a very fluid evolutionary state, not having established definite identities or constant differences from others. Of those in our area, *eurytheme* and *philodice* present the greatest problem of this sort. In the west many specimens cannot be named with any assurance. I know no other genus of butterflies that presents so many baffling, and stimulating, problems. Far, far more field, life-history, and breeding work are needed.

There is pronounced *sexual dimorphism*. Males usually have the black borders solid; but females have a row of light spots in the borders (see *eurytheme, philodice*). In some species these light spots enlarge so as to obliterate the whole inner part of the border (see *interior*), sometimes the outer part, too. In only one of our species (*nastes*) do these spots regularly occur in the male as well as in the female. In some species white females occur regularly, in others uncommonly, in others very rarely. White males are exceedingly rare. Genetical research has shown the white "character" to be Mendelian.

Food plants of one group of species are all *Fabaceæ* (Clovers, Vetches, etc.), of another group Arctic and subarctic plants as Willows, Poplars, and Heaths (*Ericaceæ*) such as Blueberry, etc.

The majority of the species belong to the typical subgenus *Colias;* two in North America form the distinct subgenus *Zerene*.

ALFALFA BUTTERFLY or ORANGE SULPHUR. *Colias eurytheme* Boisduval   pp. 49, 192

1.6—2.4 in. Although it varies greatly, the Alfalfa Butterfly in our eastern area is always recognizable by the presence of orange above, which differentiates it from its close relative, *philodice*, the Common Sulphur. Beneath, it resembles *philodice* in having at least some traces of submarginal dark spots on both wings, a postmedian costal spot on the HW, and a pearly or silvery centered, round (usually double), pink or red bordered discocellular spot on the HW. *Eurytheme* females are usually orange above; but a white form is not uncommon that cannot always be told from white *philodice* females. White males are excessively rare.

There is reason for belief that what have formerly been considered "cold weather forms" of early spring and (less consistently) late autumn, with the ground color largely yellow and the orange reduced to discal patches (*ariadne*) are really largely hybrids between *eurytheme* and *philodice*. Still other so-called hybrids are pale orange, ochreous yellow, orange yellow, etc. Until this problem is settled by genetic research we had better assign all clear yellow specimens to *philodice* and all truly orange ones to *eurytheme*, and regard as hybrids all intermediates. The *eurytheme* female which we illustrate is pale enough to warrant suspicion of hybridism in its ancestry. Most white females can be identified by the wider black borders of *eurytheme*.

The *eurytheme* — *philodice* relationship cannot be expressed by our rigid system of nomenclature. They are neither obviously separate species, nor subspecies of the same species, but something more fluid and in between these states. The work of Gerould (i.e., Annals Ent. Society of America, September 1946, 39:383–396 and earlier papers) and of Hovanitz show this condition. They hybridize, but with lowered fertility and survival values. In general, *eurytheme* grows and survives better on Alfalfa, *philodice* on White Clover. In some districts hybrids form as much as ten per cent of the population; in others, less than one per cent. And all over western North America occurs a complex assembly of yellow forms (*eriphyle*, *kootenai*, etc.) that may be regional expressions of the essentially eastern *philodice* or may be yellow forms of *eurytheme*. For the present I can see nothing for us to do but call the two forms "separate species" after qualifying our position with some such explanation as above.

Within the last thirty years *eurytheme* has greatly extended its range northeastward, doubtless hybridizing and competing with *philodice*, and handicapping it in so doing. An *eurytheme* which I caught in New York in 1918 was considered a rare prize. Now *eurytheme* has extended into Quebec, Maine, and the Maritime Provinces; and in New York it is so abundant that we hardly notice it!

One more complication enters the picture. *Eurytheme* and *philodice* are closely related to the Palæarctic *Colias chrysotheme* Esper. Some workers have placed them as merely different subspecies under this name. I approve the attempt to thus point out the relationship. But I think that, in view of the greatly overlapping ranges and the ecological and genetic differentiation of the two forms, we come closer to the facts by keeping them separate from *chrysotheme*.

Larva: — Grass green, an indistinct stripe down the back, a white stripe, edged below with black, along each side. **Food:** — Chiefly Alfalfa (*Medicago*), also White Clover (*Trifolium repens*), other Clovers, Locoweed, or Milk Vetch (*Astragalus*), Lupins (*Lupinus*), etc. Three to four or more broods. Adults in April. Hibernation as pupa, perhaps also as adult. Larva sometimes a pest on alfalfa.

Range: — Maritime Provinces w. to Pacific, s. to Florida and Mexico. Very rare in Florida, uncommon to rare in Canadian Zone northward.

COMMON or CLOUDED SULPHUR. *Colias philodice* Latreille
pp. 48, 192
1.3–1.9 in. This is the common yellow Mud Puddle Butterfly, familiar nearly the whole continent over, rising in swarms from muddy roads, or dancing by hundreds over clover fields. From other yellow *Colias* it is told by the sharply defined discocellular spot (red ring and silvery center) on the HW beneath, the presence of at least some black, submarginal spots on the wings beneath, and the wide, black borders of the females, not narrowed by enlargement of the contained yellow spots. Its relationship with *eurytheme*, with which it is much confused, is discussed under that species. Spring (*anthyale*) and late fall specimens are smaller, with narrower black borders above, and considerable fuscous or greenish dusting on the HW beneath. Several so-called "subspecies" occur in the west, but in our area all are *p. philodice*.

Philodice is preeminently a lover of open fields, meadows and roadsides. Young males gather in great swarms at mud puddles. Later in life they concentrate on flower visiting and reproduction.
Larva: — Grass green, with short hairs; a faint, darker stripe down the back and a whitish stripe along each side. **Food:** — White Clover (*Trifolium repens*) and other Clovers, Vetch (*Vicia*), Lupin (*Lupinus*), Alfalfa (*Medicago*), other *Leguminosæ*. Three broods. Adults in April. Hibernation as pupa, perhaps sometimes as adult or larva.
Range: — Newfoundland (rare), Maritime Provinces westward, s. to Florida and Texas, uncommon to rare southward. (TL Virginia.)

PINK EDGED SULPHUR. *Colias interior* Scudder p. 192
1.3–1.75 in. *Interior*, a northern species characteristic of the Canadian Zone, ranges southward well into the northernmost states. Like other *Colias* it favors open spaces, but prefers bushy or scrubby areas, especially those burned over a few years previously. Brower reports the adults in Maine to be especially fond of visiting flowers of Bristly Sarsaparilla (*Aralia hispida*). Its flight is a little slower than that of *philodice*. White females are frequent, but less common than yellow ones.
Similar Species: — *C. philodice*. The greatly reduced black borders of *interior* females are characteristic. Beneath, *interior* lacks submarginal dark spots and (usually) a dark spot on the costa of the HW; the discocellular-spot of the HW is round, single, and less sharply defined than in *philodice;* there is little or none of the dark dusting of *philodice*, the HW being a more clear, golden yellow; the fringes are more widely pink.
Larva: — Rich, dark, yellowish green; a narrow, darker dorsal stripe, bluish green along its sides; innumerable small papillæ, bearing short, dark hairs which become white down on sides; spiracular fold (along sides) white, including a bright crimson line.

Food: — Sour-top or Velvet Leaf Blueberry (*Vaccinium canadense*) is preferred; other Blueberries (*V. vacillans* and *corymbosum*) may be eaten. One brood, but a long flight season. Adults from early June through August. Hibernation as first stage larva.

Range: — Canadian Life Zone, Newfoundland westward; northern New England and New York (Adirondacks) s. in mountains to Virginia, Michigan, and Minnesota.

Subspecies: — Eastern specimens (*laurentina* Scudder, TL Cape Breton Island) are doubtfully distinct from western (*interior*, TL north shore Lake Superior, mouth of Saskatchewan River) on the basis of slightly smaller size, perhaps greater predominance of yellow females. Not a very marked subspecific difference.

PELIDNE SULPHUR. *Colias pelidne* Boisduval & Leconte p. 177
1.25–1.5 in. *Pelidne* is an Arctic species, ranging westward and northward from Labrador. Specimens from the western Arctic are curiously lacking; but a subspecies, *skinneri* Barnes, occurs southward in the Rocky Mountains into Wyoming. The male borders are wide, those of the females more reduced. Females are divided between yellow and white, about 25% yellow, 75% white. Beneath, the wings are heavily clouded and dusted with fuscous and greenish; the HW discocellular spot is small but heavily ringed with pink or red; the FW show a characteristic tendency to a discal fuscous dusting.

Range: — Labrador, Baffin Island, eastern coast Hudson Bay, James Bay.

Subspecies: — Type locality of *pelidne* ("Arctic Regions") almost certainly is Labrador. In this case all our northern population is *p. pelidne*, and *labradorensis* Scudder is a synonym.

PALÆNO SULPHUR. *Colias palæno* Linnæus   p. 192
1.4–1.75 in. A widely distributed species ranging around the Arctic and subarctic of Europe, Asia, and North America. The black borders average wide, especially in females. The HW beneath are heavily clouded with greenish-gray and, most distinctive, have no dark or red ring around the discocellular spot, which is merely a light spot. The black discocellular spot of the FW above is nearly always absent in the males. The color above averages a paler yellow in males than in other species. Females run about 50–50 white and yellow.

Range: — Arctic and subarctic, Labrador westward. Common at Churchill, Manitoba.

Subspecies: — *C. p. palæno* is European. All North American specimens are *C. p. chippewa* Kirby (TL Mackenzie River at Great Slave Lake), smaller, darker.

GIANT SULPHUR. *Colias gigantea* Strecker
1.5–1.9 in. *Gigantea* is an Arctic and subarctic species of the

northwest, which enters the eastern area only in Manitoba, although it has one southern subspecies (*harroweri* Klots) in the Rocky Mountains of Wyoming, another (*scudderi* Reakirt) in Colorado and another (*ruckesi* Klots) in New Mexico. In Manitoba it is quite large, has narrow black borders; the HW beneath are yellow, not heavily dusted with fuscous, have the discocellular spot pearly, with a usually more or less "smeared" red or pink border. Females tend to lose most or all of the dark borders above, losing the outer part of the FW border while the inner edge remains as a faint submarginal line. Northern specimens from Churchill, Manitoba (TL) average more white females than yellow ones; more southern ones (Riding Mountains, Manitoba) average more yellow than white ones.

Food: — Willow (*Salix*).

HECLA ORANGE. *Colias hecla* Lefebre   p. 177
1.4–1.8 in. A widespread species of the Old and New World Arctic, *hecla* is distinguished by its almost solid orange color above, fairly wide black borders, orange discocellular spot on HW above, heavy fuscous and greenish dusting both above and beneath, and heavily pink or red discocellular spot, elongate and pointed outwardly, on the HW beneath. In females the light spots in the dark borders are prominent and yellow tinted. Males lack the sex patch on the HW above (near base of costa) which is present in the similarly orange *C. meadi* and *elis* of the Rocky Mountains. The flight is fast and strong.

Larva: — Green, with light lateral stripes, covered with many tiny, hair-bearing, black tubercles (Lapland records). **Food:** — *Astragalus alpinus*. Hibernates as larva, possibly also as pupa; may have a two-season larval life.

Range: — Arctic of Europe, Asia, and North America, s. in the eastern area to Baffin Island and Churchill, Manitoba.

Subspecies: — *C. h. hecla* (TL Greenland) Arctic Zone in the eastern area, s. to Southampton Island and Baffin Island; color above dull orange, sometimes deep, sometimes paler; fuscous and greenish scaling heavy. *C. h. hela* Strecker (TL Churchill, Manitoba) dark borders above wider; color above bright orange; less fuscous and greenish dusting above; colors brighter and more intense.

BOOTH'S SULPHUR. *Colias boothii* Curtis   p. 177
1.3–1.7 in. *Boothii* is another species of the extreme Arctic, very rare in collections, although it may be found common when one reaches its territory. It is extremely variable, males ranging from specimens with a fairly wide, solid border to ones with practically no border. The amount of orange above is also very variable. Females are more constant, with wider borders (containing large spots) and heavier, dark dusting. *Boothii* is considered by some workers to be a hybrid between *hecla* and *nastes;*

one strong reason is its variability, which intergrades to forms of
nastes that have some orange on the FW above. Other workers
consider it a distinct and separate species, though perhaps originally a hybrid between now extinct species, and cite important
habitat and behavior differences between *nastes* and *boothii*. Or
perhaps *boothii* is a form of *hecla*. The question must be left
open. *Boothii* has a rapid flight, hugs the ground, visits flowers
avidly. Each individual tends to stay in a limited area. It
occurs mostly along the sheltered sides of ridges and hills in the
tundra.

Range: — Baffin Island w. to Bernard Harbor (Lat. 69° N,
Long. 115° W) s. to Southampton Island and Baker Lake (Lat.
64° N, Long. 97° W). (TL Boothia Peninsula.)

Subspecies: — None. *Chione* Curtis is a variety, nearly unmarked above.

NASTES SULPHUR. *Colias nastes* Boisduval   p. 177
1.1–1.6 in. Like *hecla* and *boothii*, *nastes* is a species of the far
Arctic. It is characterized by the consistent occurrence of light
spots in the borders of both sexes, and by its small size. Its color
ranges from a dirty whitish to a suffused greenish yellow; but it
is never clear, bright yellow or orange. It tends to have a large,
strongly pointed discocellular spot on the HW beneath, and a
row of submarginal black spots on both FW and HW beneath.
As may be gathered from this, it is extremely variable; but its
characters add up to a "look" that is usually unmistakable. It
shows much geographic, as well as individual, variation. It is a
strong, hard flier, not easy to capture, yet appears to be somewhat sedentary and local.

Larva: — Dark moss green, the head lighter; a pair of yellow subdorsal, and white spiracular stripes; the subdorsal stripes red
along their upper edges; the spiracular stripes light crimson along
their lower edges; body with many tubercles, bearing short, black
spines (Lapland records). **Food:** — *Astragalus alpinus*. Hibernates as full-grown larva.

Range: — Labrador northward and westward.

Subspecies: — *C. n. nastes* (TL Labrador) Labrador, Baffin
Island, w. to Hudson Bay; color above dull; with considerable
fuscous suffusion; beneath, the dark, submarginal spots are much
reduced and the basal two thirds or three quarters of the HW are
not heavily dark-dusted in strong contrast to the outer portion.
C. n. rossii Curtis (TL Boothia Peninsula) n. Hudson Bay and
northward; less suffused above, colors brighter, sometimes with
orange flush on FW; dark, submarginal spots of FW and HW
beneath, and discocellular spot of HW beneath more prominent;
basal two thirds of HW beneath contrastingly darker. *C. n.
gueneei* Avinoff (TL Southampton Island) is hardly justified as a
separate name since the orange tint of *rossii* is within the normal
variation. *C. n. moina* Strecker (TL Churchill, Manitoba) is ap-

parently quite limited to the region near Churchill; colors above and beneath much brighter; submarginal spots beneath prominent and clear-cut. *C. n. subarctica* McDunnough (TL Bernard Harbour) Baker Lake northward and westward; males especially with FW above heavily suffused with fuscous, females less so; HW beneath very heavily dark suffused for basal two thirds; submarginal spots beneath not prominent. *Nastes* shows quite a clinal gradation, both east-west and north-south. The difficulty of separating the above so-called "subspecies" arises in part from this, in part from their considerable variability, and in part from lack of material from intermediate localities.

DOG FACE. *Colias (Zerene) cesonia* Stoll   p. 192
1.8–2.4 in. The Dog Face is easily recognized by the sharp, pointed apex of the FW, and the "dog's head" in the FW border. The male has a conspicuous sex patch near the base of the costa of the HW, a structure present in some species of *C. (Colias)*. The flight is swift, so that the butterfly is not easily caught except when visiting flowers. The female has the black markings more diffuse, the border of the HW more reduced. The winter form (*rosa*) shows considerable pink on the HW beneath, lacking in the typical summer form. Common except in north.
Larva: — Green, thickly covered with small, black, hair-bearing tubercles; markings very variable; some are unmarked; others cross-banded with yellow to orange, and black; others striped lengthwise with yellow and black. **Food:** — False Indigo or Lead Plant (*Amorpha fruticosa*), Clover (*Trifolium*). Three broods in north, probably more in south. Adults in early spring. Hibernation as pupa.
Range: — New York, southern Ontario, Minnesota, Nebraska, s. to South America. Uncommon to rare northward. (TL Georgia)

Genus Anteos *Huebner:* The Angled Sulphurs

Two VERY large species of this genus occur in our area. The size and the sharply angled wings distinguish them from other New World Pierids. *Anteos* has been confused with the superficially similar Old World genus *Gonepteryx*, to which it is not even closely related. The subgenus *Anteos* consists of *clorinde* and *mærula;* the subgenus *Rhodocera* of the tropical *menippe* Huebner.

MÆRULA. *Anteos mærula* Fabricius   p. 161
2.75–3.50 in. The subspecies *lacordairei* Boisduval (TL Mexico) occurs as a breeding resident in southern Texas (H.A.F.)

north to Dallas (September–November), has strayed n. to
Omaha, Nebraska. There are also a few authentic southern
Florida records. The wings above are clear yellow. (TL
of *maerula* probably Jamaica)

CLORINDE. *Anteos clorinde* Godart

2.75–3.50 in. The so-called subspecies *nivifera* Fruhstorfer (TL
Mexico) occurs as a breeding resident in southern Texas (H.A.F.)
north to Dallas (Sept.–Nov.). The wings are white above, with a
black discocellular spot, narrowly orange ringed, on each wing;
on the FW a large, rectangular orange-yellow patch extends
from the costa across to below the cell, just basad of the end of
the cell. This patch is less marked or absent in females. (TL of
clorinde — Brazil)

Genus Phœbis *Huebner:* The Tropical Sulphurs

THE SPECIES OF *Phœbis* are medium sized to large Sulphurs, limited to the New World. They are not even closely related to the
Old World genus *Catopsilia* which some of them resemble. A few
species enter the eastern area; one, strongly migratory, ranges well
northward. All have fast, strong flights but can be caught quite
easily at flowers.

The species show a high development of various sexual characters. The genitalia offer excellent identification characters.
Male sex patches and hair pencils are highly developed on the
wings, on the FW beneath near the inner margin and on the HW
above near the costa. The *mealy border* is an area, sometimes wide,
sometimes narrow, along the outer margins, in which the scales
are fluffed up on end.

One species, *statira* belongs in the subgenus (or separate genus)
Aphrissa; the others in the typical subgenus *Phœbis*.

CLOUDLESS SULPHUR. *Phœbis sennæ* Linnæus

pp. 48, 49, 161

2.2–2.75 in. Males are clear, unmarked yellow above. Females
are deeper, more orange yellow, sometimes with much orange;
or may be pale and whitish. They have a large, dark discocellular spot on the FW above, and a more or less broken, dark brown,
marginal border. There appears to be a considerable northward
migration in the autumn. In the tropics *sennæ* is famed for its
migratory habits.

Larva: — Pale, yellowish green; a yellowish stripe along each
side; segments black dotted in crosswise rows. **Food:** — Sennas

(*Cassia*, several species), Clover, doubtless other *Fabaceæ*. Two broods, probably more southward.

Range: — nearly entire eastern area, n. to Canada. Rare northward, there chiefly in autumn migrations.

Subspecies: — *P. s. sennæ* (TL Jamaica) occurs in our area, if at all, only as a spasmodic immigrant. However, in southern Florida and Louisiana many very *sennæ*-like specimens occur. It is a warmer yellow than *eubule*, with the brownish scrawls beneath more prominent, and the dark marginal markings of the females tending to greater development. *P. s. eubule* Linnæus (TL Carolina) is the form of most of our area, most typical from the Carolina piedmont northward. *P. s. marcellina* Cramer (TL Surinam) the mainland tropical subspecies (of dubious worth) probably enters the Rio Grande valley of southern Texas; females more deeply colored, the HW often almost orange; more heavily marked beneath. The subspecific classification is extremely complex and largely statistical.

ORANGE BARRED SULPHUR. *Phœbis philea* Linnæus p. 193
2.75–3.25 in. The ♂ is illustrated. The ♀ has both a postmedian and a submarginal row of dark brown spots on the FW above, and a marginal row on both wings. In recent years *philea* has become at times common in Florida (n. to Orange Co.) where it apparently did not exist before the 1920's. Very possibly this results from an introduction. Florida is the richer for a very beautiful butterfly. The flight is swift, but the butterflies are easily caught at flowers.

Larva: — Yellowish green, darker dorsally, transversely wrinkled and tapering strongly at each end; with many fine, black granulations, these bearing small, shiny black spines; sides with a blackish or reddish black, and a more ventral, wider, yellow band containing reddish black spots ringed with whitish. **Food:** — *Cassia*, and probably other *Cassiaceæ* (notes from Brazil). At least two broods.

Range: — Georgia, Florida, Gulf Strip, southern Texas, strays n. to New York (Ithaca), Indiana, Kansas, and Nebraska.

LARGE ORANGE SULPHUR. *Phœbis agarithe* Boisduval p. 193
2.25–2.50 in. The clear, unmarked orange of the males above is distinctive. Females range from as orange above as the males to white with delicate salmon-pink clouding. The markings beneath are stronger in the winter brood. Males have a "hair pencil" near the base of the FW above. All our United States populations are *P. agarithe maxima* Neumœgen (TL Florida).

Similar Species: — *P. argante* Fabricius (may not occur in United States); see section on Casual Species, page 283.

Range: — Florida (common), Gulf Coast, Texas (common), s. into Mexico, strays n. to Illinois, Arkansas, and Kansas. (TL Mexico)

SULPHURS
Family *Pieridae*

All illustrations × 1 (natural size)

1. ALFALFA BUTTERFLY, *Colias eurytheme*, summer form *amphidusa* p. 183
    Upper side, ♂ (Ithaca, N.Y.). Large size; deep, full orange color;
    beneath much like *philodice* (see below). S. Can s. to Fla. & Tex.
    Often abundant.

2. ALFALFA BUTTERFLY, *Colias eurytheme*, summer form *amphidusa* p. 183
    Upper side, ♀ (Chicago, Ill.).

3. ALFALFA BUTTERFLY, *Colias eurytheme*, "cold weather form"
    ariadne   p. 183
    Upper side, ♂ (Coosawhatchie, S.C.). Smaller size, orange concen-
    trated in discal areas.

4. COMMON SULPHUR, *Colias philodice*   p. 185
    Upper & under sides, ♂ (Toronto, Ont.). Yellow color; wings be-
    neath with at least some dark, submarginal spots; HW beneath with
    strong, dark costal spot, and discocellular spot silvery, sharply pink-
    rimmed, usually double. Centr. Can. s. to Fla. & Tex., common to
    abundant. Open fields, mud puddles.

5. COMMON SULPHUR, *Colias philodice*   p. 185
    Upper side, ♀ (Putnam, Conn.). Wide dark borders containing
    yellow spots; otherwise with characters of male.

6. PINK EDGED SULPHUR, *Colias interior*   p. 185
    Upper & under sides, ♂ (Charlton, Ont.). Submarginal dark spots
    on wings beneath almost always missing, as is costal dark spot of HW
    beneath; HW discocellular spot less silvery, single, more diffusely
    pink-rimmed; fringes wide and pink. Can. & northern states,
    Canadian Life Zone.

7. PINK EDGED SULPHUR, *Colias interior*   p. 185
    Upper side, ♀ (Passadumkeag, Me.). Dark borders of wings greatly
    reduced (cf. *philodice* ♀ , No. 5 above); otherwise with characters of
    the ♂.

8. PALÆNO SULPHUR, *Colias palæno chippewa*   p. 186
    Upper & under sides, ♂ (Labrador). Pale yellow above; HW beneath
    with no colored rim around discocellular spot. Arctic & subarctic.

9. DOG FACE, *Colias (Zerene) cesonia*   p. 189
    Upper side, ♂ (Lake Placid, Fla.). Sharp apex of FW; "dog's head"
    outline in FW border; ♂ with sex patch on HW below costa, near
    base. N.Y. w. to Nebr., southward. Common in south.

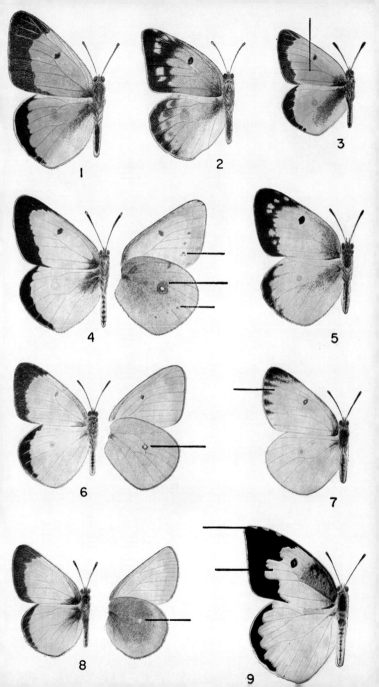

Plate 24   193

SWALLOWTAILS AND SULPHURS
Families *Papilionidae* and *Pieridae*

All are reduced to ⅜ natural size

1. PIPE VINE SWALLOWTAIL, *Papilio philenor*   p. 179
   Upper side, ♂. No median spots; submarginal spots small; HW *above*
   with no orange spots; brilliant metallic blue on HW beneath. N. Engl.
   & Nebr. southward.
2. BLACK SWALLOWTAIL, *Papilio polyxenes asterius*   p. 172
   Upper side, ♂ (Paterson, N.J.) Two rows of yellow spots; HW with
   submarginal blue band. Centr. Can. southward.
3. GIANT SWALLOWTAIL, *Papilio cresphontes*   p. 173
   Upper side, ♂ (Port Sewall, Fla.) Large; broad, yellow spot band.
   Mass. w. to Minn. & southward.
4. SPICEBUSH SWALLOWTAIL, *Papilio troilus*   p. 178
   Upper side, ♂ (Mashipicong, N.J.) No median spot band; HW
   above with a costal and an anal orange spot; in ♀ blue partly or
   wholly replaces green on HW above. S. Can. southward.
5. PALAMEDES SWALLOWTAIL, *Papilio palamedes*   p. 178
   Upper side, ♂ (Port Sewall, Fla.) Large; yellow, median spot band
   running to anal angle of HW; greenish yellow clouding. N.J. through
   Fla. & Gulf States.
6. SCHAUS' SWALLOWTAIL, *Papilio aristodemus ponceanus*   p. 174
   Under side, ♂ (Lower Matecumbe Key, Fla.) Wide, orange brown
   band followed by blue lunules. Above resembles *cresphontes*, but
   duller and browner, spots narrower. S. Fla. Nearly extinct.
7. ZEBRA SWALLOWTAIL, *Papilio marcellus*, early season form   p. 179
   Upper side, ♂ (Blair, Pa.) Greenish white; red spot at anal angle of
   HW; long tails. Mass. to Wis. & southward.
8. ZEBRA SWALLOWTAIL, *Papilio marcellus*, summer form *lecontei* p. 179
   Upper side, ♂ (Pickett Springs, Ala.) Larger, darker, longer tails.
   See text.
9. OLD WORLD SWALLOWTAIL, *Papilio machaon hudsonianus*   p. 171
   Upper side, ♂ (Riding Mts., Man.) Very wide median yellow spot
   band; short tails. Can., Hudsonian Zone, Ont. westward.
10. ORANGE BARRED SULPHUR, *Phœbis philea*   p. 191
    Upper side, ♂ (Florida City, Fla.) Large; orange bar on FW & HW.
    Fla. to Tex., strays northward.
11. STATIRA, *Phœbis statira*   p. 194
    Upper side, ♂ (Port Sewall, Fla.) Yellow, with outer "mealy
    border" paler to whitish. S. Fla. & Tex.
12. LARGE ORANGE SULPHUR, *Phœbis agarithe maxima*   p. 191
    Upper side, ♂ (Port Sewall, Fla.) Large; orange; "mealy borders"
    slightly lighter. Fla. to Tex.

STATIRA. *Phœbis statira* Cramer   p. 193
2.2–2.4 in. Widespread in the tropics, *statira* enters our area in
both southern Florida and southern Texas. Males have a very
wide, satiny "mealy border," lighter than the yellow of the
wings, and have a sex patch on the upper side of the HW near
the costa and another on the underside of the FW near the inner
margin.
Range: — Tropical America, n. into southern Florida (*floridensis*) and southern Texas (*jada* — very rare).
Subspecies: — *P. s. floridensis* Neumœgen (TL Upper Indian
River, Florida) southern Florida; outer third of wings of males
above yellow, not greatly contrasting with basal two thirds; very
little if any black edging on costa and outer margin of FW.
P. s. jada Butler (TL Guatemala) strays into Texas; basal two
thirds of wings above orange, not yellow; perhaps merely a form
of *s. statira* (TL "Coast of Coromandel and Tranquebar").

LYSIDE. *Kricogonia lyside* Latreille   p. 177
CASTALIA. *Kricogonia castalia* Fabricius
1.5–2.0 in. *Kricogonia* is a small, neotropical genus of which
two species occur in our area. These are very similar, so that
there has been much confusion. I am here following W. P.
Comstock (*Butterflies of Porto Rico*, New York Academy of
Sciences, 1944) in his analysis largely from Hispaniola material.
    (1) *lyside* — larger, average FW length, ♂, 27 mm.; ♀, 27.3
mm.; black costal bar of ♂ above narrower, tending to disappear; ♀ ♀ dimorphic, nearly half tending to be plain yellow
above, the others creamy or yellowish white with base of FW
orange yellow; this basal patch more pronounced than in white
castalia ♀ ♀ ; FW beneath basally yellow, discally creamy white,
apically slightly greenish white with definite sheen; HW beneath
slightly greenish white with definite sheen; a line of raised scales
from base of HW beneath running out through middle of cell
toward outer margin.
    (2) *castalia* — smaller, average FW length, ♂, 24 mm., ♀ 23.3
mm.; black costal bar of ♂ above broader; ♀ ♀ dimorphic, but
fewer specimens yellow; white forms with basal FW patch less
pronounced than in *lyside;* FW beneath white with yellow at
base and apex; HW beneath dull ochre, with slight, if any, sheen,
sometimes with faint, brown mark ngs.
    All Florida and most Texas *Kricogonia* appear to be *lyside;* in
southern Texas, however, a form of *castalia* occurs rarely, as
recorded by Comstock; but until a thorough study has been
made little more than the above can be said. There is much individual variation. We can trust hardly any published records.
Food: — "*castalia*" is recorded in Puerto Rico as feeding on
Lignum Vitæ (*Guaiacum officinale*).
Range: — *lyside:* southern Florida (rare) Key Largo, July,
(H. L. King); Lower Matecumbe Key, Ft. Lauderdale, July–
August 1935 (F. M. Grimshawe); Texas (abundant) straying n.

to Illinois and Nebraska. *castalia:* "several specimens from Brownsville, Tex., June 10, 1940, and elsewhere in Texas" (W.P.C.).

Genus Eurema *Huebner:* The Little Sulphurs

A LARGE, world-wide, essentially tropical genus of small Pierids. A number of species, three of which extend well to the northward, occur in our area. The species differ widely in pattern and wing shape. Seasonal dimorphism is strong, some seasonal forms having been long considered separate species; sexual dimorphism is also great.

BARRED SULPHUR. *Eurema d. daira* Latreille   p. 176
FAIRY YELLOW. *E. d. daira* summer form *jucunda* Boisduval & Leconte   p. 176
1.0–1.3 in. There is little doubt that *jucunda* is the summer form and *daira* the winter one of a single species. Absolute proof of this will only be obtained by rearing a brood of one from two known parents of the other. It is also strongly probable that a number of tropical forms, differing in having the HW white above, are all also members of the one species. These include *palmira* and *ebriola* of the Antilles and *lydia* and *eugenia* of Central America. In each case the first-named, light colored like *jucunda*, represents a summer form; and the latter-named, dark like *daira*, represents the winter form. One of the tropical forms (*palmira*) occurs in southern Florida, probably as a recent importation (see below).

In Winter Park, Florida, I found *jucunda* regularly throughout the summer, mostly in dry, open waste places. Then in September it became very scarce, and in October *daira* appeared and flew nearly throughout the winter. *Daira* seemed to keep more to the bushy areas at the edges of the same open places. Occasional intermediate forms occur, mostly in fall and spring broods (*delioides*).
Similar Species: — *Nathalis iole* is much smaller, has a dark, basal bar along costal margin of HW above, more pattern on HW beneath.
Larva: — (*daira*) Dull, light green above, beneath waxy, semi-transparent green; cross-corrugated, dotted with tiny, white spots, sparsely haired; an indistinct, darker, mid-dorsal line; a pale stripe along sides, separating the two green shades; head light green with fine hairs. **Food:** — Joint Vetch (*Æschymomene viscidula*), Pencil Flower (*Stylosanthes biflora*), probably other related *Fabaceæ*.

Range: — Florida (uncommon in southern part) n. to North Carolina (straying to Virginia) w. to Mississippi, Arkansas, Louisiana, and Texas. There seems to be a gap in Texas; records from there (Pharr, October, rare, *daira* only) may be strays of the Mexican population.

PALMIRA. *Eurema daira palmira* Poey   p. 176
0.9–1.3 in. Essentially Antillean and Central American, *palmira* is probably conspecific with *daira*. Its hind wings, white above, characterize it. ♀ ♀ have the FW above white, too. As in *jucunda*, the HW of *palmira* f. *palmira* are white beneath. In the other seasonal form, *ebriola* Poey, the border of the HW above is limited to an apical patch, and the HW and apex of the FW beneath are brown. Holland (Butterfly Book, Rev. Ed., Pl. XXXVII, fig. 12) figured a specimen of *ebriola*, calling it "*elathea* Cramer." I have seen few authentic *ebriola* from the United States. The true *E. elathea* (see section on Casual Species, page 284) does not occur in the United States. **Food:** — In Cuba, Tick Trefoil or Beggar Ticks (*Meibomia*).
Range: — Rare and spasmodic in southern Florida (Miami area and Keys, July) where it was first found by Mrs. Marguerite Forsyth in 1933. From the few specimens I cannot say whether this is the Antillean *palmira* or the Central American *lydia* Felder, or both. I have seen one possibly authentic specimen that looks like *lydia*, labeled "Brownsville, Texas, VIII–15–'34." It is quite reasonable for *lydia* to stray northward from Mexico. The Florida occurrence, which looks like a comparatively recent introduction, may die out.

BOISDUVAL'S SULPHUR. *Eurema boisduvaliana* Felder
                                                          p. 160
1.1–1.6 in. Boisduval's Sulphur is yellow above, with wide, black borders and orange along the costa of the HW in the ♂; the ♀ has a triangular, black apical border on the FW and a small apical patch on the HW. Beneath, yellow with more (winter) or less (summer) red markings. The ♂ might be confused with the rare yellow form of *E. nicippe*, but has the HW more angulate, and the black border of the FW deeply and squarely notched.
Range: — Common in Mexico; some dubious records from southern Texas, but very likely occurs there; I have seen absolutely authentic specimens (Otto Buchholz) from Royal Palm Park, Florida (May, June).

MEXICAN SULPHUR. *Eurema mexicana* Boisduval   p 160
1.3–1.8 in. Although essentially Central American, *mexicana* ranges far northward in the Mississippi Valley. The ♂ has the FW white, the HW yellowish with an orange shade along costa. The ♀ is similar, but the border of the HW consists of an apical patch and a series of black marks at the ends of the veins; and the costal orange is absent. The white "dog's head" profile in the

FW border is usually hooked downward at its tip, but sometimes is broad and square ended. Summer specimens have much reddish on the HW and the apex of the FW beneath.
Early Stages: — Not known in detail. **Food:** — Senna (*Cassia*).
Range: — Central America n., common to Oklahoma; uncommon to rare to Ontario, Michigan, Minnesota, Wisconsin, Nebraska and westward.

SLEEPY ORANGE. *Eurema nicippe* Cramer   pp. 49, 177
1.4–1.8 in. "Sleepy" may be the time-honored name for *nicippe*, but it is not very appropriate; although not a very fast flyer, *nicippe* can travel along at a good speed with a rather erratic flight, especially when frightened. It is common and widespread over most of our area south of latitude 40°. At times in the south it swarms over open meadows; and the males congregate on damp roads and around puddles. The dark borders of the ♀ are wider apically, but abruptly narrowed below veins Cu_2 of the FW and M_3 of the HW. Beneath, the apex of the FW and the whole HW are normally yellow; but a form exists in which these are deep red-brown; and intermediates are not uncommon. A yellow variety (*flava*) is known.
Larva: — Green, slender, downy; along each side a white stripe marked with yellow and bordered below with blackish. **Food:** — Senna (*Cassia* spp.), Clover, other *Fabaceæ*. At least three broods, with considerable overlapping.
Range: — Eastern area n. to New York, Ontario, Wisconsin, and Nebraska (rare northward).

PROTERPIA ORANGE. *Eurema proterpia* Fabricius   p. 160
1.3–1.7 in. Color above deep orange, the borders, vein tips and basal parts of main veins of HW black. Female duller orange, borders wider and more diffuse, considerable fuscous clouding. It presents no identification problem; but its relationship with *gundlachia* (see below) needs clarification. It is very possible that, as pointed out by Whittaker and Stallings, *proterpia* is the summer form and *gundlachia* the winter form of a single species, *proterpia*. This can be demonstrated beyond doubt by rearing a brood of one from a pair of known parents of the other.
Range: — South America n. into southern Texas and westward; well established around Pharr and Brownsville.

GUNDLACH'S ORANGE. *Eurema gundlachia* Poey   p. 160
1.3–1.7 in. As noted above, *gundlachia* is very likely the winter form of *proterpia*, having more reduced black markings above in the ♂ and a reddish-brown ground color beneath, instead of the yellow to orange of *proterpia*. The ♀ has no border on the HW and that of the FW is a triangular patch across the apex, extending down to Cu_2. There is a pronounced tail on the HW where *proterpia* has a short tail or merely an angle. The female of *gundlachia* was named *longicauda* Bates and under this name

erroneously considered a separate species (Holland, Butterfly Book, Rev. Ed., Pl. XXXVII, fig. 1).

LITTLE SULPHUR. *Eurema lisa* Boisduval & Leconte

pp. 48, 177

1.1–1.5 in. Common and widespread over most of the eastern United States. It occurs chiefly in open fields, along roadsides, and in sandy waste places; its flight is vigorous but not fast. It has been noted as flying in the windiest and most cloudy weather. Swarms occur at mud puddles. It is noted for its migratory habits; enormous flocks have been noted far out in the Atlantic and observed landing on Bermuda, some six hundred miles from the mainland.

Similar Species: — *E. nisa*, Florida and Mexican border region only, has narrower black borders, more rounded FW, no dark discocellular mark on the FW above, is more unmarked beneath, and has a clearer ground color.

Larva: — Grass green, downy, with one or two white lines along each side. **Food:** — Senna and Partridge Pea (*Cassia*), Clovers (*Trifolium*), Hog Peanut (*Amphicarpa*), probably other related *Fabaceæ*. Two broods in north, three or more in south. Adults in mid-May. Hibernation stage uncertain, perhaps both pupa and adult.

Range: — Tropical America, n. to Maine and New Hampshire (rare), New York, Ontario and Nebraska.

Subspecies: — All in the eastern area are *E. l. lisa* (TL "United States"). The Antillean subspecies *E. l. euterpe* Ménétriés has much narrower black borders above, especially in males. In Florida the population shows a tendency to resemble *euterpe.*

NISA SULPHUR. *Eurema nisa* Latreille

p. 177

1.0–1.2 in. *Nisa*, a widespread tropical species, occurs in our area only along the Mexican border and in southern Florida, in both places, apparently, as the same (nymotypical) subspecies. First found in Florida by Mrs. Marguerite Forsyth in 1933, *nisa* was common both in Royal Palm Park and on Key Largo in 1947, absent in 1948. In southern Texas it is common. Possibly the Florida population results from a recent introduction. In Florida it flies in the bushy and scrubby margins of woods, flees into the scrub when alarmed; it definitely does not fly out in the open as does the similar *lisa*.

Similar Species: — *E. lisa*, see under that species, above.

Larva: — (Brazil) Green with short, whitish down; faint, darker dorsal stripes; a whitish lateral line; head transversely wrinkled and narrowed posteriorly, with short, whitish hairs. **Food:** — Sensitive Plant (*Mimosa pudica*). At least three broods.

Range: — Southern Florida and southern Texas nearly throughout the year. Southward through Brazil.

DAINTY SULPHUR. *Nathalis iole* Boisduval p. 176

0.75–1.1 in. The tiny but fast-flying *iole* abounds in the south except east of the Appalachians, where, curiously, it is absent. Why it has not spread northward in the coastal plain is something of a mystery. In the Mississippi Valley it ranges northward in abundance to Minnesota and Nebraska. It visits flowers eagerly. Superficially it is not unlike *Eurema daira*, from which it cannot be told on the wing with certainty. ♀ ♀ have much more extensive black borders and markings, frequently have orange hindwings. I have seen (very rare) all-orange and all-white ♀ ♀. The ♂ has a distinct sex patch on the HW above near the base of costa.

Similar Species: — *Eurema daira* is larger, lacks the dark, basal bar along costal margin of the HW above.

Larva: — Variable; covered with stiff hairs; dark green, a broad purple dorsal stripe, a double, yellow and black stripe along each side; on the prothorax a pair of conical, bristly tubercles reddish and projecting forward. Pupa lacking frontal projection. **Food:** — Fetid Marigold (*Dyssodia*), Garden Marigold (*Tagetes*), Common Chickweed (*Stellaria media*), Sneezeweed (*Helenium*), Bur Marigold (*Bidens pilosa*).

Range: — Florida, Georgia and Tennessee, Texas n. to Indiana, Illinois, Michigan, Minnesota, and Nebraska, w. to Pacific (TL Mexico).

FLORIDA WHITE. *Appias drusilla* Cramer p. 161

1.60–2.3 in. Both sexes have a distinctive silky sheen on the wings above, basally. The apex of the FW is slender, the outer margin slightly concave. The ♀ ♀ are very variable; some are unmarked, creamy white; others have wide, dark borders, and the HW ochreous orange; the FW beneath is orange basally. The Florida White is common in southern Florida, where it is very distinctively an inhabitant of the shaded interiors of hardwood hammocks. The butterflies alight on the upper surfaces of large leaves with the wings folded above the back, the FW pulled down inside the HW. At times they may be migratory.

Similar Species: — See *Ascia monuste*, p. 202.

Larva: — (Brazil) Dark green, light grayish green laterally, a narrow lateral white line; dorsally many small granulations, bearing short hairs, most of these yellow, some longer and black; head yellowish green. **Food:** — Caper (*Capparis* species). At least two broods.

Range: — Widely distributed in tropics; in our area, southern Florida (strays n. to New York) and southern Texas (strays n. to Nebraska).

Subspecies: — Certainly the Florida population, probably also that of Mexico and southern Texas are *neumœgenii* (TL Florida) rather than *d. drusilla* (TL Surinam).

EUROPEAN CABBAGE BUTTERFLY. *Pieris rapæ* Linnæus
pp. 48, 208
1.3–1.8 in. Introduced into North America about 1860 in Quebec, *rapæ* has since spread over most of the continent. It is a very destructive agricultural pest on all cultivated *Cruciferæ*, even Water Cress, and Nasturtium. It is most common in cultivated areas and is strongly a denizen of open spaces; but in recent years it seems to be pushing even into small forest clearings. Specimens of the early Spring brood have the dark markings somewhat reduced, sometimes entirely absent. A rare, yellow aberration is known. The ♀ has the dark markings larger, and has another black spot on the FW.

Larva: — Green, with a mid-dorsal line and a pair of lateral lines yellow; covered with tiny, hair-bearing wartlets. **Food:** — Nearly all *Cruciferæ* (Cabbage & Mustard family), also Mignonette (*Reseda*) and, in England, Willow (*Salix*). Three brooded in north, probably more southward. Adults in late March. Hibernation as pupa.

Range: — Nearly all of North America n. to Hudsonian Zone, less common northward in Canada, s. into Mexico.

CHECKERED WHITE. *Pieris protodice* Boisduval & Leconte
pp. 49, 208
1.3–1.6 in. The "checkered" pattern is heavier in the ♀ than in the ♂. Beneath, the pattern of the upper side is repeated, with added dark scaling along the veins of the HW. In the summer form there is little of this, (or none, ♂♂); but in the smaller form emerging in Spring (*vernalis*), the brown or greenish brown scaling may be very heavy. *Protodice* is common and widely distributed in dry fields, roadsides, and waste places. Its flight is fast and erratic. When frightened it keeps to the open, never flies to woods. For former abundance, see under *Pieris napi*, below.

Larva: — Downy, striped alternately with yellow and purplish green. **Food:** — Cabbage and related plants such as Turnip, Mustard, etc. (*Brassica*), Wild Peppergrass (*Lepidium virginicum*), Shepherd's Purse (*Capsella Bursa-pastoris*), Penny Cress (*Thlaspi*), Sweet Alyssum (*Lobularia*), Fleabane (*Erigeron*), probably nearly any of the *Cruciferæ*. Three broods in north. Adults in late March. Hibernation as pupa.

Range: — Massachusetts and Rhode Island s. to Florida (rare), w. to Pacific. Less common in eastern coastal plain and piedmont than in Mississippi Valley. Less common than formerly.

Subspecies: — The entire population of our area is *P. p. protodice* (TL New York) except for possible strays of the western subspecies, *occidentalis* Reakirt (TL Colorado) along the eastern Great Plains. *Occidentalis* averages larger, more heavily marked beneath, the spring specimens with very green scaling along veins of the HW beneath.

MUSTARD WHITE. *Pieris napi* Linnæus p. 208

1.3–1.6 in. *Napi* characteristically lacks markings above except for blackish basal dustings and traces of a blackish, apical border; rarely there may be a faint dark spot in cell M_3 of the FW. Beneath, the HW and apex of the FW are yellowish white; the veins more or less (spring form) lined with gray-brown to brownish green; or (summer form) unmarked. Formerly, *napi* and *protodice* were far more abundant and occupied much greater ranges, at least east of the Appalachians. Scudder records *napi* swarming in the college yard in Cambridge, Massachusetts, about 1857. One would now have to go at least as far as the Berkshires to find it. This change certainly has coincided with the spread of *Pieris rapæ*, the introduced European Cabbage Butterfly, and is probably largely due to the failure of the native species to meet the competition of the immigrant. *Napi* has also suffered a great restriction in habitat, and probably in habits, for it is now almost entirely limited to shaded, Canadian Zone forest, and is quite shy. It seems to me that even within the last generation I have noted a tendency for *rapæ* to more and more invade even the small clearings in the forest, doubtless pushing *napi* farther toward what may some day be its "last stand." The eastern *napi* are all of the subspecies *oleracea* Harris.

Similar Species: — *P. virginiensis* lacks yellowish beneath on the HW and apex of the FW, and has the scaling along the veins of the HW and costa and apex of FW beneath much more diffuse and powdery looking. A rare spring form of *P. rapæ* lacks dark spots above, but never has the dark-lined veins of *napi*, and has heavier scaled, less fragile looking wings.

Larva: — Velvety green with a mid-dorsal stripe, and a pair of lateral stripes, greenish yellow. **Food:** — Formerly, at least, nearly any cultivated or wild *Cruciferæ;* now probably chiefly limited to native, woodland species such as Toothworts (*Dentaria*), Rock Cresses (*Arabis*), Winter and Water Cresses (*Barbarea*), etc. Three broods. Adults in late April (Massachusetts). Hibernation as pupa.

Range: — Canadian Zone of northern United States and Canada, w. to Pacific. Old records are unreliable because of both the change of range and the confusion, until very recently, with *P. virginiensis*. Not recorded s. of the Catskill Mountains in New York.

WEST VIRGINIA WHITE. *Pieris virginiensis* Edwards

p. 208

1.4–1.6 in. Until very recently, *virginiensis* has been confused with *napi*, but it is now known to be a distinct species of more southern (Transition Zone) distribution. Its dark markings are a more smoky, diffuse brown, and it lacks the yellowish tint beneath, on the HW and apex of the FW, which *napi* usually has. It is single brooded. More, even, than *napi*, it is limited to woods and very local. Of possibly a hundred specimens in the field I have never seen one elsewhere than in rich, Transition Zone deciduous woods where the food plant, Toothwort, grows. Old records are unreliable, since Scudder, Edwards, etc., confused this species with *napi*; but it is very likely that this has always been the habitat of *virginiensis* and that it has not suffered, as *napi* probably has, from the competition of the introduced *rapæ*. Perhaps it has been reduced in numbers by man's destruction of the woodlands. Perhaps, also, it suffers from the parasitic wasps that breed in great numbers in *rapæ*.

Larva: — Dark yellowish green; a narrow dorsal stripe and a pair of lateral stripes, yellowish green. Pupa slender, with frontal prominence longer than in other species of *Pieris*. **Food:** — Toothwort (*Dentaria diphylla*), probably other *Dentaria*. One brood. Adults in early May (central New York). Hibernation as pupa (pupation in mid-June).

Range: — Transition Zone, Ontario, central New England and New York, s. to Virginia (TL Kanawha, West Virginia).

GREAT SOUTHERN WHITE. *Ascia monuste* Linnæus p. 208
1.75–2.25 in. Common, at times abundant, in the far south. In Florida great migrating swarms sometimes line the coasts. The ♀ ♀ are dimorphic; one form is white, like the ♂ ♂, but with slightly wider, more diffuse dark margins; the other has a brownish gray ground color, sometimes very dark. Recent research by Dr. Erik T. Nielsen has shown that the dark form (*phileta*) marks a migratory phase. The migratory habit is not present in all populations, but instead appears only at intervals in certain breeding colonies. The forces such as overcrowding, "population pressure," attacks of parasites, etc., that may cause a colony to develop the migratory characteristics are still imperfectly known. Migrating Whites may be recognized by the way they fly steadily, almost "purposefully" in a constant direction, not stopping to visit flowers or chase each other.

Similar Species: — The Giant White, *A. josephina*, is larger, has a dark discocellular spot on the FW above, and lacks dark borders. The Florida White, *A. drusilla*, has the ♂♂ plain, unmarked white above; its ♀ ♀ vary greatly in color and dark markings but, like the ♂ ♂, always have a touch of orange at the base of the FW beneath.

Larva: — Lemon yellow with purplish green to almost blackish stripes. **Food:** — Cultivated *Cruciferæ*, Pepper Grass (*Lepidium virginicum*), Beach Cabbage (*Cakile*), Spider Flower (*Cleome spinosa*), Clammy Weed (*Polanisia*), Nasturtium, Saltwort (*Batis*), probably other wild *Cruciferæ* and *Capparidaceæ*. The use of Saltwort, a most peculiar food for a White, is connected with the migratory phase. At least three broods.

Range: — Florida, Gulf Coast and Texas straying n. in coastal plain to Virginia, in Mississippi Valley to Kansas.

Subspecies: — *A. m. monuste* (TL. Surinam) South America n. through Central America into Texas (common, Rio Grande Valley, June–Dec.); large; ♂♂ with wide borders and well marked veins on the HW beneath; ♀♀ more dusky but not largely or preponderantly so. *A. m. phileta* Fabricius (TL "America") peninsular Florida, w. along Gulf Coast, n. along coastal plain; ♂♂ with narrower borders above, less marked beneath; ♀♀ more preponderantly dusky. *A. m. cleomes* Boisduval and Leconte (TL probably Georgia) resembled *m. monuste* rather than *phileta;* possibly a now extinct or diluted subspecies of the coastal plain from Georgia northward. The variability and migratory habits make definite subspecific divisions very difficult. In the above I have largely followed W. P. Comstock (American Museum Novitates, No. 1229, May 5, 1943) adding unpublished data with Dr. Nielsen's very kind permission.

GIANT WHITE. *Ascia josephina* Latreille   p. 208
2.5–2.8 in. *A. josephina josepha* Godman & Salvin, a common Central American species, occurs in the Rio Grande Valley of Texas as a breeding resident. The principal veins of the FW and to some extent of the HW are overlaid with prominent, chalk-white scales. This and the lack of dark markings other than the black discocellular spot, characterize the species. I have been unable to find any authentic Florida records.

Superfamily Hesperioidea: The Skippers

THE SKIPPERS are a very large, world-wide group, characterized as follows: head, thorax and abdomen stout and massive, wings proportionately small. Antennæ arising far apart on top of the head. Club of the antenna often followed by a slender, tapering part, the *apiculus,* and often bent backward forming a hook. All veins of the FW arising from the discal cell, simple and unbranched. The flight is swift and darting, hence the name "skipper." The larvæ tend to be bodily plain, dull colored, and unornamented, with few hairs, but often with distinctive head patterns. The prothorax is so much more slender than either the head or the rest of the thorax that it looks like a neck. There is often a dark dorsal prothoracic shield. The pupa is typically suspended by a silk girdle, inside a loosely woven silk cocoon.

There are two families in North America, the "true" Skippers (*Hesperiidæ*) and the Giant Skippers (*Megathymidæ*). The latter are a small group limited to the New World. The families may be separated as follows:

Hesperiidæ: Head nearly as wide as, or wider than, the thorax. Hind tibia usually with two pairs of spurs. Palpi not noticeably small. Size medium to small, body not noticeably robust. Larvæ external feeders on the leaves of plants, most of them living in a rolled up or folded leaf or a nest of a number of leaves.

Megathymidæ: Head narrower than thorax. Hind tibia with only one pair of spurs. Palpi noticeably small. Size very large, body very robust. Larvæ boring in the stems of plants.

Classification and Identification of Skippers. There is a no more difficult group. In some genera the species are so extremely close, with very slight or variable color and pattern differences that they can be identified safely only by one very familiar with them. In most species, the male genitalia offer good characters. The present basis for study in the eastern area is *The Hesperioidea of North America* by A. W. Lindsey, E. L. Bell, and R. C. Williams, Jr., Denison University Bulletin (Granville, Ohio), Journal of the Scientific Laboratories, Vol. XXVI, April, 1931. No serious student can be without this work, in which are illustrated the technical characters, including the male genitalia. I have largely followed it here, with modifications suggested by Messrs. Lindsey, Bell, and H. A. Freeman. In this *Field Guide* it has not been possible, nor is it desirable, to go into technical details more than absolutely necessary. It *must* be kept in mind that in some groups positive identification of every specimen is a practical impossibility. In such cases the average collector should seek expert advice, rather than hazard a guess. Nobody thinks the worse of anyone for saying "I don't know" when it comes to some of the Skippers!

The *Hesperiidæ* of the eastern area are divided into two subfamilies, the *Pyrginæ* and *Hesperiinæ*. A third, the *Pyrrhopyginæ*, occurs in the west. In the *Pyrginæ*, vein M_2 of the FW is not markedly curved at its base, and arises from the cell about midway between veins M_1 and M_3; and the tibiæ of the middle pair of legs bear no spines. In the *Hesperiinæ*, vein M_2 is curved basally and arises closer to M_3, or the mid tibiæ are spined. In the *Pyrginæ* the chief male secondary sexual character, when present, is a long, costal fold on the FW. In the *Hesperiinæ* the males of many groups have an elongate, dark *stigma* or *brand* of sex scales on the disc of the FW. Our *Pyrginæ* average large, and run to dark browns; *Hesperiinæ* average smaller, and run more to fulvous (tawny yellow). *Hesperiinæ* are quite consistent grass feeders; *Pyrginæ* are more varied, but favor Legumes.

Much confusion is caused by the fact that the name *Hesperiinæ* has been used in the past for what we now call the *Pyrginæ*, while what we now call the *Hesperiinæ* was known as the *Pamphilinæ*.

Subfamily Pyrginæ

THE *Pyrginæ* have been characterized above in comparison with the *Hesperiinæ*. The majority of our forms are more easily identified by color and pattern and general appearance than by technical characters. I have therefore omitted a key to the genera. One that is adequate for all those of our area except a few tropical species will be found in *The Hesperioidea of North America*, mentioned above.

MANGROVE SKIPPER. *Phocides batabano* Lucas   p. 209
1.6–2.0 in. Wings above brownish black with an iridescent, blue overcast; HW with a variable, irregular, submarginal line of spots, and a streak parallel to inner margin, brighter blue. Palpi white. Not uncommon in southern Florida especially near the food plant, Red Mangrove. The adults show partiality to the Mangrove blossoms. The flight is very fast and powerful. It flies, perhaps, every month of the year.
Larva: — Head pale brown, granulated, a large, round, orange spot before eyes; body tapering to ends, bright, frosted white, thickly covered with tiny, circular pits, each bearing a minute, frosted hair. **Food:** — Red Mangrove (*Rhizophora mangle*). At least two broods.

HAMMOCK SKIPPER. *Polygonus lividus savigny* Latreille
pp. 209, 272
1.6–1.8 in. Wings above blackish brown, lighter basally; FW with a blue sheen, especially basally, and hyaline-white spots; HW with indistinct submedian and postmedian light bands. Wings beneath much lighter, with a violet-blue overcast; apex of FW and costa of HW noticeably lighter, violet-gray; markings distinct; usually a prominent, subcostal, postbasal, black spot on HW. In southern Florida I have found it consistently along shaded trails in tropical hardwood hammocks. It has a constant habit of pitching up onto the under surface of a leaf and resting there with the wings half spread out at the sides. The recent recognition of a second *Polygonus* (*manueli*, see below) occurring from Florida to Brazil on the mainland, will require re-evaluation of mainland records of *lividus*. Most previous records of *lividus* have been under the name *amyntas* Fabricius.
Similar Species: — *P. manueli*. Above, *manueli* has less blue sheen on the FW and a more distinct, pale submarginal brown band on the HW. Beneath, *manueli* has a much paler ground color, less blue sheen, and the subcostal, postbasal dark spot is very small or absent. There are distinctive genitalic differences.
Larva: — Translucent, yellow-green, a yellow, subdorsal line on segments 3–12; dense, fine, yellow, longitudinal strigulations confluent in little blotches; an ill-defined line along lower sides; body with very short, fine, white pile; head greenish white, heart-shaped, shagreened, with occiput behind, a line from over the eye upward, and a spot on front of each lobe near top, black.
Food: — Jamaica Dogwood (*Ichthyomenthia piscipula*). At least two broods.
Range: — Southern Florida, mainland and Keys, common; also Antilles.

Subspecies: — *P. l. lividus* (TL Hispaniola) not in our area.
P. l. savigny Latreille (TL Cuba) is the Florida subspecies.

MANUEL'S SKIPPER. *Polygonus manueli* Bell & Comstock

p. 209

1.6–1.8 in. The differences between *manueli* and the well-known
lividus have been noted above. Recently described (American
Museum Novitates No. 1379, June 28, 1948) *manueli* is known
to range from South America through Central America to Florida
(Royal Palm Hammock, 25 February 1925). It may occur in
southern Texas.

ZESTOS SKIPPER. *Epargyreus zestos* Geyer   p. 209
1.75–2.0 in. A widespread Antillean species that is not uncommon in southern Florida; I have seen records from January to
August.
Similar Species: — *E. clarus* (see below); *zestos* lacks the large,
white patch on the HW beneath that characterizes *clarus*.
Range: — Southern Florida, north to Sanford; Antilles.

SILVER SPOTTED SKIPPER. *Epargyreus clarus* Cramer

pp. 48, 49, 80, 209, 272

1.75–2.0 in. The brilliantly white patch on the HW beneath is
a very distinctive field mark, even in flight. Its flight is swift and
powerful. It visits flowers of many species, and is a familiar
sight on them in gardens and along roadsides. It is decidedly
pugnacious. Formerly widely known as *tityrus* Fabricius, it is
common throughout nearly all of our area.
Similar Species: — *E. zestos*, see above.
Larva: — Yellow; head brownish-red, with two eyelike orange-
red spots. Lives in a nest of leaves or leaflets of the food plant.
Pupates in a cocoon among fallen leaves and trash on the ground.
Food: — Locust (*Robinia*), *Wistaria*, Honey Locust (*Gleditsia*)
and many more *Leguminosæ* such as *Acacia*, *Amorpha*, *Lespedeza*, *Apios*, *Desmodium*, etc. One brood in north, two or three
in south. Hibernation as pupa. Adults in May (Lat. 40°).
Range: — Southern Canada s. to South America; uncommon,
rare or absent in southern Florida and Texas.

Genera Urbanus *Huebner* and
Chioides *Lindsey:* The Long-
Tailed Skippers

IN BOTH of these genera the anal angle of the HW is prolongd into
a long tail. In *Urbanus* the antennal club has a distinct, slender,
reflexed apiculus. In *Chioides* the club is relatively smaller, thicker

and more broadly curved, with a less distinct apiculus; and the apex of the FW is somewhat truncate and the outer margin concave below this. The generic names *Eudamus* and *Goniurus* have been widely used for *Urbanus*. The following key includes all our species of both genera.

1. Tails of HW white; see section on "Casual Species" page 285
.... *U. doryssus*
1. Tails of HW not white............................... **2**
2. Discal light markings of FW a transverse band, relatively unbroken, straight or gently curved, and regular.......... **3**
2. Discal markings of FW composed of well-separated spots, forming at most a broken, irregular and offset row........ **4**
3. Light band across FW wider; HW beneath very coarsely dusted and irrorated, with limbal area lighter, yellowish brown, sometimes a smeared, whitish patch; see section on Casual Species, page 285........................*U. undulatus*
3. Light band across FW much narrower; ground color of HW beneath even brown, not noticeably lighter limbally; ♂ without costal fold................................*U. eurycles*
3. Light band across FW greatly reduced and inconspicuous, or absent; ground color of HW beneath even brown; ♂ with costal fold................................*U. simplicius*
4. HW beneath with distinct white markings (*Chioides*)...... **5**
4. HW beneath sometimes with light areas, but no white lines or patches... **6**
5. HW beneath with transverse white band nearly crossing wing from about mid-costa to near anal angle.....*C. albofasciatus*
5. HW beneath with a discal white patch toward anal region, but no distinct white band............................*C. zilpa*
6. Light spots of FW large, with rounded outlines, reduced in number to one large spot at end of cell, a larger one below that, and a smaller one just outside and between these; body with green iridescence; fringes not checkered; see section on Casual Species, page 285.............*U. auginulus*
6. Light spots of FW with sharp, jagged outlines, four or five in number; fringes checkered......................... **7**
7. Body, base of FW and nearly all of HW with green, iridescent hairs...*U. proteus*
7. Without iridescent green hairs.....................*U. dorantes*

LONG TAILED SKIPPER. *Urbanus proteus* Linnæus
pp. 209, 272
1.6–2.0 in. In the far south, *proteus* is at times abundant, and may then be a bad pest on cultivated beans, the larva being called the "Bean Leaf Roller" or "Roller Worm." The flight is fast and erratic. The adults visit flowers avidly.
Similar Species: — *U. dorantes*, see below.
Larva: — Green, with a thin, dark mid-dorsal line, on either side of that a yellow lateral line, below these a pair of pale green lines. Spaces between lines gray-green, dotted with black and yellowish. Posterior segments often reddish-tinged. Head brown with two yellow spots. **Food:** — Cultivated Beans (*Phaseolus*), *Wistaria*, and various other *Fabaceæ* such as *Desmodium viridi-*

WHITES AND ORANGE TIPS
Family *Pieridae*

Note that the reductions of the illustrations vary

1. GIANT WHITE, *Ascia josephina josepha*   p. 203
   Upper side, ♂ (S.W. Arizona). × ⅔. White; large size; black discocellular spot of FW; mealy white scaling along veins. S. Tex.
2. GREAT SOUTHERN WHITE, *Ascia monuste*   p. 202
   Upper side, ♂ (Jupiter, Fla.). × ⅔. Creamy white with broken
   (and variable) dark border. Apex of FW and whole HW beneath
   yellowish, sometimes with darker streaks along veins. Fla. to Tex.,
   straying northward. Migratory.
3. GREAT SOUTHERN WHITE, *Ascia monuste*   p. 202
   Upper side, ♀ (Key Largo, Fla.). × ⅔. Much suffused with brownish
   gray; this is the migratory ♀, *phileta*. Other ♀♀ are white, like ♂♂
   but with heavier pattern.
4. MUSTARD WHITE, *Pieris napi oleracea*   p. 201
   Upper & under sides, ♂ (Magog, Que.). × 1. Veins beneath sharply
   lined with dark (spring form as illustrated) to unmarked (many
   summer specimens). Canadian Zone woodlands, Can. & Northern
   states.
5. WEST VIRGINIA WHITE, *Pieris virginiensis*   p. 201
   Under side, ♂ (McLean, N.Y.). × 1. Dirtier white than *napi*; veins
   of HW broadly but diffusely streaked with brownish. Transition
   Zone woodlands, centr. New England s. to W.Va. One-brooded.
6. OLYMPIA, *Euchloë olympia*   p. 182
   Upper & under sides, ♂ (N.E. Lake Co., Ill.). × 1. Above white,
   markings light to dark gray; HW beneath with yellow & green net-
   like marks, sometimes with rosy flush. Pa. to Minn. & westward, s.
   to Tex.
7. FALCATE ORANGE TIP, *Anthocaris genutia*   p. 181
   Upper side, ♂ (Ramapo Mts., N.Y.) × 1. Hooked apex of FW;
   apex of FW orange (white in ♀); HW beneath finely mottled with
   green & yellow. Mass. to Ga., w. to Ill. & Tex. Quite local.
8. CHECKERED WHITE, *Pieris protodice*   p. 200
   Upper side, ♂ (Birmingham, Ala.). × 1. White; brownish-black
   spots. Northward to Mass. & Nebr., very common in south.
9. CHECKERED WHITE, *Pieris protodice*   p. 200
   Upper side, ♀ (Jamesburg, N.J.). × 1. Heavier pattern than ♂.
10. EUROPEAN CABBAGE BUTTERFLY, *Pieris rapæ*   p. 200
    Upper side, ♂ (Somers, N.Y.) × 1. Creamy white; marks dark
    gray; HW beneath yellowish, with no streaks along veins. Centr.
    Can. southward throughout eastern area. Imported; injurious.

Plate 20   209

SKIPPERS
Subfamily *Pyrginae*

All illustrations are × 1 (natural size)

florum and *canescens*, *Clitoria mariana*, etc. At least three broods.
Range: —South America n. to Connecticut (casual) and Texas; northern distribution in Mississippi Valley uncertain.

DORANTES SKIPPER. *Urbanus dorantes* Stoll

1.6–1.9 in. Differs from *proteus* chiefly in lacking iridescent green above. Common in southern Texas.
Larva: — Yellowish green, with many paler spots scattered all over the body; many short, scattered hairs arise from these; head black, roughly shagreened, quite rough dorsally. **Food:** — Many *Fabaceæ*, like *proteus*.
Range: — In eastern area: Texas, Dallas southward, throughout year. Common in Greater Antilles, but not recorded from Florida.

SIMPLICIUS SKIPPER. *Urbanus simplicius* Stoll
EURYCLES SKIPPER. *Urbanus eurycles* Latreille   p. 209

1.5–1.9 in. Both these species, similar in not having the light spots on the FW separated, but differing in the amount of the light stripe across this wing (see key) are common in southern Texas. At Pharr, *simplicius* flies throughout the year; *eurycles* has been recorded from May to December.

WHITE STRIPED LONG TAIL. *Chioides albofasciatus* Hewit-
son   p. 209
ZILPA LONG TAIL. *Chioides zilpa* Butler

1.5–1.8 in. Both these species occur in southern Texas, ranging thence southward. Their distinctive characters have been cited in the generic discussion and key under *Urbanus*. *Albofasciatus* is common all along the Rio Grande Valley, flying all year. *Zilpa*, never common, has been taken at Pharr, September–November.

FLASHING ASTRAPTES. *Astraptes fulgerator* Walch   p. 209

1.8–2.1 in. The wings above are dark, brownish black, the FW crossed by partial, narrow, white hyaline bands. The head, thorax and bases of the wings are brilliant, iridescent blue-green, greener on the head and prothorax. The flight is extremely strong and fast. Two other species of the genus, casuals in Texas, are discussed in the section on Casual Species, page 285.
Range: — In eastern area, Pharr and Brownsville, Texas, "well established"; chief flights September–November and April–May.

HOARY EDGE. *Achalarus lyciades* Geyer   pp. 49, 224, 272

1.5–1.8 in. Common and widely distributed, the Hoary Edge resembles the Silver Spotted Skipper above, being brown with hyaline orange spots. However, the large, "smeared" looking, whitish patch on the HW beneath distinguishes it. Its flight is not as fast and powerful as that of *clarus*.

Similar Species: — *E. clarus*, see p. 206.

Larva: — Dark green, head black; a broad, bluish green dorsal line; heavily sprinkled with yellowish orange dots which form a narrow, lateral stripe and a duller, broader stripe below the spiracles; often black specked. **Food:** — chiefly Tick Trefoils (*Desmodium*), False Indigo (*Baptisia*) (?) and (dubious) Morning Glory (*Ipomœa*), probably other "*Leguminosæ.*" One brood in north, two in south. Hibernates as pupa. Adults in early May.

Range: — Southern New England, w. to eastern Iowa, s. to Florida, Gulf States and central Texas; rare northward and westward.

COYOTE SKIPPER. *Achalarus coyote* Skinner
1.5–1.75 in. This, the only other species of *Achalarus* in the eastern area, is plain, dark brown above, with white fringes. Some very obscure markings beneath are slightly darker.
Range: — In United States, southern Texas, fairly common, April–June, September–December.

GOLDEN BANDED SKIPPER. *Autochton cellus* Boisduval & Leconte   p. 224
1.6–2.0 in. Widely distributed, but local and mostly uncommon or rare, *cellus* is characterized by the wide, unbroken, yellow band across the FW. The HW beneath has dark and light brown transverse bands, but none of the white that characterizes *E. clarus* and *A. lyciades*. Its flight is rather sluggish, slow and near the ground. Chiefly in wet, grassy areas, along streams or ponds in or near woods. Visits flowers freely, especially those of Hydrangea, Buttonbush (*Cephalanthus*), and Ironweed (*Vernonia*).
Larva: — Yellowish green, with many small, yellow dots; along each side a broad, clear yellow line; head brown, with two yellow, eyelike spots. Lives in a shelter of leaves fastened together, emerging at night to feed. **Food:** — Hog Peanut (*Falcata* or *Amphicarpa pitcheri*), perhaps also *Breweria aquatica* (*Convolvulaceæ*). Two and a partial third broods. Hibernation as pupa. Adults in late May (Virginia).
Range: — Central America, n. to New York and Ohio, rare northward; apparently absent from Gulf States, but occurs in Florida and Texas.

CLONIUS SKIPPER. *Spathilepia clonius* Cramer   p. 209
1.6–1.8 in. Wings above dark brown. FW nearly crossed by a wide, diagonal *white* band. Apex of FW very squarely truncate, outer margin projecting strongly at vein M_2; outer margins of wings scalloped between veins.
Range: — In the eastern area: fairly well established around Pharr and Brownsville, Texas, May–June, September–October.

Genus Thorybes *Scudder:* The Cloudy Wings

Thorybes is a sizable genus of North America and the tropics, of which three species occur widely in our area. They are medium sized, dark brown skippers, with very broad wings; the FW bear a number of small, white spots in an irregular, transverse, broken, median line; the HW beneath are crossed by two rather narrow, inconspicuous, darker bands. The HW are broadly rounded; the cell of the FW is more than two thirds as long as the wing; the recurrent vein is barely indicated. The antennal club is moderately long, followed by an apiculus nearly as long. Our species may be confused with Dusky Wings, *Erynnis;* but the latter have a much shorter cell of the FW, a heavier, curved antennal club not followed by an apiculus and more mottled powdery patterns. In only one *Thorybes* (*pylades*) is the costal fold present in the ♂♂. The ♂ genitalia show good characters for species separation.

Our species may be separated as follows:

1. White spots of FW usually large, extending from vein to vein; palpi usually paler beneath; markings of HW beneath less distinct; ♂ with no costal fold; north to New England . . . *bathyllus*

2. White spots of FW usually smaller; palpi usually darker beneath; markings of HW beneath more distinct; ♂ with no costal fold; north to Arkansas and Maryland . . . *confusis*

3. White spots of FW smaller; palpi usually darker beneath; markings of HW beneath less distinct; ♂ with a costal fold; north into Canada . . . *pylades*

SOUTHERN CLOUDY WING. *Thorybes bathyllus* Abbot & Smith p. 224

1.3–1.6 in. In most of its range a common species of open spaces and roadsides, with a fast, erratic flight. Best caught at flowers. It appears somewhat later in the season than *T. pylades*.

Larva: — Dull, mahogany brown, tinged with olivaceous; thickly sprinkled with tiny, pale wartlets, each bearing a short hair; head black. **Food:** — Various *Fabaceæ* such as Wild Bean (*Strophostyles*), *Dolicholus tomentosus*, Goats Rue (*Cracca ambigua*), Butterfly Pea (*Bradburya virginiana*), etc. One brood in north, two in south. Hibernates as pupa. Adults in June.

Range: — Florida and central Texas, n. to Massachusetts, Wisconsin and Nebraska.

NORTHERN CLOUDY WING. *Thorybes pylades* Scudder pp. 48, 224

1.3–1.6 in. A more common and widespread species than

bathyllus, with much the same habits. Its pugilistic tendencies have been especially noted; Scudder describes one driving a much larger *Epargyreus clarus* from its chosen "beat."

Larva: — Green; a broken, darker stripe along the back, a dull, salmon stripe along each side, and below this another, similar, less distinct one; many minute wartlets, bearing short hairs; head black. **Food:** — probably many *Fabaceæ*; especially Clovers (*Trifolium*), *Lespedeza*, and *Desmodium*. Larva lives in a silk-lined nest (as do its relatives). Two broods in north, three or more in south. Hibernation as pupa. Adults in late May.

Range: — Entire east except northern Canada and lower Rio Grande Valley.

CONFUSED CLOUDY WING. *Thorybes confusis* Bell p. 224
1.2–1.6 in. This species was long unrecognized and confused with *pylades*. Difficult to separate from *pylades* by color and pattern; but the ♂ genitalia are distinct, and the ♂ lacks the costal fold. Information is badly needed about its habits and life history. It is sometimes common.

Range: — Florida to Texas, n. to Kansas, Missouri, and Maryland (Florida and Texas, February–October; Arkansas, May–October; Maryland, July, Aug.)

POTRILLO SKIPPER. *Cabares potrillo* Lucas p. 224
1.3–1.6 in. The short, projecting lobe on the HW at the tips of veins M_3 and Cu_1 is the most distinctive generic character. The wings above are a medium brown with vague, darker brown crossbands. The median row of hyaline white spots of the FW is broken below the cell; the outer edge of the large spot in the end of the cell is deeply indented.

Range: — In the eastern area: southern Texas, well established around Pharr, April–May, July–September.

CALCHAS SKIPPER. *Cogia calchas* Herrich-Schæffer
OUTIS SKIPPER. *Cogia outis* Skinner p. 224
1.2–1.6 in. *Cogia* is not a very distinctive looking genus, the species being medium sized, dull brown, and without prominent markings. Most characteristic is the presence in ♂♂ of a tuft of short sex scales on the HW in the fold along vein 1st A near the base. The antennal club is moderately slender; the apiculus is short, reflexed at right angles. In both our species there are many, fine, dark reticulations on the wings beneath, chiefly on the HW and the apex and outer margin of the FW. These are much stronger in *calchas* than in *outis*. The light spots above are much more distinct in *calchas* than in *outis* (which may lack them entirely). The end of the harpe of *calchas* has two blunt, straight projections; that of *outis* has a single, pointed, dorsal projection.

Range: — *Calchas* is common in Rio Grande Valley, Texas (March–June, August–October), ranges to Paraguay. *Outis* is known only from Texas (TL Round Mountain, Blanco Co.) has been recorded common around Dallas (April–July).

Genus Pyrgus *Huebner:* The Checkered Skippers

A LARGE GENUS of both Old and New Worlds ranging from the Arctic to Argentina and Chile. Some species are barely distinguishable by color and pattern, although the ♂ genitalia offer distinctive characters. In some cases we are not sure whether we are dealing with distinct *species*, *subspecies*, or very distinct *varieties*. Our species as a group are fairly well distinguished by their characteristic "checkered" appearance, lacking large, white areas above; and by the HW beneath showing the same sort of checkered pattern. See also the next genus, *Heliopetes*, and *Chiomara* and *Xenophanes*. The cell of the FW is short; the antennal club is stout, not followed by an apiculus; the palpi are prominent. The HW are evenly rounded. Most, but not all, of the forms have a costal fold and hind tibial sex tufts in ♂♂. Our species may be separated as follows:

1. Light spots of FW above squarish, well separated from each other; FW with fewer light spots, lacking (beneath, if not above), a subterminal row present in our other species... *centaureæ*
1. Light spots of FW above more elongate and crowded together; FW with more subterminal spots in addition to the usual postmedian ones.. 2
2. HW beneath with two small but distinct, slender, submarginal crescents (usually with a dark patch just basad) in cells M_1 & M_2; and with transverse markings variegated; ♂ with a hair pencil on hind tibia........................... 4
2. HW beneath with these crescents, if present, vague and fused with a marginal white patch or with each other; and with transverse markings rather uniformly greenish; ♂ with no hair pencil on hind tibia........................... 3
3. ♂ with a costal fold; harpe of ♂ genitalia with a terminal, two-toothed prolongation; ranges from very dark to very light forms, intergrading perfectly; southern Canada to Mexico, often in same localities as *albescens* and *adepta* (below).. *communis*
3. ♂ with a costal fold; harpe of ♂ genitalia lacking two-toothed prolongation; ranges from very dark to very light forms; Arizona, southern Texas (Brownsville), Mexico.......... *albescens*
3. ♂ without a costal fold; harpe of ♂ genitalia as in *albescens*; dark forms only, Mexico to Columbia; probably not in our area.. *adepta*
4. HW beneath with a prominent dark, elongate spot at midcosta; and with markings distinct and clear-cut; in eastern

area in southern Texas and Florida.................*syrichtus*
4. HW beneath lacking dark spot at mid-costa, and with
   markings pale on a pale ground, indistinct; in our area in
   southern Texas.......................................*philetas*

GRIZZLED SKIPPER. *Pyrgus centaureæ* Rambur pp. 224, 272
0.8–1.1 in. A northern, circumpolar species, of which the typical
form is found in Scandinavia. In our area it occurs as two subspecies. The northern one, *freija*, ranges southward only on
mountaintops above timberline. The southern one, *wyandot*,
flies on open, grassy hillsides. It is a difficult butterfly to see in
the field Though its flight is not particularly fast, I have more
than once had a specimen which I was watching close by, in a
short grass field, vanish as if by magic to reappear thirty feet
away. Southward it is rare and local.
Range: — In eastern area, Arctic s. to alpine summits of Gaspé
(Mt. Albert); and New York s. to North Carolina.
Subspecies: — *P. c. freija* Warren (TL Labrador), Arctic s. to
Churchill, Manitoba and Gaspé; larger and paler; HW beneath
with less of a pale, dark-edged band across postmedian area; ♂
genitalia with style of harpe shorter. *P. c. wyandot* Edwards
(TL Washington, D.C.) New York s. to North Carolina; smaller
and darker; HW beneath with a more or less prominent, pale,
dark-edged band across postmedian area; ♂ genitalia with style
of harpe longer.

CHECKERED SKIPPER. *Pyrgus communis* Grote pp. 225, 272
1.0–1.25 in. *Communis* (formerly widely known as *tessellata*
Scudder) is common and widespread over nearly all our area
except the northeastern part. It varies greatly from very dark
forms (especially ♀ ♀) to light ones (especially ♂ ♂). In southern
Texas and Mexico it overlaps broadly with *albescens*, from which
it is hardly, if at all, to be told by color and pattern. Its flight is
very fast and direct, but not long continued. There are some
very interesting observations of its pugnacity, and of males
"patrolling" a regular "beat." Individuals are prone to sun
themselves, with wings out at the sides, on leaves and stalks.
The flight season is very long.
Larva: — Body greenish, tapering posteriorly, thickest at middle; thickly covered with short, whitish, knobbed hairs; two
broad, whitish, dorsal lines and two lateral lines, all indistinct;
head and first thoracic segment brownish black. **Food:** —
Hollyhocks (*Althaea*), Indian Mallow (*Abutilon*), "Wild Tea"
(*Sida*), doubtless other Mallows (*Malvaceæ*). Three or more
broods in south, probably less in north. Hibernation as pupa
or full grown larva. Adults in March (south) to June (north).
Range: — Central Canada s. into Mexico; absent or rare in
eastern New York, New England and eastern Canada (TL Alabama).

Pyrgus albescens Plötz

1.0–1.25 in.   Opinions differ as to whether *albescens* should be considered a color variety or subspecies of *communis*, or a separate species.   Despite its name it varies through the same range from dark to light forms as *communis*.   But it appears to be constantly genitalically distinct from *communis*, with which its range overlaps.   So I treat it as a distinct species, perhaps a *sibling*.   *Adepta* Plötz appears to be either another closely allied species or else a more southern subspecies of *albescens*, once separated geographically, but now in contact in Mexico.

Range: — In eastern area, southern Texas (Dallas to Pharr); Arizona and Mexico (TL — *albescens*, Mexico; *adepta*, Colombia).

TROPICAL CHECKERED SKIPPER. *Pyrgus syrichtus* Fabricius   p. 225

1.0–1.25 in.   *Syrichtus* enters our area in southern Texas and Florida, where it is common and flies practically throughout the year.   The "form," *montivagus*, which occurs consistently in Florida, has an overscaling of brown on the HW beneath.   Its flight, like that of *communis*, is swift.

Larva: — Yellowish green, thinly haired; head black, prothoracic collar brown with three light spots.   **Food:** — Various Mallows (*Malvaceæ*).

Range: — In eastern area: southern Texas and southern Florida; s. through Central America and Antilles (TL "America").

PHILETAS SKIPPER. *Pyrgus philetas* Edwards

1.0–1.25 in.   *Philetas* is scarcely, if at all, separable from *syrichtus* (and from some *communis*) by color and pattern above; but the very pale, comparatively unmarked HW beneath is distinctive.

Range: — In eastern area, well established from Laredo to Brownsville, Texas, also westward; April–June, August–November (TL Texas).

Genus Heliopetes *Billberg:* The White Skippers

IN THE eastern area occur three species of *Heliopetes*, known by the large areas of white on the wings, but otherwise very similar to the Checkered Skippers.   Beneath, they have rather distinctive blotched patterns, quite different from those of the wings above.

ERICHSON'S SKIPPER. *Heliopetes domicella* Erichson

1.1–1.25 in.   The broad, white bands across the wings characterize *domicella*.   Superficially it might be confused with specimens of *Xenophanes tryxus*; but in the latter the light areas

are nearly transparent, and the pattern is quite different in detail.
Range: — In eastern area, southern Texas, well established around Pharr, September–December; w. to Arizona, s. to Argentina.

LAVIANA SKIPPER.   *Heliopetes laviana* Hewitson
MACAIRA SKIPPER.   *Heliopetes macaira* Reakirt   p. 225
0.9–1.5 in.   These two species are extremely similar, in fact hardly separable, on the upper sides.   On the underside of the HW there is a large, olivaceous brown, mottled patch covering most of the outer third, running from the apex nearly to the anal angle.   In *laviana* the inner edge of this patch is almost straight; in *macaira* the inner edge is curved so as to more or less parallel the curve of the edge of the wing.   In both the ♀ ♀ have more extensive dark markings than the ♂ ♂.   *Laviana* is more common in our area than *macaira*.
Ranges: — In eastern area, southern Texas, San Antonio to Brownsville, flying throughout year; w. to Arizona, s. to South America.

POWDERED SKIPPER.   *Antigonus pulverulenta* Felder   p. 225
0.9–1.1 in.   The wings above are dull orange brown, mottled with darker olivaceous brown.   The light spots of the FW are hyaline white; the submarginal light line of the HW is whitish.   The wings beneath are similarly marked, but very pale.   The strong projection in the middle of the outer margin of the HW is very distinctive.   A most unskipper-like Skipper, resembling many moths in general appearance.
Range: — In eastern area, southern Texas, common from Laredo to Brownsville, April–December.   Ranges to California.

STREAKY SKIPPER.   *Celotes nessus* Edwards   p. 225
0.75–1.0 in.   Like its close relative *pulverulenta, nessus* is a most unusual looking Skipper.   The pattern defies concise description.   The wings are yellowish brown with broken, transverse, darker bands, and darker streakings along the veins.   The fringes are strongly checkered and the outer margins somewhat crenulate, causing a pleated appearance that is enhanced by the tendency of the wing to be actually "wavy," i.e., not flat and all in one plane.
Range: — In eastern area, common to abundant in southern Texas, April–December; w. through Arizona; Georgia (once!).

Genus Pholisora *Scudder:* The Sooty Wings

A FAIRLY large genus of small, sooty brown to black Skippers, most of which have few distinct markings.   As a result the species "run

very close." The ♂ genitalia offer excellent characters for identification. Only two species are widely distributed in our area;
three others occur regularly in Texas. The following key should
be used with caution, and Texas specimens checked by the genitalia.

1. FW above with a series of darker, longitudinal dashes between veins; Texas westward........................*alpheus*
1. FW above not prominently marked with darker longitudinal
   dashes between veins................................ 2
2. Head and palpi pale, ochreous above; Texas westward..... *ceos*
2. Head and palpi no different from body................. 3
3. Wings above of an even shade of sooty black; wings narrower; outer margin of HW not crenulate (wavy) with
   checkered fringes; widespread in entire eastern area.......*catullus*
3. Wings above with faint, darker, transverse bands; wings
   broader; outer margin of HW crenulate, with fringes sometimes strongly checkered................*hayhurstii* and *mazans*

COMMON SOOTY WING. *Pholisora catullus* Fabricius

pp. 49, 225
1.0–1.2 in. Common nearly everywhere in eastern area south
of southern Canada, except in Florida. It has a rapid, erratic
flight, close to the ground. It is not very partial to flowers.
It has been noted as quite pugnacious, attacking and driving
away even such large Skippers as *Erynnis*. It varies greatly
in the number of white spots present; some females have two
transverse lines of these.
Larva: — Pale, dull, olive green, thickly covered with tiny,
yellowish granulations and a short down; head black, roughened;
first segment of thorax small, with one black, and a pair of
greenish stripes. **Food:** — Pigweed or Lambs Quarters (*Chenopodium album*), Tumbleweed (*Amaranthus græcizans*), probably
other *Chenopodiaceæ* and *Amaranthaceæ;* perhaps also Horse
Mint (*Monarda punctata*) Wild Marjoram (*Origanum vulgare*),
and *Ambrosia*. Two broods in north, three in south. Hibernates in a strong nest as full-grown larva. Adults in mid-April.
Range: — Entire east from southern Quebec, Ontario, and
Manitoba s. to Georgia and Texas; apparently absent from
Florida.

SOUTHERN SOOTY WING. *Pholisora hayhurstii* Edwards

p. 225
1.0–1.25 in. The presence of darker markings on the wings, the
more or less checkered fringes and the wavy outer margin of the
HW distinguish this species from *catullus*. From *mazans* it is
best separated by the ♂ genitalia. In *hayhurstii* the harpe has
a very long, curved, subapical, dorsad-extending arm, absent
in *mazans*. Where *catullus* is a denizen of open spaces, *hayhurstii* will be found in wooded areas, along roads and trails
where it alights mostly on leaves.
Early stages: — Not recorded in detail. **Food:** — "Pigweed"

(presumably *Chenopodium*) and *Alternanthera* (*Amaranthaceæ*). Probably at least three broods in the south.

Range: — Pennsylvania and Ohio to Nebraska, s. throughout eastern area.

MAZANS SOOTY WING. *Pholisora mazans* Reakirt

1.0–1.2 in. As noted above, *mazans* often cannot be distinguished from *hayhurstii* by color and pattern; but the ♂ genitalia are very distinct.

Range: — In eastern area: southern Texas, San Antonio to Corpus Christi, common throughout the year.

SICKLE WINGED SKIPPER. *Achlyodes thraso* Huebner p. 225

1.4–1.6 in. The wing shape alone is distinctive. The antennal club is extremely long, slender and gradually enlarged, and is but gently curved at the tip. The wings are dark, somewhat mahogany brown, with paler brown spots and blotches. One of our most unusual looking Skippers.

Range: — In eastern area: southern Texas, common, throughout the year in Rio Grande Valley; s. to Brazil.

Subspecies: — *A. t. thraso*, not in our area. *A. t. tamenund* Edwards (TL Waco, Texas) is the northern race; lighter brown, especially males.

GLASSY WINGED SKIPPER. *Xenophanes tryxus* Cramer

p. 225

1.1–1.3 in. Superficially, *tryxus* resembles a *Pyrgus;* but the broad areas of semitransparent (hyaline) spots on both wings are distinctive. It also resembles *Chiomara asychis;* but in that species the light areas are gray or white and fully scaled, not hyaline. Recorded from Brownsville, Texas, in July, on apparently good authority, but not taken there in recent years.

ASYCHIS SKIPPER. *Chiomara asychis* Cramer p. 225

1.1–1.25 in. The FW above is a slightly brownish gray, with finely reticulated cross lines and a variable amount of white banding; the HW is darker brown, with a median, transverse white band and light marks outward of this tending to pale, orange brown toward the outer margin.

Range: — In eastern area: southern Texas, common at Pharr (May–January).

FLORIDA DUSKY WING. *Ephyriades brunnea floridensis* Bell & Comstock p. 225

1.2–1.3 in. The genus is close to *Erynnis*, but differs in the wing shape: the HW is relatively larger; the outer margin of the FW is longer and more oblique, the apex more produced and sharper, and the anal angle more broadly rounded. The butterfly is of a more uniform, silkier appearance above than any *Erynnis*. Not rare in southern Florida (TL Key Largo); records range from January to August. This subspecies is smaller and darker, and has smaller hyaline spots, than the typical subspecies from Cuba.

Genus Erynnis *Schrank* (Thanaos *Boisduval*): The Dusky Wings

THE DUSKY WINGS are a sizable genus with at least fourteen species in our area. There are many more in the west and the tropics. Their classification is very difficult. Some species cannot be separated by "superficial characters," i.e., color and pattern, so that the ♂ genitalia must be used. These can often be examined by delicately brushing away the scales from the end of the abdomen, and then using a strong hand lens or binocular microscope.

The best genitalic characters are the outlines of the harpes (clasps) as seen from lateral view. A peculiarity of *Erynnis* is that these are not symmetrical, right and left sides being consistently different. Even the genitalia are not of much value with *E. persius, lucilius,* and *baptisiæ.* ♀♀ usually have more distinct patterns, with more contrasting markings, than the ♂♂.

Many are common and widespread. Some are among the earliest butterflies of spring; and some, having a partial or a full second brood, or even a third brood, fly throughout nearly the whole season. In spring they are more likely to haunt woodland areas; later they are found more in open fields and along roadsides. Their flights are often fast and erratic. Most species visit flowers freely. Larval growth is slow. As far as is known all our species hibernate as full-grown larvæ, pupating early in spring.

The following key is to be used with great caution for color and pattern characters. In any given area the females of a species can usually be associated with the males by color and pattern; but this is unsafe with specimens from different areas or different seasons.

1. Fringes of HW white; FW narrower than in other species; ♂ with a hind-tibial tuft; terminal lobe of right harpe shorter, blunt and much narrower than that of left harpe; western
                                                                                funeralis
1. Fringes of FW not distinctly white, sometimes quite pale .. 2
2. FW without distinct hyaline white spots, though sometimes with one or two indistinct spots subapically near costal margin 3
2. FW with at least a group of subapical, hyaline white spots; or with extremely dark wings (*zarucco* ♂♂) 5
3. A small species (under 1.25 in.); male with a hind tibial tuft; terminal lobe of right harpe more pointed, slightly shorter and more slender than that of left harpe . . . . *icelus*

3. Larger (usually over 1.25 in.); male with no hind-tibial tuft. **4**

4. FW with little or no gray clouding; dark marks of FW united to form distinct transverse bands; wings beneath with no distinct spots; male with no costal fold; terminal lobes of both harpes long and slender, tapering gradually to rounded tips; in eastern area in Texas only.................... *gesta*

4. FW usually quite evenly powdered with gray scales; inner part of median transverse band usually broken or indistinct; terminal lobes of both harpes broad to very near their tips, then narrowing abruptly; in eastern area in Texas only...*burgessii*

4. FW with gray clouding heavier toward apex; terminal lobes of both harpes narrowing abruptly, but that of right harpe with a shorter, broader terminal part than that of left one ...*brizo*

5.[1] HW beneath with two pale subapical spots below veins R_3 and M_1 (just basad of the subapical pale spots of the usual submarginal row) sometimes large and dark edged, but sometimes small and inconspicuous or absent, especially in ♂♂ **6**

5. HW beneath without such additional subapical spots, though with the usual marginal and submarginal rows........... **7**

6. Gray areas of FW mostly caused by presence of gray scales; terminal lobe of right harpe bluntly pointed, much wider than that of left harpe, which is very slender; widespread and common................................*juvenalis*

6. Gray areas of FW mostly caused by presence of gray hairs; terminal parts of both harpes long, thin and pointed, that of the left slightly thinner than that of the right; western, in eastern area chiefly in Texas ....*propertius*

7. Hyaline white spots larger, at least a trace of one in end of cell of FW; markings of FW contrasting (♀♀) or with spots reduced or lacking, with little or no gray vestiture (♂♂) **8**

7. Hyaline white spots smaller, often with none in end of cell of FW; color very dark, or else with gray clouding very conspicuous **9**

8. Terminal lobe of right harpe broader than that of left, obliquely truncate at tip; that of left harpe slender and tapering; widely distributed..............................*horatius*

8. Terminal lobes of both harpes slender and tapering; western, in eastern area in Texas only.......................*meridianus*

9. Very dark; hyaline white spots usually much reduced; often with a pale patch at end of cell of FW; left harpe much longer than right one, its terminal lobe long and slender, that of right harpe broad, blunt and square ended.......*zarucco*

9. Usually not very dark; markings more contrasting; males without hind tibial tuft; terminal lobes of harpes about equal in length and thickness; if one is thicker than the other it is the left one that is thicker........................ **10**

10. Dark markings conspicuous, pattern therefore quite mottled and contrasting; with a general purplish-gray appearance; terminal lobes of both harpes strongly curved, that of right harpe more slender; widespread......................*martialis*

10. Not so strongly patterned; terminal lobes of harpes not strongly curved, and about equal in thickness............. **11**

---

[1] This character is unreliable for ♂♂ and for many ♀♀ from the south, which lack the spots; the genitalia will have to be examined in many ♂ specimens.

11. Larger (over 1.25 in.); markings more or less obscured toward base of FW; FW with abundant white hairs on base and disc; a generally smooth appearance; harpes thicker and heavier; larvæ feed on willow and poplar; widely distributed

persius

11. Smaller; markings more evenly distinct over entire FW; wings (when fresh) with a purplish gloss; HW beneath with pale spots clear cut and distinct; food plant Columbine (*Aquilegia*); northeastern states............................*lucilius*

11. Larger; ground color of wings a more yellow-brown; fewer white scales in pale areas; wings with a somewhat brassy, even a greenish gloss; food plant Wild Indigo (*Baptisia*); widely distributed. ....*baptisiæ*

DREAMY DUSKY WING. *Erynnis icelus* Scudder & Burgess

pp. 240, 272

0.9–1.25 in. *Icelus* and *brizo* differ from our other *Erynnis* in almost always lacking white spots on the FW above. Of the two, *icelus* averages considerably smaller and does not have such complete, postmedian, chainlike bands crossing the FW above. Typically both have much gray shading outwardly on the FW, but this varies. Males can be distinguished by the very different genitalia. Both are early spring species, common in woodlands along roads and trails and in open clearings. Although its flight is erratic, *icelus* is one of the most easily caught of our *Erynnis*.

Larva: — Stout, tapering to ends; prothorax yellow, other segments pale green with fine, whitish granulations; a dark dorsal line on abdominal segments, and a pale lateral stripe **Food:** — Aspen (*Populus tremuloides*), probably also Willow (*Salix*); other records (Witch Hazel, Wild Indigo, Oaks, etc.) dubious. One brood. Adults in mid-May (New York and Massachusetts).

Range: — Quebec w. to Manitoba and Vancouver, s. to North Carolina and New Mexico but not in Great Plains, or states bordering them.

SLEEPY DUSKY WING. *Erynnis brizo* Boisduval & Leconte

pp. 240, 272

1.1–1.6 in. Ranging farther south than *icelus*, *brizo* is another early spring species. Its flight is swifter than that of *icelus*. Females are particularly fond of visiting violets.

Similar Species: — See *E. icelus*, above.

Larva: — Pale green; a darker green dorsal stripe, bordered with pale greenish yellow; a narrow, pale greenish yellow stigmatal band; between the two, and also below the latter, pale green flecked with darker green dots; head dark brown, paler brown above. **Food:** — Scrub Oak (*Quercus ilicifolia*); records from Wild Indigo (*Baptisia*) or *Galactia* and Beggar's Lice (*Lespedeza*) are dubious. One brood in north, two in south. Adults in early May (Massachusetts).

Range: — Southern Canada to Florida and Gulf States, w. to Manitoba and central Texas.

Subspecies: — *E. b. brizo;* range of species in our area except for Florida. *E. b. somnus* Lintner (TL Florida); much darker.

MOTTLED DUSKY WING. *Erynnis martialis* Scudder

p. 240

1.0–1.3 in. The rather strong markings, giving a definitely mottled appearance above, together with an almost purplish gloss on bright specimens, characterize *martialis*. In the east it is associated with wooded heights, westward with open prairie. It is never very common, the first brood much less so than the second.

Early Stages: — Very dubiously known.

Larva: — Supposedly pale green with darker dorsal area containing white dashes, a rather high, pale greenish yellow lateral band, below this a greenish area delicately white blotched, then a pale stigmatal band; head dark brown, each side with an upper and a lower, yellowish, oval spot. **Food:** — Records contradictory; Wild Indigo (*Baptisia*) or False Indigo (*Amorpha*) seem most probable, perhaps Pigweed (*Amaranthus*). Two broods. Adults in late May and again in mid-July.

Range: — Southern Canada s. to Alabama and (rare) Texas.

HORACE'S DUSKY WING. *Erynnis horatius* Scudder & Burgess

p. 240

1.2–1.75 in. This and the next species, *juvenalis*, are large, fairly boldly marked above, and have the hyaline spots of the FW averaging larger than in most other species. The character often cited for distinguishing them, the presence of two light subapical spots on the HW beneath in *juvenalis*, works quite well in the north for ♀ ♀, but is not very trustworthy for ♂ ♂. It is absolutely unreliable in the south where ♂ ♂ regularly lack these spots. The ♂ genitalia are quite distinctive so that this sex can be identified with assurance, and ♀ ♀ from the same localities and seasons associated with them by general similarity. *Horatius* averages a trifle darker than *juvenalis*, with fewer whitish scales on the FW above. ♂ ♂ average much darker, with less distinct patterns, than ♀ ♀. I have seen *zarucco* ♀ ♀ indistinguishable by color from *juvenalis* ♂ ♂. *Horatius* is common and widely distributed.

Larva: — Yellowish green with many pale papillæ; a dark dorsal and a bright yellow subdorsal line on abdomen; an obscure pale line on abdominal fold; head black, with a semitoothed angle on each side, the cheeks and upper face dull yellow. **Food:** — Wistaria. The above, from an old description of Chapman's, may not truly apply to *horatius*. Grossbeck and Watson listed the food plant as Oak. Someone should check

SKIPPERS
Subfamily *Pyrginae*

All illustrations are × 1 (natural size)

1. HOARY EDGE, *Achalarus lyciades*   p. 210
   Upper & under sides, ♀ (Glencarlyn, Va.). Rounded wings; HW
   beneath with large, smeary whitish patch. See also Pl. 33, fig. 2.
   New England to Iowa & southward.

2. GOLDEN BANDED SKIPPER, *Autochton cellus*   p. 211
   Upper side, ♂ (Tucson, Ariz.). Very dark brown with golden band on
   FW; no light patch beneath. N.Y. to Ohio & southward & westward.

3. SOUTHERN CLOUDY WING, *Thorybes bathyllus*   p. 212
   Upper side, ♀ (Red Bay, Ga.). Whitish spots larger than in other
   Thorybes. Mass. to Nebr. & southward.

4. CONFUSED CLOUDY WING, *Thorybes confusis*   p. 213
   Upper side, ♂ paratype (Tampa, Fla.). Male lacks costal fold; HW
   beneath more distinctly marked (cf. *pylades*, below). Md. & Kans.
   southward.

5. NORTHERN CLOUDY WING, *Thorybes pylades*   p. 212
   Upper side, side, ♂ (Ogdensburg, N.J.). Male has coastal fold; HW
   beneath less distinctly marked (cf. *confusis*, above). Throughout
   nearly entire eastern area.

6. FRITZ' SKIPPER, *Celænorrhinus fritzgærtneri*   p. 285
   Upper side, ♀ (Alvarez, Col., Mex.). Brown with whitish spots on
   FW; HW very mottled looking. Strays into Tex.

7. *Pellicia bromias*   p. 286
   Upper side, ♀ (S. Vicente, Chiapas, Mex.). Dark brown; very small
   white spots on FW; ♂ has hair pencil on costa of HW. Strays into
   Tex.

8. *Gorgythion begga pyralina*   p. 286
   Upper side, ♂ (Hacienda el Rodeo, C.R.). Dark, lustrous, strongly
   mottled; small size. Strays into Tex.

9. OUTIS SKIPPER, *Cogia outis*   p. 213
   Upper side, ♂ (Vickery, Tex.). Male has hair tuft near anal margin
   of HW; HW beneath gray-clouded with incomplete, dark transverse
   bands. Tex.

10. POTRILLO SKIPPER, *Cabares potrillo*   p. 213
    Upper side, ♀ (Brownsville, Tex.). Short projecting lobes on outer
    margin of HW. S. Tex.

11. GRIZZLED SKIPPER, *Pyrgus centaureæ freija*   p. 215
    Upper & under sides, ♀ (Mt. Albert, Gaspé, Que.). Dark ground
    color more extensive, white spots smaller, than in other eastern
    Pyrgus (Pl. 28, No. 1 & 2 and Pl. 33 No. 5 & 6). Labr. s. to Que.;
    race *wyandot* s. to N.C.

Plate 28   225

SKIPPERS
Subfamily *Pyrginae*

Illustrations × 1 (natural size) or × 1½

1. **TROPICAL CHECKERED SKIPPER,** *Pyrgus syrichtus*   p. 216
   Upper & under sides, ♂ (Florida City, Fla.) × 1. Extensive light
   spots; HW beneath with small, dark "M" at outer margin, and
   prominent dark spot at mid-costa. S. Fla. & s. Tex.

2. **CHECKERED SKIPPER,** *Pyrgus communis*   p. 215
   Upper & under sides, ♂ (Omaha, Nebr.) × 1. Extensive light spots;
   HW beneath lacks small, dark "M" at outer margin and, usually,
   prominent dark spot at mid-costa. New England & centr. Can.
   southward, abundant in south.

3. **MACAIRA SKIPPER,** *Heliopetes macaira*   p. 217
   Upper side, ♂ (Canyon del Zopilote, Gro., Mex.) × 1. Mostly white
   above; HW beneath white with olive patches. S. Tex.

4. **POWDERED SKIPPER,** *Antigonus pulverulenta*   p. 217
   Upper side, ♂ (Tucson, Ariz.) × 1. Distinctive wing shape and
   pattern. S. Tex.

5. **STREAKY SKIPPER,** *Celotes nessus*   p. 217
   Upper side, ♂ (Ingram, Tex.) × 1½. Wavy wing margins; streaky
   pattern. S. Tex.

6. **COMMON SOOTY WING,** *Pholisora catullus*   p. 218
   Upper side, ♂ (Jamaica, L.I., N.Y.) × 1½. Wings evenly blackish
   brown with smooth margins. See text. S. Can. to Ga. & Tex.
   Common.

7. **SOUTHERN SOOTY WING,** *Pholisora hayhurstii*   p. 218
   Upper side, ♂ (Omaha, Nebr.) × 1½. Wings somewhat mottled, their
   margins wavy. See text. Pa. to Nebr. & southward.

8. **SICKLE WINGED SKIPPER,** *Achlyodes thraso tamenund*   p. 219
   Upper side, ♂ (Brownsville, Tex.) × 1. Distinctive shape of FW;
   mottled pattern. S. Tex.

9. **GLASSY WINGED SKIPPER,** *Xenophanes tryxus*   p. 219
   Upper side, ♂ (Coatepec, Mex.) × 1. Powdery gray-brown above
   with very large semitransparent, light areas. S. Tex.

10. **ASYCHIS SKIPPER,** *Chiomara asychis*   p. 219
    Upper side, ♂ (Brownsville, Tex.) × 1. Light areas are whiter, less
    glassy, than in *tryxus* (No. 9, above). S. Tex.

11. **FLORIDA DUSKY WING,** *Ephyriades brunnea floridensis*   p. 219
    Upper side, ♂ paratype (Florida City, Fla.) × 1. More uniform,
    silkier, dark brown above than *Erynnis* species (see Pl. 29). HW
    broader. S. Fla.

this. Two broods in north, perhaps three in south. Adults in mid-April (Massachusetts).

Range: — Massachusetts w. to Minnesota and Colorado, s. through Florida and Texas.

JUVENAL'S DUSKY WING. *Erynnis juvenalis* Fabricius

p. 240

1.2–1.75 in. *Juvenalis* has been characterized above in comparison with *horatius*, and in the key. It is a widespread and common species, chiefly occurring in and around woods, especially where Scrub Oak grows. Like other *Erynnis* it alights on bare patches of earth and suns itself with wings held out at the sides.

Larva: — Pale, waxy green to dark green, yellow tinged by many tiny, pale yellow papillæ each bearing a very short, dark hair; no dark dorsal line; a pale, lemon yellow lateral line; prothorax yellowish green; head pale greenish brown to pale fawn, with many short, white hairs; slight, rounded, lateral lobes; sides pale salmon to orange, this sometimes broken up into as many as three light spots. **Food:** — Oaks, particularly *Quercus ilicifolia* (Scrub Oak), also *alba, muhlenbergii*, and probably *phellos;* also Hazelnut (*Corylus*); also recorded (perhaps in error?) from several *Fabaceæ* e.g., Ground Nut (*Apios*), Vetchling (*Lathyrus*) and Milk Pea (*Galactia*). Two broods in south, perhaps not always two in north. Adults in early May.

Range: — Southern Canada w. to Rocky Mountains, s. through our entire area.

PERSIUS DUSKY WING. *Erynnis persius* Scudder p. 240

1.1–1.4 in. *Persius, baptisiæ*, and *lucilius* are all rather similar to each other in genitalia as well as in pattern. Their differences are set forth in the Key. They appear to have constant food plant differences; and females may sometimes be identified by inference when taken consistently hovering around a known food plant. *Persius* is far rarer in the east than formerly supposed but is much commoner on the Pacific Coast. Its best characteristic is the considerable quantity of chiefly white hairs on the base and disc of the wings, and its generally smooth appearance. Many eastern records of *persius* really refer to the next species.

Larva: — Pale green, very profusely sprinkled with raised white dots each bearing a short white hair; a thin, dark green, mid-dorsal line, and thin, variable, yellowish white lateral lines; head variable in color and pattern, from pale, yellowish brown to black, with small spots and stripes, darker on light-headed individual, reddish brown on black-heads. **Food:** — Willow (*Salix* and Poplar (*Populus*); records of *Fabaceæ* incorrect. One brood in north and a possible full or incomplete second one. Adults in early May (Massachusetts).

Range: — New England w. to Pacific, s. to Alabama and Arkansas; data incomplete due to former confusion with *baptisiæ*.
Subspecies: — *E. p. persius* (TL New England) is the race of nearly all or all of our area. *E. p. fredericki* H. A. Freeman (TL Spearfish Canyon, South Dakota); has longer and thicker hair on both wings and more gray scales and hairs on the FW; dark markings very black, in greater contrast to ground color; fringe of HW lighter than in *p. persius* There is a slight genitalic difference. Specimens of *persius* from the east area near this may show at least intergradation to it.

WILD INDIGO DUSKY WING. *Erynnis baptisiæ* Forbes
p. 240
1.1–1.4 in. In his description of *baptisiæ* (Psyche, 1936, 43: 104–113) Forbes points out that it has in the past been lumped under *persius* by many collectors, so that many records are untrustworthy. Scudder appears to have kept his data on *persius* straight. Since the male genitalia offer no safe diagnosis, the only sure specimens that the average collector can obtain will be by breeding from the food plant Not uncommon.
Larva: — Not recorded in detail. **Food:** — Wild Indigo (*Baptisia tinctoria*).
Range: — New England s. to Florida, w. to Nebraska, Kansas, Arkansas, and Texas.

COLUMBINE DUSKY WING. *Erynnis lucilius* Scudder & Burgess
p. 240
0.9–1.2 in. Recorded only from the northern states, chiefly eastward. It has been reared from Columbine a number of times, and both sexes have been recorded as hovering over this plant.
Larva: — Somewhat pale green, with a yellowish bloom; skin very transparent; a darker dorsal line; a lateral, thin, paler, yellowish line; paler and yellower on lower sides; head black, with three reddish or whitish streaks or spots on each side.
Food: — Columbine (*Aquilegia canadensis*). Three broods, somewhat mixed due to uneven growth rates. Adults in early May (Massachusetts).
Range: — Southern Canada and New England w. to North Dakota, and Nebraska, s. to Georgia.

ZARUCCO DUSKY WING. *Erynnis zarucco* Lucas
p. 240
1.1–1.7 in. Chiefly southern, but ranges or strays northward to Massachusetts. It is quite dark, with very small hyaline spots on the FW, a more conspicuous pale patch in the end of the cell of the FW than other species, and the FW narrower. The ♂ genitalia are quite distinctive. I have found it a common butterfly of open fields and roadsides in Florida, rather addicted to flower visiting and thus easily caught. It favors flowers of

Spanish Needles (*Bidens*). Recorded widely in the literature as *Thanaos terentius* Scudder & Burgess, a synonym.

Larva: — Not known in detail. **Food:** — Legumes (*Fabaceæ*) i.e., *Baptisia* (A. H. Clark) and in Cuba *Sesbanea grandiflora*. At least two, probably three broods in Florida.

Range: — Florida w. to Mississippi and Texas (?), n. to Pennsylvania and Massachusetts (strays).

FUNEREAL DUSKY WING. *Erynnis funeralis* Scudder & Burgess

1.3–1.75 in. Not only is *funeralis* the only species in our area with distinctly white fringes on the HW, but the FW is narrower, the HW broader and rounder than in other species. Essentially western. **Food:** — Alfalfa (*Medicago sativa*) and Bur Clover (*Medicago hispida*).

Range: — In eastern area ranges eastward to w. Kansas and Texas (Rio Grande Valley, flying throughout the year); also Pensacola, Florida, October (F. E. Watson); westward to California and s. to Mexico.

BURGESS' DUSKY WING. *Erynnis burgessii* Skinner

1.1–1.5 in. *Burgessii* most resembles *brizo*, lacking distinct hyaline white spots on the FW above, but has the gray scaling more evenly distributed over the wing, and tends to have the dark transverse postmedian band on the FW broken.

Range: — In eastern area: Texas (Dallas and Palo Duro Canyon, March–May). Westward to Arizona and Utah.

PROPERTIUS' DUSKY WING. *Erynnis propertius* Scudder & Burgess

1.2–1.6 in. *Propertius*, which rather resembles *juvenalis* and *horatius*, is chiefly distinguished by the abundance of gray, hairy vestiture on the wings; rubbed specimens may not show this

Range: — May stray into eastern area. Texas (Palo Duro Canyon, April–June). W. to California.

GESTA DUSKY WING. *Erynnis gesta* Herrich Schæffer

0.9–1.3 in. A tropical species that enters the eastern area only in Texas. (Uvalde, Pharr, May, September–November).

MERIDIAN DUSKY WING. *Erynnis meridianus* Bell

1.4–1.6 in. *Meridianus* is extremely similar to *horatius* in color and pattern, so that identification is sure only by genitalia. It is western, entering the area only in Texas. (Uvalde, Palo Duro Canyon, April–June).

TIMOCHARES SKIPPER. *Timochares ruptifasciata* Plötz

1.4–1.6 in. This is another curiously mothlike Skipper. The FW are dull, light brown with irregular bands of darker spots;

the HW are a brighter, more orange brown with broken, irregular dark bands.

Range: — In eastern area, southern Texas, well established around Pharr and Brownsville, September–December.

GRAIS SKIPPER. *Grais stigmaticus* Mabille
1.8–2.1 in. A rather large, brown Skipper, with a distinctive appearance and wing shape. The FW is long, with the apex somewhat produced and truncate, and the outer margin thus bulged outward at M_2–M_3; the HW looks small and triangular. The wings are a very soft, medium brown, with hazy, transverse, darker spot bands; a light shade between the submarginal and marginal bands; and three tiny, light spots below the apex of the FW. The palpi are bright ochreous orange except on top.

Range: — In eastern area: southern Texas, well established around Pharr and Kerrville, September–December.

Subfamily Hesperiinæ

THE MAJORITY of our skippers, and likewise some of our worst problems, are *Hesperiinæ*. I have felt it advisable, therefore, to give keys to the genera. Technically four groups of genera, A, B, C, and D, are recognized. Group A contains only one genus and species in our area, *Carterocephalus palæmon*, The Arctic Skipper — distinctive and easily recognized. Group B consists of four genera with seven species in our area; small, easily recognized Skippers (p. 230). Groups C and D (p. 233) are difficult to differentiate from each other. Group C contains the great majority of genera and species. Keys to these genera are given, although they are far from satisfactory. For all but a very few experienced workers, learning the skippers consists chiefly of identifying and learning each species. As Lindsey, Bell, and Williams say: "Genera must be separated by a combination of scientific methods and intuition which only a systematic entomologist can appreciate."

The food plants of practically all of our *Hesperiinæ* are grasses and sedges; some specific preferences are shown, but many species appear to have none. The larva typically lives in a nest, feeding mostly by night. The life histories of the majority are still unknown. The larvæ seldom have very distinctive body patterns, but the shape, surface and coloration of the head and the prothoracic shield are often very characteristic.

ARCTIC SKIPPER. *Carterocephalus palæmon* Pallas   p. 272
0.9–1.1 in. Can be confused with no other species in the eastern area, the large, rounded yellow spots being distinctive. It is not truly Arctic, but more characteristic of Canadian Zone forest areas. I have taken it only along well-lit, woodland trails

and in meadows near woods. Its flight is weak and slow for a skipper, and very close to the ground. It has a wide, circumpolar range, occurring in Europe and Siberia as well.

Larva: — Uniform cream color with a faint, broad, dorsal stripe and a narrower, distinct, pale yellowish stripe along each side; dark spots along sides; head green. **Food:** — Grasses. Two broods in some southern parts of range. Adults in early June (White Mountains); mid-August (Michigan).

Range: — Central and southern Canada s. to Connecticut (Sharon) and New York (Ithaca), Pennsylvania, northern Michigan, and Minnesota.

Subspecies: — *C. p. palæmon* is European. In our area all are probably *C. p. mesapano* Scudder (TL Norway, Maine) rather than the larger western *C. p. mandan* Edwards (TL Lake Winnipeg).

The Lesser Skippers

FOUR GENERA, and in the eastern area, seven species, form a well-marked group. Technically these are Group B of the *Hesperiinæ*. They are all rather small; have the palpi upturned, with a long third joint; the antennæ short, with a blunt club; and the cell of the FW short. They all have rather weak flights, and a characteristic appearance, with wing scaling that looks (and is) soft and easily rubbed. None have prominent, raised stigmata or "brands," like so many other *Hesperiinæ*.

1. Wings broadly rounded, especially outer margin of FW and
   anal angle of HW; ♂ with no stigma....*Ancyloxypha*....   2
1. Wings not broadly rounded, all angles well marked.......   3
2. Larger (0.75–1.0 in.); FW above largely dark; FW beneath
   with discal area dark; widespread...................*A. numitor*
2. Smaller (0.6–0.7 in.); FW above and beneath with disc largely
   orange; southern Texas.............................*A. arene*
3. Wings above very largely dark; HW with very definite
   angles; club of antenna about as long as shaft; ♂ with no
   stigma...*Oarisma*....4
3. Wings above with at least some discal orange areas; HW
   more rounded; club of antenna definitely shorter than shaft;
   ♂ with a narrow, linear, black stigma on FW below cell...   5
4. Larger (0.9–1.2 in.); HW beneath with veins anterior to
   1st A lined with whitish, and anal region posterior to 1st
   A blackish; FW above with costal margin orange, rest of
   wing dark...................................*O. powesheik*
4. Smaller (0.75–1.0 in.); HW beneath with veins not so
   strikingly lined with whitish; and anal region posterior to
   1st A light colored with considerable orange; FW above
   with more scattered orange scales, costal margin not so
   contrastingly orange...............................*O. garita*

5. FW quite strongly angled, outer margin slightly concave; club of antenna short; color above largely orange-yellow with narrow dark markings (except in dark ♀ ♀); southern
Copæodes....6

5. FW more rounded; club of antenna relatively longer with a rudiment of the apiculus; dark areas above more extensive, especially along veins and margins; northern......*Adopæa lineola*

6. Smaller (0.4–0.5 in.); HW beneath with veins rusty, darker than ground color and with a pale, longitudinal shade above middle of wing; Texas and Arkansas to Florida ....*C. minima*

6. Larger (0.75–1.0 in.); HW beneath clear, almost unmarked yellow; Texas to Kansas and westward............*C. aurantiaca*

LEAST SKIPPER. *Ancyloxypha numitor* Fabricius   p. 272
0.75–1.0 in. Very common in most of the eastern area. It varies considerably in the extent of the tawny orange on the wings above, some specimens having the FW solidly dark. Its flight is weak and close to the ground among the tall grasses where it most commonly occurs. The orange color flashes quite prominently in flight.
Larva: — Grass green, covered with short, transparent setæ; head and prothoracic shield brownish black, head with light mottlings. **Food:** — Grasses. Three broods (New England), less northward.
Range: — Southern Canada s. to Florida and Texas.

TROPICAL LEAST SKIPPER. *Ancyloxypha arene* Edwards
0.6–0.7 in. A tiny species found from Arizona to southern Texas (Brownsville, July) and southward. Its small size, larger orange areas above, and an orange discal area on the FS beneath separate it from *numitor*.

GARITA SKIPPER. *Oarisma garita* Reakirt
0.75–1.0 in. Essentially a species of the northern Great Plains and of the Rockies, entering our area in Nebraska and probably the Dakotas and Manitoba. Its flight is weak and close to the ground, among grasses and low shrubs in open areas. See *powesheik*, below.
Larva (4th stage): — Head pale green, uniformly punctate, bearing many short bristles; body cylindrical, plump, tapering posteriorly, grass green; a mid-dorsal line and six pairs of lateral lines, white; lowest of these the widest, bluish. **Food:** — Grass e.g., Kentucky Blue Grass (*Poa pratensis*).

POWESHEIK SKIPPER. *Oarisma powesheik* Parker   p. 241
0.9–1.2 in. Very local, but not uncommon where it does occur. Its larger size, and clearcut, orange area along the costa of the FW, distinguish it from *garita*.
Range: — Montana e. to Iowa (TL Grinnell), Wisconsin, Michigan, and northern Illinois. Mid-June and July.

EUROPEAN SKIPPER. *Adopœa lineola* Ochsenheimer   p. 241
0.8–1.1 in. Somehow this European species became introduced
to this continent at London, Ontario, in or before 1910. From
there it has spread to southern Michigan and northern Ohio,
being at times common, but local. There is a very pale color
variety.

SOUTHERN SKIPPERLING. *Copœodes minima* Edwards p. 272
0.4–0.5 in. If we call *numitor* the "Least" Skipper we must have
some still more diminutive term for *minima*; for *numitor* looks
like a giant alongside it. It occurs commonly in open fields,
flying weakly and erratically among grasses. Its bright orange
coloration is quite distinctive, even in flight. I have taken it
flying with *numitor* many times, and have never had any difficulty in distinguishing them on the wing as far as they could
be seen.
Range: — Florida, Georgia and Gulf States through Texas, n.
to Arkansas.

ORANGE SKIPPERLING. *Copœodes aurantiaca* Hewitson
0.75–1.0 in. *Aurantiaca* is common in Texas. Its larger size
and pale, unmarked HW beneath characterize it. Females, as
in *C. minima* also, have considerable dark scaling above. This is
chiefly a mark at the end of the cell and dark lines below the cell,
along the veins and along the inner margin of the FW; and along
the costal margin and radiating from the base of the HW.
Larva: — Green; a narrow, green, mid-dorsal line; a dark purple
stripe on each side of this, and two more along each side; head
conical, with two prominent, upward projecting points, two pink
bands on face and a large, purplish area on each cheek. Pupa
with a long, slender, sharp, frontal horn. **Food:** — Bermuda
Grass (*Cynodon dactylon*).
Range: — In eastern area: Texas n. to Kansas, w. to Arizona.

The Branded Skippers

HERE, IN Groups C and D, belong the great majority of the *Hes-
periines*. Actually they are all more closely related *inter se* than
to the Lesser Skippers (above); but except by technical characters
they are very difficult to characterize as a group. In most of the
species the ♂♂ have a characteristic, raised, narrow stigma or
"brand" on the FW; but this is absent in some. In the majority
the ♂♂ are tawny, orange-brown or yellow with dark borders; but,
again, there are many exceptions to this; and the ♀♀ are usually very much darker than the ♂♂, often being dark brown with
only a few, small, light spots. Most of the species are medium

sized; a few are fairly large, and a few small. Nearly all have swift flights, the wings often beating so fast that they cannot be seen except as a blur. In practically all, the wings are definitely *trigonate*, i.e., are not rounded, but have three definite angles. Identification of many of these species is difficult; and in some genera, such as *Amblyscirtes*, the genitalia *must* be used. In some species the pattern of the upper side is distinctive, but in most the underside is better for identification; this is especially true when the upper side patterns of ♂♂ and ♀ ♀ differ strongly and the ♀ ♀ "all look alike" above. The shape of the stigma of the ♂, or its absence, is a useful character.

The key given here, a modification of that of Lindsey, Bell, and Williams, is not entirely satisfactory but is the best that can be done without either using very technical characters (such as the genitalia), or splitting some of the genera unnaturally. Used with the illustrations, it should do for most of the species. The average collector, and certainly the beginner, will do best if he merely identifies most of the species individually, by appearance.

Groups of the "Branded Skippers"

Group C — Cell of FW less than two thirds as long as wing; with no recurrent vein; majority of the genera and species.

Group D — Cell of FW about two thirds as long as wing, with at least a rudiment of a recurrent vein; three genera only.

NOTE: "Recurrent vein" — a spur sticking back toward the base from the end of the discal cell (FW).

GROUP C

The recently added tropical genus *Cobalus* is not included in the Key.

1. Club of the antenna blunt, with only a rudimentary apiculus
   Yvretta
1. Club of the antenna with a definite, sharp apiculus, sometimes very short.   2
2. Vein M_2 of FW well curved toward its base, arising from cell much nearer to M_3 than to M_1.   3
2. Vein M_2 only slightly curved, arising from cell only a little nearer to M_3 than to M_1.   12
3. Antennæ very short, scarcely longer than the width of the thorax. . . . .*Hylephila*
3. Antennæ much longer than the width of the thorax.   4
4. Tibiæ of middle pair of legs with spines.   5
4. Tibiæ of middle pair of legs without spines . . .*Problema & Atrytone*
5. Apiculus of antenna at least as long as thickness of the club, slender, either abruptly narrowing or distinctly longer than thickness of the club.   9
5. Apiculus of antenna shorter than the thickness of the club, or else not sharply narrowed.   6
6. FW with apex somewhat elongate; HW with anal angle

somewhat lobed; apiculus very short............. 7
6. FW with apex not noticeably elongate, and HW with anal angle not definitely produced or lobed; apiculus usually moderately long................................... 8
7. Stigma of ♂ slender ....*Hesperia*
7. Stigma of ♂ a broad, back patch ....*Atalopedes*
8. Vein Cu₂ of FW arising from cell slightly nearer to base of wing than to vein Cu₁; HW above well marked with yellow-fulvous; see description................................*Ochlodes*
8. Vein Cu₂ variably nearer to Cu₁ than to base of wing; when doubtful, HW above with little fulvous, at most a transverse band; see description..................................*Polites*
8. Position of vein Cu₂ variable and immaterial; club of antenna very stout with a fine apiculus, or moderate with a thick apiculus..........................*Choranthus* & *Poanes*
9. Apiculus slender, about twice as long as the thickness of the club; one species, brownish black with three clear-cut, creamy white median spots on HW beneath.............*Oligoria*
9. Apiculus shorter, or else thick; if brownish black, with either none or more than three white spots on HW beneath 10
10. Stigma of male prominent, broken into two parts; separated by an area of large, silky, gray scales...............*Wallengrenia*
10. Stigma absent or rudimentary or, if present and large, not in two separate parts......*Atrytonopsis*, *Choranthus* & *Poanes*, 11
11. Stigma present, long and very thin, black; FW largely yellow-orange above; tropical, in eastern area only in Florida
Choranthus
11. Stigma present, wide, gray; with considerable areas (♂) or prominent spots (♀) of yellow-orange above; more widespread...*Poanes yehl*
11. Stigma absent or, if present, rudimentary; wings with no prominent orange or orange brown spots or areas either above or beneath; widespread.....................*Atrytonopsis*
11. Stigma absent; wings with prominent orange or orange brown areas or patches, either above or beneath; widespead.....*Poanes*
12. Apiculus slender, shorter than thickness of the club.......*Lerodea*
12. Apiculus longer, or wings immaculate.................... 13
13. Third joint of palpus long in most species; fringes of most species checkered, or contrasting sharply with ground color of wings......................................*Amblyscirtes*
13. One species only; third joint of palpus not long; fringes neither checkered or contrasting; under surface with purplish luster... ....*Lerema*

GROUP D

The recently recorded tropical genera *Asbolis*, *Perichares*, and *Synapte* are not included in this Key.
1. Middle tibiæ without spines............*Panoquina* & *Nyctelius*
1. Middle tibiæ spined................................ 2
2. ♂ with stigma; HW beneath mottled with several colors
Thespeius
2. ♂ without stigma; HW beneath with uniform ground color and large, hyaline spots.............................*Calpodes*

SIMIUS SKIPPER. *Yvretta simius* Edwards

0.9-1.1 in. Wings above brown, somewhat golden tinted; FW with whitish yellow spots; one in end of cell, a group of smaller ones on costa subapically, and a line of three or four small ones running down to Cu_2. Beneath, the FW are pale brownish gray apically, orange-tinted discally and blackish basally, with the spots of the upperside repeated. HW beneath pale whitish gray, with a curved, postmedian band of spots and a more basal group, whitish. The extent of the spots varies considerably. Fringes very pale. The ♂ has a rudimentary stigma above vein Cu_2. The blunt antennal club, with only a rudimentary apiculus, is characteristic. Some authors consider that *simius* belongs in the genus *Amblyscirtes*. The genus was formerly known as *Chærophon*.

Range: — In eastern area, southern Texas (Palo Duro Canyon, April–June); perhaps straying in from the plains as far north as Nebraska.

Genus Hesperia *Fabricius*

Hesperia is a world-wide, Holarctic genus. The majority of the species are North American; of these, twelve occur in the eastern area. The stigma is quite distinctive; this is strong, slender, and only slightly curved, and usually shows a conspicuous, pale center stripe with black margins; it is made up of a long segment above Cu_2 and a short segment below Cu_2 that is set outside the first but continuous with it. The species differ greatly in appearance, ranging from such very dark ones as *metea* and *meskei* to light ones such as *ottoë*. There is also much variation within some of the species, both individual and geographic. The latter is not well understood, and it is probable that, with study of much more material, some of our present ideas about subspecific relationships will be considerably changed. Full details will be found in the extremely thorough work: *A Preliminary Revision of Hesperia* by A. W. Lindsey, Denison University Bulletin, Journal of the Scientific Laboratories, Vol. XXXVII, April, 1942 (Granville, Ohio). The following key to the eastern species will suffice for most specimens, but some variants will make trouble.

KEY TO THE *HESPERIA* OF EASTERN NORTH AMERICA

1. HW beneath with a transverse row of prominent spots, sharply defined and contrasting with the ground color..... 2
1. HW beneath without such prominent spots, unmarked or else with vaguely defined or scarcely contrasting spots..... 12
2. HW beneath brick red to red brown, spots well developed and very conspicuous, cream to buff; very dark above,

ground color nearly black, with light areas much reduced; widespread...................................*leonardus*

2. HW beneath otherwise, blackish to bright yellow, but not distinctly reddish................................... 3

3. Ground color of HW beneath very mottled, greenish to ochreous with blackish patches; veins white, causing the white spots to appear sharply produced along the veins toward the outer margin; fringes with terminal half whitish; large; western....................................... *uncas*

3. Ground color of HW beneath more uniform and not mottled; ranging from very dark to light yellow; veins not prominently white; if veins appear white streaked, fringes not distinctly whitish.. 4

4. Dark above and beneath, often quite blackish; pale areas above much restricted; HW beneath with light spots usually quite confluent, forming an outward-pointing, V-shaped band, and somewhat produced along veins; widespread .... *metea*

4. Never very dark; HW beneath much lighter, spots seldom confluent and not produced along veins............... 5

5. HW beneath with spots moderate to large, forming a well-developed band, in some cases scarcely contrasting with remainder of wing.................................. 7

5. HW beneath with spots never large, although often sharply contrasting, sometimes mere points..................... 6

6. Stigma with its long anterior bar slender, clean cut, diverging along its basal half from cubital stem; stigma meeting anal vein more than one third from base of wing; ♀ ♀ blackish with only scattered fulvous scales, the spots of the FW pale, but all with at least a tinge of fulvous................... *attalus*

6. Anterior bar of stigma thicker and applied to cubital stem throughout its entire length; stigma meeting anal vein one third from base of wing; ♀ ♀ sometimes very dark, but always with a conspicuous sprinkling of fulvous scales at least at base of FW; spots of FW almost white except for most posterior one; see text..................... *ottoë & pawnee*

7. HW beneath with spots moderate to large, often angular, lustrous white to yellowish white, in strong color contrast to remainder of wing................................. 8

7. HW beneath with spots large, sometimes conspicuous, but yellow, merely lighter than the yellow of the remainder of the wing.. *sassacus*

8. Wings beneath very dark; in some specimens with dark ground color partly concealed by light overscaling......... 9

8. Wings beneath not very dark appearing, the light overscaling general.. 10

9. Gaspé to Maine and Minnesota; HW beneath usually heavily overscaled with golden to greenish; FW beneath with conspicuous fulvous areas............................*laurentina*

9. Southern states; HW beneath dull and dark, with reduced and poorly defined spots; FW beneath with less fulvous... *attalus*

10. Southwestern states; paler colored generally; last light spot on HW beneath (below Cu₂) set nearer outer margin than the spots above it...................................... *viridis*

10. Labrador to Maine and Minnesota; darker colored; last

light spot on HW beneath set nearer base of wing than the
spots above it.   11

11. Overscaling of under surface usually greenish; spots tending
to form a complete band; when small, merely shortened and
not tending to become rounded and separate; often followed
by dark border without overscaling; Labrador. . . . .*borealis*

11. Overscaling golden, rarely slightly greenish; spots tending to
be rounded and separate, and without dark outer border;
Gaspé to Maine and Minnesota. . . . .*laurentina*

12. Dull and dark above, with little fulvous; HW beneath with
spots lacking to greater or lesser extent. . . . . *metea*

12. Not dark and dull; with some yellow or fulvous areas.   13

13. HW dark beneath, with more or less overlay of yellowish
scales; FW beneath dark with very restricted light areas. .*attalus*

13. HW beneath light yellow to orange fulvous.   14

14. HW immaculate beneath.   15

14. HW beneath with a vague light band, or a series of distinguishable spots slightly paler than the ground color.   16

15. Wings above with large, discal, yellow-orange areas; HW beneath with clear, pale yellow tint, not reddish or rusty tinted
yellow; northwestern; see text. . . . .*pawnee & ottoë*

15. Wings above dark, with relatively small light areas; HW
beneath with distinctly reddish or rusty tinge; southern
states. . . . . *meskei*

16. Southern states; large and dark; HW beneath with dis-
tinctly reddish or rusty tinge. . . . . *meskei*

16. Eastern and mid-western; moderate to small-sized; with
more extensive light areas above; never with reddish or
rusty tinge beneath.   17

17. Prairie states only, Manitoba s. into Iowa and e. into Illinois;
a pale and vaguely marked species; under surface of male
varying from yellowish to dull, grayish ochre, spots normally
small and vague; ♀ ♀ decidedly grayish beneath, with small,
vague spots; upper surface duller and much more vaguely
marked than *sassacus*; rare. . . . .*dacotæ*

17. Widespread, eastern; distribution overlapping that of *dacotæ*
only in Illinois and eastern Iowa; most specimens distinguishable by bright color and strong contrasts of upper
surface, and by the large, clean-cut, but sometimes not
strongly contrasting spots of HW beneath; common. . . . . .*sassacus*

LEONARDUS SKIPPER. *Hesperia leonardus* Harris   p. 273

1.1–1.4 in. Easily recognized by the dark upper side and beneath by the red HW with prominent cream spots. Common
in open fields and damp meadows. It visits flowers freely,
especially high ones. It is solely an autumn species, flying in
August and September.

Larva: — Finely and irregularly mottled, light brownish and
brownish maroon with greenish tinges; head blackish brown,
with many fine punctations and with distinctive, light markings.
Food: — Grasses. One brood. Hibernation as first-stage larva.
Adults in late August and September.

Range: — Southern Maine and Ontario w. to Iowa, s. to Florida, Missouri, and Kansas.
Subspecies: — *H. l. leonardus* (TL Massachusetts); eastern Canada and New England; spots on HW beneath white to yellowish white. *H. l. stallingsi* H. A. Freeman (TL Blendon, Ohio); s. and w. from New England; spots of HW beneath darker, ochreous. A not entirely consistent subspecies, of the "clinal" type.

INDIAN SKIPPER. *Hesperia sassacus* Harris   pp. 241, 273
1.0–1.35 in. Recognized by its bright colors and decided pattern. In the western part of its range it overlaps with *dacotæ*; most specimens of the latter are far duller and more faded looking, and have a much vaguer pattern. Open fields and meadows. One of the earliest *Hesperiinæ* of spring.
Larva: — Not well known; plumper than related forms. Food: — Grasses. One brood in north, two in south. Hibernation probably as pupa. Adults in mid-April (Georgia), late May (Massachusetts).
Range: — Maine and southern Ontario w. to Iowa, s. to Florida.
Subspecies: — In *H. s. manitoboides* Fletcher (TL Nepigon and Sudbury, Ontario) the upper side is much darker and the ground color beneath likewise darker, so that the light spots of the HW stand out more prominently. Recorded also from Minnesota. In *H. s. sassacus* (TL Massachusetts) the light areas above are much more extensive and the light spots of the HW beneath do not stand out so prominently. *Manitoboides* is not, apparently, a very consistent subspecies, even in a clinal way.

DAKOTA SKIPPER. *Hesperia dacotæ* Skinner
1.0–1.35 in. Characterized by its general lack of any decided pattern or coloration. For long considered a subspecies of *sassacus*, it is now known to be a distinct species. It is extremely rare.
Range: — Manitoba, South Dakota (TL Volga), Iowa, & Minnesota. Probably an inhabitant of wet, virgin prairie habitats, now infrequent.

COBWEB SKIPPER. *Hesperia metea* Scudder   p. 272
1.0–1.3 in. *Metea* may be told by its generally dark appearance, the angulate, white spotband on the HW beneath and the more or less white lined veins beneath. Some specimens, however, may lack the white spots beneath. It is an early spring species, found in open fields and clearings; in New England associated with Beard Grass (*Andropogon*), and visiting especially flowers of Strawberry (*Fragaria*) and Cinquefoil (*Potentilla*). I have found it particularly often in "old fields" growing up to perennials and low shrubs.
Larva: — Incompletely known. Food: — Grasses, particularly

Beard Grass (*Andropogon*). One brood with a short flight season.
Hibernates probably as pupa. Adults in early April (Georgia),
early May (New Jersey).
Range: — Southern Maine w. to Wisconsin, s. to Florida and
Texas. Very local southward.
Subspecies: — *H. m. metea* (TL Connecticut); range of the spe-
cies s. to Texas. *H. m. licinus* Edwards (TL Waco, Texas);
Texas; larger and darker, white markings beneath obscure or
absent.

DOTTED SKIPPER. *Hesperia attalus* Edwards   p. 272
1.2–1.4 in. Although widespread, *attalus* is not very well known.
It varies considerably, both individually and geographically, and
is hard to characterize. Some specimens have a full set of spots
on the HW beneath; others have none. The underside characteristically has a rather dense light overscaling; but this may
be largely lacking (especially in worn specimens) so that the
appearance is very dark. The Florida race is fairly distinctive,
but data about its northern extent are badly needed, for Georgia
specimens are frequently very unlike the nearby Florida ones.
Range: — Florida and Texas, n. to Massachusetts, Ohio, Wisconsin, and Nebraska.
Subspecies: — *H. a. attalus* (TL Waco, Texas) occupies most of
the area; underside with more light, olivaceous yellow overscaling. *H. a. slossonæ* Skinner (TL Florida); underside darker,
lacking much of the light overscaling.

MESKE'S SKIPPER. *Hesperia meskei* Edwards   p. 272
1.1–1.4 in. A large, dark, southern species with a distinctly reddish or rusty tinge beneath; the spots beneath are diffuse and
indistinct, or absent. Quite rare.
Range: — North Carolina to Florida, w. to Arkansas and Texas.
Evidently two broods.

OTTOË SKIPPER. *Hesperia ottoë* Edwards   p. 273
1.1–1.45 in. A large prairie species with very greatly reduced dark
markings above, and a pale yellow to buff, unmarked underside.
The form *ogallala* has more extensive dark markings above than
the typical form. *Ottoë* is to be found in (now rare) undisturbed
prairie areas; it visits flowers, has a strong, fast flight, and is
quite wary. In appearance it is extremely close to *pawnee;* some
males can hardly be separated except by the genitalia, in which
ottoë has a large, subterminal, dorsal tooth on the harpe, lacking
in *pawnee*. *Ottoë* flies in June and July, *pawnee* in the same regions in August and September. In *pawnee* ♀ ♀ the postmedian
spots of the FW are more whitish and clear cut than in *ottoë*.
Range: — States bordering Great Plains, South Dakota to
Texas.

Chiefly DUSKY WINGS
Erynnis, Subfamily *Pyrginae*

All illustrations are × 1½ except No. 10

1. **DREAMY DUSKY WING,** *Erynnis icelus*   p. 222
   Upper side, ♂ (Ogdensburg, N.J.). × 1½. Lacks white spots on FW
   above; postmedian markings across FW more or less interrupted;
   smaller (cf. *brizo*); see also Pl. 33, fig. 7. Can. s. to N.C. & N. Mex.
2. **SLEEPY DUSKY WING,** *Erynnis brizo*   p. 222
   Upper side, ♂ (Suffern, N.Y.). × 1½. Larger than *icelus;* chainlike
   band across FW more complete. See also Pl. 33, fig. 8 Can. southward
   through Fla. & centr. Tex.
3. **PERSIUS' DUSKY WING,** *Erynnis persius*   p. 226
   Upper side, ♂ (Rowley, Mass.). × 1½. White spots of FW not extensive; wings basally with considerable whitish hair; see text.   New
   England w. to Pacific, s. to Ark. & Ala.
4. **WILD INDIGO DUSKY WING,** *Erynnis baptisiæ*   p. 227
   Upper side, ♂ (Hempstead, L.I., N.Y.). × 1½. See text.   New
   England w. to Nebr., s. to Fla. & Tex.
5. **COLUMBINE DUSKY WING,** *Erynnis lucilius*   p. 227
   Upper side, ♂ (Great Notch, N.J.). × 1½. See text. Can. s. to Ga.
6. **MOTTLED DUSKY WING,** *Erynnis martialis*   p. 223
   Upper side, ♂ (Greenville, S.C.). × 1½. Strongly mottled; a purple
   gloss when fresh. S. Can. s. to Ala. & Tex.
7. **JUVENAL'S DUSKY WING,** *Erynnis juvenalis*   p. 226
   Upper & und.r sides, ♂ (Omaha, Nebr.). × 1½. Large size, strong
   white spots and pattern; HW beneath often with two subapical
   white spots; see text. S. Can. southward.
8. **ZARUCCO DUSKY WING,** *Erynnis zarucco*   p. 227
   Upper side, ♂ (Mobile, Ala.). × 1½. Dark; small white spots; pale
   patch in end of cell of FW. Mass & Pa. (strays). S. thru Fla. & Miss.
9. **HORACE'S DUSKY WING,** *Erynnis horatius*   p. 223
   Upper & under sides, ♂ (Tampa, Fla.). × 1½. Like *juvenalis;* lacks
   white subapical spots on HW beneath. See text. S. Can. s. thru Fla.
   & Miss.
10. **DOLORES' SKIPPER,** *Perichares philetes dolores*   p. 271
    Upper side, ♀ (San Vicente, Chiap., Mex.). × 1. Light spots pale
    yellow, semitransparent. See text. S. Tex.

Plate 30   241

LESSER AND BRANDED SKIPPERS
Subfamily *Hesperiinae*

All illustrations are × 1½ except No. 10

1. **POWESHEIK SKIPPER,** *Oarisma powesheik*   p. 231
   Upper side, ♂ (L. Okoboji, Iowa) × 1½. Powdery olivaceous brown;
   costal edge of FW fulvous; HW beneath with whitish veins. N. Ill.
   to Iowa & westward. Quite local.
2. **EUROPEAN SKIPPER,** *Adopæa lineola*   p. 23⅄
   Upper side, ♂ (Detroit, Mich.). × 1½. Dull orange-fulvous; narrow
   stigma; dark vein tips; HW beneath pale yellow. Ont. to s. Mich.
   & Ohio.
3. **INDIAN SKIPPER,** *Hesperia sassacus*   p. 238
   Upper side, ♀ (Bedford, N.Y.) × 1½. Extensive bright fulvous areas;
   HW beneath yellow with yellow spots. S. Can. s. to Fla. See ♂,
   Pl. 34, no. 4.
4. **THE SACHEM,** *Atalopedes campestris*   p. 243
   Upper side, ♀ (Tampa, Fla.) × 1½. See text and ♂, Pl. 34, Fig. 10.
   N.Y. (stray) & Dakotas w. to Pacific, s. thru Fla. & Tex.
5. **LITTLE GLASSY WING,** *Polites verna*   p. 245
   Upper side, ♂ (Northcastle, N.Y.) × 1½. Light spots of FW semi-
   transparent, the largest one very square. HW beneath brown, with
   a curved median row of small, pale spots. New England & Nebr.
   s. to Ga. & Tex. Common.
6. **LITTLE GLASSY WING,** *Polites verna*   p. 245
   Upper side, ♀ (Northcastle, N.Y.) × 1½. See ♂ above.
7. **PECK'S SKIPPER,** *Polites peckius*   p. 246
   Upper side, ♀ (Metuchen, N.J.) × 1½. HW beneath with large, clear-
   cut yellow patch; see ♂, Pl. 35, fig. 4. S. Can. s. to Ga. & Tex.
   Abundant.
8. **LONG DASH,** *Polites mystic*   p. 247
   Upper side, ♀ (Stony Clove, N.Y.). × 1½. See ♂, Pl. 35, fig. 3. S.
   Can. s. to Va. & Ill. Common.
9. **WHIRLABOUT,** *Polites vibex*   p. 247
   Upper side, ♀ (Jupiter, Fla.) × 1½. See ♂, Pl. 34, fig. 9. Conn. &
   Ark. southward. Common in south.
10. **BROAD WINGED SKIPPER,** *Poanes viator*   p. 249
    Upper side, ♂ (South Jamaica, N.Y.) × 1. See Pl. 35, fig. 10. Mass.
    & Nebr. s. to Ala. & Tex. Marshes & salt marshes.
11. **POCAHONTAS SKIPPER,** *Poanes hobomok* f. ♀ *pocahontas*   p. 250
    Upper side, ♀ (Gaylordsville, Conn.) × 1½. See Pl. 35, fig. 7 & 8
    and *zabulon* ♀, No. 12 below.
12. **ZABULON SKIPPER,** *Poanes zabulon*   p. 250
    Upper side, ♀ (Washington Heights, New York City) × 1½. Lacks
    yellow spot of spots in cell of FW, which *pocahontas* has. See ♂,
    Pl. 35, fig. 9.

PAWNEE SKIPPER. *Hesperia pawnee* Dodge   p. 273
1.1–1.5 in. As noted above, *pawnee* is very close to *ottoë*, but is shown by the male genitalia to be distinct. ♀ ♀ have very sharp, contrasting markings. The flight season, August and September, will also serve to separate specimens of the two species.
Range: — States bordering Great Plains; Minnesota and South Dakota to Kansas.

GREEN SKIPPER. *Hesperia viridis* Edwards   p. 273
1.0–1.3 in. A species of the southwest. The HW beneath shows a very decided green color, with the anal region sharply orange-yellow. The last of the white spots being set nearer the edge of the wing, the row of spots tends to bend outward and be concave externally.
Range: — In eastern area: Texas and Oklahoma; April–June, August–September.

UNCAS' SKIPPER. *Hesperia uncas* Edwards   p. 273
1.0–1.4 in. Easily recognized by the mottling of the ground color and the great extent of white scaling along the veins of the HW beneath, as noted in the key. A western, prairie species that enters the eastern area along the border of the Great Plains from Manitoba to Texas.

LAURENTIAN SKIPPER. *Hesperia laurentina* Lyman   p. 273
0.9–1.25 in. This and the next are easily distinguished from other *Hesperia* of the northeast by the clear white, often large, spots on a golden to greenish golden ground color. They are very closely related to the European *H. comma* and to a great variety of forms, variously treated as either varieties or subspecies of *comma*, or distinct species, that range from England across Europe, Asia, and North America. The relationships in this array have yet to be worked out. For the present it is perhaps wisest to call both *laurentina* and *borealis* separate species, awaiting further study. *H. manitoba* Scudder and *assiniboia* Lyman, also parts of the "*comma* complex," are western; probably do not occur in our area.
Range: — Southeastern Canada, w. to Ontario and Manitoba, s. to Maine (Bar Harbor) and Minnesota. Late July–August. Variously recorded as *H. comma laurentina*, *H. comma colorado* and *H. comma manitoba*, etc. It seems to be one-brooded.

LABRADOR SKIPPER. *Hesperia borealis* Lindsey
1.1–1.3 in. As Lindsey remarks, this may be a race of *laurentina*, presumably a subarctic subspecies. It differs in the tendency of the spots of its HW beneath, even when reduced, to form a continuous band, and by the presence of dark patches outside and, in some specimens, inside of these spots. The spots in *laurentina*

tend to become separate from each other, and rounded, and to be closely bordered by the light overscaling. Known only from Labrador (TL Nain), mid-July to early August.

FIERY SKIPPER. *Hylephila phyleus* Drury   p. 273

1.0–1.25 in. Widespread in the south. The bright colors of the ♂♂ flash in the sunlight. Distinctive characteristics are: the large amounts of bright orange-yellow above; the sharp yellow rays extending toward the margins along the veins; the characteristic pattern of the HW beneath; the yellow line along vein 2d A of the HW above; and the very short antennæ (a generic character). Some ♂♂ have the dark spots beneath reduced to tiny specks; others have them many times heavier than the one we illustrate, plus a median series of spots and some basal dashes. ♀♀ have the same pattern on the HW beneath, but the wing is much overlaid with olivaceous dusting. They vary more in darkness or lightness than ♂♂.

Similar Species: — *Polites vibex* ♂♂ are somewhat similar; they have fewer, but larger, spots on the HW beneath, lack the pointed yellow rays running out along the veins on the HW above, and have longer antennæ.

Larva: — Pale green, finely mottled with darker green except in a lighter lateral stripe; a narrow, dark green dorsal line; sometimes nearly unmarked; head dark brown. **Food:** — Grasses. At least two broods in south, probably more.

Range: — South America n. to Connecticut, Illinois, Michigan, and Nebraska, rare northward, abundant in much of the south.

SACHEM. *Atalopedes campestris* Boisduval   pp. 241, 273

1.2–1.4 in. The stigma of the ♂, a large, black blotch that distorts the cubital vein, is characteristic. The pattern beneath is difficult to characterize; in ♂♂ the transverse, postmedian spotband of the HW is broad but vague; in ♀♀ it is sharper but narrower. ♀♀ are much darker, more olivaceous beneath than ♂♂. The large postmedian spots of the FW of ♀♀ are quite glassy, a good characteristic.

Larva: — Pale green, somewhat clouded with darker green, with dark, brownish dorsal line; thickly covered with very minute, blackish papillæ, each bearing a short hair; head black, clouded below with luteous. **Food:** — Bermuda Grass (*Cynodon dactylon*). It lives in a "tent" at the base of a leaf, to which it carries pieces from the tip of the leaf. Three broods in south. Hibernation probably as adult.

Range: — Tropics, n. to New York (casual) and Dakotas, w. to California. Common except northward.

Genus Polites *Scudder*

SEVEN SPECIES of this genus occur in our area, most of them common and widespread. The following key will aid in naming most specimens, but two of the species (*themistocles* and *manataaqua*) run very close; and females are very difficult and sometimes "stump the experts."

1. HW beneath dark, unmarked or nearly so, or with a transverse band of pale spots that is never sharply bent opposite the cell nor with the spot at this point much the longest ...   2

1. HW beneath with definite markings, either a large, yellow-orange, discal patch with dark margins, or a largely yellow wing (really an enlargement of the patch) with dark spots..   6

2. HW above completely or nearly completely dark; sometimes with faint indications of light, postmedian spots, or with a slight, brassy to orange, discal tinge....................   3

2. HW above with a transverse row of light spots, or a discal patch of yellow or orange and a darker border........... *mystic*

3. Both sexes above very dark; ♂ with no yellow or orange areas on FW along costa but with small, whitish spots like ♀; these spots on FW beneath largely unscaled, glassy looking   *verna*

3. ♂ with yellow or orange areas on FW above, particularly along costal margin.................................   4

4. Small (0.90 in. or less); Florida and West Indies only; ♂ with black part of stigma very narrow; a vague, lighter, spotband on the HW beneath, more pronounced in ♀ ♀ ... *baracoa*

4. Larger (0.90 in. or more); widely distributed; ♂ with black part of stigma wider; only rarely do the HW beneath show traces of a spotband; when this is present the spots are smaller than in the above..............................   5

5. Smaller (usually under 1.1 in); stigma of ♂ tending to be somewhat broken or partially interrupted; ♀ with spots of FW more tinged with yellowish and with costal margin and cell more likely to have some yellow-orange....... *themistocles*

5. Larger (usually over 1.1 in.); stigma of ♂ tending to be continuous, less interrupted or broken looking at vein Cu_2; FW spots of ♀ paler and more whitish, with less tendency to fulvous along costa and in cell................. *manataaqua*

6. HW beneath with a postmedian, curved band of light spots, usually widely separated from light spot in base of cell; the spot in cell M_2 is not noticeably longer than those above it nor extending farther toward the margin as well as basally; northern states only................................. *mystic*

6. HW beneath with spotband enlarged so as to form a large, irregular patch; or with spotband narrower but with the spot in cell M_2 always very long so that the band angles sharply there; or with light areas occupying most of the wing   7

7. HW beneath with spotband prominent, with sharp, clear-cut edges, broadly joined to light area in cell; stigma of ♂ narrow; ♂ above with little yellow or orange on FW outside of stigma, generally dark looking; more northern........ *peckius*

7. Quite variable; if HW seems to have a narrow, light spot-band then this has blurry, diffuse edges, and is not broadly joined to any light area in cell; usually the HW beneath is mostly pale except for a few dark patches; stigma of ♂ broad; wings of ♂ above, especially FW, with extensive orange-yellow areas; southern, straying northward . . . . *vibex*

LITTLE GLASSY WING. *Polites verna* Edwards   p. 241

0.9–1.25 in. Common and widely distributed. The ♂♂ lack the yellow or orange areas above that occur in most other species of the genus. The larger, discal spots on the FW are more or less hyaline and glassy; they are very squarish and nearly lack scales, and thus aid identification of ♀♀.

Larva: — Brown, profusely flecked with minute, dark spots which bear pale, short hairs; dark stripes as follows: one mid-dorsal; three pairs on sides, fading away anteriorly and posteriorly; head dull chestnut, dark edged posteriorly. **Food:** — Grass. One brood. Hibernation stage unknown, probably larva. Adults in late June (New England).

Range: — Central New England, southern Illinois, Michigan, and Nebraska s. to Georgia, Alabama, Arkansas, and Texas.

Subspecies: — *P. v. verna* (TL Illinois); most of area; larger, spots larger; spots of HW beneath less defined. *P. v. sequoyah* H. A. Freeman (TL Arkansas); Arkansas, and Texas; smaller, spots of FW smaller, spots of HW beneath more prominent, general color tone beneath warmer.

CROSS LINE SKIPPER. *Polites manataaqua* Scudder   p. 273

1.0–1.2 in. So close to *themistocles* that many specimens cannot be separated with assurance. There are ♂ genitalic differences. In general *manataaqua* is larger and darker, has more restricted orange on the FW, has the stigma longer and more slender, but less sinuous, and tends to have faint traces of spots on the HW beneath, while *themistocles* tends to have none. The largest spot on the FW of the ♀ is very *squarish*. *Manataaqua* is seldom very common, while *themistocles* is very common to abundant.

Larva: — Dark chocolate, mottled with soiled white; many short, black tubercles, bearing short, spinelike, tawny hairs; head dull black. **Food:** — Grasses. One brood. Hibernates as fourth (sometimes third) instar larva. Adults in late June (New England).

Range: — Northern New England, w. to Dakotas, s. to Georgia, Alabama, and Arkansas.

Subspecies: — None in the eastern area.

TAWNY EDGED SKIPPER. *Polites themistocles* Latreille

p. 288

0.8–1.1 in. The Tawny Edged Skipper is widely distributed and is probably, with its congener *peckius*, our most abundant skipper. Its distinction from its close relative, *manataaqua*, is discussed above and in the key. It has had a checkered career as to specific names, having been known widely as *taumas* Fabricius and *cernes* Boisduval.

Larva: — Brownish yellow to chocolate, with very faint lines; evenly covered with short, spiny, black hairs; head black with prominent, short light stripes (that of *manataaqua* is unmarked). **Food:** — Grasses. Two broods southward, one northward. Hibernation stage probably pupa. Adults in late May (New England).

Range: — Nearly entire east, central Canada s. to Florida, Gulf States, and Arkansas.

BARACOA SKIPPER. *Polites baracoa* Lucas   p. 288
0.75–0.90 in. A small Antillean skipper that occurs not uncommonly in Florida and Georgia. Distinguishing characters are its small size, dark color, narrow stigma; and the tendency to have definite spots on the HW beneath, especially in ♀ ♀, in which the spots are more whitish.

Similar Species: — *P. themistocles;* see above, and key.

Larva: — Vinaceous buff, with a darker brown, narrow, mid-dorsal line and pair of wider, dark brown lateral lines; lighter along borders of lateral lines and spotted irregularly with dark brown, especially between dorsal and lateral lines. Head dull gold, with two white stripes and two ocellar spots. **Food:** — Grasses.

Range: — In eastern area: Florida and southern Georgia; January–April, July, September.

PECK'S SKIPPER. *Polites peckius* Kirby   pp. 241, 288
0.85–1.0 in. Easily distinguished by its small size and the characteristic light patch on the HW beneath, composed of greatly enlarged and fused spots. The sharp, clear-cut edges of this patch are distinctive; I have seen specimens of *vibex* with a patch almost identical in size and extent; but in these the markings always look blurry and "out of focus." *Peckius* is excessively common; it and *themistocles* are probably our most abundant skippers. It occurs in open spaces generally, visits flowers freely.

Larva: — Deep maroon, mottled with light brown; head black with a characteristic pattern of white streaks and areas. **Food:** — Grasses. Two broods northward, three southward; individuals of a single brood may transform straight through into adults of the next brood, or may slow down their development very erratically and hibernate as third, fourth, or fifth stage larvæ or as pupæ. There is thus a maximum of overlapping of broods. Adults in early May (New York).

Range: — Maritime Provinces westward, s. to Georgia and Texas; rare near southern limits.

LONG DASH. *Polites mystic* Scudder   pp. 241, 288

1.0–1.25 in. The connection of the upper end of the stigma with the subapical dark patch, making a long streak along the FW, gives *mystic* its common name and helps distinguish it. The HW beneath is rather reddish; the light spots form a curved band, but these are not so large as in *peckius* and *vibex*. Some *mystic* ♀ ♀ are very dark; beneath, the HW may be nearly solid reddish brown with a narrow band of small, separated, light spots.

Similar Species: — *Hesperia sassacus* has the HW beneath rather similar, but has a narrower, gray-centered stigma, seldom joined with the dark, subapical patch; has the spotband of the HW beneath more sharply angled in cell M_2; and has more extensive orange areas above, especially in the females.

Larva: — Dark chocolate with dull, white mottling; many short, black, spiny hairs arising from black tubercles; a dark brown dorsal line; head pitchy black, with surface rough. **Food:** — Grasses. One brood (New Hampshire) to two broods (New Jersey); hibernation as third or fourth stage larva. Adults in late May (New Jersey).

Range: — Maritime Provinces w. to Manitoba, s. to Virginia and Illinois.

Subspecies: — *P. m. mystic* (TL White Mountains, New Hampshire) all of above range except western edge. *P. m. dacotah* Edwards (TL Colorado); in our area in Iowa and Dakotas; HW beneath with ground color scarcely darker than light spots, pale and yellow.

WHIRLABOUT. *Polites vibex* Geyer   pp. 241, 273

0.9–1.1 in. As one would infer from the common name its flight is, indeed, fast and darting. It is an avid flower visitor The yellow of the ♂♂ is somewhat paler than in its congeners; and the stigma is noticeably broad. The pattern of the HW beneath varies greatly but is distinctive in its consistent blurriness and lack of sharp markings, as well as in the characteristic dusting of these wings in the ♀ with dark and greenish scales. Essentially southern, *vibex* has been reported at times from far northward *Vibex* and *brettus* Boisduval & Leconte have usually been considered separate species, and the latter name used for the population in the eastern area. I am assured by specialists, however, that they really should be considered as one species with at most racial distinction.

Larva: — Pale glaucous green, with obscure, dark lines; posterior half of each segment transversely roughened; head black, roughened, with white lines and patches. **Food:** — Grasses, e.g., *Paspalum ciliatifolium*. Three broods in south (Florida).

Range: — Tropics n. to Connecticut, Arkansas, and (old, dubious record) Wisconsin.

Subspecies: — *P. v. vibex* (TL "West Indies") most of our area. *P. v. præceps* Scudder (TL Tehuantepec, Mexico); from San

Antonio, Texas, southward, common all year in Rio Grande Valley; greater extent of yellow areas both above and beneath, colors lighter and brighter.

BROKEN DASH. *Wallengrenia otho* Abbot & Smith   p. 273

0.9–1.2 in. The ♂ is easily recognized by the chief generic character, the black parts of the stigma being clearly broken into a small, lower and a longer, upper part. ♂♂ of the southern race have at times considerable orange-brown above, chiefly along the costa of the FW, and some on the disc of the HW. Long, olive-green hairs basally on the FW, more extensive on the HW above, are quite distinctive. On the HW beneath, both sexes show a curved band of small, light spots, the one in cell M_2 the largest; sometimes these are quite prominent, sometimes faint. Subspecific differences cause considerable variation in color beneath (see below). Rather common in all parts of its range. Its flight is slower and its habits more sluggish than those of most related skippers. It is a consistent flower visitor.

Larva: — Pale green, hoary along mid-dorsum, profusely mottled with dark green; a dark dorsal line; a broad, yellow-green stigmatal band, broadening so as to include the dorsum beyond the 7th abdominal segment; tinged posteriorly with pinkish; a thin, green substigmatal line, followed by a yellowish green band; head chocolate, a median darker stripe bordered with paler stripes. **Food:** — Grasses, e.g. Crab Grass (*Panicum sanguinale*). One brood in north, two, perhaps three in south. Hibernates as larva. Adults in early July (New England).

Range: — Southern Quebec and Ontario, southward throughout the eastern area.

Subspecies: — *W. o. otho* (TL Georgia); Georgia, Florida, Gulf States, Texas, and southward; upper side with more fulvous; under side warm brown to chestnut brown. *W. o. egeremet* Scudder (TL Massachusetts); northern Florida and Texas northward; ♂♂ with less fulvous above; under side colder, sooty brown, markings whitish rather than yellowish. There is a considerable blend zone between the subspecies.

Genus Poanes *Scudder*

AS THIS genus now stands (even with *radians* and *haitensis* removed to *Choranthus*), it is heterogeneous and contains species not closely related. The species are, however, fairly easily distinguished from each other, however difficult it may be to characterize the genus. The dark ♀ ♀ of *hobomok* and *zabulon* cause the only real difficulties.

1. HW beneath with clear yellow areas...................   2
1. HW beneath with no large clear yellow areas, with at most small yellow spots.......................................   7

2. Yellow area on HW beneath a broad transverse band crossed by a broad ray out from end of cell....................... 3

2. Yellow area on HW beneath more extensive, not so sharply delimited...*zabulon*

3. Wings above dark brownish-black, with small, light spots only, or none; wings short and rounded...............*massasoit*

3. Wings with extensive fulvous areas above, at least with large spots and patches; wings longer, less rounded.......*hobomok*

4. HW above with only very small, light spots, or with indistinct lighter areas, or entirely dark...................... 5

4. HW above with a definite, bright yellow-orange patch..... 7

5. FW above with a pale spot in cell at least faintly indicated
   hobomok f. ♀ pocahontas

5. FW above with no pale spot in cell, although other light spots may be large and prominent...................... 6

6. Wings with pale spots above; wings longer.............*zabulon* ♀

6. Wings with no light spots or marks above; wings shorter and more rounded........................*massasoit f. suffusa*

7. FW above with definite, clear-cut spots or yellow-orange areas with sharp borders; HW beneath with or without light spots and a pale shade in cell M_2; if this shade is present it does not run out from the base of the cell.............. 8

7. FW above with borders of light areas or spots diffuse and blurry; ♂ with a pale, narrow, inconspicuous stigma.......*aaroni*

8. ♂ with a conspicuous stigma; smaller (1.3 or less); ♀ with a curved row of three or four round pale spots on HW beneath... *yehl*

8. ♂ without stigma and with orange on FW restricted to spots, not a patch; larger (1.35 in. or more); ♀ without such spots; if pale markings are present on HW beneath, they are faint repetitions of the marks of the upper side ... *viator*

BROAD WINGED SKIPPER. *Poanes viator* Edwards

pp. 241, 288
1.35–1.75 in. A large, broad-winged and robust species of wide distribution. It is, however, quite local, being found in isolated colonies; but its exact life history and habitat requirements are unknown. In coastal regions it definitely prefers salt marsh and brackish marsh environments.

Range: — Massachusetts, southern Ontario, Minnesota, and Nebraska, s. to Alabama and Texas; records scattered, not from all states within this general area.

MULBERRY WING. *Poanes massasoit* Scudder pp. 256, 288
0.9–1.1 in. Widely distributed in the north, but extremely local. Little is known about its early stages. Probably it is a grass (or sedge) feeder. It occurs in bogs or tussocky, boggy marshes. Its flight is weak and low, as it weaves through the tall grasses. It visits few flowers, but it is partial to those Swamp Milkweed (*Asclepias incarnata*). In the form *suffusa* the lower surface is suffused with rusty brown which obscures the yellow markings, and the upper side lacks the yellow spots.

Range: — Massachusetts and New Hampshire w. through Ontario, Illinois, Minnesota, and Wisconsin to Iowa; s. to Maryland and (?) Georgia.

Subspecies: — *P. m. massasoit* (TL Carver, Massachusetts) occupies most of the range. *P. m. hughi* A. H. Clark (TL Beltsville, Maryland); larger, darker above, HW beneath with ground color more reddish and yellow patch smaller. If this is a valid subspecies it cannot come from so wide an area as New Jersey, Maryland, Georgia, Nebraska, and South Dakota as cited; if it does, it is merely a color variety.

HOBOMOK SKIPPER. *Poanes hobomok* Harris   pp. 241, 288

1.1–1.3 in. Some of the older authors confused this species and the next, *zabulon*. *Hobomok* is common and widespread, essentially more northern. It has strikingly dimorphic ♀ ♀; some are yellow-orange like the ♂ ♂; others (f. ♀ *pocahontas*) are dark brown with only small light spots. This dark form is much like the normal ♀ of *zabulon;* but has always at least a trace of yellowish in the cell of the FW above; has the light spots of the FW above more blurred looking (in *zabulon* they are sharper and more clear-cut); and has the pale patch of the HW beneath at least indicated in the characteristic shape of *hobomok* (in *zabulon* ♀ ♀ it likewise shows, but not in this characteristic, restricted shape). *Pocahontas* is rare or absent in the western parts of the range of *hobomok*; it seems to occur somewhat later in the season than the normal yellow ♀.

Early stages: — Because of the confusion of *hobomok* with *zabulon* we have no full data.

Larva (third stage): — Dark green to brown with many small black tubercles in transverse lines, bearing short black spines; these interrupted to form naked bands along the sides. Head black, shagreened, with many white hairs; prothoracic shield black. **Food:** — Grass. One brood, May–September.

Range: — Maritime Provinces, Quebec, Ontario, and Manitoba s. to Georgia, Alabama, Arkansas and Kansas.

Subspecies: — *P. h. hobomok* (TL Massachusetts) nearly all of the above range. *P. h. ridingsi* Chermock & Chermock (TL Riding Mountains, Manitoba); Manitoba; slightly darker above; yellow patch on HW beneath overcast with brownish scales. According to the authors, intergrades occur in Quebec. Perhaps a clinal gradation.

ZABULON SKIPPER. *Poanes zabulon* Boisduval & Leconte
pp. 241, 288

1.1–1.3 in. Above, *zabulon* resembles *hobomok* quite closely; beneath, the much greater extent of the yellow on the HW is characteristic. A good character is the presence of a row of dark spots running from the lower, outer corner of the cell of the HW beneath straight toward the inner (anal) margin. Even in the

dark females these show through the dark suffusion. More widespread southward than *hobomok*. As noted above, many old
records and life history data cannot be trusted because the two
species were confused. Both *hobomok* and *zabulon* often occur in
woodlands and along wood roads as well as in fields. It has been
suggested that the ♂♂ favor the wooded areas, the ♀♀ open
spaces.

Early stages: — Old records and data unreliable. **Food:** —
Grasses. Two broods, perhaps three in far South. Adults in
late May, again in August.

Range: — Massachusetts w. to Iowa, s. to Georgia and Texas
(rare).

AARON'S SKIPPER. *Poanes aaroni* Skinner   p. 288
1.1–1.5 in. Limited to our central and southern Atlantic coast.
It and *Panoquina panoquin* are distinctive in being limited to salt
and brackish marshes. Above it strongly resembles *Atrytone
logan*, but with sharper-edged dark borders; but the presence of
a long, pale shade on the HW beneath, from the base of the cell
out to the margin; and the presence on the ♂ of a very thin, pale,
inconspicuous stigma, are good characters.

Range: — Atlantic Coast, New Jersey s. to Florida. June.

Subspecies: — *P. a. aaroni* (TL Cape May, New Jersey); New
Jersey s. to Georgia; smaller, paler and more yellowish. *P. a.
howardi* Skinner (TL Florida); Florida; larger; dark markings
and borders more extensive; light areas deeper orange-brown.
Doubtless there is something of a clinal gradation along the
coast.

YEHL SKIPPER. *Poanes yehl* Skinner   p. 288
1.2–1.3 in. Because of the prominent stigma, *yehl* is sometimes
placed in the genus *Paratrytone* Dyar. It is distinguished from
other *Poanes* by this and the small spots on the HW beneath.
It is more easily confused with *Atrytone conspicua*. *Conspicua*
has a heavier, blacker stigma and unspined middle tibiæ, and
tends to have the spots on the HW beneath larger and more
fused to form a patch; when these are small they are placed proportionately farther in from the wing margin than in *yehl*. ♀♀
of *conspicua* tend to be darker above, with more restricted light
spots.

Similar Species: — *A. conspicua*, see above.

Range: — Virginia and Tennessee s. through Georgia, Alabama,
and Mississippi (July–October).

Choranthus radians Lucas   p. 289
Choranthus haitensis Skinner
1.1–1.2 in. Both species occur rarely in Florida, perhaps only as
occasional introductions. Both have the stigma long, very thin,
and gently curved. Above, *haitensis* has the veins of the FW

more dark lined and the whole discal area of the HW clear orange. Beneath, *radians* has the apex of the FW and most of the HW dull, grayish olive with sharply yellow veins; the cell below the discal cell and Cu_2 is orange, the rest of the anal region gray-olive. In *haitensis* these areas beneath are bright, unmarked orange. Both are widely distributed in the Antilles. *Radians* has been reared from grasses; *haitensis* from Sugar Cane.

BYSSUS SKIPPER. *Problema byssus* Edwards   pp. 256, 288
1.2–1.4 in. The genus *Problema*, of which we have two species, is close to *Atrytone* but separated from it by genitalic characters. Our two species lack a stigma, which most of the *Atrytone* species have. *Byssus* and *bulenta* look very much alike. *Bulenta* ♂♂ may have more restricted dark markings above, especially at the base of the FW; but *bulenta* ♀♀ may have more dark above. The chief distinction is that on the HW beneath *byssus* has at least a faint trace of a lighter spotband or patch beyond the end of the cell, while *bulenta* has these wings clear, unmarked yellow, of a less rusty or orange yellow than *byssus*.
Range: — Florida to Texas and n. to Kansas and Iowa.

RARE SKIPPER. *Problema bulenta* Boisduval & Leconte   p. 256
1.2–1.7 in. *Bulenta* was for long considered a synonym of *byssus*. In 1925 Mr. F. M. Jones rediscovered it near Wilmington, North Carolina, along the edges of the marshes south and west of the city. A few specimens have been taken there since then, but none in other localities, except from Grady County, Georgia, May 7 and June 15 (Lucien Harris).

Genus Atrytone *Scudder*

SEVERAL SPECIES occur in our area, some of them widely. The generic characters, a long antennal club and the lack of spines on the tibiæ of the middle pair of legs, are distinctive. The species differ greatly in appearance. The stigma is absent in *arogos* and *logan* ♂♂, present in all others.

  1. HW beneath with no transverse bands or spots.   3
  1. HW beneath with two broad, pale rays, one in cell and beneath vein M_2, the other posterior to the cell and beneath vein Cu_2.   2
  1. HW beneath with a few diffuse spots forming a curved, transverse, postmedian row or patch; ♂ with prominent stigma; widespread. . . . . *conspicua*
  2. FW above with small, light, subapical spots just in from costal margin; chiefly northern and widespread. . . . .   *dion*
  2. FW above lacking subapical, subcostal light spots, very dark and comparatively unmarked. . . . . *dukesi*
  3. HW with the fringe along the inner (anal) margin white;

HW beneath gray-olivaceous to yellow-olivaceous, the veins
lighter; northern; rare...............................*bimacula*
3. HW with fringe of inner margin not white............... **4**
4. Wings of ♂ above unmarked, dark brown; ♀ dark, with
light spots very small to absent......................*ruricola*
4. Wings with more pale markings, sometimes very largely
yellow.. **5**
5. HW beneath very dull, ranging from olivaceous gray to
olivaceous brown; a small, very vague, pale patch at end
of cell...*palatka*
5. HW beneath bright, yellow to orange red................ **6**
6. Stigma present in ♂.................................. **7**
6. Stigma absent in ♂................................... **8**
7. HW beneath with veins narrowly but distinctly much lighter
than ground color.................................*berryi* ♂
7. HW beneath with veins very little, if any, lighter than
ground color.......................................*arpa* ♂
8. FW above largely dark, with distinct, separated, light spots **9**
8. FW above largely yellow (or orange); or with yellow patch
or shades, but these not small, distinct, separated spots.... **10**
9. HW beneath with veins narrowly but distinctly much
lighter than ground color............................*berryi* ♀
9. HW beneath with veins little, if any, lighter than ground
color..*arpa* ♀
10. HW above very dark, with at most a faint, pale, discal shade
arogos ♀
10. HW above with yellow discal patch, sometimes largely
yellow... **11**
11. FW above with veins dark against yellow ground......... *logan*
11. FW above with veins light as ground color........ *arogos* ♂

See also *A. eulogius*, section on Casual Species, page 286.

AROGOS SKIPPER. *Atrytone arogos* Boisduval & Leconte
pp. 256, 289
1.1–1.25 in. The ♂ is orange-yellow above, with wide dark margins except along the costal edge of the FW. In ♀♀ the dark margins are greatly widened so as to obliterate light areas, sometimes almost completely. The very light, bright underside, practically unmarked save for a wide dark band along the inner margin of the FW, contrasts strongly with the dull, dingy, and suffused-looking upper side. The generally suffused look and the unmarked veins of the FW above distinguish it from *logan*. It ranges widely but appears to be rather local, and is nowhere very common.
Range: — Florida and Gulf States, n. to New Jersey, Minnesota, Iowa, and Nebraska.
Subspecies: — *A. a. arogos* (TL "North America," certainly along eastern seaboard); range as above except for northwestern parts. *A. a. iowa* Scudder (TL Denison, Iowa); Kansas, Iowa, and Nebraska; appearance in general lighter; females with more yellow above; males lack dark discocellular line on FW above; lighter, brighter yellow beneath.

DELAWARE SKIPPER. *Atrytone logan* Edwards   pp. 256, 289
1.0–1.4 in. Widespread but seldom very common, *logan* is easily
recognized by the dark veins and discocellular mark of the FW
above, combined with clear, bright, yellow-orange HW beneath.
♀♀ have much more extensive dark markings above than ♂♂,
and average much larger. *Logan* occurs in open woods and, more
often, in dry, open fields. It has been called "terribly shy" and
hard to capture; but I have not found it so in either Connecticut
or Florida, especially when it is visiting flowers.
Similar Species: — *Choranthus haitensis* (in Florida) has a narrow, dark stigma in the ♂; has the FW blunter and their outer
margins more rounded; is deeper orange beneath; and has the
middle tibiæ spined. See also *Copæodes minima* (large, dark ♀♀)
and *aurantiaca*.
Larva: — Bluish white; a crescentic black band on next-to-last
segment and anal plate; thickly dotted with minute black tubercles; head smooth, white, a black band about top and sides; three
black streaks on face. **Food:** — Grasses, e.g. Woolly Beard Grass,
Erianthus divaricatus. One brood in north, perhaps three in south.
Hibernation as larva or pupa. Adults in March (Florida) to late
June (Massachusetts).
Range: — Florida, Gulf States and central Texas n. to Massa-
chusetts, Minnesota, and Dakotas.
Subspecies: — *A. l. logan* (TL Lansing, Michigan) all the above
area except western edge. *A. l. lagus* Edwards (TL Oak Creek
Canyon, Colorado); definitely in the eastern area in Texas
(Dallas, Wichita Falls, etc.), probably strays in all along western
edge; dark borders above much narrower; color beneath much
paler.

ARPA SKIPPER. *Atrytone arpa* Boisduval & Leconte
                                                    pp. 256, 289
1.3–1.6 in. A rather large species of the extreme south, *arpa* is
distinguished by its size, moderate amounts of yellow-orange
above, and clear, bright, unmarked orange-yellow to ochreous
yellow HW beneath.
Similar Species: — *A. dion* has light, longitudinal streaks on the
HW beneath. *A. berryi* has the veins of the HW beneath lined
with yellowish-white. *A. palatka* has the HW beneath very dull,
olivaceous brown; large ♂♂ of *A. conspicua* have prominent light
spots or a spotpatch on the HW beneath.
Larva: — Pale green, yellow striped; segments after the second
thickly lined with fine green and yellow streaks; collar black,
anteriorly yellow-edged; head high, narrow, blackish, white-
bordered around top and sides; two curved (externally convex)
white streaks on upper third of face, velvety black between
these. Lives in tube near bases of fanlike leaves. **Food:** — Saw
Palmetto (*Serenoa*).

Range: — Florida and Alabama. Old records of a wider range are due to confusion with other species.

BERRY'S SKIPPER. *Atrytone berryi* Bell   p. 289
1.1–1.5 in. Little is known about Berry's Skipper, named for the veteran Florida collector, Mr. Dean Berry, who has discovered most of the known specimens. The light veining on the HW beneath is a distinguishing characteristic. ♂♂ may rather resemble *A. conspicua*; but the stigma is narrower than in that species, and there is no trace of the light spots on the HW beneath that characterize *conspicua*.
Range: — Central Florida (TL Monticello)

DION SKIPPER. *Atrytone dion* Edwards   pp. 256, 289
1.3–1.6 in. *Dion* is widespread but apparently rather local and never very common. It favors marshes and marshy meadows with thick growths of sedges and tall grasses. Its chief characteristic is the presence on the HW beneath of two longitudinal pale shades, one through the cell and below vein M_2, the other below the cell and above the second anal vein.
Range: — Georgia, w. through Gulf States to Texas, n. to New York, Ontario, Wisconsin, and Nebraska. May–September. Rare northward on Atlantic Coast.
Subspecies: — *A. d. dion* (TL Indiana); most of the above range. *A. d. alabamæ* Lindsey (TL Mobile Co., Alabama); Alabama and Arkansas to Lancaster, Texas. Wings above with fulvous areas and spots very much reduced; longitudinal, light shades on HW beneath inconspicuous. A local colony of *A. d. alabamæ* has been recorded from Dahl Swamp, Accomac Co., Virginia; a most unusual record.

PALATKA SKIPPER. *Atrytone palatka* Edwards   pp. 256, 289
1.5–1.75 in. *Palatka* is the largest and most robust species of the genus. It is distinguished by its size, and by the dull and dark colors of the HW beneath.
Larva: — Yellowish green, thickly dotted with minute, dark, hair-tipped tubercles; spiracles black; ventral side bluish; head obliquely projecting, brownish; upper part of face white with three black stripes. Draws faces of saw grass leaves together, lies concealed in tube thus formed. Food: — Saw Grass (*Mariscus jamaicensis*).
Range: — Florida (TL St. Augustine) and Alabama, n. coastal to Virginia.

DUKES' SKIPPER. *Atrytone dukesi* Lindsey   pp. 256, 289
1.25–1.5 in. Beneath, *dukesi* resembles *dion* in possessing longitudinal, pale shades on the HW. Its FW are, however, much blunter and proportionately shorter and broader. The light

BRANDED SKIPPERS
Subfamily *Hesperiinae*
The illustrations are × 1 and × 1½

Plate 32   257

BRANDED SKIPPERS
Subfamily *Hesperiinae*
All illustrations are × 1½

1. **THE BLACK DASH,** *Atrytone conspicua*   p. 258
   Upper side, ♀ (Northcastle, N.Y.) × 1½. See ♂, Pl. 36, fig. 6. Prominent spot patch on HW, both above & beneath.
2. **TWO SPOTTED SKIPPER,** *Atrytone bimacula*   p. 258
   Upper side, ♀ (Ogdensburg, N.J.) × 1½. Light spots distinctly yellowish, not transparent; no spot row on HW beneath; anal margin of HW white. See ♂, Pl. 36, fig. 9.
3. **EASTERN DUN SKIPPER,** *Atrytone ruricola metacomet*   p. 258
   Upper side, ♀ (Kaaterskill Clove, N.Y.). × 1½. Very small yellowish spots on FW; HW beneath dark with faint, curved, median row of light spots. See ♂, below and Pl. 36, fig. 8.
4. **EASTERN DUN SKIPPER,** *Atrytone ruricola metacomet*   p. 258
   Upper & under side, ♂ (Flushing, L.I., N.Y.) × 1½. Very dark and unmarked above, no fulvous areas. See ♂, above, and Pl. 36, fig. 8.
5. **LOAMMI SKIPPER,** *Atrytonopsis loammi*   p. 259
   Upper & under sides, ♂ (Myakka River State Park, Fla.) × 1½. Extensive white spotting beneath; cf. with *hianna*, fig. 7, below. Fla. to N.C.
6. **TWIN SPOT SKIPPER,** *Oligoria maculata*   p. 260
   Upper side, ♂ (Chickasaw, Ala.) × 1½. Dark, uniform brown; creamy white spots; three such spots on HW beneath; wings broad. See text. Fla. to Ala., strays northward.
7. **DUSTED SKIPPER,** *Atrytonopsis hianna*   p. 259
   Upper & under sides, ♂ (Stoneham, Mass.) × 1½. Much gray dusting, especially beneath; often with one or more white spots on HW beneath; see text. New England to Nebr., s. to N.C. See also Pl. 36, fig. 13.
8. **CLOUDED SKIPPER,** *Lerema accius*   p. 260
   Upper & under sides, ♂ (Tampa, Fla.) × 1½. Male with more distinct stigma than *hianna*; discal spot of FW not so square; dark markings on HW beneath differently placed than those of *hianna*. See also Pl. 36, fig. 14. Mass. & Ill. southward.
9. **CLOUDED SKIPPER,** *Lerema accius*   p. 260
   Upper side, ♀ (Hope, Ark.) × 1½. See ♂, above. No creamy spots on HW like *O. maculata*, fig. 6.

areas of the wings, both above and beneath, are much more restricted than in even the dark *dion alabamæ*. *Dukesi* never has the small, subapical, light spots, just in from the costal margin, present in *dion* and most other *Atrytone*. Shaded swamps.

Range: — Alabama (TL vicinity Mobile) n. Virginia and Ohio.

BLACK DASH. *Atrytone conspicua* Edwards   pp. 257, 289
1.1–1.3 in. The Black Dash (formerly widely known as the Pontiac Skipper, *A. pontiac* (Edw.) is widespread in the north. It is quite local, in marshes and boggy meadows. It is relatively unwary and easy to catch. It rests much on tall grasses. Its favorite flowers are those of Buttonbush (*Cephalanthus*) and Swamp Milkweed (*Asclepias incarnata*). Its northern distribution, relatively small size, heavy stigma, and the conspicuous, small, light spot-patch on the HW beneath, distinguish it.

Similar Species: — *P. mystic* and *A. campestris* resemble *conspicua* on the upper side enough to cause occasional confusion. All but *mystic* have the ground color of the HW beneath lighter, and the spots or spotbands larger and less contrasting with the ground color. *Campestris* has the stigma very broad. The FW of *conspicua* are broader, the outer margin more rounded. In *mystic* the spots of the HW beneath are larger and sharper in outline; and there is a light spot in the cell.

Range: — Massachusetts s. to Virginia, w. through Ohio, Indiana, Illinois, Michigan, Minnesota, and Nebraska. Apparently one brood, early July–August.

TWO SPOTTED SKIPPER. *Atrytone bimacula* Grote & Robinson   pp. 257, 289
1.1–1.25 in. *Bimacula* is a rather dull and dark northern species about which little is known. ♂♂ have a little fulvous on the disc of the FW above; ♀♀ are entirely dark, with very reduced light spotting. The white fringes and edge of the anal margin of the HW are distinctive but not very prominent. The HW beneath are dull olivaceous to olivaceous yellow, with the veins distinctly lighter. What records we have point to a preference for boggy or marshy meadows, and to its occurrence in small, very local colonies. July.

Range: — Maine and Ontario s. to Virginia, northern Michigan, Iowa, and Nebraska. Old records far to the south are based on misidentifications.

DUN SKIPPER. *Atrytone ruricola* Boisduval   pp. 257, 289
1.1–1.3 in. Formerly known widely as *vestris* Boisduval, the Dun Skipper occurs throughout our area from Ontario and Quebec southward, and ranges to the Pacific Coast. It is everywhere common, occurring in open fields and along roadsides, alighting often on the ground, and visiting flowers freely. It is said to be partial to those of Mints, Fireweed, and Indian Hemp (*Apocy-

num). ♂♂ never have more than the faintest traces of light spots
on the FW; and ♀♀ are also very dark, with very small light spots
or none.   Despite its commonness, its life history is almost completely unknown.   Apparently but one brood, June–August.

Range: — Southern Quebec and Ontario s. through Florida and
Texas, w. to Pacific.

Subspecies: — The eastern population as a whole should be distinguished from that of the west as *A. r. metacomet* Harris (TL
Massachusetts); color darker and blacker, stigma of ♂ scarcely
contrasting with color of FW.   In *A. r. ruricola* (TL California)
the ground color is much lighter than that of the stigma, with
more or less fulvous tinting in the disc of the FW.

Genus Atrytonopsis *Godman*

THREE SPECIES occur in our area, fairly easily distinguished from
each other, but apt to be confused with other dull brown skippers.
In general *Atrytonopsis* are medium sized, fairly dark brown, with
a number of small, whitish spots on the FW and at least one on the
HW beneath.   One or two spots occur in the end of the cell of the
FW, and one consistently on the HW beneath near the base, above
the cell.   The whole HW and the outer margin of the FW beneath
are more or less dusted with gray; otherwise there are no mottlings,
marblings, or bandings.   ♀♀ have more and larger white spots than
♂♂.   ♂♂ have more pointed FW than ♀♀.   On the HW beneath
there is a postmedian, curved row of spots.   All, or none, of these
may be white; but they always show as at least faint dark spots.
Of this row the spot in cell M_2 (at the end of the cell) is double, and
the upper spot or part of the doublet is strongly "offset" out toward
the outer margin of the wing.

LOAMMI SKIPPER.   *Atrytonopsis loammi* Whitney   pp. 257
1.2–1.35 in.   The number and size of the whitish spots on the
FW are variable.   On the HW beneath, however, the spots are
definitely white, opaque and quite constant.   Most characteristic are the three near the base.   There is also a curved, postmedian row.

Range: — Florida, March, April, October; North Carolina, July.

DUSTED SKIPPER.   *Atrytonopsis hianna* Scudder pp. 257, 289
1.2–1.35 in.   *Hianna* is more difficult to characterize than *loammi*.   The spots of the FW are variable.   Beneath, the wings are
more heavily dusted with gray on the entire HW and the outer
margin of the FW.   The HW consistently has a single, whitish
spot near the base, just above the cell; but the other basal spots
found in *loammi* are usually represented only as indistinct, dark
spots.   In some specimens, however, all of the spots are present,

large and white, except the basal ones in and below the cell. The
life history is not known. There seems to be one brood in the
north, but perhaps two in Maryland. I have taken it only in
dry open fields.

Range: — Southern New England s. to North Carolina and
Georgia, w. to Nebraska.

TURNER'S SKIPPER. *Atrytonopsis turneri* H. A. Freeman
1.2–1.4 in. Resembles *hianna* in largely lacking white spots on
the HW beneath; most specimens have the wing unspotted, a
few have one or two light spots near the base, and a few have a
faint, submarginal row of spots. It is, however, gray-brown
above where *hianna* is brown, and beneath is much grayer.

Range: — Barber Co. (TL) & Caldwell, Kansas and Freedom,
Oklahoma, May.

TWIN SPOT SKIPPER. *Oligoria maculata* Edwards   p. 257
1.2–1.3 in. The wings are more uniform and unshaded dark
brown, both above and beneath, than in most similar skippers.
Beneath, the whole of the HW down to the anal veins, and the
costal margin and apex of the FW, are a warmer, more chocolate brown. The wings, especially the outer margin of the FW,
are more rounded than in related genera such as *Atrytonopsis*,
Lerema, and *Panoquina*. Most distinctive are the creamy white
spots on the HW beneath; one large, or double spot is in cell M_1;
there is none in cell M_2 at the end of the discal cell; and there is
one each in cells M_3 and Cu_1, close together.

Larva: — Slender, pale green, finely pubescent, the last two
segments deeper green; head oval, oblique, densely pubescent,
slightly granulated, light brown; thoracic shield lighter brown.

Food: — Presumably grass. At least two broods in Florida.

Range: — Florida (common) to Georgia and Alabama; strays to
New York, Massachusetts, and Texas.

CLOUDED SKIPPER. *Lerema accius* Abbot & Smith pp. 257, 289
1.1–1.3 in. *Accius* is quite local, from southern New England
southward, occurring in dry, open fields and meadows. Its flight
is low; and it shelters in the grass when alarmed. ♂♂ have a well-
developed but inconspicuous stigma, and very small, but usually
distinct, white spots on the FW. ♀♀ have the spots much larger,
clearly glassy white. Most distinctive is the violet-gray shading
beneath; on the FW there is a patch on the outer margin below
the apex, broadest in cells M_1 and M_2; on the HW there is a broad
outer border of the violet-gray; inside this is a dark brown shade,
widest at the costa and tapering posteriorly; inside this a broad
antemedian, violet-gray shade, running to the anal margin and
spreading out along it. The fringes are light, checkered with
dark spots at the ends of the veins.

Larva: — Slender, nearly white, mottled with very fine darker

lines and points, rings on posterior half of each segment more
prominent and less dotted; head small, flattened frontally, white
with a black band around top and sides, a black streak down
middle of face, and a short, black streak on either side of this.
Food: — Grasses, e.g., Woolly Beard Grass (*Erianthus alope-
curoides*), also "Indian Corn" (*Zea mays*) and (very dubious)
"Wistaria." Probably two broods in north and three in south,
hibernating as pupa in north.
Range: — Massachusetts s. through Florida, w. to Illinois and
Texas; s. through Central America; rare in northern states.

Genus Amblyscirtes *Scudder*

FOURTEEN SPECIES of *Amblyscirtes* occur in the eastern area, the
majority in the southern Mississippi Valley and Texas. All are
small, dark brown to brownish black, with fine, whitish spots on
the FW and sometimes the HW. In nearly all, the fringes are
whitish and checkered with dark spots at the ends of the veins. In
most, the wings are quite plain beneath, the HW and the apex of
the FW dusted with light gray and the HW with more light spots
beneath than above; but some have very decided patterns beneath.
There is practically no sexual dimorphism. A number of the species are extremely similar to one another, and are best distinguished
by the genitalia, although even these "run close." The key given
below will serve for identification of most of the species, and for
well marked, characteristic specimens of all; but inevitably a good
many specimens will be encountered that will puzzle all but the
"skipper specialists." See also *Yvretta simius*.

1. Fringes not distinctly checkered...................... 2
1. Fringes distinctly checkered........................... 3
2. Spots on wings above prominent and distinctly yellow;
beneath, HW and apex and costal margin of FW pale yellow,
the HW checkered with darker, brownish yellow; eastern .*carolina*
2. Spots on wings above very faint; HW beneath dull brown,
gray dusted, with indistinct pale spots; western........... *oslari*
3. HW beneath olivaceous or greenish-gray dusted; eastern... *hegon*
3. HW beneath brownish or gray-dusted, with no suggestion
of greenish... 4
4. Light spots on HW beneath connected by prominent pale
lines along veins..................................... *textor*
4. Spots on HW beneath not connected by pale lines along
veins, and veins not distinctly whitish................. 5
5. HW beneath with sharply defined, rounded spots, whitish,
these more or less dark-ringed......................... *eos*
5. HW beneath with light spots, if present, diffuse and not
sharply outlined, and irregular in shape................ 6
5. HW beneath strongly mottled, with large, dark and light-
dusted areas.. *nysa*

6. HW beneath lacking pale spots; or, if vague ones are present, they are along the border between a dark, basal area and a contrastingly light-dusted, outer area, often violet gray.... *vialis*

6. HW beneath with definite pale spots, these sometimes quite inconspicuous.. 7

7. Spots of FW above definitely yellowish to fulvous......... 8

7. Spots of FW above white or whitish, not distinctly yellow 11

8. FW above with a small light spot in end of cell........... 9

8. FW above with no light spot in end of cell............... 10

9. FW beneath with cell area strongly tinted with fulvous.... *ænus*

9. FW beneath with little if any fulvous in cell area........ *texanæ*

10. Wings above with considerable fulvous overscaling over entire surface, and no light spots other than two or three indistinct subapical ones; HW beneath evenly dusted with light scales but with very indistinct light markings, if any.. *erna*

10. Wings above with fulvous overscaling sparser and more restricted to basal and, on HW, discal areas; FW above with light subapical spots more consistently present, sometimes others as well; HW beneath evenly dusted with light scales, with well-developed light spots as well, although these are sometimes partly obliterated by light scaling............. *linda*

11. Wings beneath warmer brown, with light dusting very sparse and unevenly distributed; FW more produced apically, so that outer margin is proportionately longer; fringes very white; size smaller (0.90 in. or less); South Atlantic and Gulf States..*alternata*

11. Wings beneath colder, sootier brown; light dusting beneath less sparse and more evenly distributed; FW not produced apically so as to make its outer margin relatively long; fringes not noticeably white; larger (0.90 in. or more); Arkansas and Texas... 12

12. Lighter brown above; FW above often with a spot in end of cell; wings beneath more heavily light-dusted; spots on HW beneath more prominent, white......................... *celia*

12. Darker brown above; FW above never with spot in end of cell; wings beneath more sparsely light-dusted; spots on HW beneath less conspicuous, dark gray, and hoary, sometimes nearly absent................................. *belli*

ROADSIDE SKIPPER. *Amblyscirtes vialis* Edwards pp. 288, 304 0.8–1.1 in. *Vialis* is the most common and widely distributed species of our area. It is chiefly distinguished by the lilac or violet gray clouding on the outer half of the HW and the outer, apical portion of the FW beneath; and the lack of whitish spots on the HW beneath. The fringes are very strongly checkered. Like other members of the genus it visits flowers freely, and also alights frequently on stones and bare earth. Its resting action is peculiar, the wings being held out at the sides at an angle, and the antennæ waved alternately in small circles.

Larva: — Pale green, profusely dotted with pale green dots at the bases of the very short, downy hairs; head dull, frosted white with vertical, reddish stripes, rough-surfaced. Food: — Grasses, e.g., *Poa pratensis* and *Avena striata*. One brood in north, two

or more in south.   Hibernation as pupa.   Adults in late May
(Massachusetts).
Range: — Southern Canada, Maritime Provinces westward, s.
to Florida and Texas (not in Rio Grande Valley); w. to Pacific
Coast.

PEPPER AND SALT SKIPPER. *Amblyscirtes hegon* Scudder

p. 304
0.8–1.1 in.   Like *vialis*, *hegon* ranges widely in our area.   It is
much less common than *vialis*, and more northern.   The HW
beneath is heavily and coarsely dusted with light, greenish gray
on a dark background; the postmedian row of light spots is well
developed, and frequently, in part at least, confluent to form a
thin, irregular band.   *Hegon* is perhaps more associated with the
forest than *vialis*.
Larva: — Very pale green; a slender, darker green dorsal line,
and a darker line below the spiracles; head pale, the sutures
and eyespots reddish; thoracic shield short and black.   **Food:** —
Grasses. One brood in north, supposedly two southward.   Adults
in early April (West Virginia) to early June (Massachusetts).
Range: — Southeastern Canada to Georgia (chiefly in mountains)
w. to Manitoba and Iowa.   One wonders if Georgia and Texas
records may not be of some other species.

CAROLINA ROADSIDE SKIPPER. *Amblyscirtes carolina*
Skinner   pp. 288, 305
0.8–1.1 in.   Easily recognized by the pale, yellowish, and definitely checkered looking HW beneath.   The light spots above are
very yellow.   The stigma of the ♂ is very large and conspicuous
for an *Amblyscirtes*.   An interesting color variety, *reversa*, has the
HW beneath dark with the checkerings light.
Range: — Swamps and marshes in Coastal Plain; Georgia to
Virginia.

TEXTOR SKIPPER. *Amblyscirtes textor* Huebner   pp. 288, 305
1.0–1.2 in.   Somewhat larger than other *Amblyscirtes*, *textor* is
easily recognized by the weblike appearance of the markings of
the HW beneath.   The veins are prominently light; and the
transverse spot rows, connected to form irregular, narrow lines,
intersect these.
Range: — Virginia s. to Georgia and w. to Texas.

LEAST FLORIDA SKIPPER. *Amblyscirtes alternata* Grote &
Robinson   p. 304
0.75–0.9 in.   Another species of the Coastal Plain.   Its small size,
broader but not rounded FW and very sparse, irregular dusting
beneath, distinguish it.   The light spots on the HW beneath are
mere groups of light scales, with no sharp or consistent outline.
Range: — North Carolina s. through Florida, w. to Alabama.

BELL'S ROADSIDE RAMBLER. *Amblyscirtes belli* Freeman

p. 304

1.0–1.1 in. *Belli* always lacks a light spot in the cell of the FW; is rather dark; has quite sparse light dusting on the HW beneath, as well as inconspicuous light spots; and has the stigma of the ♂ very inconspicuous. It ranges rather widely in the south; probably some old records of *"vialis"* from Georgia to Texas were of this species.

Range: — Northern Georgia to Missouri, Arkansas, Oklahoma, and Texas (Dallas).

LINDA'S ROADSIDE SKIPPER. *Amblyscirtes linda* H. A. Freeman

p. 304

1.0–1.1 in. *Linda* is another small, dark species of the lower Mississippi Valley. The light spots of the FW above are yellowish; the cell area of the FW beneath has considerable fulvous scaling; the wings above have some fulvous overscaling basally on both, and discally as well on the HW; and the HW beneath are fairly heavily and evenly dusted with light scales, sometimes enough to partly obliterate the light spots.

Range: — Arkansas (May, June); Oklahoma (August, September).

ERNA'S ROADSIDE SKIPPER. *Amblyscirtes erna* H. A. Freeman

1.0–1.1 in. *Erna* enters our area only in Texas. The generally distributed, fulvous overscaling on the wings above gives it a slightly "brassy" appearance like that of *A. œnus*. From *œnus* it may be distinguished by the greater reduction of all light spots and by the lack of the reddish-fulvous tinting in the cell area of the FW beneath that marks *œnus*.

Range: — Texas (Palo Duro Canyon, Palo Pinto, and Miami; April–August).

BRONZE ROADSIDE SKIPPER. *Amblyscirtes œnus* Edwards

1.0–1.2 in. Characterized by the distinct, "brassy" luster of the wings above, caused by rather heavy, fulvous overscaling, and by the distinct, reddish-fulvous coloration of the cell area of the FW beneath.

Range: — In eastern area, Kansas, Oklahoma, and Texas (May, June, August); essentially a species of the plains and westward.

CELIA'S ROADSIDE SKIPPER. *Amblyscirtes celia* Skinner

0.9–1.1 in. The FW above usually has a light spot in the end of the cell, and the spots of the postmedian row present, although sometimes small. The HW beneath is evenly but rather sparsely and roughly powdered with gray; the basal and postmedian spots are plain, but individually irregular and not clear-cut.

Range: — In eastern area, widely distributed in southern Texas, San Antonio to Brownsville, flying throughout the year.

TEXAS ROADSIDE SKIPPER. *Amblyscirtes texanæ* Bell
0.9–1.1 in. *Texanæ* is quite noticeably paler, more fulvous tinged above than most other *Amblyscirtes*, the wings being heavily overscaled. Some specimens show a quite distinctly brighter, but diffuse, fulvous patch in the disc of the HW above. The light spots of the FW above are yellow, and there is consistently one of these in the cell.
Range: — In eastern area, Texas (Palo Duro Canyon, White Deer; May).

OSLAR'S ROADSIDE SKIPPER. *Amblyscirtes oslari* Skinner
1.0–1.15 in. Distinctly fulvous brown above, because of a heavy overscaling, *oslari* largely lacks light spots, both above and beneath. The gray dusting beneath is drab; it covers the HW, but leaves the discal region of the FW fulvous brown. *Oslari* is a widespread Rocky Mountain and western plains species that has been recorded from Caldwell, Kansas; Freedom, Oklahoma; and Palo Duro Canyon and White Deer, Texas (April–June).

EOS ROADSIDE SKIPPER. *Amblyscirtes eos* Edwards   p. 304
0.8–1.0 in. *Eos* is easily recognized by the whiteness of the spots and fringes, and by the large size and rounded and distinct shape of the spots of the HW beneath; these spots are rendered still more distinct by thin dark edges.
Range: — In eastern area, Texas (Palo Duro Canyon, Palo Pinto, Dallas; April–June, August–September). At least two broods.

NYSA ROADSIDE SKIPPER. *Amblyscirtes nysa* Edwards
0.8–0.9 in. *Nysa* is very nysally distinguished from other *Amblyscirtes* of our area by the distinctive underside pattern. On the HW are four large, dark patches; a square one slightly before mid-costa; another squarish one below the end of the cell; a marginal one in cells M_3 and Cu_1; and an apical one at the margin below veins R_3 and M_1. Between these the wing is variously colored with lighter, yellow brown or thickly powdered or irrorated with white.
Range: — In eastern area, Texas (common) n. into Kansas (Caldwell, common) May–June.

Genus Lerodea *Scudder*

OUR SPECIES of *Lerodea* are small to medium sized, brownish gray to dark brown, with small, whitish spots on the FW, or with these spots reduced or absent. The HW beneath are unmarked, dusted with pale scales in most of the species; or show pale and dark, transverse bands in others. Most of the species are so close to each other in color and pattern, and intergrade so greatly, that study of the rather distinctive male genitalia is essential for careful work. The key given below points out average differences in color and pattern; *but is not to be trusted* for perhaps half the specimens of such species as *julia*, *neamathla*, *l'herminieri* and *eufala*. The species are southern or tropical, but two range northward casually to New York and Iowa. The pupa has a long, slender, sharp, frontal horn.

1. HW beneath with transverse, dark and light patches or bands.. 2
1. HW beneath uniformly colored, with at most only faintly indicated, light, discal spots........................... 3
2. Size small (0.9 in. or less); end of harpe with a single long, slender, pointed projection............................ *tyrtæa*
2. Size larger (1.0 in. or more); end of harpe with a prominent dorsal projection that bears fine teeth along its flat, expanded edge .... *edata*
3. Color light gray-brown; spots on FW, if present, partly hyaline; end of harpe with two long, slender, rounded, fingerlike projections.. *eufala*
3. Color darker fuscous brown or olivaceous brown; end of harpe with one or two projections; if the latter, both are not rounded and fingerlike.............................. 4
4. FW nearly immaculate above, sometimes with faint traces of spots on disc; end of harpe with a single, very short, rounded projection.. *l'herminieri*
4. FW usually more distinctly spotted; end of harpe with a prominent projection at dorsal angle that bears fine teeth along its expanded edge.............................. 5
5. Spots of FW larger and clearly defined; HW beneath smoother, less dusted and powdery looking; toothed projection of harpe pointing more to rear, not bent dorsad..... *tripuncta*
5. Spots of FW smaller and less clearly defined; HW beneath more dusted and powdery looking; toothed projection bent dorsad... 6
6. Color lighter, with lighter, yellowish overscaling above and more ochreous overscaling beneath; light spots somewhat larger; toothed projection at end of harpe bent strongly dorsad; no separate, projecting lobe below this; Texas.... *julia*
6. Color darker, with darker overscaling above and beneath; light spots less prominent; end of harpe with toothed projection not bent so strongly dorsad, and with a short, projecting rounded lobe below this; Florida to Missouri (?).. *neamathla*

SWARTHY SKIPPER. *Lerodea l'herminieri* Latreille p. 305
0.8–1.0 in. The Swarthy Skipper is distinguished chiefly by its lack of distinguishing characteristics. It is merely a small, dark brownish gray Skipper with olivaceous dusting on the HW beneath, the veins slightly lighter and the anal region undusted.

Faint traces of light spots may appear on the FW above. If you
have a specimen that looks as neutral, dull, drab and undistinguished as possible, think of *l'herminieri*! It is better known in
the literature as *fusca* Grote and Robinson. Not uncommon in
the south, it ranges widely northward. It flies low, in meadows.
Range: — Florida and Texas n. to New York and Missouri.

EUFALA SKIPPER. *Lerodea eufala* Edwards   p. 305
0.9–1.1 in. *Eufala* averages somewhat lighter above than *l'herminieri*, with fairly consistently prominent, white, partly hyaline, spots on the FW, and a more even dusting on the HW beneath that is not so olivaceous or coarse, and does not leave the
veins somewhat lighter. It is common and widely distributed in
the south, and ranges, rarely or spasmodically, far northward.
Larva: — Vivid grass green, covered with small, black papillæ
bearing short hairs; a dark green, dorsal line bordered with yellow
blotching; a similar stripe above the stigmata, and another below
this; segmental creases bright yellow; head whitish with orange
brown stripes. Pupa with long, slender, frontal horn. **Food:** —
Grasses; reared once from Alfalfa. One brood in north, perhaps
two in south. Adults in April and September (Florida); late
August (Kansas); September (Iowa).
Range: — Florida to Texas, n. to Virginia and Iowa and Nebraska.

NEAMATHLA SKIPPER. *Lerodea neamathla* Skinner & Williams
                                                     p. 305
0.8–1.0 in. The spots are usually a trifle more prominent than in
l'herminieri, and less distinct than in *julia;* but practically all
identifications should be checked by the genitalia. The recent
description of *julia* from Texas makes it doubtful whether old
records of *neamathla* from the Gulf States, Texas, and north to
Missouri refer to it or to *julia.*
Range: — Florida, probably Georgia, perhaps Gulf States and
Texas. At least two broods (Florida, March, May, September).

JULIA'S SKIPPER. *Lerodea julia* H. A. Freeman   p. 305
0.9–1.1 in. *Julia* is distinguished from *neamathla* by the characters cited in the key; but checking by the genitalia is essential.
Range: — Southern Texas, widely distributed, flying all year.

THREE SPOTTED SKIPPER. *Lerodea tripuncta* Herrich-
Schæffer   p. 305
0.9–1.1 in. *Tripuncta* averages darker brown than *eufala*, and
has more conspicuous spots than *neamathla;* but the averages
break down in many specimens   It appears to be definitely established, but rare, in southern Florida. Authentic records are
Florida City and Miami, June and August, November. **Food:** —
Sugar Cane (Cuba).

TYRTÆA SKIPPER. *Lerodea tyrtæa* Plötz
EDATA SKIPPER. *Lerodea edata* Plötz

Tyrtæa 0.75–0.9 in., *edata* 0.9–1.1 in. Both of these species are well established in the lower Rio Grande Valley, Texas, where they fly throughout the year. *Tyrtæa* is quite limited to areas under the shade of tropical vegetation. They are quite different from the other *Lerodea* of our area in having a definite pattern of dark and light banding on the HW beneath. The color above is a somewhat warmer brown. They are best differentiated by size and the genitalia; *tyrtæa* is very much the smaller of the two; is, in fact, the smallest of our *Lerodea*. Both range southward through Mexico.

Genera Calpodes *Huebner*, Panoquina *Hemming*, and Nyctelius *Hayward*

THE GENERIC classification in this section of the Skippers is very confused. Perhaps of our species only *ethlius* really belongs in *Calpodes*, *panoquin* and *panoquinoides* in *Panoquina*, and the others here included in at least one other genus beside *Nyctelius*. All of the species have the FW rather narrow and produced apically and the HW produced at the anal angle. Most of the species have rather large, at least semi-hyaline, spots on the FW. The lack of knowledge of past authors regarding some of the distinctions between species makes many records dubious; so that we cannot be sure about the occurrence of *hecebolus*, *sylvicola*, and *nyctelius* in North America at all. Most identifications must be checked by the genitalia.

1. HW with prominent hyaline white spots, showing more strongly above than beneath; size large (1.75–2.0 in.)....*C. ethlius*
1. HW dark above, with no prominent light spots showing.... 2
2. Size large (1.50 in. or more)..........................*C. evansi*
2. Size smaller (1.25 in. or less).......................... 3
3. HW beneath with a prominent light streak outward from end of cell, sometimes another streak below this; veins conspicuously lighter; salt marshes of coast.............*P. panoquin*
3. HW beneath unmarked, or with spots or transverse bands, but with no prominent longitudinal streaks.............. 4
4. FW above with light spots yellowish, small, and inconspicuous, sometimes absent; upper surface heavily overlaid with tawny scales; size small (1.0 in. or less).........*P. panoquinoides*
4. FW above with light spots larger and more conspicuous, whitish and semihyaline, rarely greatly reduced; upper surface little overlaid with tawny scales, browner and more lustrous; size larger (1.1 in. or more)................... 5

5. FW above with no light spots or streaks in end of cell; HW beneath dark, unmarked; widespread in south..........*P. ocola*

5. FW above with one or two light spots or streaks in end of cell; species in extreme south only...................... 6

6. HW beneath dark and unicolorous, with at most a very faint trace of postmedian light spots...............*P. hecebolus*

6. HW beneath with a definite transverse, submarginal row of whitish spots; anterior part of HW beneath with more or less bluish luster; largest spot of FW above (below end of cell) elongate, notched externally, tapering internally..*P. sylvicola*

6. HW beneath lighter yellowish basally, with broad, transverse median dark band, lighter limbally; FW above with largest spot (below end of cell) squarish.............*N. nyctelius*

BRAZILIAN SKIPPER. *Calpodes ethlius* Stoll   p. 320
1.8–2.25 in. A common, large species of the deep south which rarely ranges far northward. The adults have a fast and powerful flight; they are best taken at flowers, which they visit freely. The larvæ feed on Cannas; sometimes they are abundant enough to be destructive. The large size and prominent hyaline spots of the HW are distinctive.

Larva: — Very translucent grayish green; a whitish line on each side of the dorsum; spiracles narrowly black rimmed, surrounded by brownish, cloudy blotches; head orange, the upper part of the frontal triangle, the ocellar band and the mandibles black.
Food: — Cannas of various species (*flaccida, indica*). Probably three or more broods in south.
Range: — South America, n. to South Carolina and Texas (breeding), straying or introduced on occasion north to Missouri and New York.

EVANS' SKIPPER. *Calpodes evansi* H. A. Freeman
1.50–1.75 in. Recently named from Pharr, Texas, and Mexico, *evansi* has in the past been confused with *P. sylvicola* (below). From *ethlius*, the only other species approaching it in size, it is distinguished by its lighter coloration as well as by the lack of hyaline white spots on the HW. Its larger size distinguishes it from *sylvicola;* in addition it has the transverse, light spots of the HW beneath broadened and diffuse so as to form a pale shade, more conspicuous than the narrower spot row of *sylvicola*.
Range: — Pharr, Texas (October) s. in Mexico.

SALT MARSH SKIPPER. *Panoquina panoquin* Scudder
                                              pp. 289, 320
1.0–1.25 in. The prominent, longitudinal, pale dash or dashes and the conspicuously lighter veins on the HW beneath are distinctive. *Panoquin* is more strikingly limited to salt and brackish marshes than any other butterfly in our area. Its flight is fairly fast, but not unusually so for a skipper; at times it may even be rather sluggish. It visits flowers freely, and may then be

netted easily. It is quite common north to New Jersey. Two broods in New Jersey (June–September) probably more in south. **Range:** — Alabama and Florida n. to New Jersey.

OBSCURE SKIPPER. *Panoquina panoquinoides* Skinner p. 320
0.8–1.0 in. *Panoquinoides* is, like *Lerodea l'herminieri,* difficult to characterize or identify because it is so lacking in character. There are usually some rather faint yellowish spots on the FW above, and two to four whitish, postmedian ones on the HW beneath; and the veins of the HW beneath are usually somewhat lined with lighter fulvous than the ground color. But I have taken specimens with not a mark on them. The upper side is usually rather heavily overscaled with fulvous. It is not uncommon along the Florida coast north to Titusville (April to July to November), occurs in the Antilles and Central America as well, and has been recorded from Texas.

OCOLA SKIPPER. *Panoquina ocola* Edwards p. 320
1.1–1.35 in. *Ocola* is common, at times abundant, in the south and ranges quite far northward. Although its flight is fast and erratic, it is easily caught at flowers. When resting it holds the wings close together over the back with the FW pulled away down inside the HW. The almost completely unmarked HW beneath, and the lack of a light spot in the cell of the FW above, with a general tendency to smaller light spots, distinguish it from the following three species. It must have three broods in Florida, perhaps less northward.
Range: — Florida and Texas n. to New York, Ohio, and Indiana, casual northward.

SYLVICOLA SKIPPER. *Panoquina sylvicola* Herrich-Schæffer
1.2–1.45 in. There are many records of this species from both Florida and Texas. Mr. Bell tells me, however, that it may not even occur in our limits; hence many or all of these records may be of the next species, *hecebolus* Scudder. Some careful study and identification of authentic specimens are badly needed.

HECEBOLUS SKIPPER. *Panoquina hecebolus* Scudder p. 320
1.2–1.45 in. Formerly regarded as a synonym of *P. ocola, hecebolus* is now believed to be a valid, but close, species. As noted above, it is possible that many or all of the records of "*P. sylvicola*" from the United States are really of *hecebolus.* From *ocola, hecebolus* may be distinguished by the presence of a small, but definite, light spot in the cell of the FW. From the true *sylvicola* it may be told by its dark unmarked HW beneath, in which it resembles *ocola*.

NYCTELIUS SKIPPER. *Nyctelius nyctelius* Latreille
1.1–1.3 in. *Nyctelius* is distinguished from its otherwise rather

similar congeners by the squarish shape of the large spot on the FW, and by the bicolored, banded lower surface of the HW. It is well established in southern Texas (Brownsville, San Antonio, May, September–December).

THE MONK. *Asbolis capucinus* Lucas

1.45–1.60 in. This well-known Antillean skipper appeared around Miami, Florida, in 1947–48 in numbers, probably as a result of an introduction, and seems to be well established. Specific records are in September (Florence Grimshawe) and July (Klots). It is very heavy bodied, and has a fast, strong flight, but visits flowers eagerly. I took one specimen so thickly dusted with orchid pollenia that on the wing it looked bright orange-brown. Wings above very dark but warm brown, the ♂ with a very thin, curved, pale stigma clearly divided by Cu_2; FW with some basal fulvous shading. HW beneath coarsely dusted with chestnut and pale scales except for a dark, submarginal shade up from anal angle inside inner margin. FW beneath similarly dusted apically; basally and discally blackish, with a light postmedian patch below Cu_2. Fringes yellowish brown. *A. sandarac* H.-S. is a synonymous name.

MALICIOUS SKIPPER. *Synapte malitiosa* Herrich-Schæffer

p. 320

1.0–1.2 in. I do not know what flight of fancy caused the specific name of this little skipper. It is rather drab, dark brown, slender bodied with broad wings, with a fulvous shade below and outside the cell of the FW above, and a more indistinct fulvous shade on the disc of the HW; both these are crossed by dark veins. Beneath, the fulvous areas are repeated, less distinctly; the HW are somewhat mottled and dusted with yellowish; and a dark patch runs from the costal margin to about two thirds way to the middle of the anal margin.

Range: — Southern Texas (Pharr and Brownsville, April–May, August–December).

DOLORES' SKIPPER. *Perichares philetes dolores* Reakirt

p. 240

1.45–1.6 in. Superficially this skipper looks much more like a member of the *Pyrginæ*, but vein M_2 of the FW is strongly curved basally and arises from the cell much closer to M_3 than to M_1. Dark brown above; FW with two large, joined spots in end of cell, four others between cell and outer margin, all hyaline yellowish. Beneath, HW and subapical region of FW mottled and more or less transversely banded with lilac gray-brown. Fringes yellowish, with brown checkerings at end of veins. Strays into our area from Mexico (Pharr, Texas, November and December).

SKIPPERS
Family *Hesperiidae*

All illustrations are × 1 (natural size)

Plate 34 273

SKIPPERS
Family *Hesperiidae*

All illustrations are × 1 (natural size)

1. LAURENTIAN SKIPPER, *Hesperia laurentina*   p. 242
   Upper & under sides, ♂ (Rangeley, Me.) HW beneath bright yellow to green, with clear, sharp spots. SE. Can. to Me. & Minn.
2. LAURENTIAN SKIPPER, *Hesperia laurentina*   p. 242
   Upper side, ♀ (Bar Harbor, Me.) See ♂, above.
3. LEONARDUS SKIPPER, *Hesperia leonardus*   p. 237
   Upper side, ♀ (Coram, L.I.). See ♂, fig. 6 below.
4. INDIAN SKIPPER, *Hesperia sassacus*   p. 238
   Upper & under sides, ♂ (Sharon, Conn.) Bright colors; HW beneath very yellow. See also ♀, Pl. 30. Me. to Iowa, s. to Fla.
5. UNCAS' SKIPPER, *Hesperia uncas*   p. 242
   Under side, ♂ (Golden, Colo.) HW beneath with black outlining the sharp, white spots. Great Plains.
6. LEONARDUS SKIPPER, *Hesperia leonardus*   p. 237
   Upper & under sides, (Bedford, N.Y.) HW beneath reddish; with distinct light spots. Me. to Iowa, s. to Fla. & Kans.
7. FIERY SKIPPER, *Hylephila phyleus*   p. 243
   Upper & under sides, ♂ (Bainbridge, Ga.) Large areas of bright yellow-orange; dark triangles along margins; spotted pattern of HW beneath. Conn., Mich. & Nebr. southward.
8. GREEN SKIPPER, *Hesperia viridis*   p. 242
   Under side, ♂ (Plainview, Colo.) HW beneath green; position of its white spots (see text). Great Plains westward.
9. THE WHIRLABOUT, *Polites vibex*   p. 247
   Upper & under sides, ♂ (Cowarts, Ala.) Darker above than *phyleus* with heavier pattern of dark spots beneath. Conn. & Ark. southward. See ♀, Pl. 30.
10. THE SACHEM, *Atalopedes campestris*   p. 243
    Upper & under sides, ♂ (Tampa, Fla.) Large; heavy dark patch on stigma; HW beneath (see text). N.Y. & N.D. south- & westward.
11. PAWNEE SKIPPER, *Hesperia pawnee*   p. 242
    Under side, ♂ (Redvers, Sask.) HW beneath unmarked; above very like *ottoë*; see text. Western; Great Plains.
12. OTTOE SKIPPER, *Hesperia ottoë*   p. 239
    Upper side, ♂ (Omaha, Nebr.). See text. Western.
13. CROSS LINE SKIPPER, *Polites manataaqua*   p. 245
    Upper & under sides, ♂ (Ramsey, N.J.) Very like *themistocles* (Pl. 35), larger & darker; see text. South to Ga. & Ark.
14. CROSS LINE SKIPPER, *Polites manataaqua*   p. 245
    Upper side, ♀ (Mobile, Ala.) See ♂, above.
15. BROKEN DASH, *Wallengrenia otho*   p. 248
    Upper & under sides, ♂ (Port Sewall, Fla.) Broken stigma of ♂; indistinct spots on HW beneath; see text. S. Can. southward.

Family *Megathymidæ:* The Giant Skippers

THE *Megathymidæ* are a small family of very large Skippers with life histories that set them apart from the *Hesperiidæ*. The larvæ bore in the stems or leaf bases of various species of Yucca (Spanish Bayonet, Bear Grass, Adam's Needle) or Agave. The adults are very large, hairy and powerful. Their flight is exceedingly swift and strong. Best collecting is done by finding the larval workings in Yucca, evidenced by accumulations of the larva's droppings, and rearing the larvæ through. The adults are said to gather sometimes at moist places to drink, and to be more easily collected then. Mating flights have been described in late afternoon or at dusk. The pupa has abdominal segments freely movable, and so is able to move along the burrow to a prepared exit hole, which was used earlier by the larva for disposal of droppings. When disturbed it flees to the far end of its burrow. The classification of the subspecies is still not too clear, due to lack of proper amounts of study material; and much life history work remains to be done.

1. On HW beneath the more basal of two white spots below costal margin is the larger; and only very small or rudimentary postmedian white spots are present; southeast and southwest.. *yuccæ*
1. On HW beneath the more basal of two white spots below costal margin is the smaller; and a well developed, or at least a more or less complete, postmedian row of white spots is present.. 2
2. HW beneath smoothly tinted, limbally and often discally powdered with bluish gray; but scarcely ever, if at all, with this gray along costal margin and apex; smaller; southeast only.. *cofaqui*
2. HW beneath coarsely and unevenly colored, gray dusting strongest limbally and along costa, often weak discally so that central area is darker; western.................... 3
3. Yellow spots above large; HW beneath with postmedian light spots greatly reduced or absent; southwestern only.. *texana*
3. Spots above greatly reduced; HW beneath with postmedian light spots large and prominent; Mexico, strays into Texas.. *smithi*

YUCCA SKIPPER. *Megathymus yuccæ* Boisduval & Leconte

p. 321

1.75–3.25 in. As with other *Megathymus*, ♂♂ are smaller than females, and occasional dwarfs occur. The life history is outlined in the genus discussion. There is but one brood.
Range: — South Carolina through Florida, w. to Kansas, Oklahoma, Texas, and westward.
Subspecies: — *M. y. yuccæ* South Carolina through Florida;

large; ground color above deep brown; wings broad; spots above deep, orange yellow. *M. y. alabamæ* H. A. Freeman (TL Anniston, Alabama); Alabama and parts of Georgia; smaller; wings above darker, blackish brown; wings broad; spots above lighter yellow than *yuccæ*. *M. y. stallingsi* H. A. Freeman (TL Caldwell, Kansas); Kansas, Oklahoma, and Texas; nearly as large as *yuccæ*; wings above still darker, black; wings narrower; spots above deeper yellow than *alabamæ*, not as deep as *yuccæ*; HW beneath with both subcostal spots large, white and crescentic, and postmedian spots larger than *alabamæ*. An east-west clinal variation is suggested.

COFAQUI SKIPPER. *Megathymus cofaqui* Strecker   p. 321
1.25–2.5 in. The very evenly and smoothly tinted HW beneath and the generally paler brown color, are the *cofaqui* characters. I have seen a dwarf ♂ with an expanse of less than an inch. The life history is as yet unknown, despite much investigation of Yucca.
Range: — Georgia and Florida; March and April.

GIANT TEXAS SKIPPER. *Megathymus texana* Barnes & McDunnough   p. 321
1.75–3.3 in. The large *texana* is perhaps a distinct species, not a subspecies of the more western *M. streckeri* as formerly supposed. *M. leussleri* Holland may be a synonym of *texana* or a subspecies of *streckeri*. The HW beneath is very much more irregularly tinted and dusted with gray than in *cofaqui*, and nearly always has the costal margin very light gray.
Range: — In eastern area, Texas (Dallas); n. to Nebraska just w. of our area, probably strays in.

SMITH'S GIANT SKIPPER. *Megathymus smithi* Druce
Rare even in Mexico, recorded once from our area, Corpus Christi, Texas, no date.

SECTION 2

Casual and Stray Species and False or Dubious Records

It has seemed best to treat separately most of the species which, because of their accidental nature in our area, will scarcely ever trouble the average collector. Nearly all of these are tropical or western. Species that definitely and consistently belong and breed in the eastern area, no matter how rare they may be, have been included in the main section.

Evaluating old, often vague records has not always been easy. Many species have been recorded as occurring in Texas or Florida. Some such records have proved to be true, but others have proved erroneous. Sometimes I have had to base judgement as much on knowledge about the sources of the records as on the butterflies themselves. Some of the records on dealers' specimens of a generation ago are known to have been deliberately falsified for the purpose of selling so-called North American specimens to collectors. The recent thorough collecting of Freeman, Stallings, Turner, and others in Texas, and of Mrs. Forsyth, Mrs. Grimshawe, Mr. Berry and others in southern Florida has done much to clarify doubtful records of "tropicals." I have also kept in mind that in some cases a species may be introduced, occur in small numbers for a while, and then die out; and that this may happen more than once with the same species.

Family *Danaidæ*

Lycorella ceres Cramer (*cleobæa* auct.) 3.3–3.7 in., a large, banded, black, brown and yellow Danaid common in the tropics, has been recorded as "Texas and the Keys of Florida." I have seen one valid specimen, which emerged from a pupa found in Miami (21 April, F. M. G.). This is apparently the Antillean race, *demeter* Felder & Felder. Texas specimens would be the continental race *atergatis* Doubleday. **Food:** — Fig (*Ficus*).

Dircenna klugii Geyer and **Ithomia anaphissa** Herrich-Schæffer have both been recorded vaguely from the United States. I think that they should be excluded from the list of species of the eastern area.

Family *Heliconiidæ*

Heliconius petiveranus Doubleday strays into southern Texas (Pharr, August, December, January). Size and wing shape as in *H. charitonius*. Above, brownish-black; FW with a broad, transverse, red bar; HW with a narrower yellow stripe from somewhat before apex across end of cell to anal margin.

Family *Nymphalidæ*

Speyeria lais Edwards of Saskatchewan, Alberta, and Manitoba barely enters our area (McCreary, Manitoba). It is regarded by dos Passos and Gray as a subspecies of *atlantis*.

Speyeria mormonia eurynome Edwards, common and widespread in the west, barely reaches this area in the Dakotas, Manitoba and (accidental) Minnesota. It is a small *Speyeria* (1.8–1.9 in.) with prominent light, submarginal spots above; and a pale, greenish ground color on the HW beneath, where the spots are sometimes yellowish and unsilvered.

Melitæa fulvia Edwards strays into our area from the west or south. 1.1–1.25 in. Above light yellowish brown; apex of the FW, narrow marginal lines and veins darker; a wide median, and a narrow, dark-bordered postmedian band of pale spots. HW beneath whitish, the veins and a double postmedian line black; apex of FW beneath like HW. One definite record, Rush Co., Kansas 28 June 1912.

Melitæa elada Hewitson (*callina* Boisduval) widespread in Mexico, strays into southern Texas (Pharr, October). It is small (1.2–1.4 in.), dingy brown above, with a number of confused rows of small, pale brownish spots on both wings; a bent, postmedian row of larger white spots on FW; a broader, median, brownish spot band on HW. The marginal light spot on the FW in cell M_3 is much larger than the others of its row, and is white. Figured in Holland, *The Butterfly Book*, Rev. Ed., Pl. LIX, fig. 21 as *M. callina*.

Melitæa theona Menetries, subspecies **thekla** Edwards, is another Mexican and southwestern species found in southern Texas (Pharr, October, March–April). 1.2–1.5 in. Larger than *elada*, dark brown, with very wide, transverse rows of orange-brown spots, the median series lighter. Figured in Holland, *The Butterfly Book*, Pl. XVII, fig. 15, 16.

Chlosyne erodyle Bates has been reported as straying into our area. I have seen no definite records. 1.6–2.1 in. Wings above black, fringes checkered with white; a number of submedian, median, and postmedian white spots; HW with a large submedian, brownish yellow patch on costal half and a large, red spot at anal angle. Figured in Holland, *The Butterfly Book*, Pl. LIX, fig. 17.

Chlosyne endeis Godman & Salvin strays into southern Texas (Pharr, October, March). Above brownish black; a few small, postbasal light spots; a narrow, light, median spot band, offset basally below vein M_3 of FW, smooth on HW; a single row of small, light spots between this and outer margin. Figured in Holland, *The Butterfly Book*, Pl. LXXVI, fig. 17, 17a.

Chlosyne janais Drury strays into southern Texas (Pharr, October). 1.6–2.2 in. Above brownish black; FW with white spots only; HW with a broad, bright orange brown, median band, tapering to a point at each end. Figured in Holland, *The Butterfly Book*, Pl. XVIII, fig. 10.

Mestra cana Erichson "subspecies **floridana**" Strecker differs from *Mestra amymone* in having the upper surface gray, with a narrow, yellowish brown border on the HW. There have been several records, all unsatisfactory, from Florida. There was an unsavory mixup about the type material, with suspicions of theft. The type series was supposedly collected by "Fred de Hart" at "Crystal River," an unlikely locality; not, as usually reported, in the "Everglades." I hesitate to exclude it from the North American list; but all records are confusing, and experienced Florida collectors whom I have consulted have never seen an authentic specimen.

Hypolimnas misippus Linnæus (The Mimic). See p. 96. A tropical, Old World species supposedly introduced into the Antilles in the early days of the African slave trade. There are a few authentic Florida records but no evidence of permanent establishment there. The larva has a number of rows of branching spines on the body and one pair on the head. Food: — various Mallows (*Malvaceæ*), Morning Glory (*Ipomœa*), and Purslane (*Portulaca*). One larva, found in Miami, was reared to the adult.

Nymphalis californica Boisduval (California Tortoise Shell). This western species was introduced near Buffalo, New York some time in the late 19th century. It survived for about twenty years before disappearing.

Metamorpha ("Victorina") **stelenes** Linnæus (The Malachite). See p. 144. A large, widespread, tropical species that enters our area in southern Texas. (Pharr, August–December) and strays n. to Kansas; and in Florida where it is casual, perhaps occasionally introduced. I have seen authentic specimens from Lower Matecumbe Key (12 October, 1936) and Miami (13 February, 1939). I cannot say what race these represent. The Texas material is the race *biplagiata* Fruhstorfer, with two green spots in the cell of the FW, not one as in *s. stelenes* and some Antillean races. Food: — (Cuba and Puerto Rico) "*Blechum Brownei.*"

Biblis hyperia aganisa Boisduval ("*Didonis biblis*") a widespread tropical species, strays into southern Texas (Pharr, February, July). 2.0 in. Above brown, the FW with a broad, limbal, pale shade; HW with a broad, submarginal, red band; outer margin of HW scalloped.

Hypanartia lethe Fabricius, common in Mexico, has been recorded as occasional in southern Texas. Recent, very thorough collecting in northern Mexico and southern Texas has not turned it up. Lacking authentic records it should be excluded from our list. The orange-brown and black butterfly has a short, sharp tail on M₃ of the HW. Illustrated in Holland, *The Butterfly Book*, Pl. XXIV, fig. 10.

Myscelia ethusa Boisduval is widespread in tropical America, but occurs only occasionally in our area in southern Texas (Pharr, May, July–November). See p. 97. The ♀ has the median spots white, as well as the apical ones, and the apex of the FW more produced.

Myscelia cyananthe Felder strays into southern Texas (Pharr, October). Similar to *M. ethusa*, but with white spots of FW reduced; bluish marks of FW reduced to short, basal bars, those in cell very narrow, that below the cell very wide; the two discal bluish bands of HW much broader, the submarginal and marginal (♀♀) ones narrow as in *ethusa*.

Dynamine dyonis Geyer strays into the eastern area from Mexico (Brownsville, Texas, 8 June 1944). Wings above shining, pale, brassy green with black marks at costa, apex, and middle of outer margin forming a much reduced border; HW with irregular, black outer-marginal border. Beneath white with transverse, brown stripes and bands, and two prominent, submarginal eyespots on HW.

Diæthria (or **Callicore**) **clymena** Huebner. Holland figures this (*The Butterfly Book*, Pl. XXI, fig. 5, 6) from a specimen probably of South American origin, stating that it is "found occasionally in Florida, but quite commonly in the Antilles, Mexico and Central America." *Clymena* is not, however, either Antillean or Mexican, nor are there any Antillean *Diæthria*. Perhaps Holland was thinking of the similar *D. anna* Guerin which is common in Mexico. The original Florida record is very old, dating from Scudder. None of the recent Florida collectors has ever seen a Florida specimen. I was just about to exclude *clymena* from the North American list when a thoroughly authentic Florida specimen turned up! It was taken by Paul Griswold Howes, curator of the Bruce Museum, in Royal Palm Park, on 26 February 1944 "apparently enjoying the damp ground just above the water, in the slough almost at the entrance to the tall growth at the entrance to the park. . . . It was quite rubbed as though it had been on the wing for a while." So we can retain *clymena* on our list. It is South American and must, therefore, have been introduced, perhaps more than once.

Diæthria asteria Godman & Salvin, common in Mexico, has been authentically recorded once (Alamo, Texas, 1 July, collected by D. Ring).

Hamadryas feronia Linnæus (White Skirted Calico) and **H. fornax** Huebner (Yellow Skirted Calico) both stray into southern Texas. See p. 145. The ground color is bluish gray, with zigzag crosslines of black and brownish gray and prominent white spots. In *feronia* the HW beneath has a white ground color; in *fornax* this is yellow. Both have been taken at Pharr, Texas, *feronia* in October and November, *fornax* in October. There is also a vague record of *H. ferox* Staudinger from southern Texas which I have been unable to verify.

Marpesia coresia Godart (The Waiter) is occasional in southern Texas (Pharr, October). It is common in the tropics. 2.0–2.6 in. Wing shape much like that of *Marpesia petreus* (p. 114) but FW not produced outwardly so far on vein M_1. Blackish brown above, lighter basally and marginally; beneath, basal half of wings white, outer half brown.

Marpesia chiron Fabricius (Many Banded Dagger Wing) is oc-

casional in southern Florida (Miami, June, July) and southern
Texas (Pharr, February) and once strayed to Kansas! 2.0–2.4 in.
Apex of FW less produced than that of *M. coresia;* above, pale
brown, with five dark, transverse bands, widest at costa of FW,
tapering to thin lines posteriorly on HW; white spots apically on
FW.

Adelpha fessonia Hewitson strays into southern Texas (Pharr,
August, October, November). Pale, grayish brown above; an
orange patch on costa before apex of FW; a smooth-edged, white,
median band across both wings from costa to anal angle, tapering
posteriorly.

Adelpha bredowii Geyer occurs in Mexico and western Texas to
California. There is a record of a stray in western Kansas, and
doubtless others may occur in our area in Oklahoma and Texas
as well. Probably the race *eulalia* Hewitson. 2.4–2.6 in. Apex
of FW less produced than *fessonia;* orange patch larger; white
band formed of separate spots, its edges irregular, and offset
below discal cell of FW.

Smyrna karwinskii Geyer has been reported as "a rare straggler
about Brownsville, Texas." It has not been taken in Texas in
recent years. Perhaps it strayed in, in the past, or was introduced and died out. 3.3–3.5 in. Dull orange brown; FW with a
large, triangular, black apical patch from mid-costa to anal
angle; in this are three yellow brown spots; ground color paler
just basad of patch; HW with a short, narrow black border. Figured in Holland, *The Butterfly Book*, Pl. LXXI, fig. 3.

Historis acheronta Fabricius is said by Holland to have been reported from southern Florida. Definite or authentic records are
lacking. Figured by Holland (as *Cœa acheronta*), *The Butterfly
Book*, Pl. LX, fig. 2.

Historis odius has been recorded from Florida a number of times,
once, at least, authentically. Widespread in the Antilles and
tropics, it doubtless does occasionally get blown or carried in.
3.4–3.6 in. Figured in Holland, *The Butterfly Book*, Pl. LX, fig. 1.

Anæa glycerium Doubleday has strayed into Texas (Pharr) from
Mexico. It has the general appearance above of *A. aidea* and
floridalis, but has stronger, apical, dark markings on the FW. Its
wing shape is distinctive. The FW is slightly concave just below
the apex, then bends out, then in again at vein Cu_1, then out
strongly at vein Cu_2, then slants in again to the anal angle.

Anæa pithyusa Felder is apparently established in southern Texas
(Pharr, March, September–December). 1.9–2.5 in. Above blackish brown with some basal iridescent blue, chiefly on the FW; on
the FW a submarginal row of light blue spots, usually five; on the
HW a more reduced row of similar, white spots; of these the one
at the base of the tail is almost always present even if the others
are lost.

Chlorippe pavon Latreille has been taken in southern Texas (Pharr,
October, December, May). Above dark brown with a faint
bluish gloss; lighter brownish, postmedian and submarginal

bands, the latter narrow; and a large orange spot on costa of FW. Apex of FW strongly and squarely produced, so that the outer margin is concave; anal angle of HW produced to form a short lobe. *Chlorippe* is the large tropical genus from which our Hackberry Butterflies were removed to form the genus *Asterocampa*. Many of the species are brilliantly iridescent.

Family *Libytheidæ*

Libytheana carinenta Cramer (Mexican Snout Butterfly) has been vaguely recorded from southern Texas. If it does occur it would be the race *mexicana* Michener (TL Jalapa, Mexico). I have found no definite records.

Family *Lycænidæ*

Strymon facuna Hewitson. A few specimens have been taken at Pharr, Texas (late July, early August). 0.8 in. Most resembles *pastor;* but lacks a tail on the HW and has the anal lobe less pronounced and the pattern beneath more reduced.

Strymon endymion cyphara Hewitson. 0.75–0.85 in. Above, looks like a *Mitoura*, having orange brown discal areas and dark margins. Beneath, strongly resembles *cecrops*, the postmedian lines being margined with red, although more narrowly than in *cecrops*. On the HW beneath it has the larger submarginal spot below Cu₁ much more orange than in *cecrops*, being in this more like *beon*. Holland figured (*The Butterfly Book*, Pl. LXIV, fig. 32) as "*endymion*" a specimen of *S. angelia boyeri* Comstock & Huntington from Haiti, stating that *endymion* might occur on the Florida Keys. I have no reliable Florida records; but the subspecies *cyphara* occurs rarely at Pharr, Texas (April–May, October–December). TL of *endymion* is Brazil; that of *cyphara*, Panama.

Strymon cestri Reakirt. 0.75–1.0 in. Rather resembles *bazochii* in color and pattern. The blue above is paler; and the wing shape is distinctive, the outer margin of the FW being strongly convex, most so between veins M₃ and Cu₁. On the HW beneath it lacks the very prominent, postbasal costal spot and the large, dark, basal and apical patches of *bazochii;* and has a prominent, round, brownish black, submarginal spot below Cu₁. Taken once at Pharr, Texas (25 March 1945).

Strymon yojoa Reakirt has been taken once at Pharr, Texas (12 December 1945), ranges south through Central America. 0.9–1.1 in. Plain, dark brown above. On the HW is a small, orange patch at the anal angle and, in the ♀, an orange and black submarginal spot in cell Cu₁. Beneath, somewhat olivaceous brown-gray; the postmedian lines thin, white, internally narrowly margined with orange-red; FW with a whitish bar at end of cell, a whitish shade beyond postmedian line and an indistinct, whitish, submarginal line; HW with a transverse, whitish, postbasal shade, a whitish submarginal shade and the submarginal spot in cell Cu₁ light orange and black.

Strymon spurina Hewitson, common and wide-ranging in the tropics, has been taken once at Pharr, Texas (25 November 1945). 1.1–1.2 in. Male above very dull, dark blue with narrow dark borders; stigma brownish black, 8-shaped. Female above grayish brown, slightly blue tinged basally, darker on outer two thirds of FW, narrowly darker outwardly on HW; a small, submarginal, orange and black lunule in cell Cu₁. Wings beneath dark brown; postmedian lines narrow, dark, outwardly whitish, forming a shallow W on HW below vein Cu₁; submarginal lines faint; an orange-red submarginal spot, outwardly pupilled with black, in cell Cu₁; anal angle with black patch narrowly capped internally with orange-red. Beneath it resembles fairly closely a dull *m-album*.

Strymon laceyi Barnes & McDunnough (Lacey's Hairstreak) is extremely rare, named from one ♀ from Del Rio, Texas (July 1909) and taken a few times at Pharr (October, December, May). Resembles the probably closely related *clytie;* but has the spots and lines beneath darker and edged with white (in *clytie* they tend to be almost clear orange brown) and the ground color beneath darker. It is certainly much more like *clytie* than *columella*, to which Holland compared it.

Strymon buchholzi H. A. Freeman (Buchholz' Hairstreak) is extremely rare in s. Texas (TL Pharr) and n. Mexico. It is described as resembling *melinus* but as being darker grey-black, especially beneath; the ♂ has a much darker stigma on the FW above; and the postmedian row of spots on the HW beneath lacks black inner edging and is proportionately farther from the inner margin and submarginal markings.

Strymon echion Linnæus Hewitson, **rufofusca** Hewitson and **zebina** Hewitson have been recorded from s. Texas (Pharr & vic.) too recently for detailed inclusion in this book. All are tropical species.

Incisalia mossii Henry Edwards (Moss' Elfin), a western species, has been recorded a few times from the east (Pennsylvania, New York). The records are regarded as very dubious, but I have included it in the Key to *Incisalia* so that eastern collectors may keep it in mind.

Family *Papilionidæ*

Papilio bairdii Edwards (Baird's Swallowtail), common in the west, occurs occasionally in the extreme western part of our area. It may be extending its range eastward. Resembling *P. polyxenes* *asterias*, it has the yellow median spots of the wings above considerably wider, and these spots beneath closer together.

Papilio lycophron pallas Gray occurs rarely in extreme southern Texas (Pharr), probably straying from Mexico. Pattern of the *cresphontes* type; the yellow spotband of the wings above is very broad, wider than the black areas; the tails are short and heavy. The ♀ is nearly all dark.

Papilio andræmon bonhotei Sharpe of the Bahamas has been recorded from Florida. Some records are dubious. Distinguished from *cresphontes* by smaller size; tails very long and slender; vein-tips along outer-anal region of HW form more projecting lobes; median yellow band of FW is a clean band, not a row of spots; submarginal spots of FW smaller, close and parallel to outer margin; a transverse, yellow mark, at right angles in from costa of FW, basad of end of cell.

Papilio rutulus Lucas (Western Tiger Swallowtail). The differences between *rutulus* and *glaucus* have been noted under *glaucus*. As stated there, there is strong reason for considering *rutulus* no more than a western race of *glaucus*. There are records of *rutulus* from Minnesota, Wisconsin, and Nebraska.

Papilio multicaudatus Kirby (Three Tailed Swallowtail). Characterized under *P. glaucus*. A rare "casual" in the western part of our area. Formerly known as *daunus* Boisduval.

Papilio celadon Lucas. Looks like a small, pale green *marcellus* with a very large, dark, Y-shaped band on the FW. A native of Cuba, it has been recorded from southern Florida (Chokoloskee). The records are extremely dubious, and there is suspicion of deliberate mis-labeling by a commercial collector.

Papilio devilliers Godart (Devilliers Swallowtail). A Cuban species that has been recorded from southern Florida. Its occurrence there, possible but doubtful, should be checked from something other than dealers' specimens.

Papilio arcas mylotes Bates. A common Central American species, erroneously cited in a popular magazine article as coming from our area.

Family *Pieridæ*

Licinia melite Huebner has been vaguely recorded from Texas. I have seen no authentic records. It occurs in Mexico as the race *jethys* Boisduval, and may well stray northward into our area.

Phœbis argante Fabricius has been variously recorded from the United States. All old records are untrustworthy because of confusion with *P. agarithe* (p. 191). It may well occur in our area, being common in Mexico n. into Tamaulipas. It is large, 2.25–2.5 in., and extremely like *agarithe;* on the FW beneath the postmedian line of dark spots is broken and zigzag; in *agarithe* this line is practically straight and even.

Phœbis neocypris bracteolata Butler (see p. 161) may well occur in the eastern area in southern Texas. The anal angle of the HW forms a short, rounded tail. The nomenclature of this group of *Phœbis* is confused, authorities differing. Perhaps this species is better known as *P. cypris* Fabricius.

Eurema salome Felder (Salome Sulphur). 1.3–1.8 in. See p. 177. The ♀ is a more brownish orange with an irregular, triangular, apical dark border on the FW, none on HW. Beneath, both sexes, HW and apex of FW somewhat ochreous yellow, marked mostly with fine, red-brown reticulations. There are various old, somewhat untrustworthy records all along the Mexican border. It definitely does occur in Arizona. The northern form, not a clear-cut race, is *limoneus* Felder. Figured in Holland, *The Butterfly Book*, Pl. XXXVII, fig. 9–10, as *"damaris* Felder."

Eurema elathea Cramer. As noted under *E. palmira*, Holland figured a specimen of *E. palmira f. ebriola*, as if from North America, calling it *elathea*. I know of no possibly accurate records of *elathea* from North America. The true *elathea* has the FW bar of the ♂ black, not gray as in *daira* and *palmira*.

Eurema messalina Fabricius is a small (0.8–1.2 in.) white species common in Cuba and the Bahamas. It has been recorded from Florida on the basis of an old record of Maynard's (*blakei*) from "Sanford" (Oct. 1, 1887) and of some specimens of very dubious authenticity labeled Chokoloskee by a dealer. Recent collecting has failed to turn it up. It should probably be excluded from the North American lists.

Eurema dina westwoodii Boisduval is a rounded-winged, orange species with a narrow black border on the FW and none, or a very narrow, broken one, on the HW. 1.0–1.5 in. It is figured by Holland, *The Butterfly Book*, Pl. XXXVII, fig. 11. It is supposed to occur in the United States along the Mexican border. Since it is common in Mexico, this is not unlikely; but I have never seen or heard of an authentic specimen. The nymotypical race, *d. dina* Poey is Cuban; it might stray to Florida.

Neophasia menapia Felder (Pine White). There is one record of this western species from Minnesota (Itasca Park, 15 August 1921) undoubtedly a stray. It ranges regularly eastward to Sioux City, Nebraska.

Family *Hesperiidæ*

Proteides mercurius Fabricius occurs rarely in southern Texas. (Pharr, ♂, 2 April 1948). 2.25–2.75 in. Dark brown above, wings basally and body light tawny. FW with three hyaline, median spots, a smaller one just beyond these, and a small, costal, subapical spot or group of spots. Wings beneath with large gray, reddish brown and white patches, chiefly along outer margins and discally on HW. Fringes pale, on the FW only below M₃. Figured in Holland (as *idas*) *The Butterfly Book*, Pl. XLIX, fig. 6, 7.

Aguna asander Hewitson is very rare in southern Texas (Pharr, September–November). Above it resembles *Epargyreus clarus* and *zestos*, but the spots are a paler hyaline yellow. Beneath, especially on HW, laved outwardly with violet-gray; on the HW is an irregular, narrow, antemedian white streak, from before middle of costa to about three quarters way out on anal margin.

Urbanus auginulus Godman & Salvin strays into southern Texas (Pharr, 10 and 11 March, 1945). 1.4–1.6 in. There are fewer yellowish hyaline spots on the FW than in our other *Urbanus*, and these are large and less sharply jagged in shape. They are: one large spot in end of cell, another below this; another, much smaller, between these but nearer outer margin. Sometimes there is a fourth spot, very small, below vein Cu₂. Beneath, darker marginally, transverse bands indistinct. Perhaps a form or race of *auginus* Hewitson, lacking the green body.

Urbanus undulatus Hewitson, taken once at Pharr, Texas (19 Sept. 1947, H. A. F.), 1.6–1.75 in. Light band across FW wider than in *U. eurycles;* HW beneath coarsely dusted and scrawled with dark and light, the dark bands very irregular; the outer area much lighter, sometimes broadly whitish brown and smeared looking.

Urbanus doryssus Swainson strays into southern Texas (Pharr, March and October), 1.7–1.8 in. Hyaline spotband of FW narrow; tails of HW short; tails and the HW at their bases white, this running narrowly up outer margin. A very striking and distinctive looking species.

Astraptes anaphus Cramer strays into southern Texas (Pharr, 1 ♀, 9 September 1944). 2.0–2.5 in. Above, brown with indistinct, darker, transverse bands; anal lobe and anal region of HW light yellowish brown, lightest terminally. No blue-green iridescence as in our other *Astraptes.*

Astraptes hopferi Ploetz strays into southern Texas (Pharr, 1 ♀, 21 October 1944). 1.8–2.1 in. Dark brown above with basal blue-green iridescence as in *fulgerator.* FW with no hyaline white spots. FW beneath with a large, triangular, white patch at inner angle; both wings beneath with dark transverse patches and bands.

Celænorrhinus fritzgætneri Bailey strays into Texas (Pharr, ♀, 20 February 1945). See p. 224. 1.7–1.9 in. The wings are fairly light brown above, marked and mottled as illustrated. The small hyaline spot on the FW below the middle of the cell is characteristic.

Celænorrhinus stallingsi Freeman has been recorded once from Texas (Pharr, 8 November 1944, allotype ♀). Darker brown than *fritzgærtneri;* the small white spot of the FW below the middle of the cell is replaced by a black dot; on the FW beneath is a white area extending from the lower end of the hyaline spot-band to the inner margin; the fringes are not checkered.

Pellicia bromias Godman & Salvin strays into southern Texas (Pharr, 23 October 1945). See p. 224. 1.25–1.45 in. Above, medium brown with very indistinct, darker, transverse bands. There are two very small, subapical, hyaline spots near the costa of the FW.

Pellicia costimacula Herrich-Schæffer has been taken at Pharr a number of times (October, December, March). 1.25–1.5 in. Darker brown than *bromias;* FW above lustrous, grayer brown on the basal half and broadly along the costa to the apex; the hyaline spots of *bromias* are absent.

Gorgythion begga Prittwitz, form or subspecies **pyralina** Moeschler has been taken once at Pharr (♀, 31 March 1946). 0.9–1.1 in. See p. 224. Its small size and extremely mottled appearance, due to the broken irregular bands of darker spots, are quite distinctive. The FW has two very small hyaline spots subapically, just in from the costa.

Pholisora ceos Edwards is rare in southern Texas (Pharr, October). 0.9–1.1 in. Plain brown above with reduced white spots. The dorsal vestiture of the collar, head and palpi is bright ochreous; the palpi are black on the sides, and whitish beneath.

Pholisora alpheus Edwards possibly enters our area from the west, having been taken at Palo Duro Canyon, near Amarillo, Texas (April–June). It is considerably powdered with whitish scales both above and beneath, and has prominent black streaks between the veins of the FW. **Food:** — (California) Pigweed, (*Atriplex expansa*).

Carrhenes canescens Godman & Salvin strays into southern Texas (Pharr, May, November). 1.2–1.3 in. Above dull, light brown, somewhat translucent looking discally, darker apically and terminally. Indistinct, irregular, darker spot-rows, chiefly showing through from beneath, cross the wings. Hyaline spots as follows: a small subapical group on FW; an irregular median band on FW; two to four discal ones on HW. These spots vary greatly, being sometimes very large, sometimes very small or nearly absent.

Atrytone eulogius Ploetz strays into Texas (Brownsville, May, November). 1.2–1.3 in. Most resembles a ♀ *A. logan* having, above, dark veins, wide dark borders and considerable dark basal suffusion. But the costal margin and most of the cell of the FW are yellow-orange, with the dark shading running out *below* the discal cell. On the HW beneath is a definite light band or patch of small spots, somewhat like that of *A. conspicua.* The ♂ lacks a stigma.

Cobalus percosius Godman & Salvin has been recorded twice from Brownsville, Texas; in April 1948 some fifty specimens were taken. Above resembles *Oligoria maculata*. 1.0–1.25 in. On the HW beneath is a postmedian row of lighter spots bordered, narrowly externally and broadly internally, with darker brown, and a series of three less distinct post-basal spots. These spots are not conspicuous, being merely slightly lighter than the ground color. The wing is broadly margined beyond the spots with slightly purplish-tinged brown.

Thespeius macareus Herrich-Schæffer has been reported from both Marco, Florida, and San Antonio, Texas. 1.3–1.5 in. Wings long and slender. FW with outer margin strongly bulged outward below apex; HW with anal angle strongly produced. FW with large, hyaline white spots; HW with a crescentic discal patch, concave outwardly, of hyaline white spots. Wings beneath complexly marked with pale gray, orange brown, and dark brown streaks and patches. Confirmation of the old records is needed.

SKIPPERS
Family *Hesperiidae*

All illustrations are × 1 (natural size)

1. **TAWNY EDGED SKIPPER,** *Polites themistocles*   p. 245
   Upper & under sides, ♂ (Stamford, Conn.) Like *manataaqua* (Pl. 34), smaller; see text. Centr. Can to Fla. & Ark.
2. **TAWNY EDGED SKIPPER,** *Polites themistocles*   **p. 245**
   Upper side, ♀ (Sharon, Conn.) See above.
3. **THE LONG DASH,** *Polites mystic*   **p. 247**
   Upper & under sides, ♂ (N. Elba, N.Y.) Long stigmal streak; HW beneath reddish tinged; spots less distinct & clear than in *peckius* (fig. 4). S. Can. to Va. & Ill.
4. **PECK'S SKIPPER,** *Polites peckius*   **p. 246**
   Upper & under sides, ♂ (Omaha, Nebr.) Small; bold patch on HW beneath; Me. & Dakotas to Ga. & Ark. See also ♀, Pl. 30.
5. **BARACOA SKIPPER,** *Polites baracoa*   **p. 246**
   Upper & under sides, ♂ (Thomasville, Ga.) Small; dark; HW beneath with weak but definite spots. Fla. & S. Ga.
6. **THE MULBERRY WING,** *Poanes massasoit*   p. 249
   Under side, ♀ (Flushing, L.I.) See also Pl. 31.
7. **HOBOMOK SKIPPER,** *Poanes hobomok*   p. 250
   Upper & under sides, ♂ (Ogdensburg, N.J.) Lacks stigma; clear-cut patch on HW beneath (cf. *zabulon*). S. Can. to Ga. & Kans.
8. **POCAHONTAS,** *Poanes hobomok* f. ♀ *pocahontas*   p. 250
   Under side, ♀ (Southboro, Mass.) Pattern of normal *hobomok* but very dark; variable; See Pl. 30.
9. **ZABULON SKIPPER,** *Poanes zabulon*   p. 250
   Upper & under sides, ♀ (Washington Hgts., N.H., N.Y.) Cf. *hobomok;* HW beneath mostly yellow, with distinctive pattern; see text. Mass. & Iowa to Ga. & Tex. See also P. 30
10. **BROAD WINGED SKIPPER,** *Poanes viator*   p. 249
    Upper side, ♂ (S. Jamaica, L.I.) Large; broad-winged; extensive dark areas above; See also Pl. 30. Mass. & Nebr. to Ala. & Tex.
11. **TEXTOR SKIPPER,** *Amblyscirtes testor*   p. 263
    Under side, ♂ (Great Dismal Swamp, Va.) Light, cobweb pattern on HW beneath. See also Pl. 38.
12. **CAROLINA SKIPPER,** *Amblyscirtes carolina*   n. 263
    Under side, ♂ (Great Dismal Swamp, Va.) Yellow spots and coloration beneath. See also Pl. 38.
13. **ROADSIDE SKIPPER,** *Amblyscirtes vialis*   p. 262
    Upper & under sides, ♂ (Mt. Equinox, Vt.) Lilac or violet-gray dusting beneath; see also Pl. 37. S. Can. southward.
14. **AARON'S SKIPPER,** *Poanes aaroni*   p. 251
    Under side, ♂ (Cape May, N.J.) Above like *Atrytone arogos* (Pl. 36) but borders clearly defined; see text. N.J. to Fla.
15. **BYSSUS SKIPPER,** *Problema byssus*   p. 252
    Upper & under sides, ♂ (Miami, Fla.) ♂ lacks stigma; heavy dark markings above; faint but definite light marks on HW beneath. Kans. to Iowa, s. to Fla. & Tex. See also Pl. 31.
16. **YEHL SKIPPER,** *Poanes yehl*   p. 251
    Upper & under sides, (Suffolk, Va.). Prominent stigma; spots on HW beneath; see text. Va. & Tenn. to Ga. & Miss.

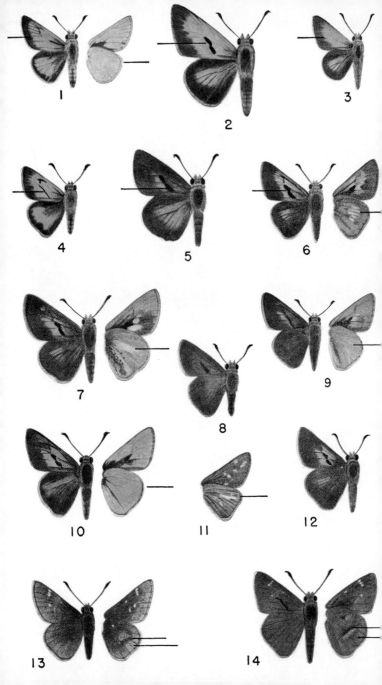

Plate 36   289

SKIPPERS
Family *Hesperiidae*

All illustrations are × 1 (natural size)

1. DELAWARE SKIPPER, *Atrytone logan*   p. 254
   Upper & under sides, ♂ (Twining, Mich.) Narrow borders; dark
   veins; HW beneath clear yellow; Mass. & N.Dak. to Fla. & Tex.
2. PALATKA SKIPPER, *Atrytone palatka*   p. 255
   Upper side, ♂ (Titusville, Fla.) Large; much fulvous above; HW
   beneath dull olive brown. Va. to Fla. See also Pl. 31.
3. AROGOS SKIPPER, *Atrytone arogos*   p. 253
   Upper side, ♂ (Cowarts, Ala.) Blurry dark borders; veins above
   light. N.J. & Nebr. to Fla. & La. See Pl. 31 (race *iowa*).
4. *Choranthus radians*   p. 251
   Upper side, ♂ (P. de Cabanas, Cuba) Large yellow areas; thin stigma
   of ♂; see text. Occasional in Fla.
5. DUKES' SKIPPER, *Atrytone dukesii*   p. 255
   Upper side, ♂ (Mobile, Ala.) Broad wings; very dark above. Ala.,
   Ohio & n. Va. Very local. See also Pl. 32.
6. THE BLACK DASH, *Atrytone conspicua*   p. 258
   Upper & under sides, ♂ (Flushing, L.I.) Heavy stigma; conspicuous patch on HW beneath. Mass. to Nebr., s. to Va. See Pl. 31.
7. DION SKIPPER, *Atrytone dion*   p. 255
   Upper & under sides, ♂ (Ohio) HW beneath reddish with yellow
   shades. N.Y. to Nebr., s. to Ala. & Tex. See Pl. 31.
8. DUN SKIPPER, *Atrytone ruricola metacomet*   p. 258
   Upper side, ♂ (Stockholm, N.J.) ♂ unmarked above. See ♂, Pl. 32.
   Can. southward.
9. TWO SPOTTED SKIPPER, *Atrytone bimacula*   p. 258
   Upper & under sides, ♂ (Catskills, N.Y.) Anal margin of HW white
   edged. S. Can. to Va. & Nebr. Very local. See also Pl. 32.
10. ARPA SKIPPER, *Atrytone arpa*   p. 254
    Upper & under sides, ♂ (Orlando, Fla.) HW beneath bright, clear
    and unmarked. Fla. & Ala.
11. SALT MARSH SKIPPER, *Panoquina panoquin*   p. 269
    Under side, ♂ (Gulfport, Fla.). HW beneath with white shade &
    veins. N.J. to Fla. & Ala. See also Pl. 39.
12. BERRY'S SKIPPER, *Atrytone berryi*   p. 255
    Upper side, ♂ (Orlando, Fla.) HW veins beneath white-lined. Fla.
13. DUSTED SKIPPER, *Atrytonopsis hianna*   p. 259
    Upper & under sides, ♂ (Ohio) Gray dusted, especially beneath;
    often with one or more whitish spots on HW beneath; N. Engl. to
    Nebr., s. to N.C. See also Pl. 32.
14. CLOUDED SKIPPER, *Lerema accius*   p. 260
    Upper & under sides, ♂ (Hope, Ark.) Grayish outer shading be-
    neath; cf. *A. hianna*. See text & Pl. 32. Mass. & Ill. to Fla. & Tex.

Plate 56

SKIPPERS
Family Hesperiidae
All illustrations are X 1 (natural size)

Part 3

APPENDICES

1. Some Principles of Classification

THE SCIENCE of classifying animals and plants is called *taxonomy*. First, it has to do with giving proper scientific names (*nomenclature*). Second, it deals with working out a system of arranging the organisms in groups, so as to serve as a convenient "indexing system" (*systematics*). This system, however, goes beyond mere convenience, for the organisms must be grouped together to bring out their true ancestral relationships (*phylogeny*).

Why Scientific Names? To people unaccustomed to using them, scientific names sometimes seem too difficult. Really, however, their use is enormously preferable. Let us see why this is so.

Chiefly, common names are often unreliable. There are no rules at all governing them, so that anybody is at liberty to change them to suit himself, coin new ones, or do whatever he pleases. This may be very satisfying to the individual, but hardly makes for understanding of what anyone means. In current books, for example, I find that for one of our butterflies the name "Common Wood Nymph" is used twice; "Grayling" is used once; "Blue Eyed Grayling" is used twice: and "Goggle Eye" is used once. Which is easier and more accurate — to remember all those, or the scientific name, *Cercyonis alope?* Think of the misunderstanding and errors if we had to cope with four or five different names (and expect new ones without rhyme or reason) for every one of our several hundred butterflies.

Scientific names, on the other hand, are relatively more stable, being given and retained according to a definite set of rules. These, the International Rules for Zoological Nomenclature, were prepared and are from time to time emended, by a committee of distinguished scientists. Actually, of course, changes arise from time to time in scientific nomenclature too. Some are due to errors dating from times before the official rules (the "Code") were adopted. These are being worked out by specialists. Others are caused by the misdeeds of present-day workers who do not follow the Code. However, scientific nomenclature is becoming more and more stabilized in better-known groups such as the butterflies; and it is not too much to hope that in the not too far distant future it may attain real stability.

People often make the mistake of thinking that scientific names are "hard to remember" and long and tongue twisting. This is just a mental hazard. There are many scientific names which people use all the time without thinking that they are hard, such as *Rhinoceros*, *Hippopotamus*, *Boa Constrictor*, *Nasturtium*, and *Rhododendron*.

How Scientific Names Are Formed. Our modern system of scientific naming dates officially from the publication in 1758 of the Tenth Edition of the *Systema Natura* by the great Swedish naturalist, Linnæus. It is to Linnæus that we owe the *binomial* form of our nomenclature.

"Binomial" refers to the fact that the name of any animal (or plant) is *double*, consisting of two names; this is easy to understand. Your own name is binomial too, and each of its parts has a different significance. One, e.g. "James" or "Helen" is individual to you; the other, "Wilson" or "Jones" is a group name, that of your closest relatives. The scientific name is double in the same way, although the *group* (genus) name is written first and the *individual* (species) name is second.

The unit is the name of the *species*, that is of the *particular kind* of animal to which the name refers. This name is written with an initial small letter. The *genus*, or *group name*, is always written with an initial capital letter. Together they make a combination that not only gives us a permanent label for the species but also tells us something about it by naming the group to which it belongs. I suggest that you turn to some of the illustrations and note some examples of genera (the plural of genus) and species. You will see that each species has certain characteristics. These are possessed in common by all the individuals that make up the population of the species, and differ from those of any other species. But it also has certain other characters in common with the other members of the same genus.

One other thing makes up the scientific name, and that is the name of the *author* of the species. He is the first person who properly published a description of the characters of the species, at the same time giving it a species name. The author's name need not be appended for every use of the species name, but it should be given at least once in every article or book. In this book the author's names are given in the Check List. It is conventional to place the name of the author in parentheses if he named the species under a different generic name than that under which it is now listed. I have not followed this last custom in this book because such a large majority of our butterflies are now placed in different genera from their original ones that it would have little meaning here.

We will discuss later the way in which a genus may be divided into *subgenera*, and a species divided into *subspecies*. When this is done we write the name of the subgenus in parentheses after that of the original genus. Thus, the genus *Colias* of the Sulphurs consists of two groups; one is composed of the typical Sulphurs, and we regard these as belonging to the "typical" or "nymotypical" subgenus, which we would write *Colias (Colias)* Fabricius. The other group composes the subgenus *Zerene* Huebner; we write this name *Colias (Zerene)* Huebner.

The subspecific name is written after the specific name, with no punctuation in between. *Colias palæno* Linnæus consists of an Old World population, that on which the name was first based (this is the "typical," or "nymotypical" subspecies) and a slightly different North American population. We call the latter subspecies *chippewa* Kirby. The full names of these two subspecies would be written *Colias (Colias) palæno palæno* (or sometimes, for short, *C. (Colias) p. palæno*) Linnæus; and *Colias (Colias) palæno chippewa* Kirby. The study of subgenera and subspecies is, however, quite involved; and many collectors, who do not go thus deeply into butterfly work, merely use the simple "binomial": "*Genus — species* Author."

Relationship (Phylogeny) and Genera. I have inferred that a genus is a group of species having some things in common. The fundamental basis for deciding what species belong together in a genus is, of course, similarity. Modern science, however, tries to make sure that the similarity shall be based on relationship, that is, on *common ancestral descent*, and not on mere superficial resemblance. Again, the analogy with human families is an apt one. One of the Jones boys may have red hair and his brother have brown hair, while their sister has yellow hair. They are, nevertheless, fundamentally closely related to each other. We would not think of transferring their sister over to the Svenson family, just because all the Svensons are yellow haired. Similarly, in classifying butterflies we try to figure out the real relationships of the species, and to be on our guard against resemblances that may be no more than "skin deep." A genus is much more, then, than a convenient way of grouping similar species; *it is a means of expressing relationship.* We may put two species together into the same genus; by doing so we indicate that we believe them to be recently descended from a common ancestral species. Or conversely, we may take a species out of a genus and put it in another, or name a new genus for it. We also may, if we consider it warranted, recognize the existence of *subgenera* within a genus, and even of *species groups* within a subgenus. This study of (ancestral) relationships in biology is called *phylogeny*. It is the genealogy of the life sciences.

Larger Groups — Families, Orders, etc. Just as we group related species together in genera, so do we group related genera together. The same principle of phylogeny, i.e., relationship based on ancestry, is followed. If we are making a very thorough classification system we may use many intermediate groups, too. A group of closely related genera is called a *tribe*. A group of tribes is a *subfamily*. There are *superfamilies*, too, and then these are grouped in categories called *orders*, and so on up into ever larger groups. Perhaps it may help to understand this if we start at the top and work

down the scale.   The following table shows where our common
Mourning Cloak butterfly fits into the system:

> Kingdom . . . . . Animal
> Phylum. . . . . . *Arthropoda* (Crabs and Lobsters, Insects, Spiders, etc.)
> Class. . . . . *Hexapoda* (Insects)
> Order . . . . *Lepidoptera* (Butterflies and Moths)
> Superfamily. . . *Papilionoidea* (True Butterflies)
> Family . . . . *Nymphalidæ* (Brush-footed Butterflies)
> Subfamily . . . . *Nymphalinæ*
> Tribe. . . . . *Nymphalini*
> Genus. . . . . *Nymphalis*
> Species. . . . . . . *antiopa* Linnæus (The Mourning Cloak)

Species and Subspecies.   The question "What is a species?" cannot be answered fully without extremely lengthy discussion.   Let
us, however, try to work out a general answer sufficient for our
purposes.

In the first place a species is a *population*, composed of individuals.   *These have certain inheritable, distinctive characteristics in
common*, which set them apart from all other populations.   They
usually vary somewhat in minor expressions of these and other
characters, but the variation is within definite limits.

The species as a whole must reproduce itself, through the reproductive activities of the individuals.   This must be done successfully enough for the survival of the species, which otherwise
will become extinct.   The reproductive power of the species must
balance the destructive powers of its enemies and of other environmental forces.   The species must, moreover, reproduce itself not
only successfully but naturally.   We are not concerned with man-
made "hybrids."

Does this mean that a species does not change as time goes on?
All evidence is to the contrary.   Species do change, otherwise there
would be no such thing as evolution.   But the changes, which arise
within the species, must be such that they can be passed on down
successfully through its inheritance mechanism.   It is these inheritable changes, not at first occurring in all individuals, that account
for much of the variation in a species.   They are the basic material
for evolution; and as such are of the greatest importance.

By the gradual accumulation of such changes, a species will in
the course of time change into something different.   This is the
simplest mechanism for evolution.   But a simple process like this
does not explain why there are so many species.   There must have
been millions of cases where a species, instead of merely changing
into a single, different species, split and gave rise to two or more
"daughter" species, differing from each other in some important
characteristics, and thenceforth maintaining their separate identities.

In such a process, we can see that the inheritable changes that
arose in the "parent" species cannot have been evenly distributed
among all members of the population.   Some changes must have

somehow been restricted to one part of the population. This one part then could evolve into one new "daughter" species, the other part into another.

When we study the whole population of nearly any species, we commonly find that it can be subdivided into different groups, which occur in *different geographic areas*. These are *geographic subspecies,* or "races." They are believed to be potential "daughter species" in the making. Some biologists, in fact, argue with excellent authority that it is only through the formation of such *geographically separated,* differing groups within a species that new "daughter species" arise.

The important factor here is *isolation*. As pointed out above, it is only through the restriction of new, inheritable characteristics to a part of a population that that part can evolve into something different from the rest of the population. There must be some *barrier* to prevent them interbreeding with all the rest of their species population; otherwise they can never develop a group identity, and the new characteristics will merely become dispersed among the whole of the species.

It is this realization of the great importance, perhaps of the necessity, of *geographic separation* in the formation of new, daughter species, that has given the great stimulus to the study of subspecies that characterizes modern taxonomy. Within the last fifty years this study has come to be a major factor in taxonomic work. In no group is this more true than in the butterflies, which are thus as important to the biologist as any other group of animals or plants.

Kinds of Subspecies. Two chief types of geographic subspecies occur. In one type, the *isolated* or *discontinuous*, there is an actual geographic or spatial separation between the subspecies, which occur in different regions separated by impassable barriers. The commonest examples of this are subspecies which occur on different land masses separated by impassable water barriers, or in mountain ranges separated by areas in which they cannot survive and which they cannot pass. The essential point is the *effective isolation of the populations from each other.*

The other type is that in which a population, occurring continuously through an area, still shows geographic differentiation. An excellent example is the Viceroy butterfly (*Limenitis archippus*) which is light brown in the northern states but dark brown in Florida, with more or less intermediate conditions all along in between. When this differentiation occurs in such a graded condition, the species is said to form a *cline.*

In the eastern area both types of subspecies occur. In a number of our butterflies one subspecies occurs in the Arctic, another in thoroughly isolated colonies southward on mountain tops or in acid bogs; or one subspecies occurs in the West Indies and another on the mainland. The great majority of our species, however, apparently show continuous or clinal subspeciation, ranging more or less uninterruptedly on the continent. Many such cases may, however, be more discontinuous than we think, due to occurrence in isolated colonies in a restricted habitat — in separated "ecological islands." This is called *ecotopic* isolation.

Forms, Varieties, Aberrations, etc. Many kinds of variations, other than geographic subspecies, occur within species. Most common is that in which males and females differ (e.g., *Colias, Eurema, Speyeria diana, Hesperia, Polites*, etc.). Or, there may be "dimorphic" forms within a single sex (e.g., *Colias, Papilio glaucus, Atrytone hobomok*) part of the individuals being of one type, and the remainder of another. There may be seasonal forms, different generations being consistently recognizable (e.g., *Polygonia, Anæa*, and *Lycænopsis*); these may be *hot* and *cold weather* forms, or *wet* and *dry season* forms. Often, however, we cannot correlate the variation with any such known factors; individuals merely occur, seemingly at random, which seem quite distinct. Such individual variations are *aberrations*. Some of them may obviously result from accidents to the larva or pupa that caused abnormal wing shapes or patterns. Others may occur over and over again, consistently enough to lead us to suspect that they may be inheritable variations.

The important thing to remember is that *such things do not represent something typifying the whole species population, but only a part of it.*

Most such variations have been given names. These may be quite convenient, especially when the variation differs enough from the normal to cause confusion in identification; or for people especially interested in such variations. But (I emphasize this, for it is a very important point) such names have no standing in official *specific and subspecific nomenclature*, and must not be given or used as though they did. They must be kept apart in their own particular section of nomenclature, and thus not allowed to cause confusion.

Aberration naming has been carried to extremes by some people, especially European workers who quite literally may count the number of scales in various spots, and name the different counts. Such work can be very interesting and valuable if properly done; for it may throw much light on problems of variation. But it must not be permitted to burden formal specific nomenclature, which has quite enough troubles of its own.

Scientific Nomenclature. Many books far larger than this one have been written about the branch of taxonomy dealing with the giving of scientific names. References to some of these will be found in the following appendix. It is essential, however, that one point be understood, the matter of priority. We have seen that a species name is given by an author who publishes a valid description and applies the name. The *first valid name* thus given to a species (or subspecies) or to a genus (or subgenus) is considered as having *priority*. It is the correct name to use. All others that may be given subsequently to the same species (or genus) are called *synonyms*. Many of our "changes" in scientific names result from someone's discovery of an older, valid name that replaces one in use at the time.

Another important concept is that of the *homonym*. By the "Code," no genus name can be repeated in the animal kingdom, for otherwise confusion could result. So, if two authors have proposed the same genus name (it does not matter what for; one could be for a bird and the other for a snail) the later one is a homonym, and invalid A substitute name can be proposed to replace it. Similarly, a *species* name must not be used twice in the same *genus;* when this does happen, the later one is a homonym, is invalid, and may have a substitute proposed. The discovery of homonyms is another fertile source of name changes. Eventually, let us hope, all will have been ferreted out and then we will be plagued no more with name changes from this source.

2. Butterfly Literature, Collections Etc.

MANY BOOKS have been written about butterflies; and the articles about them in periodicals must run into the tens of thousands. We can do no more here than to mention very briefly the chief works, combining this with an historical sketch of butterfly study in North America.

Butterfly collecting started over here at an early date. In the British Museum is a recognizable drawing of a Tiger Swallowtail which seems to have been made by John White, commander of Sir Walter Raleigh's ill-fated colonization in Virginia in 1587, and grandfather of Virginia Dare.

For long after that there are few detailed records of collectors, but various European authors undoubtedly received specimens in colonial times. Many of our eastern butterflies had been named by 1800 by such men as Linnæus, Fabricius, Cramer, Stoll, Latreille, and Drury. In the early nineteenth century appeared the great works of Jacob Huebner and Carl Geyer. To Huebner we owe a great many of our genus names, for he was the first worker to recognize the importance of detailed generic classification. You will note that he is the author of many names in our check list.

John Abbot, born in London in 1751, settled in Screven County, Georgia and collected there for many years. He reared many species, and painted their various stages and food plants. His work was published with Sir James E. Smith in 1797 and by Boisduval and Leconte (an American) in 1829–1833. These books were, by the way, the first to deal solely with North American Lepidoptera. About the end of the first quarter of the nineteenth century, however, home-grown talent began to appear; and by the middle of the century American entomologists were doing a major part of the study and publication on North American insects. Thomas Say (1787–1834), "The Father of American Zoology," published little on butterflies but very extensively in other groups. Harris' *Report on the Insects of Massachusetts Which Are Injurious to Vegetation* was of great importance. William H. Edwards' *The Butterflies of North America* and Scudder's *The Butterflies of New England . . .*, magnificent works that have not since been equaled or even approached, are still necessities today. In the number of butterflies that he named, and the exhaustive detail of his life history work, Edwards is unexcelled. Scudder, who was also a world authority on grasshoppers and fossils, was the broader taxonomist and better scientist of the two.

Up to the twentieth century many workers added greatly to the store of knowledge about our butterflies. Morris, French, Maynard, Strecker, Henry Edwards, Grote, Robinson, Reakirt, Riley, and Skinner worked and published in this country. In Europe Doubleday, Hewitson, the Felders, Godman and Salvin, Herrich-Schæffer, and Kirby were among the leading students, chiefly of the butterflies of the world in general.

By the twentieth century the great majority of North American butterfly species had been named, and a large number reared, so that considerable life history information was available. Since then the accumulation of knowledge has gone steadily on. A number of books and large works have been published. Chief of these in scope and influence were the two editions of Holland's *Butterfly Book*, the later edition of which is still almost indispensable, illustrating as it does nearly all the North American species. Unfortunately its classification and nomenclature have been so outdated that it may prove a source of confusion to anyone not fairly well acquainted with the butterflies anyway. Other works, some of them quite recent and extremely useful for certain localities and regions, are listed in the bibliography below.

Although they do not particularly cover North American butterflies, two foreign works are important: Godman and Salvin's *Biologia Centrali-Americana* and Seitz' *The Macrolepidoptera of the World*. Both cover the tropical fauna from which so many of our species have come. The *Biologia* is old enough so that many names have been changed since its publication. The same is true of Seitz, which is, besides, replete with errors which cause much confusion. Less pretentious but more recent and very valuable for the tropical elements of our fauna are: Marston Bates' *Butterflies of Cuba;* Comstock and Huntington's *Lycænidæ of the Antilles;* Comstock's *Butterflies of Porto Rico* and Hoffmann's *Catalogo Sistematico . . . de los Lepidopteros Mexicanos.*

18TH & 19TH CENTURIES

I have listed only one or two of the major works of each author. Nearly all of the books listed are quite rare and very expensive. A rough idea of their importance may be obtained by seeing how many times an author's name appears as the author of genera and species in our check list.

Boisduval, Jean Alphonse. 1836. *Histoire naturelle des insectes. Species Générale des Lépidoptères.* Paris.

 1852. *Lépidoptères de Californie.* Annales de la Societé Entomologique de France, Vol. 10.

Boisduval and John Eatton Leconte. 1829–1833. *Histoire Générale et iconographie des Lépidoptères et des chenilles de l'Amérique Septentrionale.* Paris.

Cramer, Pierre and (in part) Casper Stoll. 1775–1791. *Papillons Exotiques des trois parties du Monde L'Asie, L'Afrique et L'Amerique . . .* Amsterdam. Text in Dutch and French.

Doubleday, Edward; John O. Westwood and William C. Hewitson. 1846–1852. *The Genera of Diurnal Lepidoptera . . .* London. Text parts by Doubleday, Westwood; plates by Hewitson.

Drury, Dru. 1770–1782. *Illustrations of Natural History . . .* London.

Duponchel, P. A. J. (and Guenée). 1849. *Iconographie et Histoire Naturelle des Chenilles . . .* Paris.

Edwards, William Henry. 1868–1897. *The Butterflies of North America.*

Fabricius, Johann Christian. 1775. *Systema Entomologiæ, sistens Insectorum . . .* Flensburgi et Lipsiæ.

 1787. *Mantissa Insectorum, sistens eorum . . .* Hamburgii et Kilonii.

 1793. *Entomologica Systematica Emendata et Aucta . . .* Hafniæ.

Felder, Cajetan and Rudolph Felder. 1864–1875. *Reise der Œsterreichischen Fregatte Novara um der Erde.* Wien.

French, George H. 1886. *The Butterflies of the Eastern United States.* Philadelphia.

Godart, Jean Baptiste (and, in part, Latreille, Pierre Andre). 1819–1823. *Encyclopédie Méthodique.* Paris.

Godman, Frederick Ducane and Osbert Salvin. 1879–1901. *Biologia Centrali-Americana. Insecta, Lepidoptera-Rhopalocera.*

Gundlach, Juan. 1881. *Contribucion al la Entomologia Cubana.* Habana.

Harris, Thaddeus William. 1841 (and 1842, 1852, 1864). *A Report on the Insects of Massachusetts Which are Injurious to Vegetation.* Boston.

Herrich-Schæffer, Gottlieb August Wilhelm. 1862–1863. *Schmettlinge aus Cuba.* Regensburg.

Hewitson, William Chapman. 1862–1878. *Illustrations of Diurnal Lepidoptera. Lycænidæ.* London.

Huebner, Jacob and (in part) Carl Geyer. 1806–1838. *Sammlung exotischer Schmetterlinge.* Augsburg.

 1816–1826. *Verzeichniss bekannte Schmetlinge.* Augsburg.

 1818–1837. *Zuträge zur Sammlung exotische Schmetlinge.* Augsburg.

Kirby, William Forsell. 1871. *A Synonymical Catalogue of Diurnal Lepidoptera.* London.

Latreille, Pierre Andre (part). 1819–1823. *Encyclopédie Méthodique . . .* Paris.

Linnæus, Carolus. 1758. *Systema naturæ per Regna Tria Naturæ . . .*

Editio decima reformata. Holmiæ. (The official starting-point of our nomenclature.

1767. *Systema Naturæ ...* Editio duodecima reformata. Holmiæ.

Martyn, Thomas. 1797. *Psyche. Figures of Nondescript Lepidopterous Insects ...* London.

Maynard, Charles Johnson. 1891. *The Butterflies of New England ...* 2d ed. Newtonville, Massachusetts. (1st ed. 1886).

Morris, John G. 1860. *Catalogue of the Described Lepidoptera of North America.* Smithsonian Institute, Washington.

Poey, Felipe. 1851. *Memorias sobre la historia natural de la isla de Cuba ...* Habana.

Reakirt, Tryon. 1863. *Notes on Central American Lepidoptera ...* Proceedings of the Entomological Society of Philadelphia, Vol. 2.

Scopoli, Johann Anton. 1777. *Introductio ad historiam naturalem, sistens genera Lapidum, Plantarum et Animalium ...* Pragæ.

Scudder, Samuel Hubbard. 1872. *A Systematic revision of some of the American Butterflies; with brief notes on those known to occur in Essex County, Mass.* Salem, Massachusetts.

1889. *The Butterflies of the eastern United States and Canada with special reference to New England.* Cambridge, Massachusetts.

Smith, James Edward and John Abbot. 1797. *The natural history of the rarer lepidopterous insects of Georgia.* London.

Strecker, Herman. 1878. *Butterflies and Moths of North America. A Complete Synonymical Catalog ...* Reading, Pennsylvania.

Swainson, William. 1821–1823. *Zoological Illustrations ...* London.

20TH CENTURY

Only a small number of the most important butterfly references are given. There are, of course, hundreds more, chiefly articles in scientific journals, which cover more restricted fields than those we list.

Barnes, William and Foster H. Benjamin. 1926. *List of the Diurnal Lepidoptera of Boreal America North of Mexico.* Bulletin of the Southern California Academy of Sciences, Vol. 25.

Barnes, William and J. McDunnough. 1917. *Check-list of the Lepidoptera of Boreal America.* Decatur, Illinois.

Barnes, William (and others, chiefly J. McDunnough). 1911–1924. *Contributions to the Natural History of the Lepidoptera of North America.* Decatur, Illinois.

Bates, Marston. 1935. *The Butterflies of Cuba.* Bulletin of the Museum of Comparative Zoology at Harvard College, Vol. 78, No. 2. Cambridge, Massachusetts.

Bell, Ernest L. 1938. *The Hesperioidea.* Part One of a Catalog of the Original Descriptions of the Rhopalocera found north of the Mexican border. Edited by F. Martin Brown. Bulletin of the Cheyenne Mountain Museum, Vol. 1, Part 1. Colorado Springs, Colorado.

Clark, Austin H. 1932. *The Butterflies of the District of Columbia and Vicinity.* Smithsonian Institution, United States National Museum, Bulletin 157. Washington, D.C. (Government Printing Office, price $1.50).

Comstock, John Henry and Anna Botsford Comstock 1904 (reprinted

1936). *How to Know the Butterflies.* Ithaca, New York.

Comstock, William P. 1940. *Butterflies of New Jersey.* Journal of the New York Entomological Society. Vol. 48: 47–84.

Comstock, William Phillips. 1944. *Insects of Porto Rico and the Virgin Islands. Rhopalocera or Butterflies. Scientific Survey of Porto Rico and the Virgin Islands.* Volume 12, Part 4. New York Academy of Sciences, New York, New York.

Comstock, William P. and **E. Irving Huntington.** 1943. *Lycænidæ of the Antilles . . .* Annals of the New York Academy of Sciences, Vol. 45. New York, New York.

Davenport, Demarest and **V. G. Dethier.** 1938. *Bibliography of the Described Life Histories of the Rhopalocera of America North of Mexico 1889–1937.* Entomologica Americana, Vol. 17 (new series) No. 4 (Brooklyn Entomological Society). (See also Edwards, Henry; and Dethier, V. G.

Dethier, V. G. 1946. *Supplement to the Bibliography of the Described Life-histories of the Rhopalocera of America North of Mexico.* Psyche. Vol. 53, Nos. 1–2.

dos Passos, Cyril F. 1939. *The Satyridæ.* Part Two of *A Catalog of the Original Descriptions of the Rhopalocera found north of the Mexican Border.* Edited by F. Martin Brown. Bulletin of the Cheyenne Mountain Museum, Vol. 1, Part 2. Colorado Springs, Colorado.

Dyar, Harrison G. 1902. *A List of the North American Lepidoptera and Key to the Literature of This Order of Insects.* Bulletin No. 53, United States National Museum, Washington, D.C.

Edwards, Henry. 1889. *Bibliographical Catalog of the Described Transformations of North American Lepidoptera.* Bulletin of the United States National Museum, No. 35. Washington, D.C. (Although not a 20th century publication it is listed here because of its continuing value, with its supplements — see Davenport and Dethier.)

Field, William D. 1938. *A Manual of the Butterflies and Skippers of Kansas . . .* Bulletin of the University of Kansas, Lawrence, Kansas.

Forbes, W. T. M. 1906. *Field Tables of Lepidoptera.* Worcester, Massachusetts.

Grossbeck, John A. 1917. *Insects of Florida. IV. Lepidoptera.* Bulletin of the American Museum of Natural History, Vol. 37, Art. 1. New York, New York. (Edited and with addenda by **Frank E. Watson.**)

Hoffmann, Carlos C. 1940–1941. *Catalogo sistematico y zoogeografico de los Lepidopteros Mexicanos.* Sobretiro Annales Instituto Biologica Universidad Nacional de Mexico. Mexico, D.F.

Holland, W. J. 1898, revised edition 1931. *The Butterfly Book.* Garden City, New York.

Lindsey, A. W.; E. L. Bell and **R. C. Williams, Jr.** 1931. *The Hesperioidea of North America.* Denison University Bulletin, Vol. 26. Granville, Ohio.

Macy, Ralph W. and **Harold H. Shepard.** 1941. *Butterflies . . .* University of Minnesota Press, Minneapolis, Minnesota.

McDunnough, J. 1938. *Check List of the Lepidoptera of Canada and the United States of America.* Part 1, Macrolepidoptera. Memoirs of the Southern California Academy of Science, Vol. 1. Los Angeles, California.

Rothschild, Walter and **Karl Jordan.** 1906. *A Revision of the American Papilios.* Novitates Zoologica, Tring, England. Vol. 13.

ROADSIDE SKIPPERS
Genus *Amblyscirtes*

All illustrations are × 1½

1. ROADSIDE SKIPPER, *Amblyscirtes vialis*   p. 262
   Upper & under sides, ♂ (Randolph, N.H.). Fringes strongly checkered;
   much violet-gray dusting outwardly on wings beneath. Common.
   See text. S. Can. southward. See also Pl. 35, fig. 13.
2. BELL'S ROADSIDE SKIPPER, *Amblyscirtes belli*   p. 264
   Upper side, ♂ paratype (Vickery, Tex.). Dark brown above; no light
   spot in cell of FW; beneath sparsely dusted, light spots of HW inconspicuous. See Fig. 4, below. W. Ga. & Mo., s. to Tex.
3. PEPPER AND SALT SKIPPER, *Amblyscirtes hegon*   p. 263
   Upper & under sides, ♂ (Ogdensburg, N.J.). Fringes strongly
   checkered; light spots prominent, those of HW beneath, large; wings
   beneath heavily dusted with greenish-gray. Not uncommon. Can. s.
   to Ga.
4. BELL'S ROADSIDE SKIPPER, *Amblyscirtes belli*   p. 264
   Under side, ♂ paratype (Vickery, Tex.). See fig. 2, above.
5. LINDA'S ROADSIDE SKIPPER, *Amblyscirtes linda*   p. 264
   Upper side, ♂ (Quitman, Ark.). Fringes checkered; FW above with
   no light spot in cell; HW beneath well dusted, with definite light spots
   See text & fig. 7, below. Ark.
6. LEAST FLORIDA SKIPPER, *Amblyscirtes alternata*   p. 263
   Upper & under sides, ♂ (Cowarts, Ala.). Fringes checkered; small
   size; HW beneath with very sparse dusting. See text. N.C. s. thru
   Fla., w. to Ala.
7. LINDA'S ROADSIDE SKIPPER, *Amblyscirtes linda*   p. 264
   Under side, ♂ (Quitman, Ark.) See fig. 5 above.
8. EOS ROADSIDE SKIPPER, *Amblyscirtes eos*   p. 265
   Upper & under sides, ♂ (Kerrville, Tex.). Fringes very whitish; Spots
   well developed, especially on HW beneath, there large, prominent,
   dark-ringed. See text. Tex. & westward.

Note: *Amblyscirtes* is a *very* difficult genus. Many specimens of some of the
      species can be identified surely only by studying the genitalia, and then
      only by an authority.

Plate 38   305

SKIPPERS
Subfamily *Hesperiinae*

All illustrations are × 1½

1. **TEXTOR SKIPPER,** *Amblyscirtes textor*   p. 263
   Upper & under sides, ♂ (Suffolk, Va.). Distinctive, strong pattern of
   underside. Va. s. to Ga., w. to Tex. See also Pl. 35, fig. 11.
2. **CAROLINA ROADSIDE SKIPPER,** *Amblyscirtes carolina*   p. 263
   Upper & under sides, ♂ (Suffolk, Va.). Light spots distinctly yellow;
   strongly patterned, yellow underside of HW. Va. to N.C. See also
   Pl. 35, fig. 12.
3. SWARTHY SKIPPER, *Lerodea l'herminieri*   p. 266
   Upper & under sides, ♂ (Staten I., N.Y.). Small, brownish olivaceous;
   very undistinguished; HW beneath well dusted, its veins lighter; see
   text. N.Y. & Mo. to Fla. & Tex. Common.
4. **THREE SPOTTED SKIPPER,** *Lerodea tripuncta*   p. 267
   Upper side, ♂ (Florida City, Fla.). Small light spots above; very
   faint light spots on HW beneath. See text. S. Fla., rare.
5. **NEAMATHLA SKIPPER,** *Lerodea neamathla*   p. 267
   Upper & under sides, ♂ (Mobile, Ala.). Faint light spots above; HW
   beneath olivaceous dusted, the veins lighter. See text. Fla. to Tex.
   Common.
6. EUFALA SKIPPER, *Lerodea eufala*   p. 267
   Upper side, ♂ (St. Petersburg, Fla.). See text. Va. & Nebr. s. to Fla.
   & Tex. Common. See fig. 8, below.
7. **JULIA'S SKIPPER** *Lerodea julia*   p. 267
   Upper & under sides, ♂ paratype (Uvalde, Tex.). Lighter coloring,
   with more lighter, yellowish overscaling above & beneath; light spots
   slightly more prominent. See text. Tex.
8. EUFALA SKIPPER. *Lerodea eufala*   p. 267
   Under side, ♀ (St. Petersburg, Fla.). See fig. 6, above.

Note: *Lerodea* is another very difficult genus. Many specimens of some of the
   species can be identified surely only by studying the genitalia, and then
   only by an authority.

Skinner, Henry. 1898. *A Synonymic Catalogue of the North American Rhopalocera.* Philadelphia and Supplement No. 1, 1904.

Seitz, Adalbert. 1907–1924 (editor). *The Macrolepidoptera of the World.* Vol. V. The American Rhopalocera. Stuttgart. (Various authors.)

Williams, C. B. 1930. *The Migration of Butterflies.* Edinburgh and London.

GENERAL ENTOMOLOGY

Comstock, J. H. 1940. *An Introduction to Entomology.* Comstock Publishing Co., Ithaca, New York. *The* standard for over fifty years.

Frost, S. W. 1942. *General Entomology.* McGraw-Hill Book Co. A standard text.

Essig, E. O. 1942. *College Entomology.* Macmillan Co. A standard text.

Lutz, F. E. 1935. *Fieldbook of Insects.* G. P. Putnam's Sons. The most widely used, popular guide to insects, chiefly of eastern North America.

Swain, Ralph B. 1948. *The Insect Guide.* Doubleday and Co. A finely illustrated and thoroughly authentic popular book on the orders and major families of North American insects.

Torre-Bueno, J. R. de la. 1937. *A Glossary of Entomology.* Brooklyn Entomological Society, Brooklyn, New York. A very complete, illustrated dictionary of entomological terms.

INSECT TAXONOMY AND NOMENCLATURE

Ferris, G. F. 1928. *The Principles of Systematic Entomology.* Stanford University Press.

Jaeger, E. C. 1944. *A Source Book of Biological Names and Terms.*

Mayr, Ernst. 1942. *Systematics and the Origin of Species.* Columbia University Press. Although not concerned solely with entomology, this is a "must" for every serious student of taxonomy.

Schenk, E. T. and John H. McMasters. 1936. *Procedure in Taxonomy.* Stanford University Press.

Woods, R. S. 1944. *The Naturalist's Lexicon.* Abbey Garden Press, Pasadena.

COLLECTING AND PRESERVING SPECIMENS

Gray, Alice. Direction Leaflets: 1. How to Make and Use Safe Insect-Killing Jars. 2. How to Make and Use Insect Nets. 3. How to Collect Insects and Spiders for Scientific Study. 5. How to Make and Use Spreading Boards for Insects. Others in course of preparation. Department of Insects and Spiders, American Museum of Natural History, New York City, New York. Available upon request.

Oman, P. W. and A. D. Cushman. 1946. *Collection and Preservation of Insects.* United States Department of Agriculture, Misc. Publication 601, Washington, D.C. (25¢.)

Peterson, A. M. *A Manual of Entomological Equipment and Methods.* Part 1 (1934), Edwards Bros., Ann Arbor, Michigan. Part 2 (1937), John S. Swift and Co., St. Louis, Missouri.

Ward's Natural Science Establishment, Rochester, N. Y. *How to Make an Insect Collection.*

DEALERS IN ENTOMOLOGICAL SUPPLIES AND BOOKS

Ward's Natural Science Establishment, Inc., Rochester, New York.
General Biological Supply Co., Chicago, Illinois.
John D. Sherman, Jr., 132 Primrose Ave., Mt. Vernon, New York, is *the* dealer in entomological literature.

ENTOMOLOGICAL SOCIETIES AND PERIODICALS

We have in North America a number of entomological societies, most of them of long standing. The major ones publish purely entomological journals. With the exception of the *Lepidopterists' News*, all are devoted to the study of all groups of insects. For anyone interested in butterflies we advise primarily the *Lepidopterists' News*, secondarily the *Entomological News*. Only one periodical that is not strictly entomological has been included; that, the *Bulletin of the Southern California Academy of Science*, publishes many articles of the greatest value to the student of butterflies. Other entomological journals, now defunct, have contained much valuable information.

American Entomological Society, Philadelphia, Pennsylvania. *Entomological News* and *Transactions*.
Entomological Society of America, Columbus, Ohio. *Annals.*
Brooklyn Entomological Society, Brooklyn, New York. *Bulletin* and *Entomologica Americana.*
Cambridge Entomological Club, Cambridge, Massachusetts. *Psyche.*
Florida Entomological Society, Gainesville, Fla. *The Florida Entomologist.*
Kansas Entomological Society, Lawrence and Manhattan, Kansas. *Journal.*
Lepidopterists' Society, Osborn Zoological Laboratory, New Haven, Connecticut. *Lepidopterists' News.*
New York Entomological Society, New York. *Journal.*
Entomological Society of Ontario, Guelph, Ontario. *Canadian Entomologist.*
Pacific Coast Entomological Society, San Francisco. *Pan-Pacific Entomologist.*
Southern California Academy of Sciences, Los Angeles. *Bulletin.*
Entomological Society of Washington, Washington, D.C. *Annals.*

MUSEUMS AND COLLECTIONS

Nearly all the large public natural history museums, and some colleges and universities, have important collections of butterflies and libraries of entomological books and periodicals. These are available for study by qualified persons. Most of these institutions publish scientific periodicals in which entomological works often appear. The chief ones in our area are:

United States National Museum, and Library of Congress, Washington, D.C.
Academy of Natural Sciences, Philadelphia, Pennsylvania
American Museum of Natural History, New York City, New York
Boston Society of Natural History, Boston, Massachusetts
Canadian National Collection, Ottawa, Ontario
Carnegie Museum, Pittsburgh, Pennsylvania

Cornell University, Department of Entomology, Ithaca, New York
Chicago Natural History Museum, Chicago, Illinois
Kansas State College, Manhattan, Kansas
University of Kansas, Lawrence, Kansas
Michigan State College, East Lansing, Michigan
University of Michigan, Ann Arbor, Michigan
Museum of Comparative Zoology, Cambridge, Massachusetts
New York State Museum, Albany, New York
Peabody Museum, Yale University, New Haven, Connecticut

3. Check List of the Butterflies of Eastern North America

ALL SPECIES and subspecies known to have been recorded from the eastern area have been listed. A few of uncertain status, or for which records from our area are dubious, have been queried. Subgeneric names are in parentheses. Subspecific names are prefixed by "a," "b," etc. and indented under species. An asterisk before a name marks a nymotypical subspecies that does not occur in our area. No real synonymy has been included. The occasional names *printed in italics* are names formerly widely used, included here to avoid confusion when a recent name change has been made.

Superfamily *Papilionoidea* — The True Butterflies

Family *Satyridæ* — The Satyrs and Wood Nymphs

LETHE Huebner (subgenus ENODIA) Huebner
  1. portlandia Fabricius — Pearly Eye
    a. borealis A. H. Clark
    b. anthedon A. H. Clark
  2. creola Skinner — Creole Pearly Eye
  3. eurydice Johannson — Eyed Brown
     canthus Linnæus
    a. appalachia R. L. Chermock
EUPTYCHIA (EUPTYCHIA) Huebner. The Satyrs
  1. cymela Cramer — Little Wood Satyr
    eurytus Fabricius
    a. viola Maynard
 *2. hermes Fabricius
    a. sosybia Fabricius — Carolina Satyr
  3. mitchellii French — Mitchell's Satyr

4. areolata Abbot & Smith — Georgia Satyr
    a. septentrionalis Davis — Lakehurst Satyr
5. rubricata Edwards — Red Satyr
EUPTYCHIA (CYLLOPSIS) Felder
6. gemma Huebner — Gemmed Satyr
    a. freemani Stallings & Turner
CŒNONYMPHA Huebner. Ringlets
*1. tullia Muller — Widespread Ringlet
    a. inornata Edwards — Inornate Ringlet
        ochracea Edwards
    b. benjamini McDunnough — Prairie Ringlet
    c. mcisaaci dos Passos — McIsaac's Ringlet
    d. brenda Edwards — Ochre Ringlet
        ochracea auct.
    e. nipisiquit McDunnough — Maritime Ringlet
CERCYONIS Scudder. The Wood Nymphs or Graylings
1. pegala Fabricius — Southern Wood Nymph
    a. nephele Kirby — Northern Wood Nymph
    b. maritima Edwards — Maritime Wood Nymph
    c. alope Fabricius — Blue Eyed Grayling
    d. carolina Chermock & Chermock — Carolina Wood Nymph
    e. texana Edwards — Texas Wood Nymph
ŒNEIS Huebner. The Arctics
1. macounii Edwards — Macoun's Arctic
*2. chryxus Doubleday — Chryxus Arctic
    a. calais Scudder
    b. strigulosus McDunnough
3. taygete Geyer — White Veined Arctic
    a. gaspeensis dos Passos
*4. jutta Huebner — Jutta Arctic
    a. ridingiana Chermock & Chermock
    b. terra-novæ dos Passos
5. polixenes Fabricius — Polixenes Arctic
    a. katahdin Newcomb — Mt. Katahdin Arctic
6. melissa Fabricius — Melissa Arctic
    a. assimilis Butler
    b. semplei Holland
    c. semidea Say — White Mountain Butterfly
EREBIA Dalman. The Alpines
1. discoidalis Kirby — Red Disked Alpine
2. rossii Curtis — Ross' Alpine
*3. theano Tauschenberg
    a. canadensis Warren — Churchill Alpine
4. epipsodea Butler — Common Alpine
*5. disa Thunberg — Disa Alpine
    a. mancina Westwood

Family *Danaiidæ* — The Monarchs

DANAUS (DANAUS) Huebner
*1. gilippus Cramer — The Queen
    a. berenice Cramer
    b. strigosus Bates

*2. eresimus Cramer
    a. montezuma Talbot
    b. tethys Forbes
DANAUS (DIOGAS) D'Almeida
   3. plexippus Linnæus — The Monarch or Milkweed Butterfly
LYCORELLA Hemming
  *1. ceres Cramer
    a. demeter Felder
    b. atergatis Doubleday ??
DIRCENNA Doubleday
  1. klugii Geyer ??
ITHOMIA Huebner
  1. anaphissa Herrich-Schæffer ??

Family *Heliconiidæ* — The Heliconians

HELICONIUS Kluk
  *1. charitonius Linnæus — The Zebra
    a. tuckeri Comstock & Brown
    b. vazquezæ Comstock & Brown
  2. petiveranus Doubleday
AGRAULIS Boisduval and Leconte
    Dione auct.
  *1. vanillæ Linnæus — Gulf Fritillary
    a. nigrior Michener
    b. incarnata Riley
DRYAS Huebner
    Colænis Huebner
  *1. julia Fabricius — Julia
    a. cillene Cramer
    b. delila Fabricius

Family *Nymphalidæ* — The Brush Footed Butterflies

EUPTOIETA Doubleday
  1. claudia Cramer — Variegated Fritillary
  *2. hegesia Cramer — Mexican Fritillary
    a. hoffmanni W. P. Comstock
SPEYERIA (SPEYERIA) Scudder. The Greater Fritillaries
    Argynnis auct.
  1. idalia Drury — Regal Fritillary
  2. atlantis Edwards — Atlantis Fritillary
    a. canadensis dos Passos
    b. hollandi Chermock & Chermock
  3. lais Edwards — Lais Fritillary
  *4. mormonia Edwards
    a. eurynome Edwards — Eurynome Fritillary

SPEYERIA (SEMNOPSYCHE) Scudder
  5. diana Cramer — Diana
  6. cybele Fabricius — Great Spangled Fritillary
    a. novascotiæ McDunnough
    b. krautwurmi Holland
    c. pseudocarpenteri Chermock & Chermock
  7. aphrodite Fabricius — Aphrodite
    a. winni Gunder
    b. alcestis Edwards
    c. manitoba Chermock & Chermock
BOLORIA Moore (subgenus CLOSSIANA) Reuss. The Lesser Fritil-
    laries
      Brenthis auct.
  *1. selene Schiffermueller
    a. myrina Cramer — Silver Bordered Fritillary
    b. atrocostalis Huard
    c. terra-novæ Holland
    d. nebraskensis Holland
    e. marilandica A. H. Clark ?
  *2. eunomia Esper — Bog Fritillary
    a. triclaris Huebner
    b. dawsoni Barnes & McDunnough
  *3. titania Esper — Purple Lesser Fritillary
    a. boisduvalii Duponchel
    b. grandis Barnes & McDunnough
    c. montina Scudder — White Mountain Fritillary
  *4. chariclea Schneider — Arctic Fritillary
    a. arctica Zetterstedt
    b. butleri Edwards
  5. polaris Boisduval — Polaris Fritillary
  6. freija Thunberg — Freija
    a. tarquinius Curtis
  7. toddi Holland — Meadow Fritillary
    a. ammiralis Hemming
      bellona Fabricius
  *8. frigga Thunberg
    a. saga Staudinger — Saga Fritillary
  9. improba Butler — Dingy Fritillary
EUPHYDRYAS Scudder. Checkerspots
  1. phæton Drury — The Baltimore
    a. borealis Chermock & Chermock
MELITÆA Fabricius (subgenus MICROTIA) Bates. The Checkerspots
  1. fulvia Edwards
  2. harrissii Scudder — Harris' Checkerspot
    a. hanhami Fletcher
    b. albimontana Avinoff
    c. liggetti Avinoff
  3. ismeria Boisduval & Leconte — Ismeria Checkerspot
  4. gorgone Huebner — Gorgone Checkerspot
    a. carlota Reakirt
  5. nycteis Doubleday — Silvery Checkerspot
    a. drusius Edwards
    b. reversa Chermock & Chermock
  6. elada Hewitson
  *7. theona Menetries
    a. thekla Edwards

PHYCIODES (PHYCIODES) Huebner. The Crescents
1. picta Edwards — Painted Crescent
2. phaon Edwards — Phaon Crescent
3. vesta Edwards — Vesta Crescent
4. camillus Edwards — Camillus Crescent
5. batesii Reakirt — Tawny Crescent
6. tharos Drury — Pearl Crescent
   a. arctica dos Passos — Newfoundland Crescent

PHYCIODES (ERESIA) Doubleday
7. frisia Poey — Cuban Crescent
   a. tulcis Bates

PHYCIODES (TRITANASSA) Forbes
8. texana Edwards — Texan Crescent
   a. seminole Skinner — Seminole Crescent

CHLOSYNE Butler. The Patched Butterflies
*1. lacinia Geyer
   a. adjutrix Scudder — Scudder's Patched Butterfly
2. erodyle Bates
3. endeis Godman & Salvin
4. janais Drury

HYPOLIMNAS Huebner
1. misippus Linnæus — The Mimic

POLYGONIA Huebner. The Angle Wings
1. interrogationis Fabricius — Question Mark or Violet Tip
2. comma Harris — Hop Merchant
3. satyrus Edwards — Satyr Anglewing
   f. marsyas Edwards
4. faunus Edwards — Green Comma
   a. smythi A. H. Clark
5. progne Cramer — Grey Comma
6. gracilis Edwards — Hoary Comma

NYMPHALIS Kluk. The Tortoise Shells
1. j-album Boisduval & Leconte — Compton Tortoise Shell
2. milberti Latreille — Milbert's Tortoise Shell
   a. viola dos Passos
3. antiopa Linnæus — Mourning Cloak
4. californica Boisduval — California Tortoise Shell

VANESSA Fabricius. Thistle Butterflies
1. atalanta Linnæus — Red Admiral
2. cardui Linnæus — Painted Lady
3. virginiensis Drury — American Painted Lady

PRECIS Huebner
   Junonia Huebner
*1. lavinia Cramer
   a. cœnia Huebner — The Buckeye
   b. zonalis Felder — Tropical Buckeye

ANARTIA Huebner
*1. jatrophæ Johannson — White Peacock
   a. guantanamo Munroe
   b. luteipicta Fruhstorfer
2. fatima Fabricius

METAMORPHA Huebner
*1. stelenes Linnæus — The Malachite
   a. biplagiata Fruhstorfer

HYPANARTIA Huebner
1. lethe Fabricius ??

MYSCELIA Doubleday
  1. ethusa Boisduval
  2. cyananthe Felder
DYNAMINE Huebner
  1. dyonis Geyer
DIÆTHRIA Billberg. The "88's"
  1. clymena Cramer
  2. asteria Godman & Salvin
EUNICA Huebner. The Purple Wings
  1. tatila Herrich-Schæffer — ??
    a. tatilista Kaye — Florida Purple Wing
  2. monima Stoll — Dingy Purple Wing
MESTRA Huebner
  1. amymone Menetries — Amymone
 *2. cana Erichson
    a. floridana Strecker ??
BIBLIS Fabricius
 *1. hyperia Cramer
    a. aganisa Boisduval
HAMADRYAS Huebner. The Calicoes
  1. feronia Linnæus — White Skirted Calico
  2. fornax Linnæus
  3. ferox Staudinger ??
MARPESIA Huebner. The Dagger Wings
  1. coresia Godart — The Waiter
  2. chiron Fabricius — Many Banded Dagger Wing
 *3. petreus Cramer — Ruddy Dagger Wing
    a. thetys Fabricius
LIMENITIS Fabricius. The Viceroys & Admirals
  1. arthemis Drury — White Admiral
    a. rubrofasciata Barnes & McDunnough
    b. astyanax Fabricius — Red Spotted Purple
  2. archippus Cramer — The Viceroy
    a. floridensis Strecker — Florida Viceroy
    b. watsoni dos Passos — Watson's Viceroy
ADELPHA (ADELPHA) Huebner. The Sisters
  1. fessonia Hewitson
ADELPHA (HETEROCHROA) Boisduval
  2. bredowii Geyer — Mexican Sister
SMYRNA Huebner
  1. karwinskii Geyer
HISTORIS Huebner
  1. odius Fabricius
  2. acheronta Fabricius ??
ANÆA Huebner. The Leaf Wings
  1. andria Scudder — Goatweed Butterfly
  2. floridalis Johnson & Comstock — Florida Leaf Wing
  3. aidea Guerin — Tropical Leaf Wing
  4. glycerium Doubleday
  5. pithyusa Felder
CHLORIPPE Boisduval. The Reflecting Butterflies
  1. pavon Latreille
ASTEROCAMPA Roeber. The Hackberry Butterflies
  1. clyton Boisduval & Leconte — Tawny Emperor
    a. flora Edwards
    b. texana Skinner

     c. louisa Stallings & Turner
2. celtis Boisduval & Leconte — Hackberry Butterfly
     a. alicia Edwards
     b. antonia Edwards
     c. montis Edwards
*3. leilia Edwards — Leilia
     a. cocles Lintner

Family *Libytheidæ* — The Snout Butterflies

LIBYTHEANA Michener
1. bachmannii Kirtland — Snout Butterfly
     a. larvata Strecker
2. carinenta Cramer ??

Family *Riodinidæ* — The Metalmarks

APODEMIA Felder
1. walkeri Godman & Salvin — Walker's Metalmark
EMESIS Fabricius
1. emesia Hewitson — Emesia Metalmark
LASAIA Bates
1. sessilis Schaus — Blue Metalmark
CARIA Huebner
1. domitianus Fabricius — Domitian Metalmark
LEPHELISCA Barnes and Lindsey
     Calephelis auct. & *Nymphidia* auct.
1. virginiensis Guerin — Little Metalmark
     pumila Boisduval & Leconte
2. borealis Grote & Robinson — Northern Metalmark
3. muticum McAlpine — Swamp Metalmark
4. rawsoni McAlpine — Rawson's Metalmark
5. nemesis Edwards — Fatal Metalmark
6. perditalis Barnes & McDunnough — Lost Metalmark

Family *Lycænidæ* — The Gossamer Winged Butterflies

Subfamily *Theclinæ* — The Hairstreaks

EUMÆUS Huebner
*1. atala Poey — Atala
     a. florida Roeber — Florida Atala

ATLIDES Huebner
   1. halesus Cramer — Great Purple Hairstreak
     a. estesi Clench ?
STRYMON Huebner
     Thecla auct.
   1. m-album Boisduval & Leconte — White "M" Hairstreak
   2. cecrops Fabricius — Red Banded Hairstreak
   3. beon Cramer — Beon Hairstreak
   4. titus Fabricius — Coral Hairstreak
     a. mopsus Huebner
     b. watsoni Barnes & Benjamin
   5. melinus Huebner — Gray Hairstreak
     a. humuli Harris
     b. franki Field
   6. buchholzi H. A. Freeman
   7. favonius Abbot & Smith — Southern Hairstreak
   8. ontario Edwards — Northern Hairstreak
     a. autolycus Edwards
   9. alcestis Edwards — Alcestis Hairstreak
  10. acadica Edwards — Acadian Hairstreak
     a. watrini Dufrane
  11. edwardsii Grote & Robinson — Edwards' Hairstreak
  12. falacer Godart — Banded Hairstreak
     calanus auct., not Huebner
  13. calanus Huebner — Florida Hairstreak
  14. caryævorus McDunnough — Hickory Hairstreak
  15. liparops Boisduval & Leconte — Striped Hairstreak
     a. strigosus Harris
     b. fletcheri Michener & dos Passos
  16. martialis Herrich-Schæffer — Martial Hairstreak
*17. acis Drury
     a. bartrami Comstock & Huntington — Bartram's Hairstreak
*18. simæthis Drury
     a. sarita Skinner — Sarita Hairstreak
  19. pastor Butler & Druce — Pastor Hairstreak
  20. facuna Hewitson — Facuna Hairstreak
  21. mæsites Herrich-Schæffer — Mæsites Hairstreak
     a. telea Hewitson
*22. columella Fabricius — Columella Hairstreak
     a. modesta Maynard
     b. istapa Reakirt
  23. bazochii Godart — Bazochii Hairstreak
  24. clytie Edwards — Clytie Hairstreak
  25. azia Hewitson — Azia Hairstreak
*26. endymion Fabricius — Endymion Hairstreak
     a. cyphara Hewitson
  27. cestri Reakirt — Cestri Hairstreak
  28. yojoa Reakirt — Yojoa Hairstreak
  29. spurina Hewitson — Spurina Hairstreak
  30. laceyi Barnes & McDunnough — Lacey's Hairstreak
  31. zebina Hewitson — Zebina Hairstreak
  32. rufofusca Hewitson — Reddish Hairstreak
  33. echion Linnæus — Echion Hairstreak
MITOURA Scudder
   1. gryneus Huebner — Olive Hairstreak

  a. sweadneri Chermock
  b. castalis Edwards
 2. hesseli Rawson & Ziegler — Hessel's Hairstreak
 3. xami Reakirt — Xami Hairstreak
ERORA Scudder
 1. læta Edwards — Early Hairstreak
INCISALIA Scudder. The Elfins
 1. augustinus Westwood — Brown Elfin
   augustus Kirby (homonym)
  a. crœsioides Scudder
  b. helenæ dos Passos
 2. polios Cook & Watson — Hoary Elfin
 3. henrici Grote & Robinson — Henry's Elfin
  a. margaretæ dos Passos
  b. turneri Clench
  c. solatus Cook & Watson
 4. irus Godart — Frosted Elfin
  a. hadros Cook & Watson
 5. lanoraieensis Sheppard — Bog Elfin
 6 niphon Huebner — Pine Elfin
  a. clarki T. N. Freeman
 7. mossii H. Edwards — Moss' Elfin ??

Subfamily *Gerydinæ* — The Harvesters

FENISECA Grote
 1. tarquinius Fabricius — The Harvester
  a. nova-scotiæ McDunnough

Subfamily *Lycæninæ* — The Coppers

LYCÆNA (LYCÆNA) Fabricius
 *1. phlæas Linnæus
  a. americana Harris — American Copper
   hypophlæus auct. not Boisduval
  b. feildeni McLachlan — Arctic Copper
LYCÆNA (THARSALEA) Scudder
 1. thoë Guerin — Bronze Copper
 2. epixanthe Boisduval & Leconte — Bog Copper
  a. phædra Hall
  b. michiganensis Rawson
 3. helloides Boisduval — Purplish Copper
 4. dorcas Kirby — Dorcas Copper
  a. dospassosi McDunnough

b. claytoni Brower
*5. xanthoides Boisduval — Great Copper
   a. dione Scudder

Subfamily *Plebeiinæ* — The Blues

LEPTOTES Scudder. The Tropical Blues
*1. cassius Cramer — Cassius' Blue
   a. theonus Lucas
   b. striatus Edwards
  2. marinus Reakirt — Marine Blue
HEMIARGUS (HEMIARGUS) Huebner. The Eyed Blues
*1. ceraunus Fabricius — Ceraunus Blue
   a. antibubastus Huebner
   b. zacheinus Butler & Druce
HEMIARGUS (CYCLARGUS) Nabokov
*2. thomasi Clench
   a. bethune-bakeri Comstock & Huntington — Miami Blue
HEMIARGUS (ECHINARGUS) Nabokov
  3. isolus Reakirt — Reakirt's Blue
   a. alce Edwards ?
BREPHIDIUM Scudder. The Pygmy Blues
  1. exilis Boisduval — Western Pygmy Blue
   a. fea Edwards ?
  2. pseudofea Morrison — Eastern Pygmy Blue
   isophthalma auct.
ZIZULA Chapman
  1. gaika Trimen — Imported Blue
   cyna Edwards
EVERES Huebner. The Tailed Blues
  1. comyntas Godart — Eastern Tailed Blue
   a. valeriæ Clench ?
   b. texana F. H. Chermock ?
  2. amyntula Boisduval — Western Tailed Blue
LYCÆIDES Huebner. The Orange Margined Blues
*1. argyrognomon Bergstræsser — Northern Blue
   a. scudderii Edwards — Scudder's Blue
   b. empetri T. N. Freeman — Crowberry Blue
   c. aster Edwards — Newfoundland Blue
  2. melissa Edwards — Melissa Blue
   a. samuelis Nabokov — Karner Blue
PLEBEIUS Kluk
  1. aquilo Boisduval — Arctic Blue
   a. lacustris T. N. Freeman
  2. sæpiolus Boisduval — Sæpiolus Blue
  3. acmon Westwood — Acmon Blue
GLAUCOPSYCHE Scudder
  1. lygdamus Doubleday — Silvery Blue
   a. couperi Grote
   b. mildredæ F. H. Chermock
   c. jacki Stallings & Turner
   d. afra Edwards ?
   e. oro Scudder ?

LYCÆNOPSIS Felder
*1. argiolus Linnæus — Spring Azure
   a. lucia Kirby
   b. pseudargiolus Boisduval & Leconte

Family *Papilionidæ* — The Swallowtails

PAPILIO (PAPILIO) Linnæus
*1. machaon Linnæus — Old World Swallowtail
   a. hudsonianus A. H. Clark
   b. dodi McDunnough ?
 2. brevicauda Saunders — Short Tailed Swallowtail
   a. bretonensis McDunnough
   b. gaspeensis McDunnough
*3. polyxenes Fabricius — Black Swallowtail
   a. asterius Stoll
 4. bairdii Edwards — Baird's Swallowtail
 5. cresphontes Cramer — Giant Swallowtail
   a. pennsylvanicus Chermock & Chermock
*6. thoas Linnæus — Thoas Swallowtail
   a. autocles Rothschild & Jordan
*7. lycophron Huebner — Lycophron Swallowtail
   a. pallas Gray
*8. aristodemus Esper
   a. ponceanus Schaus — Schaus' Swallowtail
 9. ornythion Boisduval — Ornythion Swallowtail
*10. andræmon Huebner — Andræmon Swallowtail
   a. bonhotei Sharpe
 11. glaucus Linnæus — Tiger Swallowtail
   a. canadensis Rothschild & Jordan
   b. australis Maynard
 12. rutulus Lucas — Western Tiger Swallowtail
 13. multicaudatus Kirby — Three Tailed Swallowtail ?
 14. troilus Linnæus — Spicebush Swallowtail
   a. ilioneus Abbot & Smith
 15. palamedes Drury — Palamedes Swallowtail
   a. leontis Rothschild & Jordan ?
*16. anchisiades Esper
   a. idæus Fabricius — Idæus Swallowtail
PAPILIO (GRAPHIUM) Scopoli. The Kite Swallowtails
 17. marcellus Cramer — Zebra Swallowtail
   a. floridensis Holland
 18. celadon Lucas ???
PAPILIO (BATTUS) Scopoli. The Aristolochia Swallowtails
 19. philenor Linnæus — Pipe Vine Swallowtail
 20. polydamas Linnæus — Polydamas Swallowtail
   a. lucayus Rothschild & Jordan
 21. devilliers Godart ???

Family *Pieridæ* — The Whites and Sulphurs

Subfamily — *Dismorphiinæ*

LICINIA Huebner
  1. melite Huebner?

Subfamily *Pierinæ*

ANTHOCARIS Boisduval (subgenus **FALCAPICA**) **Klots**
  1. genutia Fabricius — Falcate Orange Tip
    a. midea Huebner
EUCHLOË Huebner
  1. olympia Edwards — Olympia
    a. rosa Edwards
COLIAS (COLIAS) Fabricius. The Northern Sulphurs
  1. eurytheme Boisduval — Alfalfa Butterfly
  2. philodice Latreille — Common Sulphur
  3. interior Scudder — Pink Edged Sulphur
  4. pelidne Boisduval & Leconte — Pelidne Sulphur
 *5. palæno Linnæus — Palæno Sulphur
    a. chippewa Kirby
  6. gigantea Strecker — Giant Sulphur
  7. hecla Lefebre — Hecla Orange
    a. hela Strecker
  8. boothii Curtis — Booth's Sulphur
  9. nastes Boisduval — Nastes Sulphur
    a. rossii Curtis
    b. gueneei Avinoff
    c. moina Strecker
    d. subarctica McDunnough
COLIAS (ZERENE) Huebner. The Dog Faces
  10. cesonia Stoll — The Dog Face
ANTEOS Huebner. The Angled Sulphurs
 *1. mærula Fabricius — Mærula
    a. lacordairei Boisduval
 *2. clorinde Godart — Clorinde
    a. nivifera Fruhstorfer
PHŒBIS (PHŒBIS) Huebner. The Tropical Sulphurs
  1. sennæ Linnæus — Cloudless Sulphur
    a. eubule Linnæus
    b. marcellina Cramer ?
  2. philea Linnæus — Orange Barred Sulphur
 *3. agarithe Boisduval — Large Orange Sulphur
    a. maxima Neumœgen
  4. argante Fabricius ?

SKIPPERS

Subfamily *Hesperiinae*

The illustrations are all × 1½ except fig. 7

1. SALT MARSH SKIPPER, *Panoquina panoquin*   p. 269
   Upper & under sides, ♂ (Cape May, N.J.). Light veins and streaks
   between veins on HW beneath. Salt marshes along coast, N.J. s. to
   Ala. & Fla. See also Pl. 36, fig. 11.
2. SALT MARSH SKIPPER, *Panoquina panoquin*   p. 269
   Upper side, ♀ (Port Sewall, Fla.). See ♂, above.
3. OBSCURE SKIPPER, *Panoquina panoquinoides*   p. 270
   Upper & under sides, ♂ (Puerto Plata, Dominican Republic). Small;
   heavily dusted with tawny scales; spots of FW small or absent. S. Fla.
4. OBSCURE SKIPPER, *Panoquina panoquinoides*   p. 270
   Upper side, ♀ (Cabanas, P. de R., Cuba). See ♂, above.
5. OCOLA SKIPPER, *Panoquina ocola*   p. 270
   Upper side, ♂ (Tampa, Fla.). Larger size than *panoquinoides;* FW
   with no light spot in cell (cf. *hecebolus*, below). Fla. & Tex. n. to N.Y.
   & Ind., casual in north. Common.
6. HECEBOLUS SKIPPER, *Panoquina hecebolus*   p. 270
   Upper side, ♂ (Pharr, Tex.). FW above with light spot in cell (cf.
   ocola, above); HW beneath nearly or entirely unmarked; largest spot
   of FW not squarish. S. Fla. & S. Tex.
7. BRAZILIAN SKIPPER, *Calpodes ethlius*   p. 269
   Upper side, ♂ (Hope, Ark.) × 1 (natural size). Large size; very
   robust; prominent transparent spots on HW. N.Y. & Mo. (strays)
   southward, common in south.
8. MALICIOUS SKIPPER, *Synapte malitiosa*   p. 271
   Upper side, ♂ (Pharr, Tex.). Dark brown, marked with orange-
   fulvous; longitudinal dark discal shade on FW nearly black. S. Tex.
   Shady areas.

Note: *Panoquina* and *Calpodes* are very difficult genera, with numerous tropical
      species. Many specimens of some of the species can be identified surely
      only by studying the genitalia, and then only by an authority well ac-
      quainted with all the species.

1

2

3

4

5

6

Plate 40   321

GIANT SKIPPERS
Family *Megathymidae*

All the illustrations are × 1 (natural size)

1. YUCCA SKIPPER, *Megathymus yuccœ*   p. 274
   Upper side, ♂ (Gulfport, Fla.). HW beneath has the more basal of
   the two white spots below costa larger than the outer one; and has at
   most very small postmedian, discal spots. S.C. thru Fla., w. thru
   Kans., Okla. & Tex.
2. YUCCA SKIPPER, *Megathymus yuccœ*   p. 275
   Upper side, ♀ (St. Petersburg, Fla.). See ♂, above.
3. COFAQUI SKIPPER, *Megathymus cofaqui*   p. 275
   Upper side, ♂ (Sarasota, Fla.). Smaller size; pale ground color; HW
   beneath smoothly tinted, with distal and limbal gray powdering,
   but little, if any, gray along costal margin. Ga. & Fla.
4. COFAQUI SKIPPER, *Megathymus cofaqui*   p. 275
   Upper side, ♀ (Sarasota, Fla.). See ♂, above.
5. LEUSSLER'S SKIPPER, *Megathymus leussleri*   p. 275
   Upper side, ♂ (Valentine, Nebr.). Large size; HW beneath very
   coarsely dusted and marked, with prominent gray dusting along costa.
   Perhaps conspecific with *M. texana;* see text. Strays along w. border
   of the eastern area, Nebr. to Tex.
6. LEUSSLER'S SKIPPER, *Megathymus leussleri*   p. 275
   Upper side, ♀ (Valentine, Nebr.). See ♂, above.

*5. neocypris Huebner — Tailed Sulphur
   a. bracteolata Butler ?

PHŒBIS (APHRISSA) Butler
*6. statira Cramer
   a. floridensis Neumœgen — Florida Sulphur
   b. jada Butler

KRICOGONIA Reakirt
1. lyside Latreille — Lyside
2. castalia Fabricius — Castalia

EUREMA (EUREMA) Huebner. The Little Sulphurs
1. daira Latreille — Barred Sulphur
   f. æst. jucunda Boisduval & Leconte — Fairy Yellow
   a. palmira Poey — Palmira
2. boisduvaliana Felder — Boisduval's Sulphur
3. mexicana Boisduval — Mexican Sulphur
4. salome Felder — Salome

EUREMA (ABÆIS) Huebner
5. nicippe Cramer — Sleepy Orange

EUREMA (PYRISITIA) Butler
6. proterpia Fabricius — Proterpia Orange
7. gundlachia Poey — Gundlach's Orange
8. lisa Boisduval & Leconte — Little Sulphur
9. nise Latreille — Nise Sulphur
*10. messalina Fabricius
   a. blakei Maynard ?
*11. dina Poey
   a. westwoodi Boisduval ?

NATHALIS Boisduval
1. iole Boisduval — Dainty Sulphur

APPIAS Huebner (subgenus GLUTOPHRISSA) Butler
*1. drusilla Cramer
   a. neumœgenii Skinner — Florida White

PIERIS Schrank (subgenus SYNCHLOE) Huebner
1. rapæ Linnæus — European Cabbage Butterfly
2. protodice Boisduval & Leconte — Checkered White
   a. occidentalis Reakirt ?
*3. napi Linnæus — Mustard White
   a. oleracea Harris
4. virginiensis Edwards — West Virginia White

ASCIA (ASCIA) Linnæus
1. monuste Linnæus — Great Southern White
   a. phileta Fabricius
   b. cleomes Boisduval & Leconte ?

ASCIA (GANYRA) Dalman
*2. josephina Latreille — Giant White
   a. josepha Godman & Salvin

NEOPHASIA Behr
1. menapia Felder — Pine White

Superfamily *Hesperioidea* — The Skippers

Family *Hesperiidæ* — The True Skippers

Subfamily *Pyrginæ*

PHOCIDES Huebner
  *1. batabano Lucas — Mangrove Skipper
    a. okeechobee Worthington
POLYGONUS Huebner
  *1. lividus Huebner
    a. savigny Latreille — Hammock Skipper
      amyntas Fabricius
  2. manueli Bell & Comstock — Manuel's Skipper
PROTEIDES Huebner
  1. mercurius Fabricius
AGUNA Williams
  1. asander Hewitson
EPARGYREUS Huebner
  1. zestos Geyer — Zestos Skipper
  2. clarus Cramer — Silver Spotted Skipper
    tityrus Fabricius
URBANUS Huebner
  1. proteus Linnæus — Long Tailed Skipper
  2. dorantes Stoll — Dorantes Skipper
  3. simplicius Stoll — Simplicius Skipper
  4. eurycles Stoll — Eurycles Skipper
  5. auginulus Godman & Salvin
  6. undulatus Hewitson
  7. doryssus Swainson — White Tailed Skipper
CHIOIDES Lindsey
  1. albofasciatus Hewitson — White Striped Long Tail
  2. zilpa Butler — Zilpa Skipper
ASTRAPTES Huebner
  1. fulgerator Walch — Flashing Astraptes
  2. anaphus Cramer
  3. hopferi Plœtz
ACHALARUS Scudder
  1. lyciades Geyer — Hoary Edge
  2. coyote Skinner — Coyote Skipper
AUTOCHTON Huebner
  1. cellus Boisduval & Leconte — Golden Banded Skipper
SPATHILEPIA Butler
  1. clonius Cramer — Clonius Skipper
THORYBES Scudder. The Cloudy Wings

1. bathyllus Abbot & Smith — Southern Cloudy Wing
2. pylades Scudder — Northern Cloudy Wing
3. confusis Bell — Confused Cloudy Wing

CELÆNORRHINUS Huebner
1. fritzgærtneri Bailey — Fritz' Skipper
2. stallingsi Freeman

PELLICIA Herrich-Schæffer
1. bromias Godman & Salvin
2. costimacula Herrich-Schæffer

GORGYTHION Godman and Salvin
*1. begga Prittwitz
  a. pyralina Mœschler

CABARES Godman and Salvin
1. potrillo Lucas — Potrillo Skipper

COGIA Butler
1. calchas Herrich-Schæffer
2. outis Skinner — Outis Skipper

PYRGUS Huebner. The Checkered Skippers
*1. centaureæ Rambur — Grizzled Skipper
  a. freija Warren
  b. wyandot Edwards
2. communis Grote — Checkered Skipper
3. albescens Plœtz
4. syrichtus Fabricius — Tropical Checkered Skipper
5. philetas Edwards — Philetas Skipper

HELIOPETES Billberg
1. domicella Erichson — Erichson's Skipper
2. laviana Hewitson — Laviana Skipper
3. macaira Reakirt — Macaira Skipper

ANTIGONUS Huebner
1. pulverulenta Felder — Powdered Skipper

CELOTES Godman and Salvin
1. nessus Edwards — Streaky Skipper

PHOLISORA Scudder. The Sooty Wings
1. catullus Fabricius — Common Sooty Wing
2. hayhurstii Edwards — Southern Sooty Wing
3. mazans Reakirt — Mazans Sooty Wing
4. ceos Edwards — Ochre Headed Sooty Wing
5. alpheus Edwards — Alpheus Sooty Wing

ACHLYODES Huebner
*1. thraso Huebner — Sickle Winged Skipper
  a. tamenund Edwards

XENOPHANES Godman and Salvin
1. tryxus Stoll — Glassy Winged Skipper

CHIOMARA Godman and Salvin
1. asychis Cramer — Asychis Skipper

EPHYRIADES Huebner
*1. brunnea Huebner
  a. floridensis Bell & Comstock — Florida Dusky Wing

ERYNNIS Schrank. The Dusky Wings
    Thanaos Boisduval
1. icelus Scudder & Burgess — Dreamy Dusky Wing
2. brizo Boisduval & Leconte — Sleepy Dusky Wing
  a. somnus Lintner
3. martialis Scudder — Mottled Dusky Wing

4. horatius Scudder & Burgess — Horace's Dusky Wing
5. juvenalis Fabricius — Juvenal's Dusky Wing
6. persius Scudder — Perseus' Dusky Wing
   a. fredericki H. A. Freeman ?
/. baptisiæ Forbes — Wild Indigo Dusky Wing
8. lucilius Scudder & Burgess — Columbine Dusky Wing
9. zarucco Lucas — Zarucco Dusky Wing
10. funeralis Scudder & Burgess — Funereal Dusky Wing
11. burgessi Skinner — Burgess' Dusky Wing
12. propertius Scudder & Burgess — Propertius' Dusky Wing
13. gesta Herrich-Schæffer — Gesta Dusky Wing
14. meridianus Bell — Meridian Dusky Wing

TIMOCHARES Godman and Salvin
   1. ruptifasciata Plœtz — Timochares Skipper

GRAIS Godman and Salvin
   1. stigmaticus Mabille — Grais Skipper

CARRHENES Godman and Salvin
   1. canescens Felder

Subfamily *Hesperiinæ*

CARTEROCEPHALUS Lederer
*1. palæmon Pallas — Arctic Skipper
   a. mesapano Scudder

ANCYLOXYPHA Felder
   1. numitor Fabricius — Least Skipper
   2. arene Edwards — Tropical Least Skipper

OARISMA Scudder
   1. garita Reakirt — Garita Skipper
   2. powesheik Parker — Poweshiek Skipper

ADOPÆA Billberg
   1. lineola Ochsenheimer — European Skipper

COPÆODES Edwards
   1. aurantiaca Hewitson — Orange Skipperling
   2. minima Edwards — Southern Skipperling

YVRETTA Hemming
   1. simius Edwards — Simius Skipper

HESPERIA Fabricius
   1. leonardus Harris — Leonard's Skipper
      a. stallingsi H. A. Freeman
   2. sassacus Harris — Indian Skipper
      a. manitoboides Fletcher
   3. dacotae Skinner — Dakota Skipper
   4. metea Scudder — Cobweb Skipper
      a. licinus Edwards
   5. attalus Edwards — Dotted Skipper
      a. slossonæ Skinner
   6. meskei Edwards — Meske's Skipper
   7. ottoë Edwards — Ottoë Skipper

8. pawnee Dodge — Pawnee Skipper
9. viridis Edwards — Green Skipper
10. uncas Edwards — Uncas' Skipper
11. laurentina Lyman — Laurentian Skipper
12. borealis Lindsey — Labrador Skipper

HYLEPHILA Billberg
1. phyleus Drury — Fiery Skipper

ATALOPEDES Scudder
1. campestris Boisduval — The Sachem

POLITES Scudder
1. verna Edwards — Little Glassy Wing
   a. sequoyah H. A. Freeman
2. manataaqua Scudder — Cross Line Skipper
3. themistocles Latreille — Tawny Edged Skipper
   cernes Boisduval
   taumas Fabricius
4. baracoa Lucas — Baracoa Skipper
5. peckius Kirby — Peck's Skipper
6. mystic Scudder — The Long Dash
   a. dacotah Edwards
7. vibex Geyer — The Whirlabout
   a. præceps Scudder

WALLENGRENIA Berg
1. otho Abbot & Smith — The Broken Dash
   a. egeremet Scudder

POANES Scudder
1. viator Edwards — Broad Winged Skipper
2. massasoit Scudder — The Mulberry Wing
   a. hughi A. H. Clark ?
3. hobomok Harris — Hobomok Skipper
   f. ♀ pocahontas Scudder — Pocahontas' Skipper
   a. ridingsi Chermock & Chermock
4. zabulon Boisduval & Leconte — Zabulon Skipper
5. aaroni Skinner — Aaron's Skipper
   a. howardi Skinner
6. yehl Skinner — Yehl Skipper

CHORANTHUS Scudder
1. radians Lucas — Radiate Skipper
2. haitensis Skinner — Haitian Skipper

PROBLEMA Skinner and Williams
1. byssus Edwards — Byssus Skipper
2. bulenta Boisduval & Leconte — Rare Skipper

ATRYTONE Scudder
1. arogos Boisduval & Leconte — Arogos Skipper
   a. iowa Scudder
2. logan Edwards — Delaware Skipper
   a. lagus Edwards
3. arpa Boisduval & Leconte — Arpa Skipper
4. berryi Bell — Berry's Skipper
5. dion Edwards — Dion Skipper
   a. alabamæ Lindsey
6. palatka Edwards — Palatka Skipper
7. dukesi Lindsey — Dukes' Skipper
8. conspicua Edwards — The Black Dash
9. bimacula Grote & Robinson — Two Spotted Skipper

*10. ruricola Boisduval
    a. metacomet Harris — Eastern Dun Skipper
  11. eulogius Plœtz
ATRYTONOPSIS Godman
    1. loammi Whitney — Loammi Skipper
    2. hianna Scudder — Dusted Skipper
    3. turneri H. A. Freeman — Turner's Skipper
OLIGORIA Scudder
    1. maculata Edwards — Twin Spot Skipper
COBALUS Huebner
    1. percosius Godman & Salvin
LEREMA Scudder
    1. accius Abbot & Smith — Clouded Skipper
AMBLYSCIRTES Scudder. The Roadside Skippers
    1. vialis Edwards — Roadside Skipper
    2. hegon Scudder — Pepper & Salt Skipper
    3. carolina Skinner — Carolina Roadside Skipper
    4. textor Huebner — Textor Skipper
    5. alternata Grote & Robinson — Least Florida Skipper
    6. belli H. A. Freeman — Bell's Roadside Skipper
    7. linda H. A. Freeman — Linda's Roadside Skipper
    8. erna H. A. Freeman — Erna's Roadside Skipper
    9. ænus Edwards — Bronze Roadside Skipper
  10. celia Skinner — Celia's Roadside Skipper
  11. texanæ Bell — Texas Roadside Skipper
  12. oslari Skinner — Oslar's Roadside Skipper
  13. eos Edwards — Eos Roadside Skipper
  14. nysa Edwards — Nysa Roadside Skipper
LERODEA Scudder
    1. l'herminieri Latreille — Swarthy Skipper
      fusca Grote & Robinson
    2. eufala Edwards — Eufala Skipper
    3. neamathla Skinner & Williams — Neamathla Skipper
    4. julia H. A. Freeman — Julia's Skipper
    5. tripunctata Herrich-Schæffer — Three Spotted Skipper
    6. tyrtæa Plœtz — Tyrtæa Skipper
    7. edata Plœtz — Edata Skipper
CALPODES Huebner
    1. ethlius Stoll — Brazilian Skipper
    2. evansi H. A. Freeman — Evans' Skipper
PANOQUINA Hemming
    1. panoquin Scudder — Salt Marsh Skipper
    2. panoquinoides Skinner — Obscure Skipper
    3. ocola Edwards — Ocola Skipper
    4. sylvicola Herrich-Schæffer ?
    5. hecebolus Scudder ? — Hecebolus Skipper
NYCTELIUS Hayward
    1. nyctelius Latreille — Nyctelius Skipper
ASBOLIS Mabille
    1. capucinus Lucas — The Monk
THESPEIUS Godman
    1. macareus Herrich-Schæffer
SYNAPTE Mabille
    1. malitiosa Herrich-Schæffer — Malicious Skipper

PERICHARES Scudder
 *1. philetes Gmelin
    a. dolores Reakirt — Dolores' Skipper

Family *Megathymidæ* — The Giant Skippers

MEGATHYMUS Scudder
 1. yuccæ Boisduval and Leconte — Yucca Skipper
    a. alabamæ H. A. Freeman
    b. stallingsi H. A. Freeman
 2. cofaqui Strecker — Cofaqui Skipper
 3. texana Barnes & McDunnough ? — Giant Texas Skipper
 4. leussleri Holland ? — Leussler's Skipper
 5. smithi Druce — Smith's Giant Skipper

INDICES

Index to Technical Terms
and General Subjects

IN PART this index serves the purpose of a glossary, since it refers to the chief explanations and illustrations of technical terms. It is also an index to the most important references to subjects other than the butterflies themselves and their food plants.

Transition life zone, 23, 25
tribes, 295
trigonate (wing shape), 233
trochanter, 46
Tropical life zone, 23, 26
truncate, 92

uncus, 54
urea, 55

vannal veins, 53
varieties, 298
variety names, 66
venation, wing, 50, 51
ventral, 46
vinculum, 54

waste places, 28
wings, 47

Index to Larval Food Plants

I HAVE TRIED to establish some uniformity in the plant names by following, as nearly as possible, the nomenclature of *Gray's New Manual of Botany* (7th ed.), Small's *Flora of the Southeastern United States* and Bailey's *Manual of Cultivated Plants* (rev. ed.). This has not always been possible. Sometimes the authorities differ. Again, many records culled from the entomological literature, especially old ones, have been under names which I have been unable to reconcile with accepted usage. In such cases I have been forced merely to repeat the record, unintelligible though it be, rather than take the risk of falsifying it. As always common names are a fruitful source of misunderstanding. Note that only larval food plants are indexed, not plants referred to as part of the general environment, or flowers visited by adult butterflies.

Index to Butterflies

REFERENCES ARE GIVEN in this index to every important mention of each butterfly, by both common and scientific names, but not to unimportant, casual mentions. Families, subfamilies, genera, etc., have been indexed likewise. No distinction is made here between genus and subgenus names, nor between species, subspecies, form and variety names. Page references in bold-face type are to illustrations. The Check List has not been indexed.